THE HISTORICAL
ATLAS
OF
WORLD
WAR II

A Quantum book

This edition published in 2014 by
Chartwell Books
an imprint of Book Sales
a division of Quarto Publishing Group USA Inc.
276 Fifth Avenue Suite 206
New York, New York 10001 USA

ISBN-13: 978-0-7858-3146-4

This book is produced by
Quantum Books Limited
6 Blundell Street
London, N7 9BH

Publisher: Kerry Enzor
Quantum editorial: Hazel Eriksson, Sam Kennedy
Production manager: Rohana Yusof

Edited & designed by Therefore Publishing Limited
www.thereforepublishing.com

Printed in China

THE HISTORICAL
ATLAS
OF
WORLD
WAR II

ALEXANDER SWANSTON
& MALCOLM SWANSTON

**CHARTWELL
BOOKS**

CONTENTS

FIGHT THEM ON THE BEACHES
The D-Day landings were one of the turning-points of the war,
and also one of the great martial undertakings of human history.

KEY TO MAPS

Military units–types

- ⊠ infantry
- ▬ armored
- ◠ airlanding and Luftwaffe field
- ⊕ airborne
- ⊡ artillery

Military units–size

- XXXXX army group
- XXXX army
- XXX corps
- XX division
- X brigade
- III regiment
- II battalion
- I company

Military unit colours

- British / Canadian / U.S / Polish
- German
- French
- training
- refitting
- Chinese
- Japanese
- Finnish
- Polish
- Soviet Union

General military symbols

- —XXXXX— army group boundary
- —XXXX— army boundary
- —XXX— corps boundary
- ⬯ pocket or position
- ⬤ paratroop drop
- ⛵ sunken ship
- ⊥ mobile gun
- ⊥ anti tank gun
- ⅄ light machine gun
- ⊥ heavy machine gun / other infantry weapon
- ⊞ gun emplacement
- ⊓ gun in casement
- ● heavy AA gun
- ○ light AA gun
- ⚔ 20mm anti-aircraft gun
- ▨ German strongpoints
- ⊔ pillbox for guns
- □ concrete shelter
- ⊡ shelter with cupola
- ✸ sea mine
- ◸ land mine
- ×××××× barbed wire
- ⊓⊔ major defensive line
- ⋀⋁⋀ entrenchment
- ◯ radar station
- ⚕ church

Military movements

- ➤ attack
- ➤ retreat
- ✛ bombers
- ✳ explosion
- ⊕ airfield

Geographical symbols

- buildings
- urban area
- road
- railway
- river
- seasonal river
- canal
- border
- ⋈ bridge or pass
- marsh/swamp
- rocks and beach
- woodland

7

MAP LIST

INTRODUCTION

At the Armistice of 11 November 1918, German armies were in retreat, beaten on the battlefield. While the Allies grew stronger by the day, Germany grew weaker. The massive contribution by the United States from April 1917 in materials and men, tipped the scales in the Allies' favor. Nevertheless the German Army still stood on foreign soil, Germany was not invaded and German industry still functioned almost undamaged by war.

World War I ended officially with the Treaty of Versailles, signed in 1919. Germany was not consulted about the terms, she was sent the details on the proposed treaty and allowed to comment but these were largely ignored. When the terms of the Treaty of Versailles became known, many Germans were astounded, war guilt and loss of territory all came as a shock, especially after President Wilson's "Fourteen Points" were grasped by Germany as a fair end to a terrible war. In these circumstances the myth of the "stab in the back" by defeatists in Germany began to grow.

With the rise of the Nazis, these myths were propagandized, demands for territorial restitution were soon realized. However, Hitler wanted more. Italy and Japan also developed their expansionist agendas. The World War began as a series of regional conflicts which, by the signing of the Tripartite Pact on 27 September 1940 between Germany, Italy, and Japan, created a full global military alliance. The Rome-Berlin-Tokyo Axis connected wars in Europe, in the Mediterranean, Africa, and Atlantic, to wars in Asia and the Pacific. It eventually drew in the majority of the sovereign nations that existed in 1939.

The Asian war began in 1933 with Japan's invasion of China from their puppet state of Manchuria (Manchukuo). The war in Africa began in 1936 with the Italian invasion of Abyssinia (Ethiopia). In Europe in 1939 with the invasion of Poland, which drew in Britain and France with both their empires. It began in the Pacific in 1941 with the Japanese attack on Pearl Harbor. This brought the United States into the war against Germany, with Hitler declaring war on the US in the aftermath of the Japanese attack. Over 60 million people would perish in this global conflict, making it the most cataclysmic event in the whole of human history.

In this single volume it is our intention to bring all of the major events into focus, our maps throw spotlights onto crucial battles and campaigns—this was a total struggle of decency against darkness, as British Prime Minister Winston Churchill stated in 1940, "If the light of Freedom … should be finally quenched, it might well herald a return to the Dark Ages, when every vestige of human progress during two thousand years would be engulfed." But as history demonstrated he was not just talking to Britain but the whole free world. It was a simple struggle between darkness and light. If our forefathers had failed, the consequences would have been unbearable for most—and certain death for many.

To those who saved our freedom, this book is respectfully dedicated.

Alexander Swanston
& Malcolm Swanston

Europe
11 November 1918

- Central Powers
- Allied
- Neutral
- Armistice lines

Arctic Circle

Iceland
to Denmark

Norwegian Sea

Faeroe Islands to Denmark

N O R W A Y

S W E D E N

Finland
(Independent from 1917)

Helsingfors

St. Petersburg

Christiania

Stockholm

North Sea

Baltic Sea

Riga

S O V I E T

Vitebsk

R U S S I A

Glasgow   Edinburgh

DENMARK
Copenhagen

Königsberg

Minsk

UNITED KINGDOM

Dublin   Liverpool   Hull

Hamburg

Berlin

Warsaw

Poland

Birmingham

Amsterdam   **NETHERLANDS**

GERMAN EMPIRE

Lemberg

Bristol

London

Calais

Brussels

BELGIUM

L

Frankfurt

Prague

Cracow

Rhine

Brest

Paris

L

Orléans

Munich

Vienna

Budapest

A T L A N T I C

O C E A N

F R A N C E

L

Bern
SWITZERLAND

AUSTRO-HUNGARIAN EMPIRE

Danube

ROMANIA

Lyon

Milan

Trieste

Bucharest

Black Sea

Bordeaux

Venice

Belgrade

Corunna

Genoa

Sarajevo

SERBIA

BULGARIA

MONACO

ANDORRA

Marseille

SAN MARINO

Adriatic Sea

MONTE-NEGRO

Sofia
*Occupied by Allies
Sept. – Oct. 1918*

ALBANIA

OTTOMAN EMPIRE

Corsica

I T A L Y

Rome

PORTUGAL

Barcelona

Madrid

S P A I N

Sardinia

Naples

Aegean Sea

GREECE

Smyrna

Lisbon

Balearic Is.

Alicante

Athens

Cádiz

Almería

M e d i t e r r a n e a n   S e a

Sicily

Italian occupied

Gibraltar
to Great Britain

Tangier

A l g e r i a
to France

Tunis

Tunisia
to France

Crete

THE PEACE OF VERSAILLES 1919–20

"You hold in your hands the future of the world."

PRESIDENT POINCARÉ, JANUARY 1919

On 28 June 1919 in the Hall of Mirrors, within the Palace of Versailles, the treaty was signed that ended the war to end wars. Between August 1914 and November 1918 a confident Imperial Europe tore itself to pieces. Four empires collapsed: the Russian, Austro-Hungarian, Ottoman, and German. From their ashes emerged new states: Czechoslovakia and Yugoslavia. Some old states, Poland, Lithuania, Latvia, and Estonia, reemerged from years of domination.

The peacemakers had gathered in Paris in January 1919 after the Armistice of 11 November 1918. President Wilson arrived in the port of Brest the previous December aboard the liner George Washington to cries of "Vive Wilson" and "Vive l'Amerique." He and the American delegation were greeted by the French foreign minister, before they caught the special night train to Paris. There they were met by the French government. Clemenceau, President Poincaré, and their ministers greeted Wilson; the crowds cheered, bands played, and flags waved. Amid wild cheering, the President and his wife were driven in an open carriage along the Champs-Elysées to their residence. The President, happy with his reception, also came armed with his "Fourteen Points." This vision of a new world order included the withdrawal of troops from Russia and elsewhere; the restoration of some pre-war borders and the re-drawing of others; a commitment to transparent diplomacy, as well as to free trade, disarmament, and open access to the world's seas.

Many in Europe hoped Wilson's plan would bring a fair solution to their ancient and deeply-held prejudices.

Clemenceau's France was a sad place in the spring of 1919, a quarter of Frenchmen between the ages of 18 and 30 were dead, a further quarter were maimed, the northern industrial zone including the coal mines, the power for what was left of its industry, was in ruins. Thousands of square miles were pitted with shell holes, and scarred by lines of abandoned trenches. So bad was the damage to the land, especially around Verdun, that nothing would grow.

Fourteen Points or not, so much was at stake for France: Clemenceau's raison d'être was to make sure that Germany paid in full. France needed a secure future from a more populous Germany, whose industry was undamaged by war.

The British had already achieved almost all of its desires: the German High Seas Fleet was destroyed and Germany's colonies were now mostly in British and a few more in Allied hands. The Americans, however, were eager to get the job of peacemaking done and go home, protected by their powerful navy and the wide expanses of the Atlantic and Pacific Oceans.

British Prime Minister Lloyd George's view was clear; he wanted to achieve a balance of power in Europe. Germany must not be destroyed, leaving the way open for a strong and revolutionary Russia; it must be left with some kind of strength. Britain would then be free, with its

Europe 1920–21
Postwar Settlements

unchallenged naval dominance, to pursue its trade and enjoy the benefits of its recently extended and already vast empire.

The day after his arrival in Paris, Lloyd George met Wilson, Clemenceau, and Vittorio Orlando, the Italian Prime Minister, at the French Foreign Ministry on the Quai d'Orsay. Each leader brought along his Foreign Minister and a small group of advisors. On 13 January, in line with British wishes, two representatives from Japan joined the group. This became known as the Council of Ten, although some referred to it as the Supreme Council, since smaller states and allies were not included. This group would meet more than 100 times. By March, as negotiations became more difficult, the Supreme Council met without the Foreign Ministers and the Japanese, to become the Council of Four: Wilson, Lloyd George, Clemenceau, and Orlando.

The peacemakers had taken on, at least for a short term, the administration and feeding of much of Europe and the Near East. If they did not undertake the work it seemed no one would, or perhaps worse Socialist or right-wing revolutionaries might.

Apart from destroying human life, hope, and expectation on an immense scale, the war had disrupted the world economy. It would not be easy to repair this and deal with a host of problems created by emerging new states changing ownership of territory, populations, and raw materials.

The absentee in all of these deliberations was Russia, an ally from 1914 until March 1918. After the first revolution of February 1917, Russia continued to fight alongside the Allies, though with decreasing effectiveness. By October 1917 the Bolsheviks had seized power. The Treaty of Brest-Litovsk ended the war between the Central Powers and Russia on 3 March 1918. The Armistice of 11 November 1918 between the Allies and

Germany effectively ended the Treaty of Brest-Litovsk. When German and Austrian forces withdrew from occupied lands in the east a mixed bag of nationalists and revolutionaries claimed territory for their causes.

In January the American government sent William Bullitt, a self-confident, upper-class product of Yale, on a mission to the revolutionary government in Russia. He was to search out acceptable grounds upon which a peace might be made with the Western Allies. They had previously supported the counterrevolutionary governments by sending forces to support "the Whites," of whom there were quite a number. However, it was the "Reds," the Bolsheviks, that held the Russian heartlands.

Various communications and discussions with the Bolsheviks came to nothing. On 23 May 1919, the Allies decided on partial recognition of the White, Kolchack government, but by June the Reds were defeating Kolchack's forces on all fronts. Nothing more could be done about Russia's possible interests. A clause was added to the treaty that was then being finalized, stating that in future any treaty made between the Allies and Russia, or any parts of it, would be binding on any future Russian government. After a few final days of discussion and last-minute amendments, the final Treaty of Versailles, with its 440 clauses, went off to the printers. Two days later a final session was called to vote on the terms but, alas, no printed version was yet available. It had to be read out aloud to the gathering in French. The non-French speakers are reputed to have nodded off, while others voiced objections; China complained that the Japanese were given German holdings and concessions in China; other issues were raised but ignored. Then Marshal Foch, Head of the French army, rose and asked to be heard. He pleaded, once again, that the River Rhine should be the frontier, a barrier between France and Germany. He said later to a *New York Times* reporter, "…remember, the next time the Germans will make no mistake, they will break through into northern France and capture the Channel ports and use these as a base of operations against England." The peacemakers ignored his pleas and seemed satisfied with their final draft. The German delegation was led by Ulrich von Brockdorff-Rantzau, the Foreign Minister, who put his faith in the Americans and in Wilson's Fourteen Points as, indeed, did most Germans.

On 7 May, the terms were handed over to the German delegation, with two weeks to reply. The Germans were soon at work on the treaty: translations were printed and distributed. The shock was instantaneous. Loss of land to Poland and France, all the overseas colonies confiscated, millions in gold to be paid. Germany would not be allowed to join the newly-forming League of Nations, would face the loss of almost all of its merchant fleet, and almost complete disarmament.

Within the specified time the Germans replied, with page after page of carefully argued objections and proposals. They considered that the Treaty was not a fair one; by taking territory from Germany it denied the right of self-determination, as laid out in the Fourteen Points. Reparations were unsustainable, Germans would be turned into a nation of slaves. Brockdorff-Rantzau strenuously rejected Clause 251, believing that it implied Germany's war guilt. When the peacemakers read the terms in full some were uneasy. Herbert Hoover, then working as American Relief Administrator, recalled some years later, "many parts of the proposed Treaty would ultimately bring destruction."

After further discussions, the Allies ratified the final Treaty, with little changed. This was presented to the Germans on 16 June. They were informed they had three days to accept and this was later extended to six days. The Germans left immediately for Weimar, the seat of Germany's shaky coalition government. The German cabinet, which had been inclined to sign, became deadlocked and on 20 June resigned. Brockdorff-Rantzau resigned his position as head of the German peace delegation. President Friedrich Ebert was left high and dry, with no government and no spokesman. He almost resigned himself but was persuaded to stay. He cobbled together another government by 22 June and, after another debate in the National Assembly, a vote was taken in favor of signing, with the proviso that Germany would not accept Clause 251, articles on the surrender and trial of those responsible for the war and the war guilt. The reply from Paris was unequivocal: the German government must accept or refuse. Finally the Germans accepted. The formal signing was set for 28 June in the Hall of Mirrors at the Palace of Versailles and, without further delay, it was signed. Dignitaries posed for the camera, a few speeches were made and crowds cheered. President Wilson left the same day for Le Havre and a ship home.

While the Allies cheered, Germany mourned, and flags flew at half-mast. The myth of Germany's "undefeated" army prospered; others blamed traitors at home who had "stabbed Germany in the back." In the beer halls of Bavaria an unemployed ex-soldier and would-be politician drew crowds with his speeches on the "peace of shame." Hitler was just beginning to make his mark.

THE RISE OF FASCISM

"Fascism accepts the individual only insofar as his interests coincide with the state's."

BENITO MUSSOLINI, ITALIAN DICTATOR

The aftermath of World War I, with its peace treaties created between 1919 and 1921, redrew Europe into a patchwork of small, precariously viable states. President Wilson's Fourteen Points intended to create states based on ethnic-cultural identities. The reality of the Treaty of Versailles, however, was ethnic minorities in almost all of the new states. The resentment felt by the defeated powers manifested itself in the growth of new nationalist regimes. The economic crisis of the early 1930s persuaded ordinary men and women to look in new directions, leaving traditional leaders and institutions in favor of radical new movements and parties.

In Italy, as early as October 1922, Benito Mussolini seized power, as the leader of Fasci di Combattimento—the Fascist Party. His authoritarian oratory and right-wing policies appealed to many in Italy and across Europe, especially those who feared the spread of Communism and detested the inability of democratic governments to deal with this threat and the economic crisis of the early 1930s. This feeling ran deep in Germany where Communist groups tried to seize power as early as 1919.

In 1923 a little-known leader of the National Socialist German Workers' Party, Adolf Hitler, attempted a coup in Bavaria. It failed and he was imprisoned. This brought attention to his right-wing ideals and gave him time to write *Mein Kampf* ("My Struggle"). The emphasis of this book was the restoration of German "greatness," defying the terms of the Treaty of Versailles, ridding Germany of the detested Weimar Republic and what he regarded as the international troublesome non-aryan Jews.

All right-wing nationalist movements benefited from the parlous economic situation. Investors left Europe in search of higher interest rates elsewhere and the cycle of indebtedness established around German reparations payments merely confused matters further. American loans were made to Germany to help reparations payments to France and Britain, who could then repay interest to the U.S. for their own wartime loans. In this situation the Wall Street crash caused severe hardship, especially with the recall of U.S. European loans, damaging Germany in particular. Many European countries suffered unemployment rates of 25 percent or more. In Germany,

CLOSE TIES
A poster from 1938 celebrating the Hitler-Mussolini Pact.

The Fascist States
1922–36

Democratic countries

Repressive or conservative countries

Fascist countries

Communist dictatorship

Right-wing activity

industrial production fell to 53 percent of the 1929 figure and social distress was immense. Malnutrition was rife, meat consumption fell and the death rate increased, while in England there were hunger marches from the Jarrow shipyards to London. Government reactions to the Depression sometimes exacerbated the distress. Import tariffs were strictly applied all over Europe, and even Britain ended its eighty-six years of free trade by the 1932 Import Duties Act. The Ottawa Imperial Conference granted preferential treatment to Dominion agricultural products, while British manufactured goods received reciprocal treatment in Dominion markets. France adopted similar tactics regarding her own colonies. European states adopted deflationary policies, especially in Germany and France; there was budgetary control in Britain; and government intervention in Nazi Germany, concentrating on promoting heavy industry, a public works program and a secret rearmament program.

In Britain the revival of domestic consumer demand provided with cheap money helped private enterprise and gradually turned around the economy. The Depression had a significant impact on domestic and international

politics. Democracies experienced unusual political tendencies. Ministerial crises in France and the development of Fascist leagues, the Croix de Feu, led in 1936 to Léon Blum's Popular Front government, a sister system to that in Spain. Britain ended the normal single-party government and switched to a multi-party national government in the face of international events and Oswald Mosley's British Union of Fascists. Support for right-wing extremist parties grew, from the Lapua movement in Finland to the Hungarian Arrow Cross and the Iron Guard in Romania. Ruined farming interests backed the right (Romania's League of the Archangel Michael) and many ruined and worried middle-class voters in Germany helped bring Hitler to power.

After being appointed Chancellor of Germany, Adolf Hitler mentioned to a newspaper editor, who opposed the Nazis, that he, Hitler, intended to come to power by winning seats in the Reichstag: after he had achieved this it might as well close its doors and become a museum. Four weeks later, on the morning of 27 February, the Reichstag went up in flames. Hitler at once blamed the Communists, many of whom blamed Hitler. Hitler's governmental position was less secure than may be imagined; he was head of a coalition government with only two other Nazis in the Cabinet. Much to his distaste, he needed other parties' support to win a majority in the Reichstag. The overthrow of Germany's parliamentary system began with the Reichstag Fire Decree, which gave Hitler or "the government" emergency powers that were used against the enemies of the Nazi Party, the Communists in particular.

The German economy was already recovering from the worst effects of the depression, but new measures speeded things up. The state funded a motorway network that would connect the major cities to newly-created towns and under-developed areas. New industrial sites sprang up and flagging industries benefited from state support. The armaments industry, in particular, enjoyed

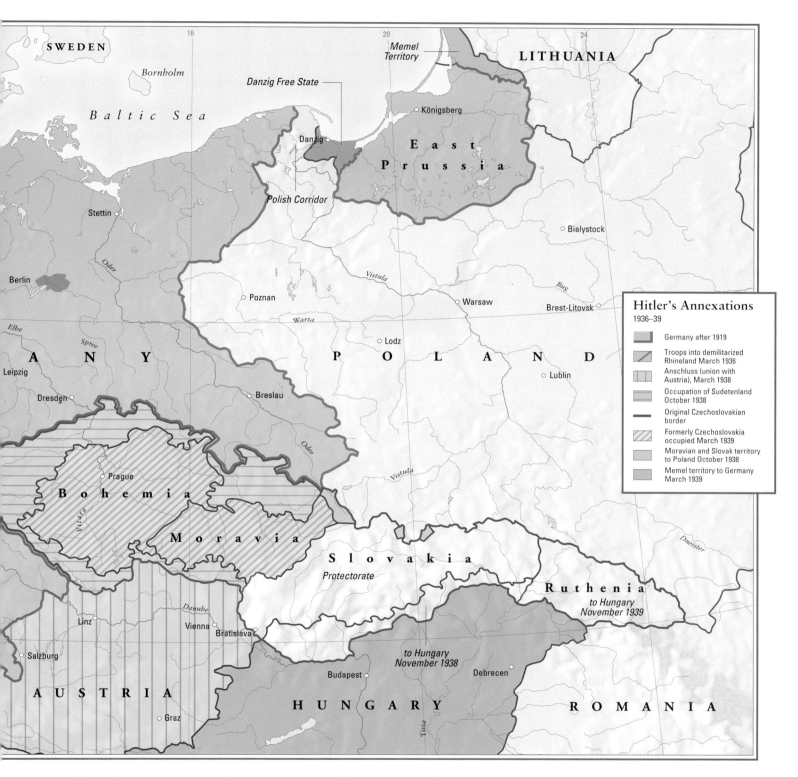

SWEDEN

Bornholm

Baltic Sea

Memel
Territory

LITHUANIA

Danzig Free State

○ Königsberg

Danzig

E a s t

Stettin

P r u s s i a

Oder

Polish Corridor

○ Bialystock

Berlin

Vistula

Bug

Elbe

○ Poznan

○ Warsaw

Brest-Litovsk

A N Y

Spree

Warta

P O L A N D

Leipzig

○ Lodz

Dresden ○

○ Breslau

○ Lublin

Oder

B o h e m i a

○ Prague

Vltava

Vistula

M o r a v i a

Dneister

S l o v a k i a

R u t h e n i a

Protectorate

to Hungary
November 1939

Danube

Linz ○

Vienna ○

Bratislava ○

to Hungary
November 1938

Salzburg ○

Budapest ○

Debrecen ○

A U S T R I A

H U N G A R Y

R O M A N I A

○ Graz

Tisza

Hitler's Annexations
1936–39

	Germany after 1919
	Troops into demilitarized Rhineland March 1936
	Anschluss (union with Austria), March 1938
	Occupation of Sudetenland October 1938
	Original Czechoslovakian border
	Formerly Czechoslovakia occupied March 1939
	Moravian and Slovak territory to Poland October 1938
	Memel territory to Germany March 1939

full order books, especially now the cursed Treaty of Versailles was cast aside. All of this activity created a massive boost to the German economy.

Hints of a new and more aggressive foreign-policy direction came when Hitler took Germany out of the League of Nations in 1933. He also agreed to continue with secret plans to expand the armed forces. However,

Hitler remained prudent at this point. He knew that Germany must continue to recover before provoking any possible military reaction. In 1934, Germany signed a Non-Aggression Pact with Poland, an attempt to sidetrack the French security agreements and, for a period, Hitler persuaded Europe that he just wanted to negotiate a restitution of Germany's grievances.

INVASION OF POLAND 1939

"The battlefront disappeared, and with it the illusion that there had ever been a battlefront. For this was no war of occupation, but a war of quick penetration and obliteration—Blitzkrieg, lightning war."

JOURNALIST WORKING FOR TIME MAGAZINE, 25 SEPTEMBER 1939

With the rearmament of Germany, Poland realized the possibility of invasion. This caused major concern for the military for two main reasons. Firstly its army and airforce were ill-equipped, the airforce having very few modern types of aircraft, particularly interceptors essential for defending the cities and troop concentrations from bomber attacks. Worse was the state of the army, still reliant on the horse cavalry and with a severe lack of motorized transport for its infantry, though this did not mean that these units fought with any lack of conviction. The second problem facing the Poles was where and how to defend. Germany had annexed Czechoslovakia in 1938, allowing the Germans to enter from the south through Slovakia. There was also the problem of East Prussia, allowing the Germans to enter from the north. This effectively surrounded Poland, with the unsympathetic U.S.S.R. on the east. With such a huge front to cover and most of the important industry in the west of the country, the Poles would have to fight a holding battle on the borders for as long as possible in order to mobilize the maximum number of troops. The problem with this tactic was that forward formations could be easily surrounded and cut off but Poland had

hopes that France would intervene before this came about. They could then fall back onto a defense using the river system of Poland.

The Germans held all the advantages, having started a process of rearmament that had been running for many years, breaking the Treaty of Versailles and equipping its army and airforce with the best weapons and vehicles available. They also had another advantage, a new tactic, Blitzkrieg. This entailed rapid control of the skies and comprehensive bombing of enemy lines of communication and transport. It was followed by a concentrated thrust by armored units on a small front to punch a hole in the defense allowing for mechanized troops to spill into the rear of the enemy's position. All these movements were covered by the airforce preventing counterstrikes by the enemy, and by mobile artillery which could be called upon to destroy any strong defensive pockets. However, many German infantry units still depended on horse transport to consolidate captured positions.

Using this new technique from 1 September 1939, the Germans enjoyed rapid success. Dive-bombers wiped out much of the Polish Air Force while it was still on the ground, though some Polish pilots bravely succeeded in

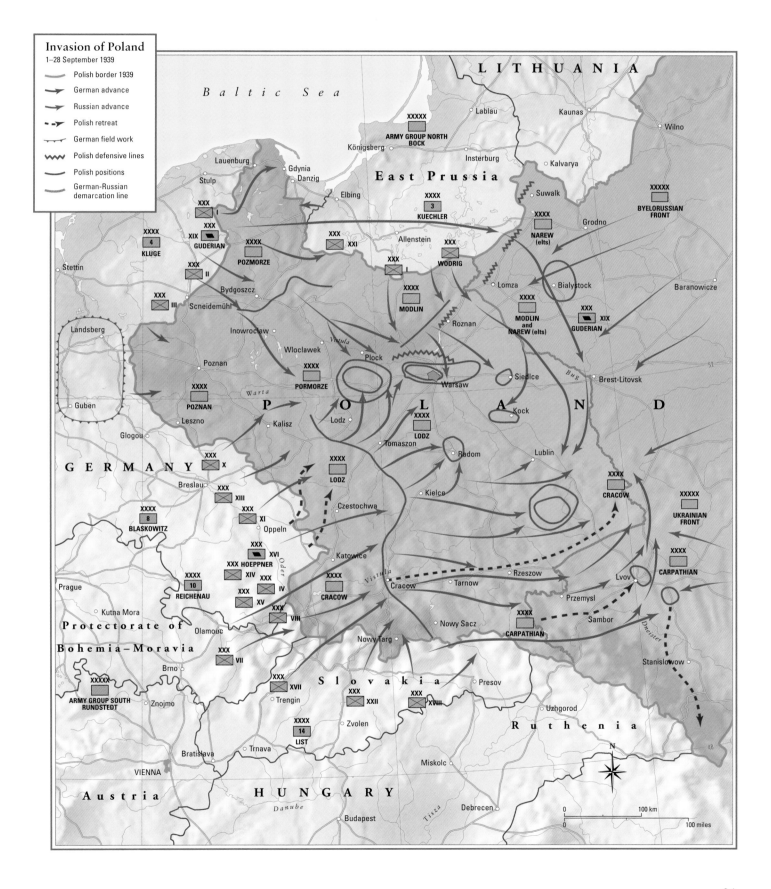

In the two centuries up to 1812 Poland had been steadily reduced from a once great empire to a Grand Duchy.

At the end of the Napoleonic Wars the Duchy was finally shared out between Prussia, Russia, and the Austrian Empire. Poland, as an independent state, disappeared from the map for more than one hundred years.

At the end of World War I Poland was reestablished as a state by the Treaty of Versailles. This Treaty granted sizeable areas of Germany to the new Poland, including a corridor to the Baltic Sea. Poland also acquired territories east of Brest-Litovsk from Soviet Russia, stabilizing its frontier at the end of 1921.

As German and Soviet power expanded in the 1930s, Poland's position between these two states became increasingly difficult. Treaties with Britain and France meant very little in real terms. After the German and Soviet attacks in 1939, Poland once again disappeared from the map for over five years. After the end of World War II, Poland was restored by the Allies. At Stalin's behest, the country's boundaries were moved westward, losing its eastern provinces but gaining large areas of German territory. Millions of Germans were displaced westward; millions of Poles, mostly from the eastern territories, took their place.

making a few effective sorties. The Luftwaffe could then concentrate on supporting the advancing divisions. Army Group North, commanded by the arrogant but ambitious General von Bock gave the order to take the ground between Pomerania and East Prussia, cutting off what became known as the "Polish Corridor." This maneuver was entrusted to General Heinz Guderian, a proponent of tank warfare, who quickly accomplished his goal. He then continued on through East Prussia and back into the north-east of Poland in order to meet up with the advancing Army Group South. Meanwhile, the 3rd Army pressed south-east toward Warsaw from East Prussia. The 8th, 10th, and 14th Armies, under the command of General von Rundstedt, who had recently been pulled out of retirement, pushed north-eastward from Silesia and Slovakia, creating a gigantic pincer movement.

By 6 September, the 3rd and 4th Armies from the north and the 8th and 10th from the south were advancing on Warsaw, while the 14th Army took Cracow. The Wehrmacht (Nazi armed forces) proceeded to make probing attacks on the outskirts of Warsaw, but were beaten back by a stubborn defense, the 4th Army losing

nearly 60 tanks in action that showed the Poles had developed an effective anti-tank strategy. During these attacks the Poles attempted a risky counterattack on the flank of the advancing 8th Army, which took the Germans by surprise, incurring large casualties on both sides before being beaten back, thanks in part to the Luftwaffe's control of the skies and the high degree of skill shown by the German artillery support.

On 15 September Warsaw was surrounded, as were many other cities and army units in western Poland. This was a grave time for the Poles, but they still refused to accept the German call to surrender. German commanders now sat back awaiting the capitulation of Warsaw, which was being starved out. Hitler could not wait for this and ordered an extensive artillery and air bombardment of the city. On 17 September the Red Army entered eastern Poland against minimal resistance, since almost all available Polish forces were involved in the fight in the west. This action had been arranged between Germany and U.S.S.R. before the invasion, with Stalin proclaiming that Poland no longer existed as an independent state. Poland had been subsumed into the Nazi Reich and the Soviet Union.

Warsaw managed to combat the onslaught until 27 September, with other pockets of resistance managing to hold out until 2 October, this final surrender marking the end of the campaign. During a month of vicious fighting the Poles suffered over 200,000 casualties, with a further one million servicemen becoming prisoners of war. More than 100,000 men managed to escape through Romania and make the arduous journey to western Europe to carry on the fight against Fascism. The Germans suffered 40,000 casualties, killed and wounded—fewer than the Poles—demonstrating the success of the Blitzkrieg. Now Hitler looked to expand westward but first he had to secure his northern flank: Scandinavia.

RAIN OF TERROR
German planes rained bombs on residential areas of Warsaw, so as to sow panic among the civilian population. Non-combatants were targets and victims from the very start of the Nazi occupation of Poland.

GOOSE-STEP TO VICTORY
Warsaw capitulated on 1 October, 1939, a month to the day after the invasion of Poland began. German troops paraded through the streets, a scene that was later to be repeated in other capitals across Europe.

THE WINTER WAR

"Men were thrown headlong at Finnish guns. Tanks and their crews were shelled and burned, whole regiments of infantry encircled. Entire battalions of troops, the spearhead of the Red Army, were cut off from their reinforcements and supplies."

ANONYMOUS SOVIET SOLDIER

Soviet interest in Finland in 1939 was due to Stalin's desire to strengthen the Soviet Union's northern border. He also wanted to lease the port of Henko for a 30-year period but talks between Finland and Soviet Russia did not go to plan, even when the Soviet Union offered territorial compensation in Soviet Karelia.

The Finns thought that any leeway towards the Soviets, after only gaining independence in 1917, would only lead to Stalin wanting more. After the bargaining failed, Stalin fell back on military intervention, thinking that it would be an easy conflict to conclude, even setting up an interim Finnish government before the invasion had begun. Stalin felt that the workers would welcome the Communists with open arms. However, this was not to be the case.

Defending Finland was an army of 10 divisions supplemented with a few specialist units. These divisions were poorly equipped, lacking automatic weapons, artillery and, most importantly, anti-tank weapons. Each division had only 30-odd pieces of pre-1918 artillery with a severe lack of ammunition.

But what they lacked in equipment they made up for in training. They were particularly skilled in maneuvering in the heavily forested and snow-covered countryside, using ski troops to mount surprise attacks then quickly melting back into the forest. These troops were also highly motivated to retain the independence of Finland and were led by intelligent officers and N.C.O.s. The commander of the defense of Finland was Marshal Carl Gustaf von Mannerheim. He had begun constructing a defensive line earlier in the 1930s, based on a 40 mile front, blocking the main route for an attacking army hoping to take Finland's most populous region. This defensive line was made up of modern pill boxes and anti-tank ditches along the Karelian Isthmus. It was a strong position to defend but could by no means hold out indefinitely against the sheer numbers the Soviets could throw at it and was designed to give time for outside assistance to arrive.

Facing these defenses were 1.2 million men of the Soviet Army, comprising 26 divisions, supported by 1,500 tanks and 3,000 aircraft of all types. But with all this abundance the Soviets soon ran into problems with communication between men and machines, as well as the problem of supply. The Russian plan was to advance on all fronts and for the total occupation of Finland. This could not be possible as there was only room to maneuver in the south and the north.

Mannerheim managed to check the advance of the Soviets on the Karelian Isthmus with relative ease and did not even have to deploy his strategic reserve. This was partly due to the lack of leadership on the Soviet side

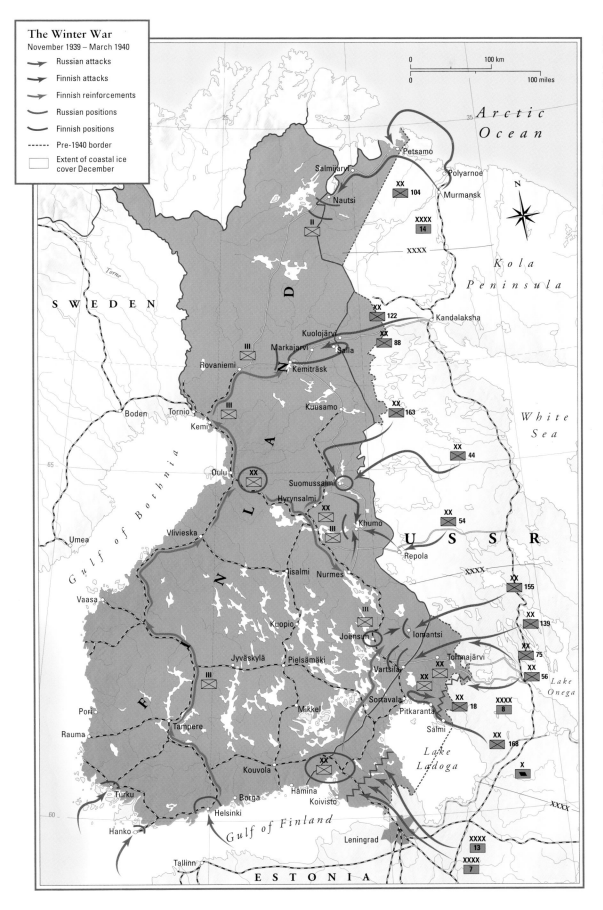

The Winter War
November 1939 – March 1940

→ Russian attacks
→ Finnish attacks
→ Finnish reinforcements
⌒ Russian positions
⌒ Finnish positions
--- Pre-1940 border
☐ Extent of coastal ice cover December

FINNISH WAR
*The first real test for
Stalin's Army came at
the end of 1939. On
30 November, Soviet
troops invaded Finland.
The campaign was a
disaster, after initial
Finnish successes.
However, sheer numbers
of men and heavy guns
were ultimately reflected
in the Soviets' favor.*

thanks to Stalin's earlier purges of the officer class. The advantage of having so many aircraft did not assist the Soviets either; the short winter days offered few daylight hours to fly, resulting in heavy losses and little strategic gain. The number of tanks facing the Finns could have created a huge problem: they had little or no anti-armor weapons and scant knowledge of armored warfare. This was soon learnt in the harsh conditions and the Finns employed many improvised weapons such as the Molotov cocktail, a bottle filled with petrol with a simple fuse, lit before throwing.

The Soviets employed their tanks independently of their infantry so the Finns could sneak up on them at night and attack with relative ease. Up in the north the Murmansk troops had taken the port of Petsamo and began moving south towards Nautsi, cutting Finland off from the Arctic Ocean.

In late December the Finnish army counterattacked all along the Eastern Front, using ski troops to penetrate around and behind the Russians, who were having to use the road network. These attacks created isolated pockets of resistance, which were slowly destroyed one by one. The Soviets suffered heavy losses—almost four divisions—with the Finns using captured equipment against their former owners.

At the start of February, after intensive training in tank infantry cooperation, the Soviets launched a fresh attack against the Mannerheim Line, and broke through on 11 February. The Finns fell back to a second line of defense but this was again broken by the massive attacking force. The Soviets then launched an attack into the rear positions of the Finnish lines across the frozen sea west of Viipuri. With bleak prospects Mannerheim urged his government to make peace.

The Soviet terms were for the port of Hanko as well as the whole of the Karelian Isthmus including Viipuri and the northern portion of Lake Ladoga. The Finns hoped for Anglo-French intervention but when this was found

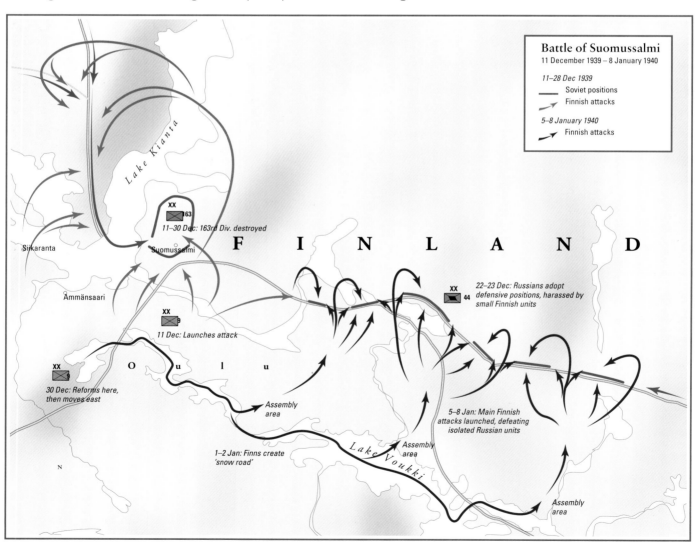

lacking they eventually signed the Treaty of Moscow on 12 March 1940. The Russians lost more than 126,000 men and almost 300,000 more were evacuated through injury and frostbite. Much material was lost, but more importantly it showed a lack of military competence in beating the tiny Finnish army. The Soviets' credibility had been tarnished, leading commanders to set about a serious reorganization of the army. The lessons of this campaign were not lost on the German observers.

MOLOTOV'S BREAD BASKET

The RRAB-3 (above right) was a Soviet cluster bomb used against Finnish cities in the Winter War. On being dropped, it could scatter up to a hundred incendiary devices over a large area. The bread-basket nickname was an ironical coinage of the Finnish people, a reference to Soviet foreign minister Molotov's claims that Russian planes were dropping food parcels, not bombs, on Finland. As for the Finns, they had a secret weapon of their own. Their white-clad ski patrols (right) were extremely adept at approaching Soviet columns unseen, launching an ambush, and sliding away into the featureless snowfields before the enemy could strike back. The Red Army learned from this experience, and later deployed similar tactics against the Germans in the snowy landscape of the Eastern Front.

THE PHONEY WAR

"We're gonna hang out the washing on the Siegfried Line
Have you any dirty washing, mother dear?
We're gonna hang out the washing on the Siegfried Line
'Cos the washing day is here.
Whether the weather may be wet or fine,
We'll just rub along without a care.
We're gonna hang out the washing on the Siegfried Line
If the Siegfried Line's still there."

BRITISH "PHONEY WAR" HIT SONG

The day Poland capitulated, 27 September 1939, Hitler announced his intention to attack the Western powers. A blueprint for this attack—named Plan Yellow—was submitted by Oberkommando des Heeres (O.K.H.) on 19 October. This called for a drive to Dutch and Belgian coastlines, creating a secure base for further operations against British and French forces in northern France. As far as Hitler was concerned this was a completely inadequate plan. He required something much more decisive. Bad weather forced a series of postponements and O.K.H. gave in. Plan Yellow was cancelled when a small group of German officers, carrying copies of the plan, force-landed in Belgium on 9 January 1940.

A new plan was drawn up by General Manstein. It was codenamed *Sichelschnitt*—"Sickle Cut"—and was much more in line with Hitler's own ideas. It became the master plan to encircle the French and British armies. The

detailed plan was drawn up by O.K.H. and was ready by 24 February 1940.

The Allies, the French and British, depended on the Maginot Line to defend the Franco-German frontier. France had poured an enormous amount of its national wealth into the construction of this defensive line. The country's major problem with Germany was a demographic one; Germany's existing population and birth rates were substantially higher than France's. If these trends continued Germany could always field more troops than France. Therefore an essentially defensive war was the best hope for France. Belgium was to be covered, in the event of a German advance in that direction, by mobile forces advancing to the line of the River Dyle with its right flank in the Ardennes Forest, which the allies considered impassible by armored forces.

However, what the Allies considered impassible was the subject of extensive German exercises, to drive an

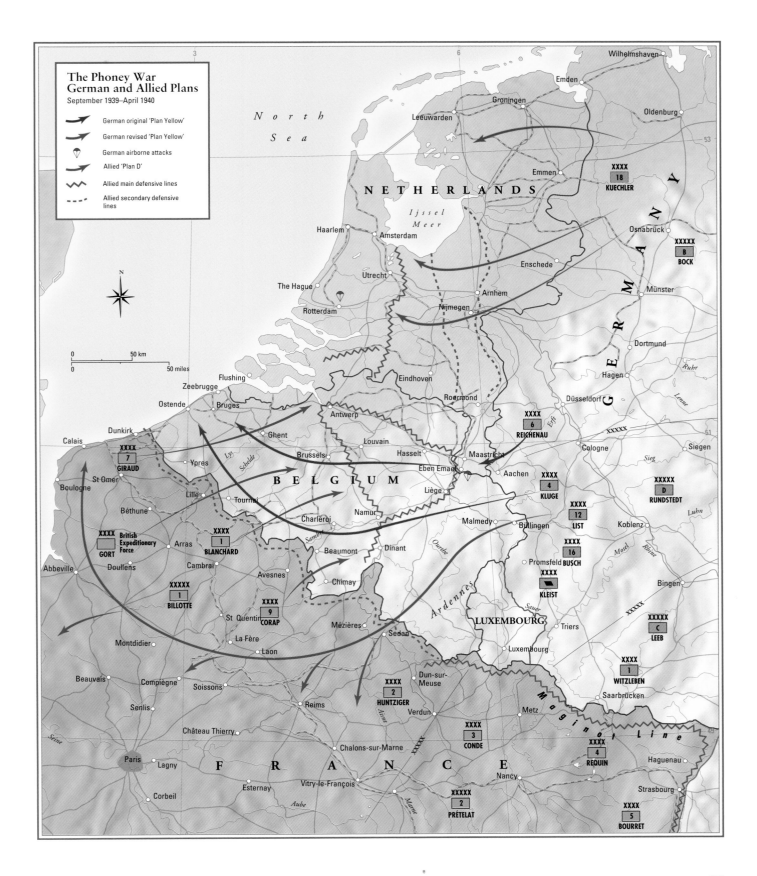

The Phoney War
German and Allied Plans
September 1939–April 1940

➤ German original 'Plan Yellow'

➤ German revised 'Plan Yellow'

⛟ German airborne attacks

➤ Allied 'Plan D'

〰 Allied main defensive lines

╌╌ Allied secondary defensive lines

armored thrust and bypass the Maginot Line was a critical part of Manstein's plan. Sickle Cut planned to drive armored columns through the Ardennes Forest and cross the formidable River Meuse at Dinant, Sedan, and Monthermé. The columns would then turn northwest and drive as hard as possible for the Channel coast, trapping the British Expeditionary Force (B.E.F.) together with the French First Army Group and surviving Belgians. German Army Group B would attack in the Netherlands and eastern Belgium, backed by the specialist airborne forces, especially at the key Belgium fortress of Eben Emael. The southern Army Group C, under von Leeb, was to engage the garrison of the Maginot Line and penetrate. It was not allotted any tanks to achieve this.

Both sides were about equal in divisions: 94 French, 12 British, 9 Dutch, and 22 Belgian opposed 136 German. The Allies, however, had few dedicated tank formations. The Germans concentrated their tank force into ten dedicated divisions, so their 2,500 tanks were far more effectively controlled than the dispersed 3,000 Allied tanks. The Germans could also deploy over 3,200 modern

aircraft in support of their armies. The Allies had around 2,000 aircraft, though many of them were of doubtful quality. Perhaps the most decisive part of the operation was the German doctrine of Blitzkrieg, while Allied forces practiced only defensive war and its High Command lacked a firm, clear structure of command and control, thinking in terms of a slightly updated war of 1918. In September 1939, the British and French had mobilized

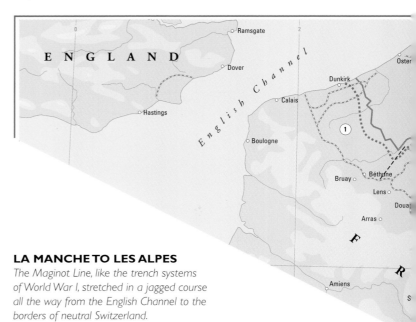

THE DECAYING MAGINOT LINE
The Line took the form of a long string of fortifications, gun emplacements, and underground communications tunnels. Vast resources were devoted to building the Maginot Line but when the invasion came much of it was bypassed. All that is left is some forlorn twentieth-century archaeology.

LA MANCHE TO LES ALPES
The Maginot Line, like the trench systems of World War I, stretched in a jagged course all the way from the English Channel to the borders of neutral Switzerland.

their armies, approximately 3,000,000 for France and almost 450,000 for Britain, of which some 300,000 were sent to France as the B.E.F. This was almost all of Britain's mobile army and it was the entirety of its tank force. During September, October and the following months British forces took their places at the 'front' that stretched from Switzerland along the Maginot Line, the Belgian border and to the Channel coast.

During the winter of 1939 and spring of 1940, British and French troops expected to replay tactics of the last war, but on a more sensible defensive line, in the expectation that the Germans would wear themselves out. But this time the German enemy was not playing by the same rules. The Treaty of Versailles had removed the old plan, persuading the Germans to develop new tactics. On 10 May 1940 these tactics would be tested.

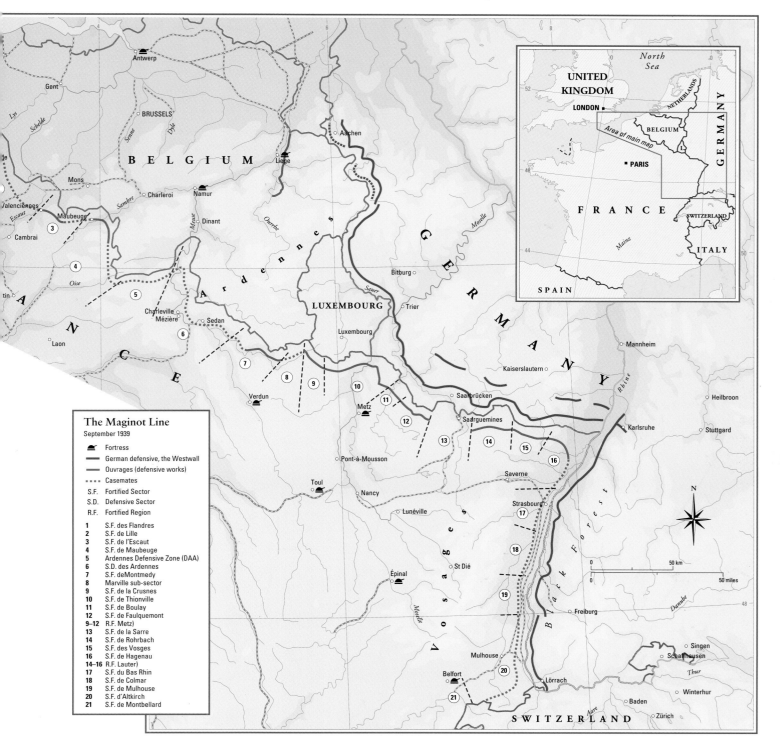

The Maginot Line
September 1939

⚓ Fortress
▬▬▬ German defensive, the Westwall
▬▬▬ Ouvrages (defensive works)
••••• Casemates
S.F.   Fortified Sector
S.D.   Defensive Sector
R.F.   Fortified Region

1	S.F. des Flandres
2	S.F. de Lille
3	S.F. de l'Escaut
4	S.F. de Maubeuge
5	Ardennes Defensive Zone (DAA)
6	S.D. des Ardennes
7	S.F. de Montmedy
8	Marville sub-sector
9	S.F. de la Crusnes
10	S.F. de Thionville
11	S.F. de Boulay
12	S.F. de Faulquemont
9–12	R.F. Metz)
13	S.F. de la Sarre
14	S.F. de Rohrbach
15	S.F. des Vosges
16	S.F. de Hagenau
14–16	R.F. Lauter)
17	S.F. du Bas Rhin
18	S.F. de Colmar
19	S.F. de Mulhouse
20	S.F. d'Altkirch
21	S.F. de Montbellard

INVASIONS OF DENMARK & NORWAY 1940

"The whole of northern Norway was covered with snow to depths which none of our soldiers had ever seen, felt, or imagined. There were neither snow-shoes nor skis—still less skiers. We must do our best. Thus began this ramshackle campaign."

WINSTON CHURCHILL, 1940

In order to sustain Hitler's expansion of the Reich, Germany required the raw materials to fuel it. Most pressing was the iron ore that Germany imported from the neutral country of Sweden. The French and the British were well aware of the importance of this material, and both sides raced for control of it. The German plan would mean the invasion of Norway. In order for Germany to do this it first had to deal with Denmark.

Denmark had only a tiny army and even smaller airforce and navy. This was not going to be the Wehrmacht's toughest assignment. In the early hours of 9 April, 1940 Germany invaded. It faced some small resistance in North Schleswig, but this was quickly overpowered. The Danish navy, in charge of defending the numerous ports of Denmark, allowed German troop ships to enter Copenhagen at will. The very first airborne attacks occurred during this fleeting campaign, with the fort at Madneso and the airport of Aalborg north of Jutland being swiftly taken by the elite Fallschirmjäger (German parachute troops). With Copenhagen occupied by the morning, the Danish government ordered a ceasefire and the Danish invasion ended.

France and Britain had been planning to send an expeditionary force to the northern Norwegian port of Narvik since the beginning of hostilities between the Finns and the Soviets. This was really a cover so they could secure the port and control the all important iron ore from Sweden. The Nazis beat them to it. As German forces were taking Denmark with relative ease another German combined force was on its way to Norway. Surprise was total with troops coming in by air and sea, the airborne troops taking the airports of Stavanger and Oslo, which were vital for the follow-up transports to land more troops and material. The coastal cities were also taken stretching from Kristiansand in the south to Narvik in the very north of the country. The Norwegians defending these ports were soon overwhelmed but did manage to sink the German cruiser Blücher with torpedoes and artillery fire from the Oscarsborg fortress in the Oslofjord.

After these setbacks, the Norwegian government retreated into the interior of the country and King Haakon VII, gave command of the army to Major-General Otto Ruge, who quickly set up plans for a fighting retreat to slow down the German advance long enough for

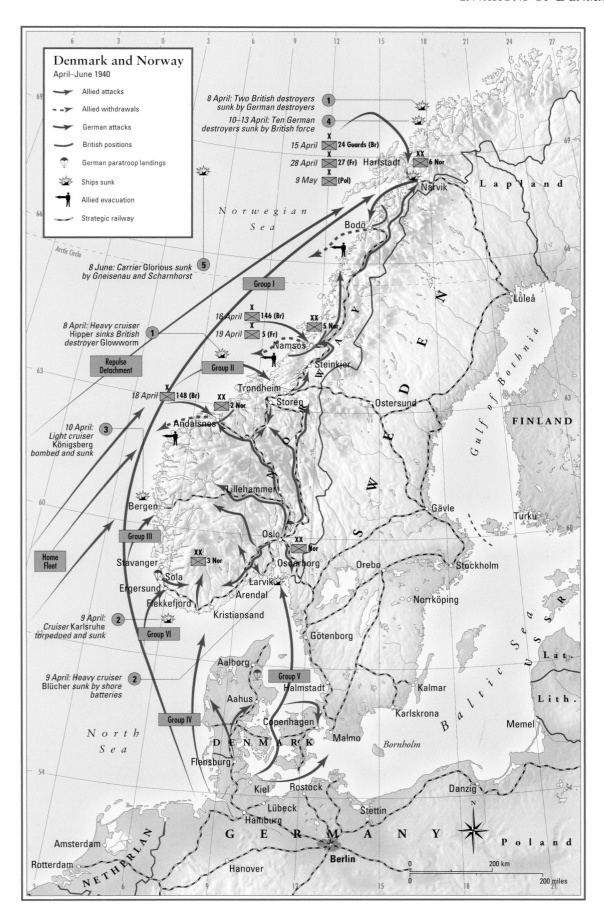

Denmark and Norway
April–June 1940

→ Allied attacks
⇢ Allied withdrawals
➤ German attacks
⌣ British positions
⛉ German paratroop landings
✺ Ships sunk
⚓ Allied evacuation
〜 Strategic railway

8 April: Two British destroyers sunk by German destroyers
10–13 April: Ten German destroyers sunk by British force

1

4

15 April: 24 Guards (Br)
28 April: 27 (Fr)
9 May: (Pol)

Harstadt

6 Nor

Narvik

Lapland

Norwegian Sea

Bodö

8 June: Carrier Glorious sunk by Gneisenau and Scharnhorst

5

Arctic Circle

Group I

16 April: 146 (Br)
19 April: 5 (Fr)

5 Nor

8 April: Heavy cruiser Hipper sinks British destroyer Glowworm

1

Namsos

Repulse Detachment

Group II

Steinkjer

Luleå

Gulf of Bothnia

18 April: 148 (Br)

2 Nor

Trondheim

Storen

Ostersund

FINLAND

10 April: Light cruiser Königsberg bombed and sunk

3

Andalsnes

Lillehammer

Bergen

Gävle

Turku

Group III

Oslo

Nor

Oscarborg

Orebo

Stockholm

Home Fleet

Stavanger

3 Nor

Norrköping

Sola

Larvik

Ergersund

Arendal

9 April: Cruiser Karlsruhe torpedoed and sunk

2

Flekkefjord

Kristiansand

Group VI

USSR

Göteborg

Lat.

9 April: Heavy cruiser Blücher sunk by shore batteries

2

Aalborg

Group V

Halmstadt

Kalmar

Lith.

Aahus

Karlskrona

Memel

Copenhagen

Malmo

Bornholm

Group IV

North Sea

DENMARK

Baltic Sea

Flensburg

Kiel

Rostock

Danzig

Lübeck

Stettin

Hamburg

GERMANY

Poland

Amsterdam

NETHERLAND

Berlin

0   200 km
0   200 miles

Rotterdam

Hanover

33

outside assistance to arrive. When this arrived in the form of a British Expeditionary Force south of the port of Trondheim they were sent to reinforce the Norwegian troops in that sector but were soon evacuated after a poorly attempted attack on the city. From this stage all Allied resistance was based in the north of the country.

In the north the Allied forces were trying desperately to eject German forces from the Narvik area. The Royal Navy had done its part well by driving off the German navy in the area. The port was eventually re-taken on 28 May by French and Norwegian troops. But the invasion of Belgium, Holland, and France now had the Allies looking elsewhere and suddenly Norway was not as important as originally thought. The Royal Navy began to evacuate troops at the beginning of June, along with the Norwegian government and the King, who would sit out the rest of the war in exile in London. This was not to be the last large scale evacuation the Allies would have to cope with.

The Germans suffered the heaviest casualties, losing 5,500 men and 200 aircraft. Crucially they also lost two major modern warships that would never quite allow the German surface fleet to recover. The British lost about 4,000 men, including 1,500 men lost with the sinking of the carrier Glorious. The Norwegians lost 1,800 men and the French about 500.

FLATTENED CITIES

The invasion of Norway was as ruthless and destructive as any Blitzkrieg operation. The town of Steinkjer (above) was severely damaged, as were Namsos and Bodø.

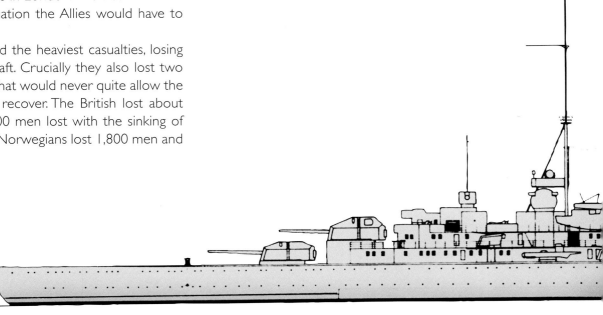

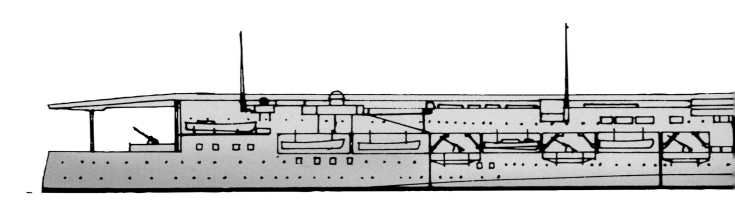

THE SHIPS OF THE BATTLE OF NORWAY

The intense seaborne campaign waged by both the British and the German navies resulted in the loss of many ships. The British destroyer Glowworm spotted the German heavy cruiser Admiral Hipper on 8 April, immediately engaging it. After inflicting serious damage on the German ship, she was lost with few survivors. The Blücher, one of Germany's new heavy cruisers, was the lead ship for Task Force 5 heading for Oslo. On board were many Gestapo officers intended for the new administration, and 900 men of the 163rd Infantry Division. The Blücher was engaged at short range by shore batteries in the Dröbak Narrows as she attempted to approach Oslo. She was also hit by two torpedoes fired from a shore battery. She sank with great loss of life. The Glorious operated as part of a British Task Force and was caught unawares by the German battlecruisers Scharnhorst and Gneisenau, which sank her.

HMS GLOWWORM

Destroyer	launched 1935
Displacement	1370 tons
Length	323 feet
Armament	4 x 4.7 inch guns
	10 x 21 inch torpedoes
Crew	145

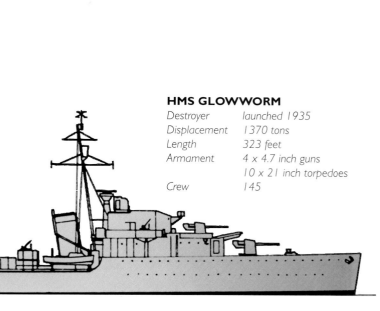

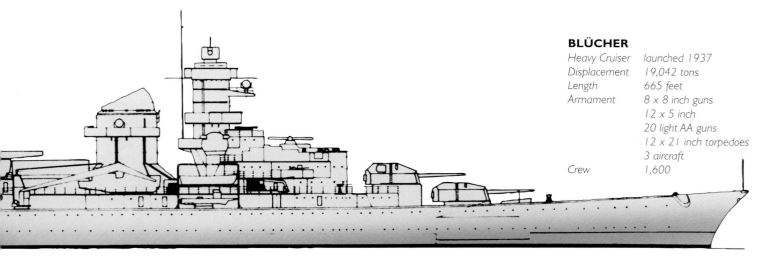

BLÜCHER

Heavy Cruiser	launched 1937
Displacement	19,042 tons
Length	665 feet
Armament	8 x 8 inch guns
	12 x 5 inch
	20 light AA guns
	12 x 21 inch torpedoes
	3 aircraft
Crew	1,600

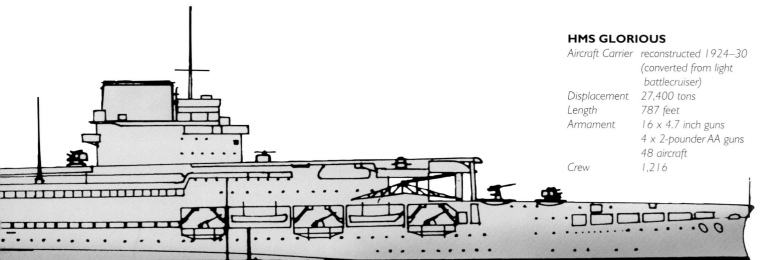

HMS GLORIOUS

Aircraft Carrier	reconstructed 1924–30
	(converted from light
	battlecruiser)
Displacement	27,400 tons
Length	787 feet
Armament	16 x 4.7 inch guns
	4 x 2-pounder AA guns
	48 aircraft
Crew	1,216

THE BATTLE OF SEDAN 1940

"Schützenregiment I has at 22:40 taken high hill just to the north of Cheveuges. Last enemy blockhouse in our hands. A complete breakthrough!"

LIEUTENANT-COLONEL HERMANN BALCK, NEAR SEDAN

The key to the German attack in the West was the advance through the "impassable" Ardennes Forest and the capture of the river crossings along the Meuse River. After the German attack on 10 May, a major consequence of the French theory of the "impassable" Ardennes was that their failure to move the full complement of men and guns assigned to this sector and to Namur, in Belgium, to link up with forces in Givet, in France, before the German armored columns arrived.

Erwin Rommel and Heinz Guderian were given the task of making the initial breakthrough. Guderian stated that it was vital for his force to be on the Meuse within five days of the start of the campaign. In fact, both commanders' units were on the Meuse in two and a half days. The first attempt to cross was made just after 4:00 pm on 12 May at Dinant. Four tanks of the 7th Panzer rushed to seize the bridge. At least one got within 33 feet of the bridge when it was blown up. German aerial reconnaissance revealed another bridge still standing almost four and a half miles to the north, near Yvoir. The commander of 31st Panzer Regiment, part of the 5th Panzer Division, immediately ordered armored vehicles forward to attempt to capture it. The column reached the bridge and the leading vehicle, an armored car, was about halfway across when a sole Belgian soldier

manning a 47 mm anti-tank gun fired, hitting the armored car. It swerved sideways and burst into flames. French forces were in the process of taking over the defense of the bridge from their Belgian allies, but it was left to a Belgian lieutenant to blow the bridge. In much confusion the bridge was blown up, taking two German armored cars with it. The Germans, for a moment, fell back.

Another attempt to cross the river on the remains of a blown railroad bridge between Houx and Yvoir by the German infantry was beaten back by Belgian infantry. After these initial failures the Germans sent reconnaissance patrols to locate suitable crossing points. One of these patrols found an island connected by a weir and lock: the French had not been able to destroy this because the level of the river would have been lowered, making the sector fordable in many places. The Germans waited until nightfall then, around 11:00 pm, their infantry crossed and much to their surprise were not fired on; the immediate area on the west bank was undefended. The French had identified this weir as a possible problem but, such was the poor quality of their command and control, they had not reacted until it was too late. Eventually the French opened fire on the weir but despite this the Germans continued to feed soldiers across, gaining their first foothold on the west bank of the Meuse.

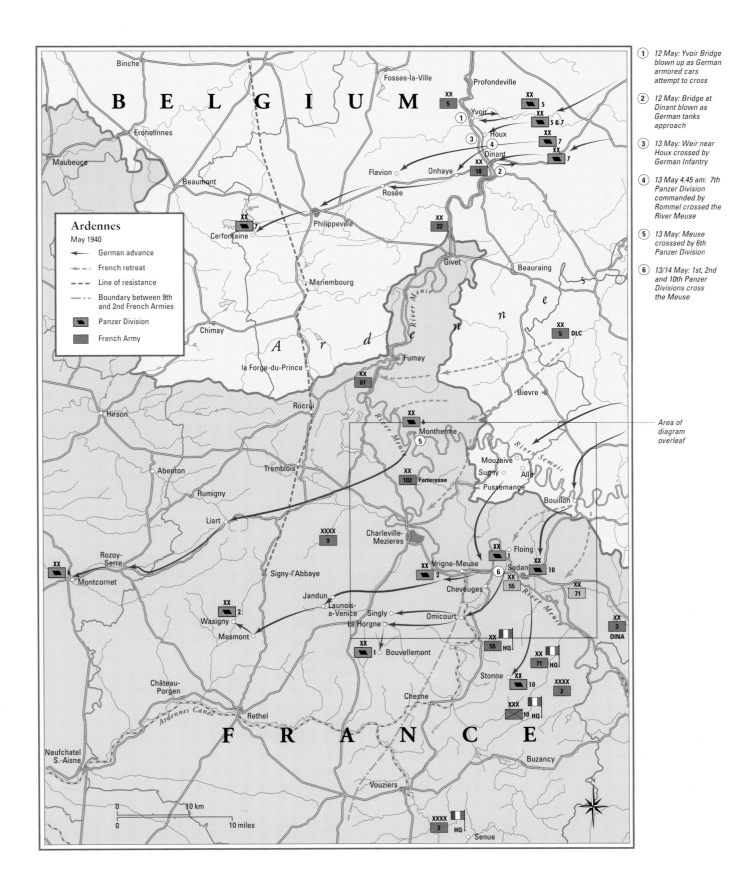

① 12 May: Yvoir Bridge blown up as German armored cars attempt to cross

② 12 May: Bridge at Dinant blown as German tanks approach

③ 13 May: Weir near Houx crossed by German Infantry

④ 13 May 4.45 am: 7th Panzer Division commanded by Rommel crossed the River Meuse

⑤ 13 May: Meuse crosssed by 6th Panzer Division

⑥ 13/14 May: 1st, 2nd and 10th Panzer Divisions cross the Meuse

Area of diagram overleaf

Ardennes
May 1940

⟵ German advance

⟵ French retreat

--- Line of resistance

--- Boundary between 9th and 2nd French Armies

▮ Panzer Division

▮ French Army

Meanwhile, on the night of 12 May, the French commanders of this sector, including General Gamelin, slept soundly in their headquarters believing all was well. German commanders were not so comfortable knowing the next 24 hours could be critical. Once again failures in the French command aided the Germans. General Huntziger, commander of the French 2nd Army, knew from reports coming from the 5th Division Légère de Cavalerie (D.L.C.), a French cavalry unit forming an advance screen about 18½ miles north east of Sedan, that the Germans were well on their way to the line of the Meuse. Huntziger ordered the 71st Division, held in reserve, north to support the 55th Division and 147th Fortress Regiment.

The 71st, some 31 miles behind the first line, lacked transport and an order from Huntziger to make best speed to the front. Advance units of the 71st arrived on the night of 13/14 May, but too late for the 55th to redeploy and consolidate its positions. These second line French units, which were made up of elderly reservists who had perhaps hoped to see out the war in a quiet sector, lacked equipment. They should have had 100,000 mines to defend the most exposed positions but only had 2,000, none of which worked. Planned equipment

also called for over 100 anti-tank guns but by 10 May they had received just nine. Heading for the elderly reservists was one of the best-trained, most-determined armored forces yet created.

Some time after 7:00 am the first of many air attacks began. The bombers were joined by Stuka dive-bombers attacking out of a cloudless sky. The French line was cracked but not broken. At 3:00 pm German troops attempted to cross the river in rubber boats, and were met by a fierce artillery barrage. Of the 96 rubber boats setting out, only 15 made it to the Allied bank. After such loss the Germans launched smaller raiding parties, to some extent, were covered by the smoke of explosions and suffered a much lower rate of loss. These small parties of infantry pushed forward, capturing and destroying French positions and creating a gap in the French defenses. German units followed, exploiting and expanding the breach. By 5:45 am on 14 May, a bridge was built over the river, just south of the destroyed Pont de la Gare at Sedan.

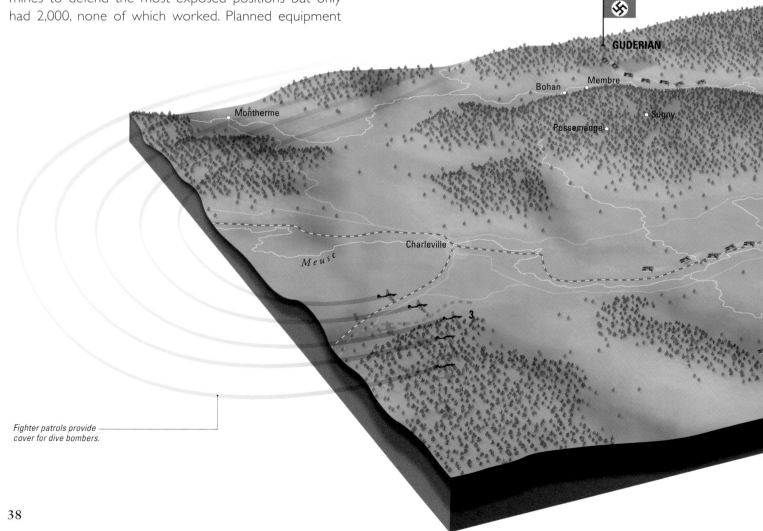

Fighter patrols provide cover for dive bombers.

RIVER CROSSING
A German pontoon bridge over the Meuse. Forlorn French prisoners can be seen among the German troops. The river was key to the Battle of Sedan: the French had to stop the Germans getting across, but failed to do so.

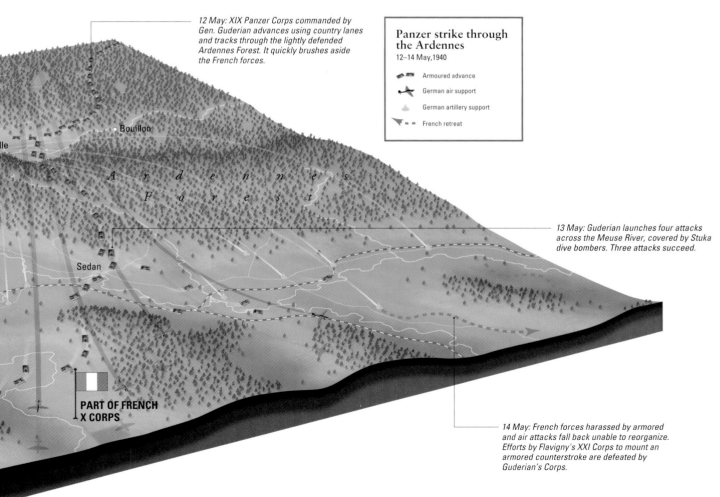

12 May: XIX Panzer Corps commanded by Gen. Guderian advances using country lanes and tracks through the lightly defended Ardennes Forest. It quickly brushes aside the French forces.

Panzer strike through the Ardennes
12–14 May, 1940

- Armoured advance
- German air support
- German artillery support
- French retreat

Bouillon

Ile

A r d e n n e s F o r e s t

Sedan

13 May: Guderian launches four attacks across the Meuse River, covered by Stuka dive bombers. Three attacks succeed.

PART OF FRENCH X CORPS

14 May: French forces harassed by armored and air attacks fall back unable to reorganize. Efforts by Flavigny's XXI Corps to mount an armored counterstroke are defeated by Guderian's Corps.

BLITZKRIEG IN THE WEST

"Gentlemen, you are about to witness the most famous victory in history."

ADOLF HITLER, 9 JUNE 1940

After many months of the Phoney War, Hitler was now ready to strike in the west. Predicting that the Allies would expect the main offensive through Belgium and northern France, General von Manstein drew up a plan that would entail a diversionary thrust through Holland and Belgium, drawing Allied strength and reserves north, while the main Panzer attack would drive through the "impassable" forests of the Ardennes and head for the coast, catching the main body of the Allied armies in an enormous pocket.

Von Bock was to lead Army Group B, consisting of 29 divisions of regular infantry, into Belgium and Holland drawing the main Allied defense force toward him. Meanwhile von Rundstedt's Army Group A had charge of 44 divisions, including almost all the Panzer divisions: sufficient to strike through the Ardennes. General von Leeb had Army Group C, 17 divisions, between Switzerland and Luxembourg, which was holding the French on the Maginot Line.

The French army was similar in size to that opposing it, if not stronger. This advantage was to become void as the command structure, under General Gamelin, was poorly thought through and slow to respond to changing situations. They also had great confidence in the truly giant defenses of the Maginot Line, never expecting them to be merely bypassed. The British had sent over an expeditionary force consisting of ten divisions to bolster the French defense and under French command. The Allies always thought that the main German advance would come through Belgium, just as they had done in

1914, and based their defensive maneuvers on this. Together the British and French came up with the Dyle Plan, which entailed the main forces of the Allies advancing to a line drawn by the River Dyle to Wavre, just east of Brussels, the Belgian capital. In 1940 this line was extended to the River Maas in Holland in order to create one long line from the Channel coast to the Franco-Belgian border.

On the morning of 10 May the town of Eben Emael was attacked by an airborne force that landed on the roof of the fortress. Arriving in gliders the specialist engineers used shaped charges to destroy the gun cupolas that were placed commanding the approaches to the strategic bridges, where the Meuse met with the Albert Canal. While the engineers dealt with the fort, parachute troops landed next to these bridges and captured them quickly. Within 24 hours the 4th Armored Division arrived to consolidate the bridgehead; meanwhile the rest of the Belgian forces still trying to defend the fort capitulated. The Germans lost six troops in this outstanding maneuver, the most successful airborne attack of the entire war.

Von Manstein's plan to lure the Allied armies into a defensive line in northern Belgium achieved great success. Von Rundstedt proceeded to advance through the Ardennes with the bridge crossing the Meuse at Sedan his target. The Panzers rolled through the heavily forested area on extremely narrow roads and met only cursory opposition. Because of the German air superiority, the French and British had no chance of seeing the enormous traffic jam occurring before them. By the evening of the

12 May, seven Panzer divisions stretched from Dinant in the north to Sedan in the south, ready to forge ahead. On 13 May Guderian received the order to force a crossing of the Meuse, under a massive aerial umbrella, with Stukas dive-bombing any defenses and terrifying the French Second Army under the command of General Huntziger. By the end of the day 1st Panzer held a bridgehead three miles wide and four miles deep. The French were slow to attempt to counter-attack, with the 3rd Armored Division keen to strike the weak flank of the German advance, but held back and spread along a thin defensive line. With the Allies now aware of the German bridgehead they attempted to destroy the pontoon that the 1st Panzer had used to force a crossing, sending out a force of obsolete Fairey Battle light bombers. Losses were catastrophic, and the bridge remained intact. With the point of the German advance on the boundary of two French armies the pace of the advance quickened, helped by command and control problems on the French side.

After this failure by the French to contain the Panzers on the Meuse, the German commanders exploited it for all its worth, turning westward toward the Channel. The French commanders were in complete disarray, not knowing what the enemy's main objective was: Paris or the Channel. No major counterattacks were mounted, except for a local offensive action near the town of Montcornet, led by the brilliant young tactician Colonel Charles de Gaulle. However this was soon beaten back by a superior German force.

FORTRESS WITHOUT A ROOF

German paratroopers pose at Eben Emael fort. It was almost impregnable from the outside, but the Germans bypassed its defenses by simply dropping in from the skies. It took only 78 crack troops to capture the fort along with its garrison.

Guderian's Panzers arrived at the Channel on 19 May ending an advance of nearly 200 miles in ten days. This meant that the majority of the Allies' best fighting units were now caught in a pocket in northern France and Belgium with little chance of escape and almost assured destruction.

The Allies attempted a counterattack on 24 May into the flank of the 2nd Panzer and achieved some success before the Germans eventually beat them back to the start line by the end of the day. Then the shocking news came through to the Panzer commanders from the Führer himself for all armored advances to cease; he wanted to let the supply line catch up to the tanks and save them for the rest of France. Hitler preferred to leave the destruction of the B.E.F. to Goering's Luftwaffe, which would simply flatten the army from the air.

The evacuation of an army was a massive undertaking, with all arms playing vital roles. General Gort, leading the B.E.F., set up a perimeter to stop any infantry from penetrating to the beach along the Aa, Scarpe, and Yser canals. Churchill placed Vice-Admiral Ramsey in charge of the naval evacuation and duly sent an order to scrape, borrow, and steal any vessels between nine and 30 feet long on the south coast. These boats, usually piloted by their owners, braved the bombing and strafing to go right

HITLER'S DAY IN PARIS

The Führer visited Paris for the first time on 25 June, some days after his troops had taken the city. He went to various famous locations, and lingered long at the tomb of Napoleon. "I have often considered whether we would have to destroy Paris," he later said to Albert Speer (left).

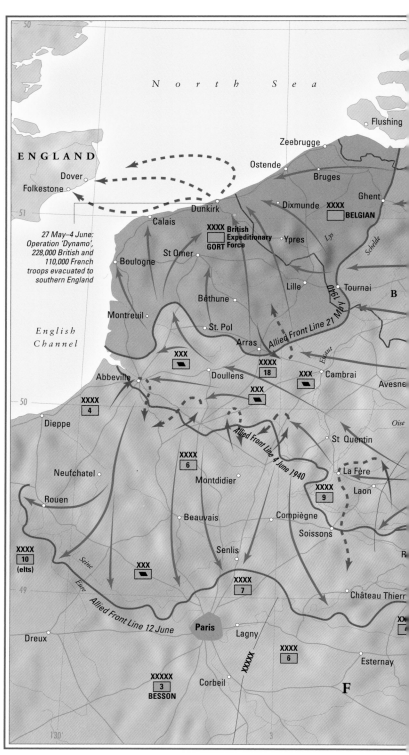

into the beach to pick up the beleaguered troops, who had to stand in the sea sometimes up to their chests for many hours. Boats' crews sometimes had to physically push back the desperate soldiers for fear of overloading and sinking. Over the next eight days, with the R.A.F. vigorously trying to stave off the Luftwaffe and achieving many victories, although vastly outnumbered, the navy and its assorted craft managed to lift off 338,226 men, a third of these being of foreign services. The evacuation had been a success in bringing back the B.E.F.; all arms of the services had worked in unison and achieved an almost impossible task. But it did cost all of the B.E.F.'s equipment, from small-arms to artillery.

After the evacuation and the surrender of Belgium on 28 May, the French were not only on their own but they were in disarray. The Wehrmacht now turned their attentions southward and to the rest of France, with the French digging in on the line of the Somme and the Aisne. The French fought heroically but they were facing overwhelming odds and the Germans soon broke

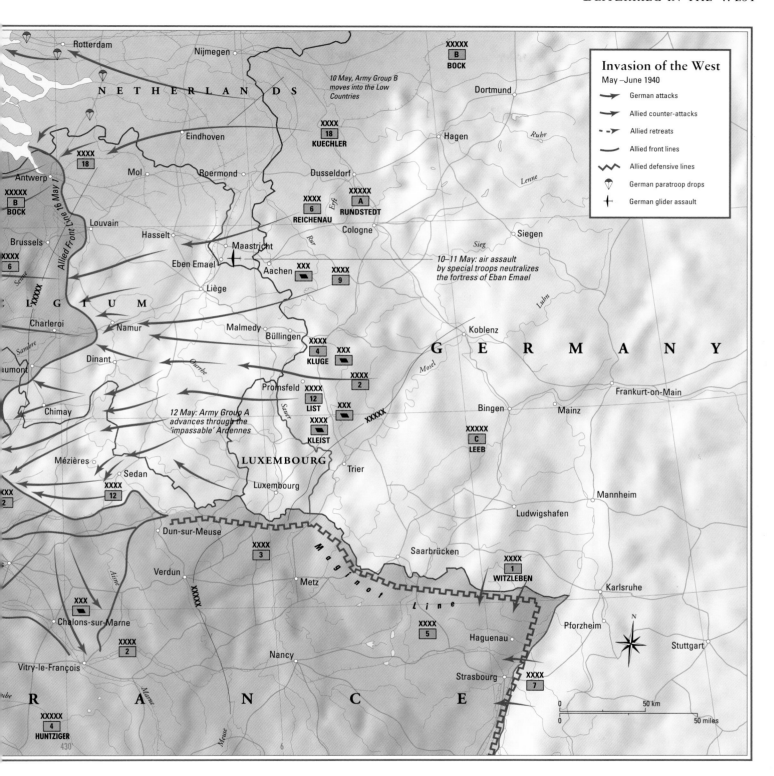

Invasion of the West
May–June 1940

→ German attacks
→ Allied counter-attacks
-→ Allied retreats
⌢ Allied front lines
⌵ Allied defensive lines
☂ German paratroop drops
† German glider assault

10 May, Army Group B moves into the Low Countries

10–11 May: air assault by special troops neutralizes the fortress of Eban Emael

12 May: Army Group A advances through the 'impassable' Ardennes

through and on 14 June entered Paris, which had been proclaimed an open city by the French government for fear of aerial attack and annihilation. With nothing to hold them back the French were forced to agree to an armistice, which was signed on 22 June in the same railroad carriage where they had accepted the German surrender in 1918.

Within six weeks Holland, Belgium, and France were all brought under Nazi control. The human cost of these victories were 30,000 dead German soldiers and airmen and casualties reaching 160,000. The French losses were greater still, with an estimated 90,000 dead, 200,000 wounded and nearly two million missing or taken prisoner by the Germans.

DUNKIRK 1940

"By now dive-bombers seemed to be eternally dropping out of the cloud of enemy aircraft overhead. Within half a mile of the pierheads a two-funneled gray-painted transport had overhauled and was just passing up to port when two salvoes were dropped in quick succession right along her port side. For a few minutes she was hid in smoke and I certainly thought they had got her. Then she reappeared, still gaily heading for the piers, and entered just ahead of us."

COMMANDER C.H. LIGHTOLLER (RETIRED)

After the German attacks on 10 May 1940, the rapid advance, particularly of the Panzer divisions, made a nonsense of the Allied defense plan. By 15 May the British and the Belgians were being outflanked in the north by German advances in the Netherlands. Appearing out of the Ardennes Forest, German Army Group A crossed the River Meuse at Sedan and Dinant, French resistance collapsed at these weakly-held points, allowing the Germans to advance into northern France. Trying to realign his armies Maurice Gamelin, the French commander, agreed to the withdrawal of the French First Army Group and the British Expeditionary Force from the line of the Dyle to the River Scheldt on 16 May. French armored attacks on the 17–19 May, and British on 21 May, gave the Germans a scare and a few temporary problems. But their advance continued, reaching Abbeville by 20 May and then the Channel coast on 22 May. A German attack separated most of the Belgian army from the British on 25 May, leading to Belgian capitulation on 28 May. The British and the French First Army were being squeezed into what would become the Dunkirk perimeter. By Hitler's direct command, the Panzer divisions were halted from 26 to 28 May. The Allies took this moment to draw breath and consider their position. The Germans could not believe their luck, they needed time for infantry to catch up and to service their tanks and transport. Meanwhile, on 27 May the decision to withdraw the Allied forces from Dunkirk was taken. A miracle of improvisation was about to begin.

Under the command of Admiral Ramsey a fleet of ships was assembled, which ranged from pleasure steamers, coasters, family riverboats, and fishing boats to Royal Navy warships. This fleet of all shapes and sizes sailed across the Channel. The smaller craft picked men off the beaches and ferried them to larger vessels in the deeper water, the Royal Navy took men from the Mole, a long jetty in the port of Dunkirk. Above, the R.A.F. home-based fighter force battled to keep the Luftwaffe at bay. Despite their losses the Luftwaffe broke through the British fighter screen, sinking many ships and killing many soldiers on the beaches.

But discipline and training held up: men formed up to take their place on the ships. Somehow they managed to get aboard under air attack, wounded and hungry. Between 26 May and 4 June 222 Royal Navy ships and 665 other commandeered vessels succeeded in bringing back 112,546 French and Belgian soldiers, and 224,585 British troops to British soil. Most of the B.E.F.'s equipment lay abandoned and smashed in France but the men escaped to form the cadre of a new and better army. Most of all, Britain's resolve not to give in was confirmed in the sight of enemy and friends alike.

The remaining British forces in France, mainly the 51st Highland Division, and units of the R.A.F., together with the French forces, were given little respite. On 5 June the German army renewed its attacks and on 20 June Italy attacked south-eastern France.

INTO CAPTIVITY

Though most escaped back to Britain, about 40,000 British soldiers were captured at Dunkirk. They were not kindly treated. They were forced to march to Germany, where those below the rank of corporal were put to work in factories for the duration of the war.

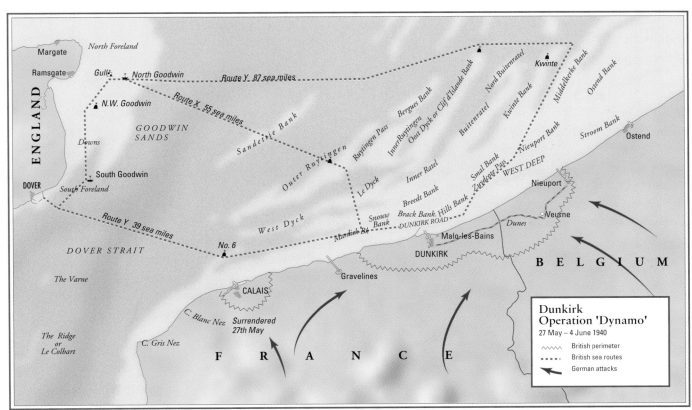

THE FALL OF FRANCE

*"There is nothing preventing the enemy reaching Paris.
We were fighting on our last line and it has been breached.
I am helpless, I cannot intervene ..."*

GENERAL WEYGAND

British and French counterattacks on 17, 18, and 21 May 1940 failed to halt the German advance. Meanwhile, Weygand, the French Supreme Commander, had been organizing a new defensive line along the River Somme and River Aisne. Reinforcements and surviving units from the battles in northern France and Belgium were deployed in the new 4th Army Group formed under the command of General Huntziger which, together with the 2nd and 3rd Army Groups—a total of 50 divisions—held a front line of 230 miles facing a German strength of 120 divisions. Many other French troops manned the static defenses of the outflanked Maginot Line. The French airforce had received limited reinforcement from the British Royal Air Force and mustered over 1,000 aircraft to face the Luftwaffe's complement of almost 3,000 aircraft.

The Germans concentrated almost all of the Panzer divisions in Army Groups A and B to form armored spearheads commanded by Guderian and von Kleist respectively. Von Kleist launched his attack on 5 June and Guderian launched his on 9 June. The French army, facing the onslaught launched by Army Group B, resisted with great valor. Among them was the British 51st Highland Division, the only part of the British Expeditionary Forces still fighting, apart from the R.A.F. However, by the night of 8 June units of Army Group B had broken through the French line and were heading for Paris. On 9 June von Rundstedt's Army Group A launched a series of attacks towards Rheims, meeting fierce resistance. On 11 June the French units facing von Bock's Army Group B attacks collapsed. This forced French units facing von Rundstedt to retreat, falling back behind the River Marne. The continued pressure on the French was maintained by the German ability to drive the armored spearheads forward, protected and supported by the Luftwaffe. The French command structure was not up to facing such a fluid situation and failed to organize defense lines effectively or organize any strategy that would defeat German tactics. On 12 June Guderian's Panzer Group, now joined by von Kleist, broke through east of Paris. On the same day elements of the Tenth Army and surviving units of British forces surrendered at St. Valéry-en-Caux.

However, two days earlier on 10 June the French government under Paul Reynaud left Paris for Tours, leading a vast column of followers and refugees: l'exode. Reynaud was visited at Tours on 11 June by Churchill, who urged continued resistance. On Churchill's return to England, General Charles de Gaulle had risen to his new position as Under-secretary for war, after his valiant effort to stop the German advance at Laon on 17–19 May. De Gaulle was an ardent supporter of the pro-war party in the French Cabinet and at his urging Churchill, on 16 June, made a remarkable proposal to the French government, an 'indissoluble union of Britain and France'. This, it was stated, would be a testimony of their joint determination to fight Germany to the end. It might also

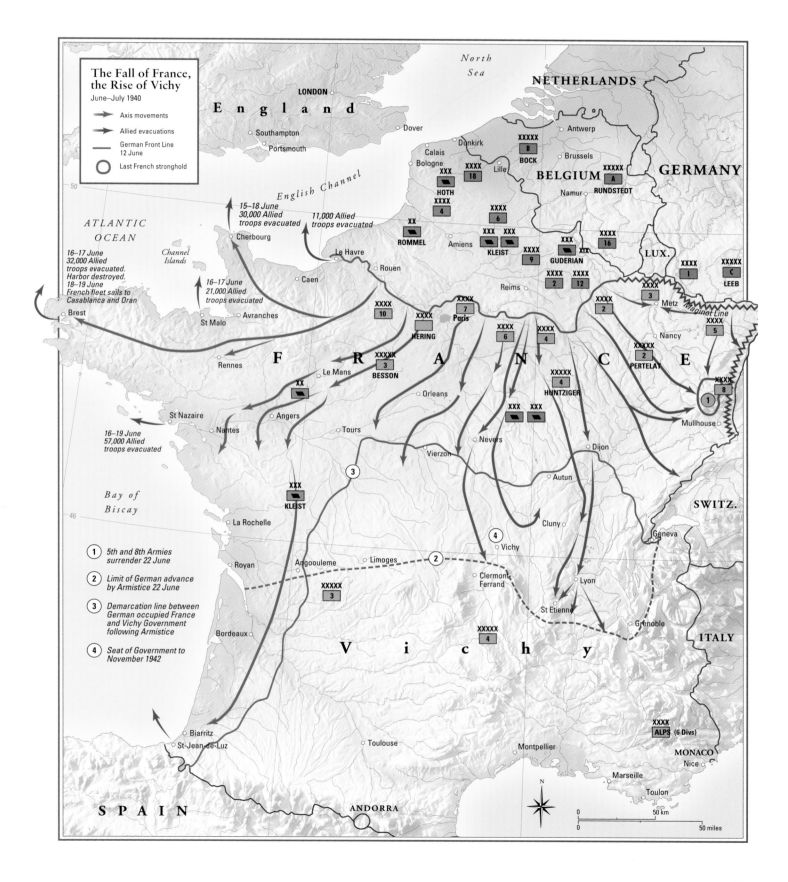

The Fall of France,
the Rise of Vichy
June–July 1940

→ Axis movements
→ Allied evacuations
— German Front Line
  12 June
◯ Last French stronghold

North
Sea

NETHERLANDS

LONDON

England

Southampton   Dover
Portsmouth

English Channel

ATLANTIC
OCEAN

Channel
Islands

Cherbourg

15–18 June
30,000 Allied
troops evacuated

11,000 Allied
troops evacuated

Le Havre

16–17 June
32,000 Allied
troops evacuated.
Harbor destroyed.
18–19 June
French fleet sails to
Casablanca and Oran

16–17 June
21,000 Allied
troops evacuated

Rouen

Caen

Brest

St Malo   Avranches

Rennes

16–19 June
57,000 Allied
troops evacuated

St Nazaire

Nantes

Angers

Le Mans

BESSON
XXXXX
3

NERING
XXXX

Paris
XXXX
7

Reims

Calais
Bologne
Dunkirk
Lille

BOCK
XXXXX
B

Brussels

Antwerp

BELGIUM

Namur

HOTH
XXX

XXXX
18

XXXX
4

XXXX
6

KLEIST
XXX XXX

XXXX
9

GUDERIAN
XXX
XIX

XXXX
2   XXXX
12

GERMANY

RUNDSTEDT
XXXXX
A

LUX.

XXXX
16

XXXX
1

LEEB
XXXXX
C

XXXX
3

Metz

Maginot Line

XXXX
2

Nancy

XXXX
5

PERTELAT
XXXX
2

XXXX
8
◯ 1

Mullhouse

ROMMEL
XX

Amiens

XXXX
10

XXXX
6

XXXX
4

HUNTZIGER
XXXXX
4

XXX XXX

XX

Orleans

Tours

Vierzon

Nevers

Autun

Dijon

Cluny

SWITZ.

Geneva

Bay of
Biscay

KLEIST
XXX

La Rochelle

3

4   Vichy

Lyon

St Etienne

Grenoble

ITALY

1 5th and 8th Armies
   surrender 22 June

2 Limit of German advance
   by Armistice 22 June

3 Demarcation line between
   German occupied France
   and Vichy Government
   following Armistice

4 Seat of Government to
   November 1942

Royan   Angoouleme   Limoges

2

Clermont
Ferrand

XXXXX
3

Bordeaux

V i c h y

XXXXX
4

Biarritz
St-Jean-de-Luz

Toulouse

Montpellier

Marseille

Toulon

SPAIN

ANDORRA

XXXX
ALPS (6 Divs)

MONACO
Nice

N

50 km
0
0
50 miles

50

46

F R A N C E

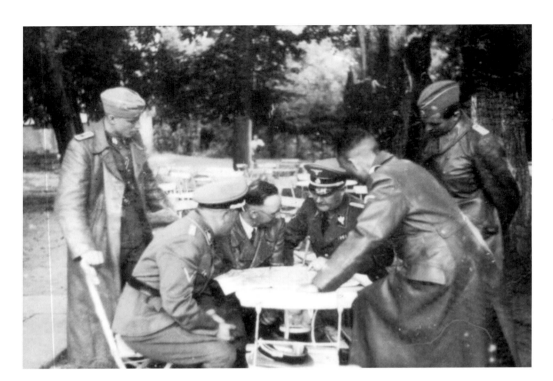

HIMMLER IN FRANCE
*Heinrich Himmler, the head of the
Gestapo, visited France in August
1940, once the fighting was over.
By that time the apparatus of the
Gestapo was falling into place, its
job to root out resistance.*

serve, should France fall, as a way of saving a large portion of the French army and especially the powerful French fleet, thus keeping them in a continued war with Germany from British and French colonial bases.

By this time a large area of France containing over 30 percent of its industrial base was overrun. It was this industry that supplied the French Field Army. Another large portion lay under German gunfire. Many of the French army's supply depots were overrun. If the line could be stabilized, which was doubtful, how could a continued French army of 50–60 divisions be supplied? Equipment and men were being used faster than they could be replaced. The British could only just rearm the returned B.E.F. and could do little or nothing to help further. Any commitment from the United States was unlikely to be effective quickly enough. The French High Command realized this terrible reality very quickly. The British, mesmerized by the size of the French army, were slower to come to terms with this horrific situation. Set against this situation the British proposal of union was unacceptable to the French government, now dominated by their peace party which, on 16 June, appointed the hero of Verdun, Marshall Philippe Pétain, as its new Head of Government.

Pétain immediately formed a new government and that same evening sued through Spanish diplomatic connections for an armistice. The war dragged on for another six days. By 17 June the last British forces were withdrawn from France. There was talk of the French government moving to its colonies in North Africa but in the end no ministers went.

After Hitler and Mussolini, whose army invaded south-eastern France on 20 June, met in Munich, their terms were presented to the new French government on 22 June at Compiègne, on the same train that Germany had signed its armistice with the Allied powers in November 1918.

The 1918 signing had been a quiet, secret affair but this time it was done in the full glare of German propaganda—bands played, soldiers presented arms, photographs were taken, cine films rolled—and amongst all this Hitler arrived to take the surrender. Two days later an agreement was signed with Italy confirming its possession of Nice and parts of Savoy. The zone of German occupation was somewhat smaller than the area conquered by the advancing army. The zone libre (free zone), its capital at Vichy, ran south of the River Loire, less its Atlantic and Alpine frontiers. The French empire and its fleet remained in the hands of the Vichy government. The provinces of Alsace-Lorraine were ceded to Germany. The French war was over. France would be drained of its productive resources and its young men sent to labor in Germany. However, it was not the end, many Frenchmen fought on at home and abroad with the hope that one day they would see a liberated France. It would take four long and bloody years.

France
After end of June 1940

Germany after June 1940

Occupied by Germany from June 1940

France (Vichy) from end of June 1940

Italy and Italian-occupied end of June 1940

Neutral

GREAT BRITAIN

London
Free French base from 17 June 1940

North Sea

NETHERLANDS

Dover

Dunkirk

Antwerp

Calais

Brussels

Bologne

Lille

BELGIUM

Namur

English Channel

ATLANTIC OCEAN

GERMANY

Cherbourg

Amiens

Le Havre

Rouen

Channel Islands occupied June 1940–May 1945

Caen

Rheims

Metz

Brest

Avranches

Paris

Government evacuated to Tours then Bordeaux 9 June 1940

St Malo

Nancy

Rennes

F R A N C E

occupied France from 22 June 1940

Le Mans

Orleans

Mullhouse

St Nazaire

Angers

Tours

Nevers

Nantes

Dijon

Vierzon

Autun

SWITZERLAND

Bay of Biscay

La Rochelle

Cluny

Royan

Limoges

Vichy

Geneva
Savoy

Angouleme

seat of government 10 June 1940–Nov. 1942

Lyon

St Etienne

N

V i c h y

Grenoble

ITALY

Bordeaux

under Vichy administration; occupied by German 11 November 1942

Genoa

0   50 km

0   50 miles

Biarritz

Toulouse

St-Jean-de-Luz

Montpellier

MONACO

Nice

Marseille

Toulon

ANDORRA

Corsica occupied by Germany 1942

July 1940 elements of French fleet return from N. Africa; 27 November 1942 French fleet scuttled

SPAIN

49

THE BATTLE OF BRITAIN

"The Battle of France is over.
The Battle of Britain is about to begin.
Upon this battle depends the future of Christian civilization."

WINSTON CHURCHILL, JUNE 1940

After the British withdrawal from Dunkirk and the fall of France, Hitler expected that Britain would sue for peace and end the war in Europe. However, Churchill, with the support of the British people, committed Britain and its Commonwealth to see the war through to a victorious conclusion, no matter how desperate the circumstances seemed. On 16 July Hitler ordered the directive for Operation Sealion as a prelude to a full cross-channel invasion, and the Luftwaffe was instructed to destroy the air defense of Great Britain.

Hitler was entirely confident of his overwhelming advantage, so much so that he seemed somewhat puzzled by Churchill's refusal to discuss terms. "As England, in spite of the hopelessness of the military position, has so far shown herself unwilling to come to any compromise," announced the Führer, "I have decided to begin to prepare for, and if necessary to carry out the invasion of England. This operation is dictated by the necessity of eliminating Great Britain as a base from which the war against Germany can be fought, and if necessary, the island will be occupied."

The campaign would be decided for the first time by air power alone. German control of the air would be crucial in protecting German seaborne forces as they crossed the English Channel. The might of the British Navy would have to be defeated, or at least held at bay, by the Luftwaffe in order that the invasion fleet could land its troops without suffering a complete disaster.

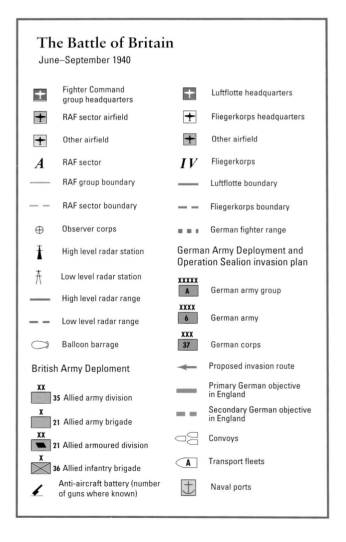

The Battle of Britain
June–September 1940

Fighter Command group headquarters		Luftflotte headquarters	
RAF sector airfield		Fliegerkorps headquarters	
Other airfield		Other airfield	
A RAF sector		*IV* Fliegerkorps	
RAF group boundary		Luftflotte boundary	
RAF sector boundary		Fliegerkorps boundary	
Observer corps		German fighter range	

High level radar station

Low level radar station

High level radar range

Low level radar range

Balloon barrage

German Army Deployment and Operation Sealion invasion plan

XXXXX A — German army group

XXXX 6 — German army

XXX 37 — German corps

British Army Deploment

XX 35 Allied army division

X 21 Allied army brigade

XX 21 Allied armoured division

X 36 Allied infantry brigade

Anti-aircraft battery (number of guns where known)

Proposed invasion route

Primary German objective in England

Secondary German objective in England

Convoys

Transport fleets

Naval ports

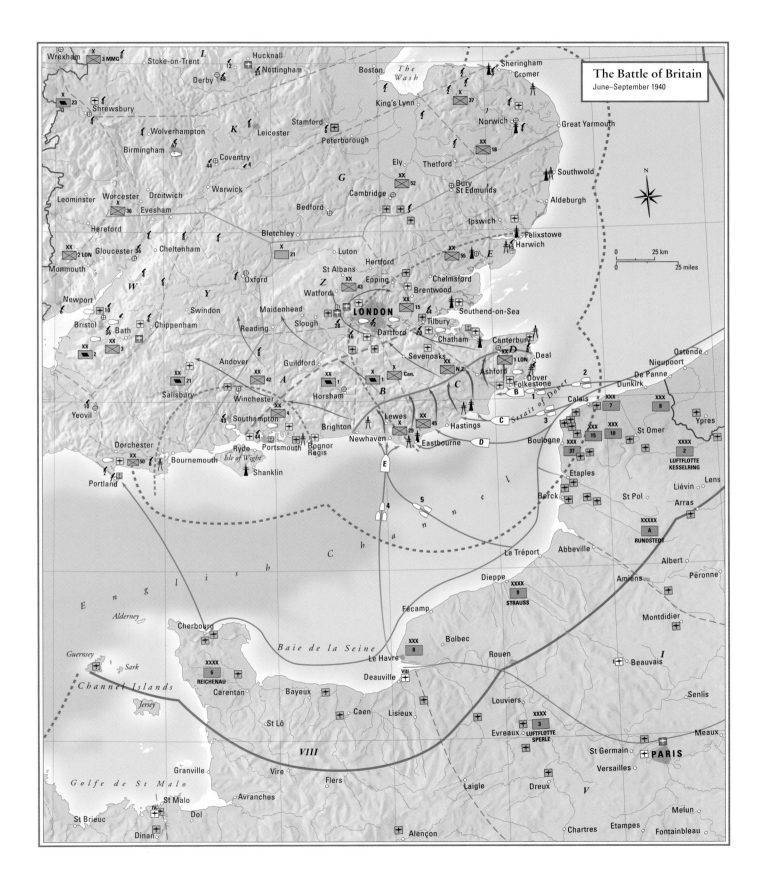

The Battle of Britain
June–September 1940

Although the Luftwaffe was still recovering from its losses in the French campaign, it could still command 2,669 aircraft, of which 993 were single-engine fighters, 375 long-range twin-engine fighters protecting a force of 1,015 bombers and 346 dive-bombers.

Facing this threat the R.A.F. had 704 fighters, mostly single-engine Hurricanes and Spitfires, but including some slower, older aircraft and around 440 bombers. The bombers would have to bomb German transport concentrations in the Channel ports and the invasion force, should it appear.

The figures may seem to have been heavily in favor of the Luftwaffe, but the British had been preparing their air defense for a number of years. The key element was Radio Location (Radar) and the command and control structure based around it. This would allow the British to keep their fighters on the ground until directed against specific targets. Those targets were German formations "spotted" by radar forming up over northern France and tracked as they approached southern England.

The Germans, however, were unprepared for long-range operations, since their airforce had been designed for the support of ground forces. Their fighter escort for the bomber formations had limited range and could only escort the bombers for some 20 minutes over England, leaving them at the mercy of British fighters. The Royal Air Force also had the inestimable advantage of fighting on (or rather above) home turf. The Luftwaffe was operating over enemy territory and any aircraft shot

down meant the loss of a trained crew, while the British crewman, if he survived, could rejoin his unit. In some cases, R.A.F. pilots downed in the morning found themselves back in action the same afternoon.

The first phase of the Battle of Britain opened in July with Luftwaffe attacks on Channel convoys, radar stations, and other targets, mainly along the south coast. German strategy was to draw the British fighter force into combat, destroying the aircraft by sheer force of numbers, competence, and the experience of their aircrews, together with the superiority of their aircraft. However, Britain's command and control system worked too well. Air Vice Marshal Hugh Dowding, the commander of Britain's air defense, was almost always able to concentrate his available aircraft. With the aid of radar, fighters were in the right place at the right time to intercept incoming German raids.

By early August, German raids had become focussed on British airfields and aircraft industry. On 1 August, Hitler issued First Directive No. 17, "for the conduct of air and sea warfare against England [meaning Great Britain]." Aerial battles, however, were already a daily occurrence over southern England. On 13 August—"Adlertag" (Eagle Day)—approximately 1500 German aircraft were launched against England. Despite many previous attacks, the radar-directed air defense system was still intact. On 15 August this massive German force of 1,270 fighters and 520 bombers was directed at British air bases and the support structure that supplied air defense, airfields, repair depots, aircraft factories, and antiaircraft sites.

Thanks to radar, Dowding was able to concentrate his aircraft at crucial locations along the front of the enemy's approach. To the Germans it seemed as though the R.A.F. had an uncanny ability to attack or at least disrupt their every move.

The campaign to destroy the Royal Air Force continued for another month. By mid-August Luftwaffe intelligence had reported that the task was almost complete. However, German pilots reported the opposite. By now British industry was producing 400 fighters per month, against the German's 200. The truth of the matter was the Luftwaffe was weakening while the R.A.F. was growing stronger, though its lack of trained pilots remained a real weakness. However, as the battle progressed, pilots from other commands of the R.A.F. were transferred to Dowding's fighter command. These, together with foreign contingents—French, Czechs, and particularly Poles—made a major contribution to the outcome of the battle.

HAWKER HURRICANES OVERHEAD

The Hurricane was the workhorse of Fighter Command. It was less glamorous than the Spitfire, but inflicted more damage on the Luftwaffe during the Battle of Britain. It was easier to repair than the Spitfire, and the tightly grouped guns in its wings made it a better killing machine.

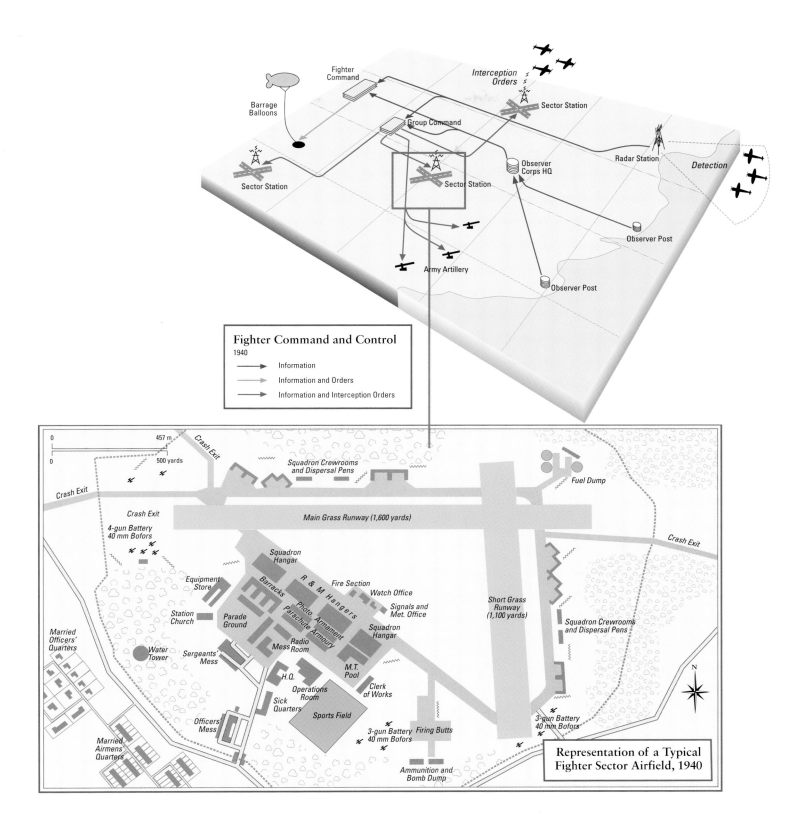

Fighter Command and Control
1940

→ Information
→ Information and Orders
→ Information and Interception Orders

Fighter Command

Interception Orders

Barrage Balloons

Group Command

Sector Station

Radar Station

Detection

Sector Station

Observer Corps HQ

Sector Station

Observer Post

Army Artillery

Observer Post

Representation of a Typical Fighter Sector Airfield, 1940

0 — 457 m
0 — 500 yards

Crash Exit

Crash Exit

Crash Exit

Squadron Crewrooms and Dispersal Pens

Fuel Dump

Main Grass Runway (1,600 yards)

Crash Exit

4-gun Battery 40 mm Bofors

Squadron Hangar

Short Grass Runway (1,100 yards)

Equipment Store

R & M Hangers

Fire Section

Watch Office

Squadron Crewrooms and Dispersal Pens

Barracks

Photo. Armament

Signals and Met. Office

Station Church

Parade Ground

Parachute Armoury

Squadron Hangar

Radio Room

Mess

Water Tower

Sergeants' Mess

H.Q.

M.T. Pool

Clerk of Works

Married Officers' Quarters

Operations Room

Sports Field

3-gun Battery 40 mm Bofors

Sick Quarters

Officers' Mess

3-gun Battery 40 mm Bofors

Firing Butts

Married Airmens' Quarters

Ammunition and Bomb Dump

N

THE BRITISH AIR DEFENSE SYSTEM, SUMMER 1940

Fighter Command controlled its force of interceptors based on information supplied by radar and supported by the Royal Observer Corps. On receiving this information it ordered "scrambles" from sector airfields to intercept incoming German formations. On the night of 24 August, 1940, German bombers attacked London and other British cities. This change of tactics provoked the British to attack Berlin, on the night of 25/26 August, forcing the Luftwaffe to defend its own cities. Attacks on cities became the norm thereafter. Fighter Command's structure, its bases, and systems were no longer targeted, allowing it to rebuild, reinforce, and recover.

THE BLITZ 1940–41

"A string of bombs fell right beside the Thames, their white glare was reflected in the black, lazy water near the banks, and faded in midstream where the moon cut a golden swathe broken only by the arches of famous bridges ..."

EDWARD R. MURROW, AMERICAN REPORTER

The bombing campaign began on the night of 24/25 August 1940, known more by its popular name, "The Blitz" and was aimed at Britain's capacity to make war. Industrial targets of all kinds were repeatedly bombed: factories, shipyards, oil terminals, and any domestic homes that might be in their way. Urban centers were bombed without restriction from August 1940 to May 1941, after which large numbers of German bombers were transferred east in preparation for the attack on Russia.

This event was not unexpected, since Britain had prepared for the possibility, or probability, of air attacks. Most citizens had been issued with gas masks, trained air raid wardens patrolled every city street and country lane enforcing the black-out that had been introduced. No chink of light must show from factory, home, or chicken shed, which might guide German bombers to their targets. Children and young mothers had been evacuated from major cities to the countryside in one of the largest movements of civilian population ever undertaken. Around key centers, barrage balloons, searchlights, and anti-aircraft guns were deployed. Most of this valuable and scarce equipment was deployed in the south-east and London, although 42 guns were still found to defend the town of Derby, home to the Rolls-Royce Works producing engines for Spitfire and Hurricane fighters.

CHILDREN OF THE BLITZ
Some young Londoners, sitting in the ruins of the street where they lived. The East End of the city bore the brunt of the Blitz, as bombs fell in their thousands on the tight and densely populated areas around the London docks, which were a primary target.

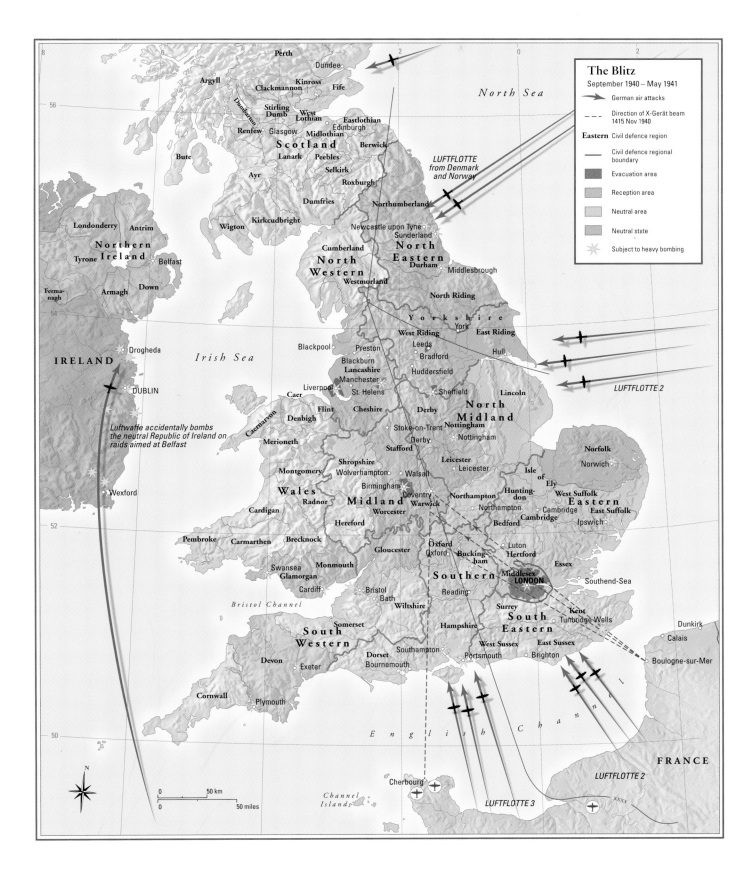

During August, the Luftwaffe concentrated its efforts on London. The Germans attacked in broad daylight, but lost many aircraft in the process. By the middle of September night raids on London had become the norm. Their attacks were therefore less precise and bombs aimed in the darkness fell on a much wider area, hitting homes as often as factories.

Despite all the preparations, the weight of attacks shocked the civilian population and some people in provincial cities, such as Plymouth, migrated to the nearby countryside each night, camping to avoid the bombs. In

APPROACHING THE TARGET

Dorniers follow the bend of the River Thames. These light bombers, dubbed "flying pencils," were designed to be nimble enough to outrun fighters if engaged in enemy territory.

London the Underground system became a haven each night for people sleeping on the platforms deep beneath the street, seeking shelter from the nightly raiders. Nevertheless, by the end of September almost 7,000 civilians were dead, thousands wounded, and tens of thousands homeless.

On the night of 14/15 November 1940, German "pathfinder" bombers flying along radio direction beams, known as "X-Gerät," hit Coventry, a provincial manufacturing city heavily involved in Britain's war effort. Following the pathfinders were over 400 bombers. Aiming at the fires already created, they dropped 503 tons of high explosive bombs and some 30,000 incendiary bombs. Hundreds were killed, over 1,200 badly wounded, and thousands more made homeless. Thousands of buildings were destroyed or badly damaged. Yet, despite all the horror, within a few days factories were back in production and morale had recovered quickly. It seemed that bombing could not destroy a nation's will to fight and survive. It became a matter of pride, an indication of the national mood. Small signs displayed in broken shop windows defiantly announced "Business as usual."

By Christmas 1940, the raids covered most of Britain. Glasgow, Belfast, Liverpool, and Sheffield had all been badly hit, and London had not been spared. Just after Christmas, on the night of 29/30 December, more than 130 bombers attacked London. The area between the Guildhall and St Paul's Cathedral was ablaze; it seemed for a moment, that the great cathedral itself would be lost, until brave action by firewatchers saved the building. It was not the same for the homes and offices in the surrounding area; ancient dwellings and Wren churches were turned to ashes; hundreds of years of building, and history were lost. Despite this bleak time the country survived, and new equipment came out of battered factories—including radar-directed guns that could predict the height and direction of bombers. Night fighters were now equipped with radar and began to intercept the night raiders with increasing success; fire and rescue teams became more expert; and bomb disposal units carried out their lonely, dangerous tasks. It was now clear to all that Britain was not going to crack.

FIGHTING FIRE
In the first phase of the Blitz, London was bombed 57 nights in a row. The fire service dealt with countless blazes, and were helped out by "street fire parties," volunteers trained to use stirrup pumps.

THE HUMAN COST OF THE BLITZ
Between July and December 1940, in the first phase of the Blitz, the Luftwaffe dropped a total of 27,486 tons of bombs on British cities, killing 23,002 British civilians and injuring a further 39,096.

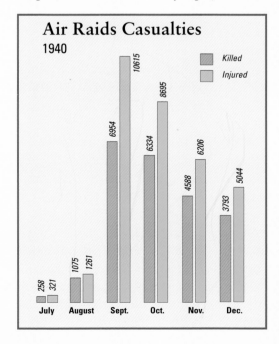

Air Raids Casualties 1940

Killed / Injured

Month	Killed	Injured
July	258	321
August	1075	1261
Sept.	6954	10615
Oct.	6334	8695
Nov.	4588	6206
Dec.	3793	5044

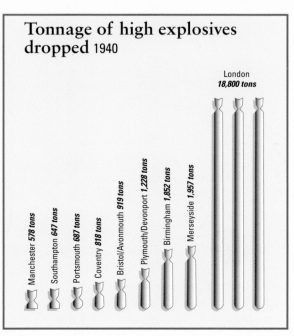

Tonnage of high explosives dropped 1940

- Manchester **578 tons**
- Southampton **647 tons**
- Portsmouth **687 tons**
- Coventry **818 tons**
- Bristol/Avonmouth **919 tons**
- Plymouth/Devonport **1,228 tons**
- Birmingham **1,852 tons**
- Merseyside **1,957 tons**
- London **18,800 tons**

THE BOMBING OF GERMANY 1940–41

"The sirens suddenly screamed out over the city. Immediately there was a dead silence all around. Shops closed, business people and gossiping women stopped talking. They began to run through the street ... all of them ran, and no one spoke at all."

ELSE WENDEL, HOUSEWIFE

Britain's Royal Air Force, the first such organization in the world to function independently of an army or a navy, had been formed around the proposition of taking the war to the enemy by bombing its industrial centers. The R.A.F. had done this in 1918, operating from bases in northern France. Its fleet of strategic bombers was just coming into meaningful service when the World War I ended.

Through to the 1920s and 30s, the R.A.F.'s main role had been imperialist and policeman-like—bombing rebellious colonies with a fleet of light biplanes. Its strategic role was relegated to theory and discussion in training schools. By the mid-30s rearmament was underway, which included new aircraft for R.A.F. Bomber Command. In September 1939 this Command was ready to operate from bases in eastern England, following its "Western Air Plans" (originated by the Combined Services Planning Section in 1936). These plans assumed immediate military operations by German forces in the west. From the beginning of an offensive, R.A.F. attacks would be mounted against Luftwaffe bases and supply

depots. It was assumed that, as German attacks developed against France, raids by the R.A.F. would be focussed on the German lines of supply. Following these attacks, raids would then be directed on German war industry, especially oil refineries and oil storage facilities.

Bomber Command lost part of its strength two days before Britain's declaration of war when, as planned previously, No. 1 Group, with ten squadrons of Fairey Battle light bombers, moved to France together with two Blenheim squadrons from another group to form the Advanced Air Striking Force. Five more squadrons of Battles were left in England but were reduced to a training and reserve basis. The restricted nature of operations after the outbreak of war gave Bomber Command the opportunity to withdraw a further nine of its squadrons from the home-based groups and add these to the reserve, leaving only 23 front line squadrons that contained approximately 280 aircraft with trained crews. That part of Bomber Command which now stood ready to proceed with war operations was organized in the following manner:

The Bombing of Europe
1939–41

- Bomber Command Headquarters
- Bomber Group Headquarters

Weight of bombs

- 25 – 1000 tons
- 1000 – 3000 tons
- 3000 – 4000 tons

Inset (Ruhr region):
Wesel
Starkade Bottrapp Gielen-Kirchen Lunen
Homberg
Huls Essen Wanne-Eickel Dortmund
Duisberg Schwerte
Krefeld R u h r
Munchen-gladbach Dusseldorf
Reisholz

Norway

SWEDEN

Denmark
Copenhagen

Sylt
Flensburg
Kiel Warnemunde
Lubeck Rostock
Cuxhaven Wismar
Wilhelmshaven Hamburg Stettin
Emden Bremerhaven
Oldenburg Bremen
Berlin
Salzbergen
Osnabruck Brunswick Magdeburg
Bielefeld
Munster Merseburg
Hamm Paderborn
Soest Kassel
Emmerich

Irish Sea

UNITED KINGDOM
York

North Sea

NETH.
Amsterdam
Schipol
Soesterberg
Rotterdam

Grantham

Huntingdon Exning

Abingdon High Wycombe
London

Haamstede
Flushing
Ostend Eindhoven
Dunkirk Zeebrugge Munchen-gladbach *See inset*
Calais Hazebrouck Monheim
Bologne Merville Brussels Cologne

GERMANY

Koblenz
Frankfurt
Prague

English Channel

Belgium

Cherbourg
Dieppe
Le Havre

Mannheim
Nuremberg
Karlsruhe
Stuttgart

Paris

Brest

Lorient

Munich

St Nazaire

F r a n c e

Austria

Bern
SWITZERLAND

Bay of Biscay

La Pallice/
La Rochelle

Royan

Geneva

Ambares

Bordeaux
Airfield Bordeaux

Vichy
Occupied 11 Nov. 1942

Turin Milan Venice

Genoa

I T A L Y

SPAIN

Bomber Command Headquarters at Richings Park, Langley, Buckinghamshire (but due to move in March 1940 to a new location being prepared at High Wycombe). The Commander-in-Chief was Air Chief Marshal Sir Edgar Ludlow-Hewitt.

2 Group HQ: Wyton. Commander: Air Vice-Marshal C.T. Maclean. Squadrons: Nos. 21, 82, 107, 110, 114, and 139, equipped with Bristol Blenheims; 101 Squadron non-operational.

3 Group HQ: Mildenhall. Commander: Air Vice-Marshal J.E.A. Baldwin. Squadrons: Nos. 9, 37, 38, 39, 99, 115, and 149, equipped with Vickers Wellingtons; 214 and 215 Squadrons non-operational.

4 Group HQ: Linton-on-Ouse. Commander: Air Vice-Marshal A. Coningham. Squadrons: Nos. 10, 51, 58, 77, and 102, equipped with Armstrong-Whitworth Whitleys; 78 Squadron non-operational.

5 Group HQ: St Vincent's House, Grantham. Commander: Air Commodore W.B. Callaway (Air Vice-Marshal A.T. Harris from 11 September). Squadrons: Nos. 44, 49, 50, 61, 83, and 144, equipped with Handley Page Hampdens; 106 and 185 Squadrons non-operational.

THE VICKERS WELLINGTON

The Wellington (below left and right) was designed by Barnes Wallace, the inventor of the "bouncing bomb." Wellingtons flew the first R.A.F. bombing raid of the war, on September 4, 1939. They were still frontline aircraft when the war came to an end. The first production variant had a crew consisting of a pilot; a radio operator, a navigator who was also a bomb aimer, a nose gunner, a tail gunner and a waist gunner. The post-mission debrief (above right) was an essential corollary to every bombing mission.

The four types of aircraft in use were the Blenheim, Hampden, Wellington, and Whitley, all of reasonable design and without major mechanical drawbacks. Maximum bomb loads varied from 1,000 pounds for the Blenheim to 8,000 pounds for the Whitley. The Blenheim had only a restricted range but the other three types could reach any part of Germany except the extreme east. It had always been intended that the main bombing operations would be carried out by tight, self-defending daylight formations and only the Whitley squadrons of 4 Group were trained in night bombing.

On 1 September, the U.S. President Franklin D. Roosevelt called for restraint from bombing operations where civilians might be hit. France and Britain agreed at once. On 18 September, Germany also agreed, but only as the Polish Campaign drew to a close. Meanwhile, the R.A.F. was cleared to attack German shipping as long as it

was not alongside a wharf or dock. Bombers could also fly over enemy territory for the purpose of dropping propaganda leaflets. Many R.A.F. Commanders felt this was a waste of time, but it did build up experience of operating over enemy territory before actually being committed to an all-out bombing campaign. It also bought time to build up aircraft numbers and train aircrews beyond the number immediately available.

After the fall of France, Germany controlled the Atlantic coast from the Spanish border to the north of Norway. During the Battle of Britain, the British Bomber Command's main task was to bomb barge concentrations along the occupied Channel coast. Their planned attack on German industry was secondary to the needs of that moment. Despite this, a small number of bombers were sent to Germany night after night; oil-related targets were still their priority.

Virtually all night raids were carried out by small groups of aircraft directed to various targets, with each crew navigating its own way. Though navigation equipment and skills were lacking, on moonlit nights visual sightings of rivers or other identifiable landmarks helped the bomber crews to locate their targets. As German flak and searchlights became more effective, however, the bombers were forced to fly at higher altitudes, making identification of the target even more difficult. A small number of aircraft were fitted with bombing cameras and these were given to the best crews, since the interpretation between claims of the crews indicated massive discrepancies.

On the night of 23/24 September a unique raid was launched against Berlin, when 129 aircraft were dispatched to 18 targets within the city: railroad yards, factories, gasworks, and power stations. Of the 129 aircraft dispatched, 112 reported bombing the city, while three aircraft were lost. Very few details from the German side are available, possibly having been removed from the records for security purposes, although it is known that most of the bombs fell in the Moabit district, where the power stations were hit and the baroque palace, Schloss Charlottenburg, was damaged.

During the Battle of Britain and for many months after, Germany was visited by British bombers, but numbers were small, and sometimes the missions involved only the dropping of leaflets. However, during the winter of 1940 the raids became much larger. On the night 16/17 December 134 bombers—the largest raid sent to a single target—flew to Mannheim in retaliation for the devastating attacks on Coventry.

BOMBING STATISTICS 1940–42

Bomber Production

	GERMANY	BRITAIN	U.S.
1940	2,852	3,488	—
1941	3,373	4,668	—
1942	4,502	6,253	12,627

These figures include all bomber types.

Bomber Losses

	GERMANY	BRITAIN	U.S.
1940	1,653	494	—
1941	1,814	914	—
1942	2,338	1,400	30

German losses are for all bomber types and from all causes. British and American losses are for aircraft involved in operations from only British bases against Europe, all causes.

Bombing Tonnage

	LUFTWAFFE ON U.K.	R.A.F. ON GERMANY AND OCCUPIED EUROPE	U.S.A.A.F. ON GERMANY AND OCCUPIED EUROPE
1940	36,844	13,033	—
1941	21,848	31,704	—
1942	3,260	45,561	1,561

Figures for U.K. cover Bomber Command flying from British bases; figures for the United States cover the 8th Air Force flying from British bases.

The R.A.F. raid began with eight chosen bomber crews attacking Mannheim city center. Their payload consisted of incendiaries. The bombers following would use the resulting fires as a target marker to drop high explosive bombs in order to cause maximum destruction. The raid, however, was not a success, with bombs being scattered all over the city rather than concentrated in the center as planned. For the first time the target was not primarily industrial or military in nature. The raid left 34 dead, 81 wounded, 476 buildings destroyed or severely damaged and 1,266 people lost their homes. Four aircraft failed to return.

Cities in Britain had been badly hit, including Liverpool, Manchester, Plymouth, and many others. The bombing of London was still an almost nightly occurrence. It was felt strongly by High Command that R.A.F. Bomber Command should take war to the heart of the German cities, what the R.A.F. would later call "area bombing." The concerted terror bombing of the Germans was about to begin.

WAR IN EAST AFRICA 1941

"War alone can carry to the maximum tension all human energies and imprint with the seal of nobility those people who have the courage to confront it; every other test is a mere substitute."

The German invasion of France in May 1940 transformed the strategic situation in the Mediterranean and North Africa. Eager to profit from this new situation, Italy declared war on Britain and France on 10 June 1940. Eleven days later, the Italian Prime Minister and dictator Benito Mussolini authorized his troops to cross the border into France. By staking a claim in Hitler's conquest of the country, Mussolini hoped to win a say in the peace that followed the glorious victory. Hitler had other ideas, however, and he reached an armistice with France without any reference to his Italian ally.

The surrender of France seriously weakened the British position in the Mediterranean. Moreover, the neutralization of the French fleet meant that Italy was the de facto dominant naval power. Added to this, Italian ground forces based in Italian Somaliland, as well as in Eritrea, Ethiopia, and Libya, now formed the largest fighting force in Africa. Some 300,000 Italian troops, and a further 150,000 locally-recruited fighting men, found themselves facing approximately 75,000 British troops scattered across north and eastern Africa.

Hoping to seize the initiative, Mussolini ordered attacks on Sudan and Kenya and an all-out attack to seize British Somaliland, which was occupied from 5–19 August. Along the North African coast a force of six Italian divisions marched 60 miles into Egypt, where it dug in, building a forward base at Sidi Barrani. General Sir Archibald Wavell, the British Commander-in-Chief, gave priority to the Italian invasion of Egypt, launching the first

ITALIAN CRUISERS LIE IN WAIT
Four cruisers of the Italian Fleet lay at anchor in Naples harbor. The Italian Fleet was built to turn the Mediterranean Sea into an Italian lake. However, three of these four cruisers were sunk by the British at the Battle of Matapan.

attacks on 9 December in a five-day operation. Its success encouraged Wavell to advance into Libya in early January 1941, capturing Tobruk on 22 January. He then divided his forces, one part following the coast road, the other part advancing across the desert, linking up at Beda Fomm. His force had advanced 500 miles, capturing 130,000 prisoners and most of their equipment.

Meanwhile, the British offensive in East Africa began. On 19 January the 4th and 5th Indian Divisions advanced into Eritrea from Sudan. Commanded by Major-General William Platt, this force slowly advanced through difficult terrain, oppressive heat, and bitter fighting. The vital port of Massawa fell to them on 8 April. A new front had opened on 11 February. Three divisions, commanded by Lt-General Alan Cunningham, advanced into Italian Somaliland. Fourteen days later, Mogadishu, the capital, was captured. This force then pushed on, advancing across the Ogadem Desert deep into Ethiopia from the south, entering the town of Jijiga unopposed.

On 25 February, yet another British force landed at Berbera, recapturing British Somaliland. Part of this force advanced to Jijiga joining British Commonwealth units already there. This united force faced formidable Italian

defenses at Harar. As it turned out, the Italian forces put up a token resistance before withdrawing. On 28 March Dire Dawa fell, opening the way to the capital city of Ethiopia, Addis Ababa. The city fell to British and Commonwealth troops on 6 April after an eight-week fighting advance covering over 1,700 miles.

The Italian defenders of Addis Ababa withdrew northward. Their commander concentrated his surviving forces at Amba Alagi, a mountain stronghold, and there the Italians would make their last stand. On 3 May attacks were launched by Indian troops from the north, joined by Cunningham's troops attacking from the south. By 19 May the Duke of Aosta, realizing his situation was hopeless, surrendered. Scattered resistance continued until 3 July and clearing-up operations were completed in November. This victory liberated the ancient state of Ethiopia and returned Emperor Haile Selassie to his throne. The end of this campaign ensured vital supply routes through the Red Sea were under Allied control.

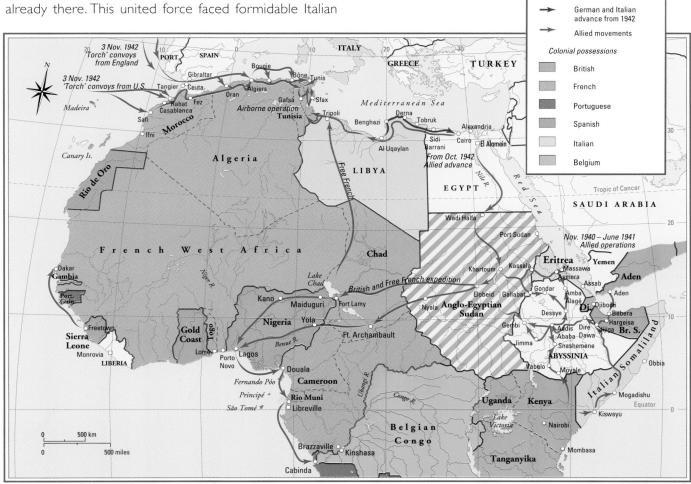

Africa in the Second World War

→ German and Italian advance from 1942

→ Allied movements

Colonial possessions

British

French

Portuguese

Spanish

Italian

Belgium

Iraq, Syria, & Persia 1941

"You do not need to bother too much about the long future in Iraq. Your immediate task is to get a friendly government set up in Baghdad, and to beat down Rashid Ali's forces with the utmost vigor."

CHURCHILL TO WAVELL, 9 MAY 1941

Despite a run of victories in north-east Africa, the British position in the region remained extremely precarious. The German invasion of Yugoslavia and Greece had forced the British to withdraw to the island of Crete, though Crete was itself under threat of invasion. Rommel and his Afrika Korps had advanced from El Agheila, in Libya, all the way to the western border of Egypt. The British garrison in the Libyan town of Tobruk was at this point also besieged by the Axis forces.

In April 1941, in addition to all these separate campaigns faced by the British and Commonwealth forces, another problem arose. This new and thorny issue was Iraq, which had been a British mandate until it gained full independence in 1932.

By agreement with Iraq, British garrisons still remained in the country. The pro-British regent, Emir Abdullah, and his government wished to declare war on Germany. But nationalist factions wanted concessions from the British first. On 3 April the Emir was overthrown in a coup led by the pro-Axis General, Rashid Ali. The General objected to the arrival of the 10th Indian Division sent to secure the vital oilfields around Basra. The British had treaty rights to the port of Basra and his objections were ignored, so he ordered his troops to surround the British airbase at Habbaniya, some 50 miles west of Baghdad. On 2 May British aircraft bombed Iraqi positions, and the Iraqi forces replied with artillery fire bombarding the British base. After some intense pressure from London, General Wavell, the area commander, agreed to send a relief force to Habbaniya.

"Habforce" was created out of the scarce troops available. It consisted mostly units of the 1st British Cavalry Division, based in Palestine. This scratch force left on 13 May, crossing the desert terrain in temperatures of 120°F, arriving at Habbaniya on 18 May in time to find the Iraqis already withdrawing. The British advance was attacked by Luftwaffe aircraft operating from bases in Syria and northern Iraq, but nevertheless they secured Habbaniya and continued on to take Baghdad. In the south the 10th Indian Division pacified the area around Basra. Meanwhile General Rashid Ali and his pro-Axis clique fled to Persia (Iran) and Emir Abdullah was restored on 30 May.

Evidence of German involvement in the region caused British Prime Minister Churchill grave concern. He was anxious that the Germans should not be allowed the opportunity to develop a new front from the Vichy French-controlled Syria and Lebanon. Churchill overruled the reluctance of Wavell (commander of the Middle East) to become involved in a new campaign. Charles de Gaulle, leader of the Free French forces, also lobbied for the invasion of Vichy-held Lebanon and Syria.

Wavell reluctantly did agree to commit part of the British 1st Cavalry Division, most of the 7th Australian Division and the Free French units—a total of 34,000 troops—to Operation Exporter. This operation began on 8 June, advancing along the coast road towards Beirut and over the mountains into Syria. Initially the advance was successful, but by 13 June the advance had stalled, allowing time for the Vichy French forces to launch a counterattack. Bitter fighting followed but British control of the air and Habforce from Iraq, advancing toward Homs and Aleppo, as well as two extra British Brigades from Palestine, overwhelmed the Vichy French forces who fell back from Damascus. Supported by naval gunfire the Australians broke through into the outskirts of Beirut and, in a fierce five-day battle, captured the city. With Vichy French forces already surrendering in eastern Syria, Dentz, the Vichy commander, was in a hopeless situation

and signed an armistice on 14 July. Of the surviving 38,000 men, only 5,700 joined de Gaulle's Free French forces, despite his appeals,

On 22 June Germany invaded the U.S.S.R. creating a new ally for the hard-pressed British. Determined to support its new ally, Britain in concert with the Soviets, entered the neutral country of Persia (Iran) on the night 24/25 August 1941. Soviet columns advanced southward from the Caucasus Mountains and from central Asia, east of the Caspian Sea. A British force advanced northward from the Persian Gulf and westward from Iraq and overland from India. Tehran was occupied on 17 September. The ruler of Persia, the Shah, put up only a token resistance and then ordered a ceasefire on 28 August. He abdicated and was taken by the British, firstly to a remote island in the Indian Ocean, and then to South Africa, where he died. Meanwhile his son, Mohammed Reza Pahlavi, had taken the throne. The strategic supply route to Soviet Russia and valuable oilfields were safely under Allied control.

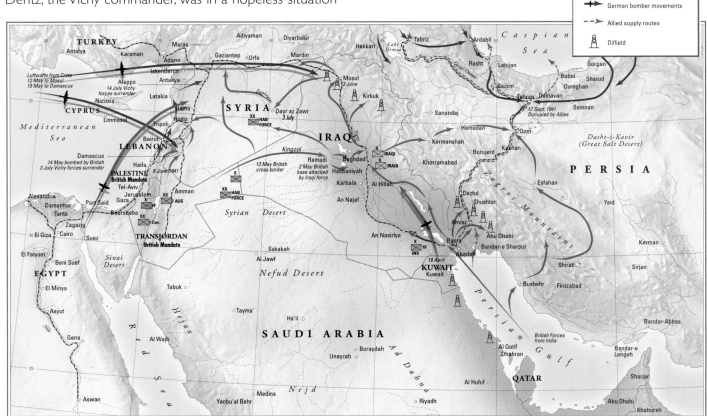

Iraq, Syria and Persia
April – September 1941

- Allied forces movements
- Free French forces movements
- Russian forces movements
- Allied bomber movements
- German bomber movements
- Allied supply routes
- Oilfield

THE WESTERN DESERT 1940–43

"Before Alamein, we had no victories. After Alamein, we had no defeats."

WINSTON CHURCHILL

On 13 September Marshal d'Armata Rodolfo Graziani crossed into Egypt with five divisions of his 10th Army. Facing him was Lt-Gen Richard O'Connor, commanding the tough and experienced 4th Indian Division and the 7th Armored Division. O'Connor's plan was to allow the Italians to advance to Mersa-Matruh and then punch north and cut their lines. But the Italians stopped short at Sidi Barini, apparently having run short of fuel. Here they began to fortify their positions, and await a counterattack.

It came with Operation Compass on 9 December. O'Connor's intention was to push the Italians back to their original start line, then withdraw into the desert with as many prisoners as possible. The Royal Air Force and Royal Navy pounded the Italian positions prior to the attack, while the forward units of 7th Armored probed the Italian defenses. Surprise was total. Elements of 7th Royal Tank Regiment stormed past the Italian line and into their rear, reaching the border wire on 10 December.

O'Connor realized that he could exploit the reduction in Italian positions in Egypt. On 3 January the seaport of Bardia was assaulted by the newly-arrived Australian 6th Division; the Italian defenders capitulated in three days. The Australians were ready to assault Tobruk on 21 January, and within 36 hours the city had fallen. O'Connor once again saw an opportunity: perhaps he could push Italy out of North Africa altogether. He gave the order for the Australians to push on to take Derna and for 7th Armored to take Mechili.

Both these objectives were achieved by 2 February but by now the forces needed a rest and a refit. Instead, they were ordered to advance yet again. The orders were for the Australians to chase the Italians into the guns of an armored force that would motor across the desert and cut the road from Benghazi to Tripoli at Beda Fomm. By 5 February a rifle brigade had established a road block, just in time to intercept the retreating Italian forces. The Italians took many losses under intense and accurate rifle and artillery fire. Soon more Italian troops were piling up behind the devastated first elements. White flags began to be flown as night fell, and—after a desperate final attack on the morning of the 6 February—the entire Italian column surrendered.

It was an immense victory for the British and Commonwealth troops. O'Connor's desert army had taken 500 miles of territory, destroyed the Italian 10th Army and captured 130,000 prisoners. Losses on the Allied side amounted to 550 killed and 1,300 wounded. O'Connor felt that they could push on, but Churchill had other plans: he was looking toward Greece and the Balkans. Thus the opportunity for O'Connor to press home his advantage was lost.

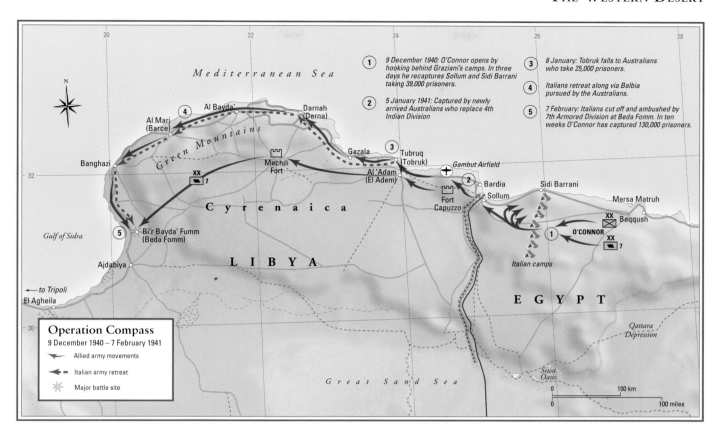

Operation Compass
9 December 1940 – 7 February 1941

➤ Allied army movements

◄ Italian army retreat

✳ Major battle site

① 9 December 1940: O'Connor opens by hooking behind Graziani's camps. In three days he recaptures Sollum and Sidi Barrani taking 39,000 prisoners.

② 5 January 1941: Captured by newly arrived Australians who replace 4th Indian Division

③ 8 January: Tobruk falls to Australians who take 25,000 prisoners.

④ Italians retreat along via Balbia pursued by the Australians.

⑤ 7 February: Italians cut off and ambushed by 7th Armored Division at Beda Fomm. In ten weeks O'Connor has captured 130,000 prisoners.

Hitler saw that the Italians were close to a humiliating defeat in the desert, and took steps to reinforce the Axis armies. On 12 February the first units of a German army arrived in Tripoli. These were the 5th Light Division and the 15th Panzer Division. They were under the command of Major-General Erwin Rommel, who had orders to block the British advance in the area of Buerat.

On the British front, 7th Armored had pulled back to Cairo, and 6th Australian had been transferred to Greece. O'Connor was out of the fighting due to illness, and his replacement, General Philip Neame, lacked tactical understanding. Under Neame's command was a battered brigade of the 2nd Armored Division, and a brigade of Australian infantry. When General Wavell saw the state of these forces he quickly moved them into a more defensible position. Then, confident that the Germans would need time to build up stocks of fuel and ammunition, Wavell left for Cairo.

But Rommel was not a general who liked to sit around. He was convinced that the positions opposite him were weak. On 24 March he gave the order for the 5th Light Division to take the fort and landing strip at El Agheila. A week later Rommel advanced to Mersa el Brega. When he heard from his reconnaissance aircraft that there was no opposition at Agedabia he ordered 5th Light to move up to the town. Though he only had limited

troops (the bulk of his Panzer Division had yet to arrive), Rommel prepared to advance further. Against orders from Berlin, Rommel sent the 5th Light Division on a rightward-flanking movement through the desert, This took the British by surprise. Forces started to withdraw toward Egypt rather than be encircled. Disastrously for the British, German troops captured O'Connor (now returned to the front) and Neame, as they were on their way to take charge of the developing catastrophe. Rommel took Benghazi on 4 April and Derna on 7 April. Everything achieved by Operation Compass had been lost. By 9 April reconnaissance units of the German 5th Light were almost at the Egyptian border.

A large contingent of Allied forces had stayed behind in Tobruk, their numbers swollen by Australian stragglers who had been holed up in Benghazi. Rommel wanted to take this port so as to shorten his supply lines. He attacked the town on 10 April, and again on 16 April, but was repelled both times. After this he decided to bypass Tobruk for the time being.

With Allied attention on the campaign in the Balkans, it was difficult for General Gott, the commander of 7th Armored, to achieve much against the rapidly growing Afrika Korps. The most he could do was probe and harry their defenses with "Jock Columns," mixed armored units named after his second-in-command Jock Campbell.

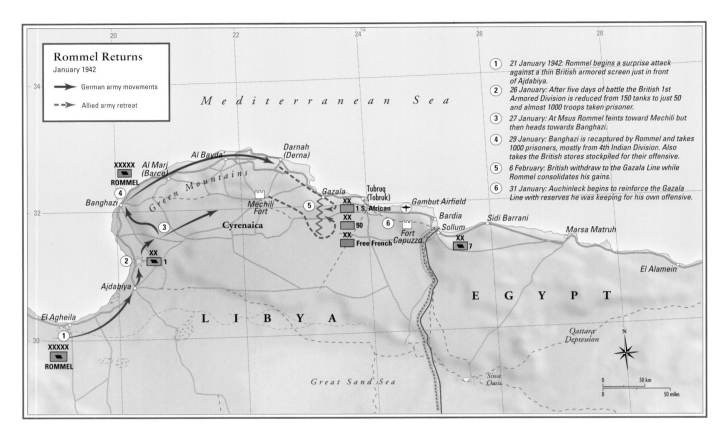

Rommel Returns

January 1942

→ German army movements

- - → Allied army retreat

① 21 January 1942: Rommel begins a surprise attack against a thin British armored screen just in front of Ajdabiya.

② 26 January: After five days of battle the British 1st Armored Division is reduced from 150 tanks to just 50 and almost 1000 troops taken prisoner.

③ 27 January: At Msus Rommel feints toward Mechili but then heads towards Banghazi.

④ 29 January: Banghazi is recaptured by Rommel and takes 1000 prisoners, mostly from 4th Indian Division. Also takes the British stores stockpiled for their offensive.

⑤ 6 February: British withdraw to the Gazala Line while Rommel consolidates his gains.

⑥ 31 January: Auchinleck begins to reinforce the Gazala Line with reserves he was keeping for his own offensive.

More ambitious was Operation Brevity, an assault on the still untested 15th Panzer Division. The division was still short of the majority of its armor, but it had many anti-tank guns which ripped apart the British advance.

On 27 May Rommel took the Halfaya Pass and set up a massive anti-tank ring armed with the formidable 88 mm cannon. The Allied position was now terrible, both in the Balkans and in the western desert. Churchill responded by stripping Britain of all the armor and aircraft that she could spare. In due course, 300 new tanks arrived along with 50 Hurricanes.

These new assets were deployed as part of Operation Battleaxe, intended to relieve Tobruk. Allied tank formations swarmed forward to engage the Panzers, but the Germans merely withdrew, luring the Allied tanks within sight of the anti-tank guns. Within three days Wavell called off the assault. The Allies had lost half their tanks for no gain. Churchill, sorely disappointed, removed Wavell, appointing General Auchinleck in his place.

Auchinleck's brief was to mount an offensive as soon as possible. But he insisted on waiting until he had accumulated sufficient troops and tanks to ensure success. This new force, the 8th Army, was made up of two Corps: the 8th and 30th. It was placed under the command of Lt-General Sir Alan Cunningham. On the morning of 19 November, Auchinleck unleashed the 8th Army. The 8th Corps drove north to attack the German and Italian garrisons from Sidi Omar all the way to the coast. The 7th Armored advanced north-west toward Bir el Gubi and to the relief of Tobruk. The 4th Armored Brigade held the ground between these two forces to the east of Gabr Saleh. By the end of the day 7th Armored were only ten miles from Tobruk but were not to get any closer, as the Italians defenders were well dug in with anti-tank support.

Rommel saw that Tobruk was the goal of the Allied attack, and personally led the counterattack at El Duda. He ordered 15th Panzer and 21st Panzer to strike the 4th Armored Brigade, sending them reeling back. The Panzer Divisions then swung north-west to strike the 7th at Sidi Rezegh. The 8th Army was left in disarray, and Rommel took this chance to "race for the wire" with 21st Panzer in the lead and 15th Panzer in close support. These formations crossed the British lines with relative ease, but the Allied units that had been bypassed were now reforming behind him. They managed to link up with the defenders of Tobruk on 26 November. With an undefeated Allied army to his rear, Rommel gave the order for his two Panzer Divisions to retreat as far as Gazala. When he saw that there was no suitable defense line he fell back to the Gulf of Sirte.

The Afrika Korps was quick to regroup. Rommel realized that the Allied supply lines were now overstretched, and he made ready for a counteroffensive. He struck on 21 January. By the second day he had reached Agedabia, and broke through the disorganized Allied columns. By 2 February Barce, Marawa, and Derna had been recaptured. Timini and Mechili fell on 6 February.

Rommel halted in a line with Timini to prepare for the final push into Egypt. Meanwhile he sent reconnaissance units forward to probe Allied defenses. The Allies were digging in along a line running south from the Gazala inlet to the Foreign Legion outpost at Bir Hakeim. They laid deep minefields in front of their positions.

Auchinleck wanted the 8th Army to go on the offensive, and began to move men and material up. He also placed a strong reserve force in the center of the defense, thinking that this was where Rommel would attack. Ritchie felt otherwise, considering that Rommel would try to swing south into the open desert and strike their rear. He came up with a compromise: reserves were positioned in "boxes" both center and south, behind the main line of defense but within easy reach.

As Ritchie had predicted, Rommel launched his attack around the southern end of the defenses and was soon devastating the "boxes" of reserve formations. Many were simply annihilated. These moves were made by

21st Panzer and 15th Panzer with the 90th Light and the Italian Ariete Divisions covering their flanks. Their attack was brought to a halt, as so often, by lack of fuel and ammunition. The problem was exacerbated by the fact that bypassed troops of the 8th Army were able to attack the German supply columns. But for the most part Allied units were retreating in disarray through Tobruk and onward to the Egyptian border.

On 15 June, Auchinleck ordered a defensive line to be held from Tobruk through El Adem to El Gubi. Rommel was obsessed with the capture of this port, which had been denied him several times before. To take it he needed fuel and supplies, and thought that the huge Allied supply dump near the R.A.F. airfield at Gambut could serve this purpose. Rommel ordered the 21st, 90th Light, and the Ariete Divisions to move through the scattered Allied defenses and take the dump from the south. It was in German hands by the early afternoon. With the airfield at Gambut also in his hands, Rommel was once again ready to assault Tobruk.

The port of Tobruk was defended by the 2nd South African Division commanded by Major-General Klopper. The German attack began early on 20 June, and by lunchtime Rommel himself was in the center of the town.

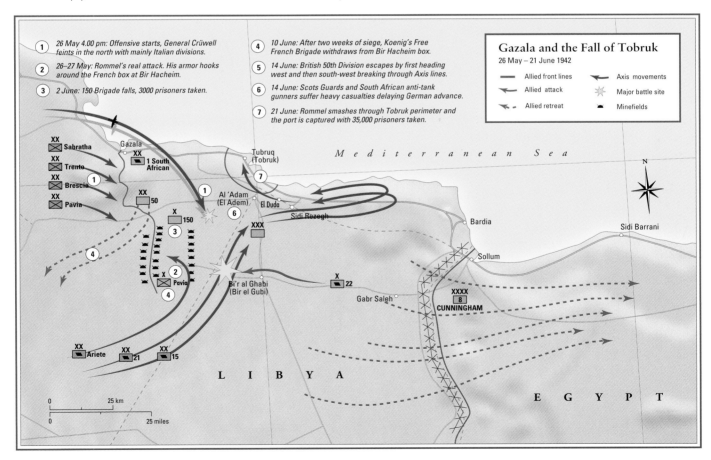

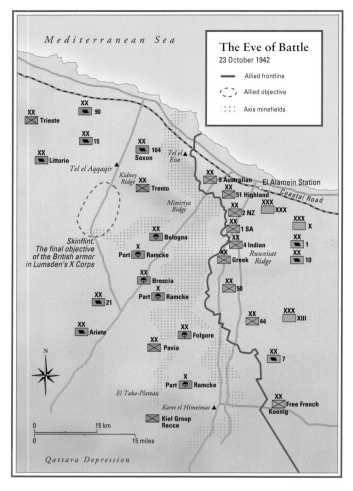

The Eve of Battle
23 October 1942

— Allied frontline

⌐ ⌐ Allied objective

∷ ∷ Axis minefields

Mediterranean Sea

XX
90
XX Trieste

XX
15

XX Littorio

XX
164
Saxon

Tel el Aqqaqir

Kidney Ridge

XX Trento

Miteiriya Ridge

Tel el Eisa

XX
9 Australian

El Alamein Station

Coastal Road

XX
51 Highland

XX
2 NZ

XXX
XXX

XX
1 SA

XXX
X

XX
4 Indian

XX
1

XX Bologna

X
Part Ramcke

Skinflint.
The final objective
of the British armor
in Lumsden's X Corps

XX Greek

Ruweisat Ridge

XX
10

X
Brescia

X
Part Ramcke

XX
50

XX
21

XX
44

XXX
XIII

XX Ariete

XX Folgore

XX Pavia

XX
7

N

X
Part Ramcke

El Taka-Plateau

Karet el Himeimat

XX
Free French
Koenig

XX
Kiel Group
Recce

0   15 km

0   15 miles

Qattara Depression

Klopper surrendered the next day, to the disgust of the his men, who had been waiting for the order to counter. Rommel's success saw him promoted to Field Marshal.

Rommel now wanted to advance all the way to the Nile. The Allies tried to create a holding line south of Mersa-Matruh but this did not hold for long. By 29 June, Italian and German forces were past Mersa-Matruh and the two Panzer divisions were striking south-west toward El Quseir. The only thing between Rommel and victory was a defense line around a railroad station at El Alamein. Rommel saw no reason why the Afrika Korps could not push through one last defense and reach the Nile delta.

As the 90th Light Division set off on this final push they were hit by bombs from the desert airforce and then by a massive bombardment from every artillery piece Auchinleck could muster. This stopped the 90th in their tracks. Both sides withdrew a short distance to catch their breath, but then the British artillery opened up again, tearing apart the Axis troops. In the wake of the bombardment the 9th Australian Division pushed the Germans further back. Auchinleck had succeeded in halting the Afrika Korps—but had not defeated it.

At this moment Auchinleck was replaced by General Alexander. Lt-General Bernard Law Montgomery was given command of the 8th Army. Montgomery knew Rommel would try to break the line. Sure enough, the German general attacked on 30 August, and immediately ran into trouble. The Germans were subjected to relentless aerial bombing from R.A.F Wellington bombers, and a wall of anti-tank and artillery fire from the Royal Artillery. This time, the British tanks were not lured into open ground, but were used instead as mobile artillery, supporting any waning defense. On 4 September, Rommel ordered a withdrawal, leaving behind hundreds of destroyed vehicles and thousands of dead. Rommel himself was ill, and had to return to Germany, leaving the Afrika Korps in the care of General Stumme.

On 23 October nearly 900 guns of the Royal Artillery opened fire on the German and Italian rear echelon, causing massive disruption to command and supply lines. Allied troops began to creep forward. On the right of the advance was 9th Australian Division; to their left was the 51st Highland Division, then two brigades of New Zealanders with the 9th Armored Brigade. The Miteiraya Ridge was their main objective. The sappers were the first to go forward to clear paths through the minefields, which were sometimes two miles deep. This was not an easy task as the German counter barrage was stepping up. Through paths, marked by white tape, the infantry advanced and started to clear positions of the enemy.

By the morning of 24 October, most of the objectives had been taken, and the infantry began to dig in and wait for the armor to move up and support them. But behind the infantry there was absolute chaos as the armor tried to advance up the narrow tracks through the minefields. If one was blocked by a damaged or destroyed vehicle this would cause massive bottlenecks, becoming easy prey for the German long-range artillery. With the armor still not able to reach the infantry in the front, the battle was beginning to stall. However, Montgomery still wanted them to advance to reach more defensible positions for the inevitable Axis counterattack.

Rommel returned to the fray on 25 October and immediately ordered 21st Panzer north to hold the Allied advance Montgomery, meanwhile, organized his own armor in such a way as to draw in as many Axis tanks and infantry as possible. He outnumbered his enemy, and was sure to win in any war of attrition. He ordered the 9th Australian Division to break out towards Tel el Eisa, a maneuver that succeeded in drawing many Axis tanks and infantry into that sector.

The 2nd Battalion, the Rifle Brigade, advanced to a forward position known as "Snipe" on the night of 26 October. Their orders were to hold a defensive position until relieved by advancing armor. This armor arrived, but attracted so much artillery fire that they had to retire. All around the Snipe position were advancing Axis armor, and the 2nd Battalion inflicted heavy damage on the enemy thanks to the 19 6-pounders attached to the unit. After a hard engagement that lasted all day the Snipe position claimed 34 armored vehicles, damaging many more and causing the counterattack to falter.

Rommel began to prepare to fall back but first had to break his troops out of a salient holding out near Tel el Eisa. For this task he made an assault group from 21st and 90th Light Divisions, which were immediately attacked by bombers, but still went forward into the attack. They took a heavy toll of the defending Australians with the support of some Rhodesian Valentine tanks and succeeded in opening up a gap for their troops to escape.

While this action was going on, Montgomery prepared another massive thrust, again to be preceded by an enormous barrage. This, the opening of Operation Supercharge, was a lesser version of Operation Lightfoot. The infantry was to march forward, followed by an armored push to break out into the enemy's rear. But once again the armor got hopelessly bogged down in the small tracks through the minefields. However, some units did get through and were led by the infantry through the night and over the Aqqaqir Ridge. By this time the sun was rising behind the tanks, silhouetting them and making easy prey for the German anti-tank gunners.

But the advance had achieved what Montgomery required, as Rommel gave the order for the Afrika Korps to retreat just as Hitler's order to "Halt" came in. Rommel had no choice but to launch the 21st and 15th toward the enemy on 2 November and great losses were incurred on both sides. Montgomery had more reserves and Rommel now had fewer than 40 serviceable tanks. The Afrika Korps had been beaten and by 4 November the Argyll and Sutherland Highlanders were at Tel Aqqaqir. The Battle of El Alamein was over, and the tide of war was about to turn.

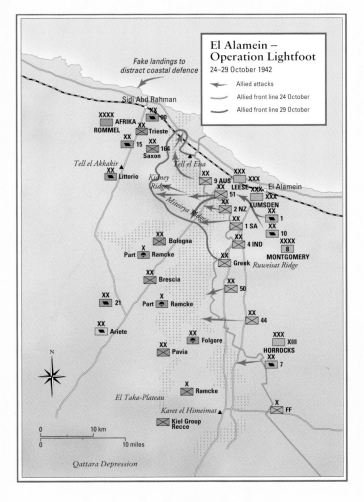

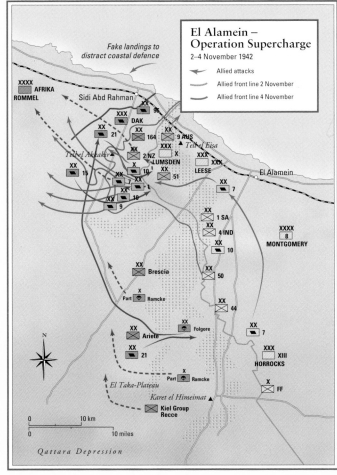

Northwest Africa 1943

"Even without the Allied offensive, I should have had to capitulate by 1 June at the latest as I had no more food to eat."

COLONEL-GENERAL HANS-JÜRGEN VON ARNIM, MAY 1943, AFTER AXIS SURRENDER IN TUNISIA

After the British victory at the Battle of El Alamein, British forces pursued Rommel's Afrika Korps and their allies, the Italians, across north Africa from the Egyptian border, then across Libya and into Tunisia. Rommel was organizing yet another defensive line when news arrived that an Anglo-American landing had been made along the northwest coast of Africa from Casablanca to Algiers. This was Operation Torch. The landing involved three task forces. The Western Task Force, which landed on the Moroccan coast between Safi and Mehdia, was under the command of Major-General Patton. Center Task Force landed at Oran under the command of Major-General Fredenhall. Eastern Task Force landed at Algiers under the command of Lt-General Anderson.

The Allies were unsure where the loyalties of the Vichy French troops lay, so Major-General Mark Clark was smuggled ashore before the landings to clarify matters. But for security reasons the information that Clark gave the French commanders was vague. When the forces landed French troops opened fire sporadically, but all resistance ended on 10 November.

The Allied advance across northwest Africa was rapid, and the invading forces quickly linked up with British and American paratroops who had been dropped to secure the airfields at Bone and Gafsa. Hitler saw the new threat in north Africa and swiftly flew in reinforcements. By January there were over 100,000 German troops in western Tunisia. The Afrika Korps had now withdrawn behind the French-made defenses known

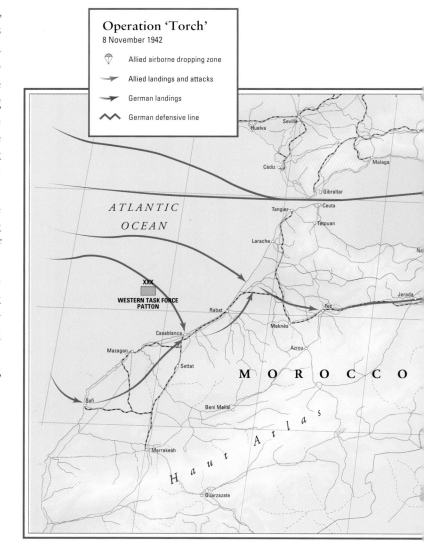

Operation 'Torch'
8 November 1942

⬦ Allied airborne dropping zone

➤ Allied landings and attacks

➤ German landings

〰 German defensive line

as the Mereth Line, while Montgomery continued to regroup in Libya. But as winter rains turned the desert into an impassable bog, the advance slowed.

While Montgomery built up his forces, Rommel turned his attention to the U.S. 1st Army at Kesserine Pass. This was to be a harsh induction for the unblooded troops of the American Army. Rommel left north Africa and his beloved Afrika Korps in secret, so as not to affect the morale of his troops. On 9 March the Afrika Korps came under the command of the Italian General Giovanni Messe's 1st Italo-German Panzer Army. The Germans, now under the command of General von Arnim, wanted to emerge in this sector in order to break apart the two ends of the pincer that was closing in on them. Faid was assaulted by the 21st Panzer and taken. Then, using the same trick that had fooled the British two years earlier, the Germans drew the U.S. tanks onto their anti-tank guns and destroyed more than 100 of them. The Allies retreated, but the Germans stopped the follow-up due to a disagreement between Rommel and his superiors. This allowed the Allies to regroup, enabling them to take up new positions, hold off the renewed German assault and, within days, to recapture the ground they had lost.

On 20 March Montgomery opened up his attack on the Mereth Line. Just over a week later the 1st Army took the offensive in the west, and by early April elements of the U.S. 2nd Corps met with the 8th Army. With this link-up, the Germans and Italians were trapped in an ever decreasing bridgehead, and had nowhere to retreat to. The Royal Navy was hampering an evacuation by sinking any ship that put out to sea.

The final push of the Allied armies was all that was required to evict the enemy from Africa. All the Allied armies now linked up: U.S. 2nd Corps in the north, the 1st Army in the center and the 8th Army in the southern sector. The final battle commenced on 6 May with a massive artillery bombardment of the enemy positions in the center section, and the leading Indian division accomplished their task by the end of the day. With the road now open all the way to Tunis, von Arnim realized that the game was nearly up and, heavily outnumbered, he was captured on the 12 May. By then over 250,000 Axis troops had surrendered to the Allies and would take no further part in the fighting. After three hard years of fighting in extreme conditions, the war in the north African deserts was at last at an end.

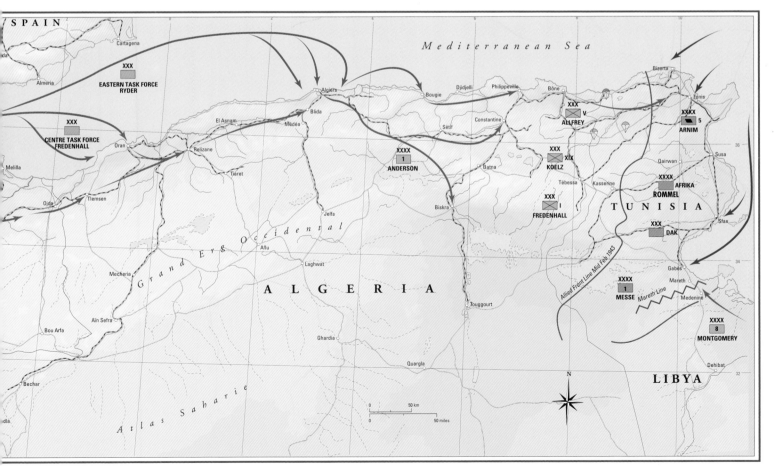

BATTLE OF THE ATLANTIC 1939–45

"As the bows went higher, so did the shrieks. I clung to a stanchion feeling sick and helpless as I had to look on while the children were swept out into the darkness below by the torrent of water which roared through the smoking-room."

ADMIRAL SIR K. CREIGHTON, CONVOY COMMODORE

At the outbreak of the war in Europe, the German Navy began to apply the same war of attrition that had failed it in World War I. This was based on the calculation that if 750,000 tons of Allied shipping, mostly British, could be sunk per month for twelve months then Britain would be forced into surrender by starvation.

Germany began the war with 57 U-boats. German naval planners required 350 but with the help of mines, aircraft, warships, and surface raiders, this total might be achieved. Against this force Britain could deploy 12 battleships and battlecruisers, six aircraft carriers, 58 cruisers and, most importantly, over 200 destroyers, and escorts with antisubmarine capabilities, as well as some 69 submarines. The French navy could also help but its main task at the outbreak of war was to face the Italian Fleet in the Mediterranean.

In September 1939 the German navy, apart from two surface raiders out in the Atlantic, were unable to operate much further west than a few hundred miles off the British coast, an area known as the Western Approaches to the British Admiralty. The North Sea and the English Channel were about the limits of U-boat operations. Thus, the bulk of ships lost were in these areas. In the period from September 1939 to June 1940, 702 merchant ships were lost.

One of the raiders loose in the Atlantic Ocean was the Admiral Graf Spee commanded by Captain Hans Langsdorff. She had left her German port before war broke out and was well positioned to raid Allied commerce. She was supported by a supply ship, the Altmark. During her cruise in the Indian Ocean and the South Atlantic, the Graf Spee sank nine merchant ships, then began to have problems with her engines. Captain Langsdorff planned a route back to Germany, but this would include a visit to the River Plate off the coast of South America where Langsdorff knew Allied convoys would gather.

The British anticipated this and sent "Force G" (one of eight such groups formed to hunt down the surface raider). On sighting the three cruisers of "Force G" Langsdorff assumed they were merchant ships and steamed straight for them. Too late, he realized they were warships, although of inferior gun power. In the brief

80-minute battle all three cruisers were damaged but so was the Graf Spee. She sought the safety of Montevideo, in neutral Uruguay, to make repairs and bury her dead. The Uruguayans gave her permission for just 72 hours in port. Meanwhile the British reinforcements were on their way. Another cruiser arrived but Langsdorff was forbidden to intern his ship and, if he could not fight his way back to the Fatherland, was instructed to scuttle the ship. He was also misled by British radio signals into believing that a larger force awaited him. He scuttled the Graf Spee on 17 December and a few days later committed suicide. These events were greeted as a great victory by the British but the real threat to lines of supply and survival still lurked beneath the waves.

With the German conquest of Norway and France in 1940, the nature of the U-boat war in the Atlantic changed. In July at Lorient in western France the first U-boat base came into operation. Immediately the U-boats' route to their patrol area was reduced by some 450 miles. Not only could more of the available U-boats be on patrol for longer periods but a greater number of them could be kept in action. From the start of the war

THE DEATH OF THE GRAF SPEE

Large crowds gathered to watch the scuttling of the German heavy cruiser. Its sinking was a diversion for the onlookers, but a tragedy for ship's captain. Days later, wearing full dress uniform and lying on the ship's battle ensign, he shot himself.

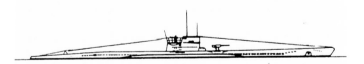

The Type VIIc U-boat was the mainstay of the German U-boat service throughout most of the war. They required a crew of 44 men and were armed with five 533 mm torpedoes, four bow tubes, one stern tube. They also carried one 88 mm gun and one 20 mm gun. The vessel was 220 feet long and had a displacement of between 750 and 850 tons. Though subject to various improvement as the war progressed, by 1943 they were out-classed by Allied submarine counter-measures. Five hundred and ninety-three of these submarines were completed and commissioned.

25 U-boats had been lost but production had increased so, despite these losses, there were now 51 in service. In addition to the U-boats, the Germans possessed the first Focke-Wulf Condors—four-engine, long-range aircraft. These began operations from an airfield near Bordeaux in August 1940. Ranging far out into the Atlantic, they acted primarily as reconnaissance, reporting the positions and directions of Allied convoys. This task completed, they were then free to unload their bombs on any target of opportunity.

At this time most convoys had one or two escorts; these were primarily antisubmarine and could not perform any meaningful antiaircraft role. In the sky and below the waves, the Germans seemed to hold the key to victory. Thousands of Allied merchant seamen lost their lives and cargoes which meant survival to Britain, ended up on the seabed.

German sinkings of Allied merchant ships reached a peak in April 1941, but as the convoy system became more widespread sinkings began to decline. The German naval code was now being read, thanks to the work of the cryptanalysts at Bletchley Park in England. The German plan to sink 750,000 tons of shipping per month was never consistently achieved. Britain also instituted careful rationing at home and a strict control of shipping space, reducing the country's import requirements by half during the course of the war.

British escorts became more effective, now being joined by the growing Canadian Navy. This forced U-boats further out into the Atlantic beyond the range of patrol aircraft. As the U-boats moved west there was, however, the danger of meeting more U.S. merchant ships and warships, which created the possibility of a clash with the U.S. Already U.S. warships were patrolling towards Britain and it was obvious that the Americans were determined to aid Britain's survival. Hitler did not want to have any problems with the U.S.—not at this time—and with his armies gathering on the borders of the Soviet Union, he was happy for the U-boats to do their duty in the Atlantic. Hitler was looking eastward.

From 7 December 1941 the United States was officially in the war, and this presented the U-boats with rich pickings off the east coast of the U.S. The U.S. Navy was initially unwilling to instigate a convoy policy, then suffered difficulties in organizing it. This left their ships prey to U-boat attack and losses soared, reaching a peak in summer and fall of 1942.

American surface escorts rallied and fought back, and U-boat losses also increased in the same period. By September 1942, with New York as the focus and western terminus for transatlantic convoys, the U.S. now introduced convoys in the Gulf of Mexico and along the eastern seaboard, and the main battle zone swung back to the mid-Atlantic.

First introduced in the spring of 1941 "Wolfpacks"—U-boats organized into patrol lines across the usual

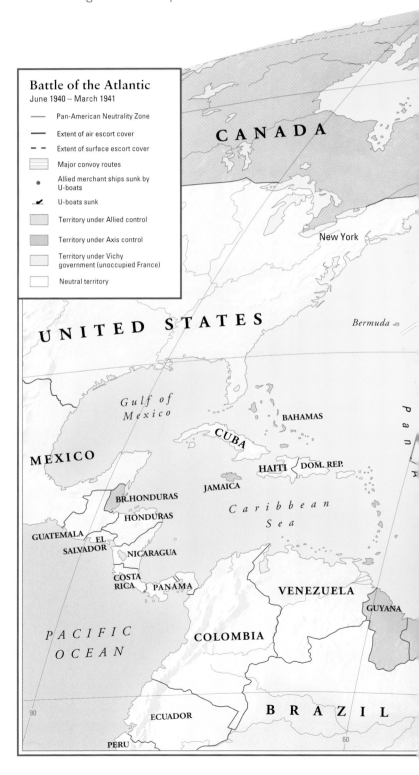

Battle of the Atlantic
June 1940 – March 1941

— Pan-American Neutrality Zone
— Extent of air escort cover
- - Extent of surface escort cover
▭ Major convoy routes
• Allied merchant ships sunk by U-boats
↙ U-boats sunk
▨ Territory under Allied control
▨ Territory under Axis control
▨ Territory under Vichy government (unoccupied France)
▭ Neutral territory

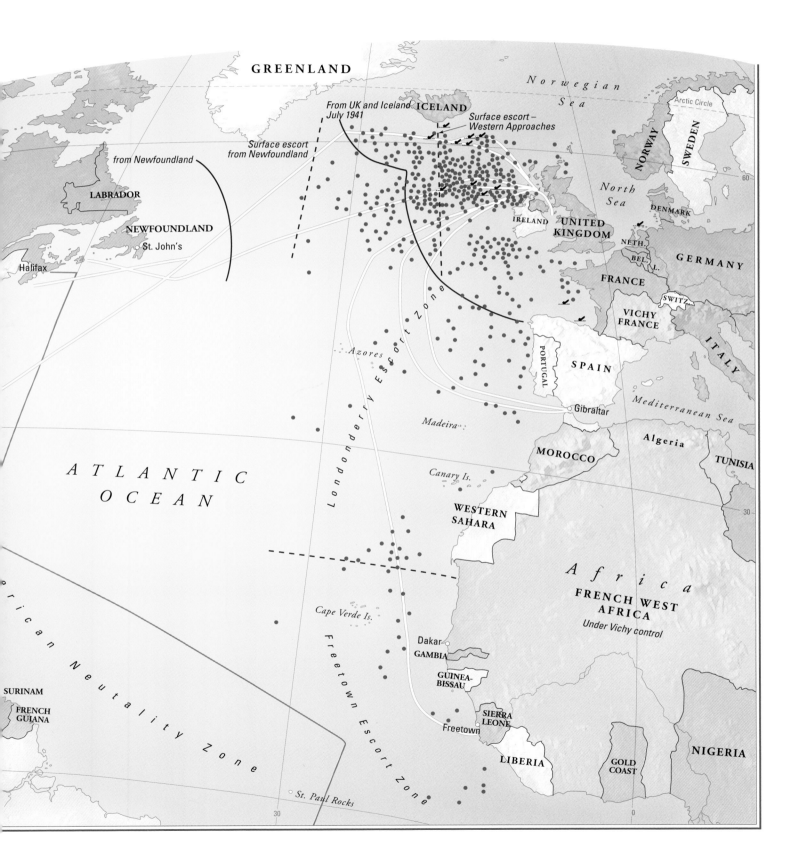

GREENLAND

Norwegian Sea

ICELAND

From UK and Iceland
July 1941

Surface escort –
Western Approaches

Arctic Circle

NORWAY

SWEDEN

Surface escort
from Newfoundland

60

North Sea

from Newfoundland

LABRADOR

DENMARK

NEWFOUNDLAND

IRELAND

UNITED
KINGDOM

NETH.

St. John's

BEL.
L.

GERMANY

Halifax

FRANCE

Azores

VICHY
FRANCE

SWITZ.

ITALY

PORTUGAL

SPAIN

ATLANTIC
OCEAN

Londonderry Escort Zone

Gibraltar

Mediterranean Sea

Madeira

Algeria

TUNISIA

Canary Is.

MOROCCO

30

WESTERN
SAHARA

Africa

FRENCH WEST
AFRICA

Under Vichy control

Freetown Escort Zone

Cape Verde Is.

Dakar

GAMBIA

GUINEA-
BISSAU

SURINAM

FRENCH
GUIANA

SIERRA
LEONE

NIGERIA

Freetown

LIBERIA

GOLD
COAST

erican Neutality Zone

St. Paul Rocks

30

0

convoy routes—grew larger. More U-boats than ever patrolled the airgap: the mid-Atlantic area beyond the range of Allied patrol aircraft. As the Germans concentrated their forces in the mid-Atlantic, they met better armed and equipped Allied escorts, who were using improved tactics. By August even the airgap itself was reduced by the introduction of V.L.R. (very long range) Liberator patrol bombers. Their patrols were now more carefully coordinated with the convoys themselves; instead of circling over the convoy or a suspected area, they flew just ahead or on either side: sightings and sinkings of U-boats increased.

The surface escorts' 10-centimeter radar, with a 360° sweep, for the first time made it possible to establish a radar watch completely around a convoy, day and night, in good weather. The assembly of Wolfpacks around the convoy could also be detected by high frequency direction-finding sets, which picked up U-boats sending reports to each other and to their base. The convoy battles of late 1942 and early 1943 were positively affected by these developments. Major victories were scored over the Wolfpacks in May 1943, when 41 U-boats were sunk.

The Allies, via ULTRA, were able to read the German naval code again after January 1943, except for a brief period in the first three weeks of March. During the March period half of all convoys located by the Germans were attacked and 22 percent were lost. By this time Admiral Dönitz, now head of the Kriegsmarine, had between 400 and 435 U-boats available for operations. Despite successes, the U-boat-arm was still losing U-boats at an alarming rate. ULTRA intelligence continued to penetrate the German codes.

At the Casablanca Conference between Roosevelt and Churchill in January 1943, the Allies gave the Atlantic first priority. By late March, support groups had been established to assist convoy escorts, especially through the still existing airgap. More V.L.R. Liberators finally closed the gap in May. ULTRA decrypts had a devastating effect at this point, routing convoys clear of U-boats patrol lines and diverting escort reinforcements into attack positions where it was possible to take an enormous toll. Almost 100 U-boats were sunk in the first five months of 1943. At the end of May, Admiral Dönitz withdrew almost all of the mauled U-boat fleet back to base. The Battle of the Atlantic had been won. Though ships continued to be sunk until May 1945, never would the supply of materials and food be threatened again. The U-boat force was now used to tie down the massive

Allied naval escort force, while new and improved U-boats could be designed and built. It was not until 30 April 1945 that this new generation sailed on its first patrol, a Type 23 with high-speed underwater performance. On the same day in Berlin, Hitler committed suicide.

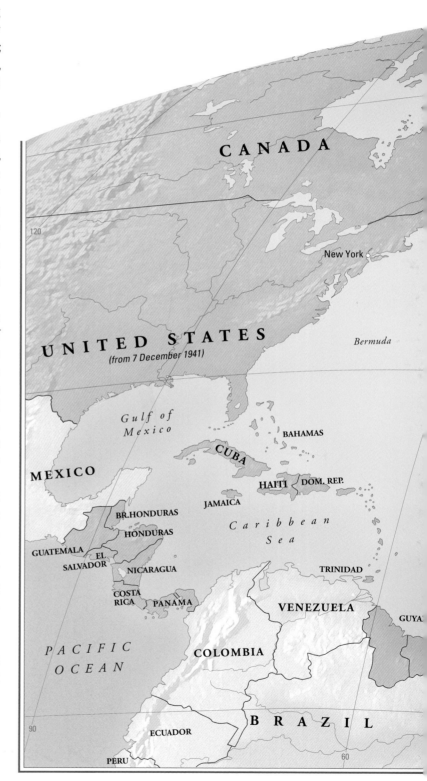

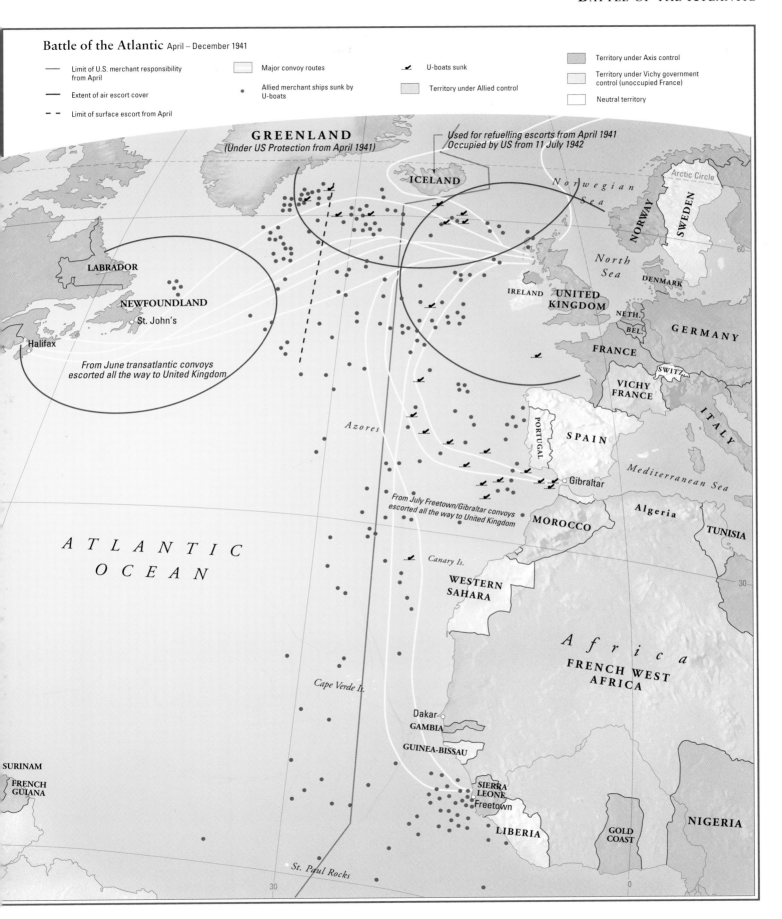

Battle of the Atlantic April – December 1941

——	Limit of U.S. merchant responsibility from April
——	Extent of air escort cover
– – –	Limit of surface escort from April
☐	Major convoy routes
•	Allied merchant ships sunk by U-boats
⚓	U-boats sunk
☐	Territory under Allied control
☐	Territory under Axis control
☐	Territory under Vichy government control (unoccupied France)
☐	Neutral territory

GREENLAND
(Under US Protection from April 1941)

Used for refuelling escorts from April 1941
Occupied by US from 11 July 1942

ICELAND

Norwegian Sea

Arctic Circle

NORWAY

SWEDEN

LABRADOR

NEWFOUNDLAND

St. John's

North Sea

DENMARK

IRELAND

UNITED KINGDOM

NETH.

BEL.

GERMANY

Halifax

From June transatlantic convoys escorted all the way to United Kingdom

FRANCE

SWITZ.

VICHY FRANCE

ITALY

Azores

PORTUGAL

SPAIN

Mediterranean Sea

Gibraltar

From July Freetown/Gibraltar convoys escorted all the way to United Kingdom

MOROCCO

Algeria

TUNISIA

ATLANTIC OCEAN

Canary Is.

WESTERN SAHARA

30

A f r i c a

FRENCH WEST AFRICA

SURINAM

FRENCH GUIANA

Cape Verde Is.

Dakar

GAMBIA

GUINEA-BISSAU

SIERRA LEONE

Freetown

LIBERIA

GOLD COAST

NIGERIA

30

St. Paul Rocks

0

THE INTELLIGENCE WAR

"The knowledge not only of the enemy's precise strength and disposition, but also how, when, and where he intends to carry out his operations, brought a new dimension to the prosecution of war."

FIELD MARSHAL SIR HAROLD ALEXANDER, ON ULTRA

Secure communications are a vital part of political and military organizations: they have to be able to send messages in secret. To meet this requirement, Germany invested in an encoding machine developed in the Netherlands. The original machine was intended for commercial use. However, with further development, it could be made into an unbreakable encoding machine for use on the field of battle, or so the Germans thought.

The "Enigma" machine was a kind of typewriter equipped with notched rotors that utterly scrambled any message. The rotor settings could produce hundreds of millions of possibilities in any given message. But another Enigma machine, having the same rotor settings, could easily decode the message. And it was a simple matter to change the settings every day, or as often as required.

The French and Belgians knew a little about the military version of the Enigma machine, and the breaking of the Enigma code began in Belgium, with some help from the French. With the aid of secret agents, the French began to read simple messages but the complexity of the machine daunted even their most gifted cryptographers. The French tried to involve the British, who proved disinterested. The French then turned to their new allies, the Polish, passing on all they had learned. By 1932, the Poles had constructed a reproduction of the Enigma machine. French agents continued to supply information

INFINITE KEYS
The genius of the Enigma machine, the thing that made it apparently undecryptable, was the vast number of possible settings engineered into a typewriter-sized box. A standard machine with three rotors and a ten-way plugboard had 15 billion potential settings.

as the Germans worked to improve their machines. With the updated information, the Poles worked on the cracking of encoded messages and, by 1938, had constructed what they termed a "bombe"—this consisted of a number of linked Enigma machines. By the end of 1938 the French agents' supply of codes ceased but, by this time, the code-breakers had developed their own techniques and were capable of cracking a limited number of encoded transmissions.

With Europe on the brink of war, the Poles held a meeting in Warsaw with their French and British Allies where they demonstrated their new methods of breaking the Enigma codes. Some of the most important work was carried out by a brilliant mathematician, Marian Rejewski, perhaps one of the most gifted cryptanalysts of the twentieth century. When the French and British left the meeting they were presented with Polish-built replicas of the Enigma machine. Given how little preparation the British had made for an intelligence war against Germany, this gift was of incalculable importance.

After the invasion of Poland, the Polish code-breakers escaped to France to continue their work. Following the invasion and fall of France the code-breakers again escaped and, for a time, worked in the Vichy zone of France, sending the results of their work—encoded on their Enigma machines—to London. By this time some French and Polish cryptographers had fallen into German hands. The captives, however, had been able to convince their German interrogators that the Enigma, with its millions of variables, was impossible to break, a story the Germans were eager to believe.

In Britain, at a country house called Bletchley Park, a code-breaking center had been established that continued the work of the French and the Poles. Academics were recruited and the establishment quickly expanded. By 1941 new, improved "bombes" were installed, ten-feet tall electro-mechanical giants. With amazing speed, the machines searched through the millions of possible rotor and key settings made by the German Enigma operators. The "bombe" came to a stop when it found the letter matches for which the cryptographer was searching. This could then be tried out on a British version of the Enigma machine. If these settings worked out they could lead to a group of messages being broken. It would then be sent to either the Navy, Army, or Air Force departments to turn into a meaningful message in English. The message was assessed for importance, and any person or unit mentioned was entered in an archive, a vast collage of German personnel and operations. Other information

THE INTELLIGENT BOMBE

Alan Turing devised a machine, based on the Polish bombe, that could be loaded with sets of rotors which mimicked the function of an Enigma machine. The Turing bombe could very quickly test thousands of possible settings, and so decrypt Enigma daily.

was gathered from German shortwave radio traffic and compared to Enigma decrypts. Perhaps the most important factor in this intelligence gathering was German carelessness. Luftwaffe operators often used recognizable chains of letter codes. The German Navy, meanwhile, proved much more difficult to break.

Bletchley Park and its team of academics still relied on captured material from the enemy. Such an incident occurred when the British destroyer HMS Somali engaged and damaged the German trawler Krebs. The sinking Krebs was beached and the Somali's Signals Officer boarded and searched the German vessel, recovering spare rotors and the Enigma settings for February 1941. Further captures, especially the occasional German weather ship out in the Atlantic, provided more rotor settings and data. In May 1941 HMS Bulldog, escorting Convoy OB318, was some seven days out of Liverpool when the convoy was attacked by U-110, commanded by Kapitänleutnant Lemp (the U-boat commander who had sunk the passenger liner Athenia at the beginning of the war). Lemp fired three torpedoes at the convoy and two merchant ships were hit. The periscope of U-110 was spotted and depth charges were fired. A second volley damaged the U-boat, which started to sink. Lemp ordered the ballast tank to be blown, which brought the U-boat back to the surface. As the crew abandoned ship, Lemp should have given orders to scuttle the U-boat, but either this was not done, or else the explosive charges were faulty. HMS Bulldog immediately sent a boarding party onto the U-boat. It consisted of a young sub-lieutenant

ENIGMA IN ACTION

It took three men to operate Enigma. The first typed the message; the second noted the apparently random letter that each keystroke illuminated on the alphabet board above the machine's keyboard; the third sent the message to its recipient in Morse code.

and five seamen. They boarded the abandoned and dark U-boat aware that charges had probably been set but calmly searched for any useful information. They found charts, code-books and a complete Enigma machine, which they carefully unscrewed from its mounting. It took some three hours to recover everything of potential value and get back to HMS Bulldog. The British ship attempted to tow the damaged U-110 back to port but the attempt failed. However, the most valuable cargo got home to port. The Bletchley Park staff could hardly believe their luck: a new machine with all its codes for the length of the U-boat's cruise, some three months, plus material that would help them to read the German Navy's Hydra Code for the rest of the war.

In the Pacific, however, the American cryptographers working on Japan's diplomatic and military codes, known to the Americans as "Purple" codes, did not enjoy the benefit of captured machines. They were led in their endeavors by William Friedman, chief cryptanalyst of the United States Army Signal Intelligence Service. He was an expert in statistics and probability, and by 1941 he had

over 20 years experience of code-breaking. With Friedman was a carefully gathered team who had worked on the "Purple" problem since 1939.

The Japanese used a mechanical device to encode their messages. It consisted of two typewriter keyboards connected by switches, plugs, and circuits. The Japanese machine did not use rotors but "stepping switches" as used in the telephone systems of the day. It was the realization, by cryptanalyst Harry Clark, that ordinary telephone stepping switches could be used in this way that led to the American breakthrough in reading the "Purple" codes.

With agonizing slowness, separating encrypted text in segments representing possible key settings, looking for letters in known frequency of use, skilled translators could form a complete message. Missing letters sometimes required educated guesswork on the part of the translator. The first message to be decrypted was completed on 25 September 1940. With experience, the American cryptanalysts built a machine that would duplicate "Purple's" functions. By early 1941 four machines were at work, two in Washington, one in the Philippines and one at Bletchley Park. Using the gift of this machine, the British began to intercept messages sent between Japanese embassies in Europe and the Middle East. By June 1941, a second machine had been sent for British use in Singapore.

So important had the decoding of Japanese messages become to the prosecution of the war that the information was distributed under the codename "Magic." In Britain, information gleaned from Enigma was known as "ULTRA." The information distributed under Magic and ULTRA had an incalculable impact, allowing the Allies to prepare moves on all fronts, to preempt Yamamoto's plans at Midway in June 1942, and also to enable General Montgomery to change his plans for Normandy in June 1944, when it became known that the Second S.S. Panzer Corps was to be deployed in that area.

The Axis powers never came close to winning this secret war, and they placed too much faith in their own encoding machines. But they had their moments. Germany compromised the Special Operations Executive's entire operation in the Netherlands; Japanese spies operated for years before the Pacific War, reporting on Allied defenses in Singapore, Hong Kong, Manila, and Pearl Harbor. But in the end, the Allied ability to break the Axis codes was a trump card. It made it possible to flout the enemy at many a turn, and always to deploy Allied military power in the right place at the right time.

The Wireless War

Germany

Allied to Germany

German/Axis occupied

Allied states or under Allied control

Neutral states

German Army wireless links using Enigma coding machine

Parr British codename for penetrated German wireless link

German listening post

British listening post

German Army, Navy, Luftwaffe HQ

Geheimschreiber station (encryption-decryption station)

Arctic Circle

Narvik

Arkhangelsk

Luleå

Norwegian Sea

FINLAND

L. Onega

Oslo

SWEDEN

Stockholm

Helsinki

Leningrad

L. Ladoga

SOVIET UNION

Estonia

Moscow

Mullet

Baltic Sea

Memel

Latvia

Riga

Whiting

North Sea

Denmark

Copenhagen

Trout

Lithuania

REICHKOMMISSARIAT OSTLAND

Rastenburg *Messages received from Eastern Front*

Königberg

Dace

East Prussia

Perch

Turbot

to U-boat wolf packs

Dublin

IRELAND

UNITED KINGDOM

Amsterdam

Neth.

Wilhelmshaven

Hamburg

Grilse

Berlin

Dace

Warsaw

Gen. Gov. of Poland

REICHKOMMISSARIAT UKRAINE

Kiev

Parr

Shad

Vinmitsa

to Caucasus

Octopus

London

GERMAN EMPIRE

Brussels

Belgium

Jellyfish

Frankfurt

Pollack

Prague

Prot. of Bohemia-Moravia

SLOVAKIA

Roach

Paris

St. Cloud

ATLANTIC OCEAN

France

Stuttgart

Munich

Salzburg

Vienna

Tarpot

ROMANIA

Crimea

Sebastopol

Bern SWITZ.

Austria

HUNGARY

Grayling

Budapest

Geneva

Milan

Venice

CROATIA

Banat

Bucharest

Black Sea

Genoa

Danube

Belgrade

Serbia

Sofia

BULGARIA

Gurnard

Mont.

ALBANIA

Marseille

Bream

SPAIN

PORTUGAL

Corsica

Rome

ITALY

Adriatic Sea

Istanbul

TURKEY

Lisbon

Madrid

Sardinia

Taranto

Greece

Aegean Sea

Athens

to Italy

Balearic Is.

Gibraltar to Britain

Algiers

Bone

Tunis

Sicily

Mediterranean Sea

Malta to Britain

Crete

French North Africa

Tripoli

Libya to Italy

Benghazi

Libya

64

60

56

52

48

44

40

36

32

MEDITERRANEAN NAVAL WAR 1940–43

"The Mediterranean will be turned into an Italian lake."

BENITO MUSSOLINI

The Mediterranean naval war was fought to keep open supply routes to North Africa and (for the Allies) to the Suez Canal. When France capitulated in the summer of 1940, Britain attempted to persuade the French Fleet in Algeria to surrender its ships to the Royal Navy, who would then sail them out of reach of the Germans. When the French refused to surrender their navy, the British felt that they had no choice but to destroy the fleet rather than allow it to fall into German hands. On 3 July the Royal Navy opened fire on the French ships. The attacks resulted in the deaths of 1,297 French sailors, and led to extremely bad relations between the French and British. It also impressed upon the United States the determination of Britain to survive.

Later that year, on the night of 11 November, the Royal Navy launched an attack against a large part of the Italian fleet at Taranto harbor. In the harbor were six battleships, seven heavy cruisers, two light cruisers, and eight destroyers—a formidable force that could strike a blow against British transports supplying the army in Egypt. Two waves of elderly biplanes, Fairey Swordfish, attacked the ships using torpedoes adapted to run in shallow water. They succeeded in hitting three battleships, for the loss of two aircraft. The raid alarmed the Italians so much that they moved the remainder of the fleet to safer ports in northern Italy. The Japanese Navy also took a great interest in the attack; it influenced their developing plan to strike the American fleet in Pearl Harbor.

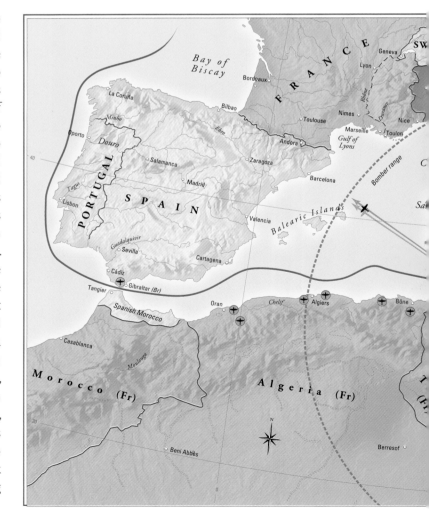

Late in March 1941 the Royal Navy received information, via ULTRA intercepts, that an Italian force, was near Crete on its way east, to intercept troop ships taking Allied soldiers to Greece. When the British came in sight of the Italian ships, the Italians gave chase, believing that the British were attempting to escape. But once the Italian cruisers broke off the pursuit, the British launched an airstrike, crippling some ships and sinking others. Two more Italian destroyers were sunk during a failed counterattack the next day. The longterm outcome of this sea battle was that the Italians never dared sail into the eastern Mediterreanean again, giving the lie to Mussolini's empty boast that the whole sea would be turned into an "Italian lake."

The British possession of Malta was a troublesome island in that lake. Its position between Italy and North Africa meant that Malta had potential to disrupt supply lines. This fact was recognized by Italy, which began bombing the island as soon as it declared war on Britain. The island's defenses consisted of outmoded Gloster Gladiator biplane fighters and antiaircraft guns. This weak defense still caused the Italians to be cautious, and the British decided that Malta must be defended. In June 1941, the Luftwaffe arrived in the form of Fliegerkorps X, covering the Afrika Korps sailing to Tunisia. This increased the intensity of the bombing campaign and the island was almost cut off. Convoys continued to reach Malta but experienced horrendous losses. As a result, the island's population and garrison were surviving on limited rations. During a respite, HMS Furious managed to fly in 61 Spitfires to aid the defense, but supplies of food, oil, and medicine were also urgently required. In August 1942, Operation Pedestal was carried out: 14 merchantmen were escorted by a massive naval force including three carriers, two battleships, and 32 destroyers. Just five transports survived. One carrier, two cruisers, and a destroyer were lost defending the convoy. As the war moved in the Allies' favor, the siege of Malta eased. In recognition of their bravery, the people of Malta received the George Cross, Britain's highest civilian decoration.

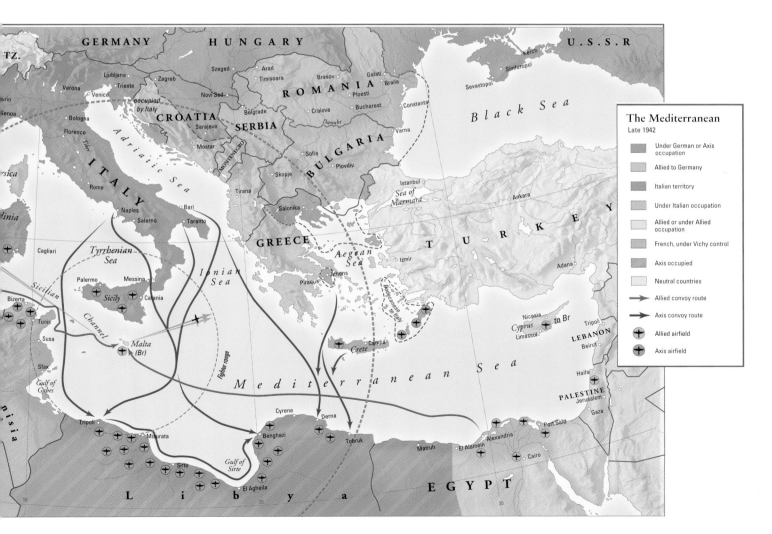

THE BALKAN CAMPAIGN 1941

"Führer, we are on the march!"

BENITO MUSSOLINI TO ADOLF HITLER, 28 OCTOBER 1940

On 7 April 1939 Italy annexed Albania, giving Mussolini a foothold in the Balkans, Italy's backyard. The Russo-German Non-Aggression Pact of 1939 also reorganized the Soviet Union's interest in the Balkans. This treaty assigned northern Bukovina and Bessarabia, parts of Romania, to the U.S.S.R.

In the Vienna Award of 30 August 1940 Germany and Italy recognized these annexations. The treaty also awarded southern Dobruja to Bulgaria and northern Transylvania to Hungary. This vastly reduced Romania was guaranteed by Germany and Italy. Germany was anxious to protect its supply of oil from the Ploesti region. Hitler's plan to secure the region for the Tripartite Pact was thrown off balance by Mussolini's attack on Greece from Albania. Mussolini expected Greece to fall within a few days but, much to his surprise, the Greeks resisted and forced the Italians back into Albania. The British sent an expeditionary force to aid the Greeks, which placed further pressure on the Italians.

Hitler was infuriated by his Italian ally's incompetence, as it provided the British with a reason to enter Greece and it alarmed the Soviet Union. Stalin was suspicious of Axis armies operating in the region, especially with regard to Bulgaria, which he viewed as a potential satellite of the U.S.S.R. At a meeting in Berlin in November 1940, Foreign Minister Molotov announced the Soviet Union's intention of declaring a unilateral guarantee of the existing Bulgarian borders. Hitler was increasingly convinced that his plan to

attack the Soviet Union was correct but first he must sort out the situation in the Balkans. He ordered the Army General Staff to prepare a plan for the invasion of Greece. The plan called for attacks to be launched from Bulgaria but he was far more unsure of Yugoslavia, which was wavering. Its ruler, Regent Paul, encouraged by the British and Americans, was resisting German diplomatic pressure. He eventually gave in, and signed up to the Tripartite Pact on 25 March 1941. Germany would enjoy transit rights for its troops for the planned attack on Greece, thus widening the front and outflanking Greek defenses north and west of Salonika. However, two days after Regent Paul signed, he was deposed by General Simovic, leader of an antiroyalist military coup. His supporters wanted to steer a neutral course. Hitler quickly resolved to include Yugoslavia in his plans for Greece, thereby ending any possibility of Britain, or any other power, interfering in his arrangements for the future of the Balkans.

On 6 April 1941, German forces launched their attack on Yugoslavia from the north and east. A massive air attack on Belgrade killed some 17,000 people. Four days into the campaign Yugoslavia's resistance began to fall apart when the predominantly Croatian 4th and 7th Armies mutinied. Croatia's semiautonomous government welcomed Axis forces in Zagreb the same day. The Serbian part of the country fought on for two more days before asking for an armistice.

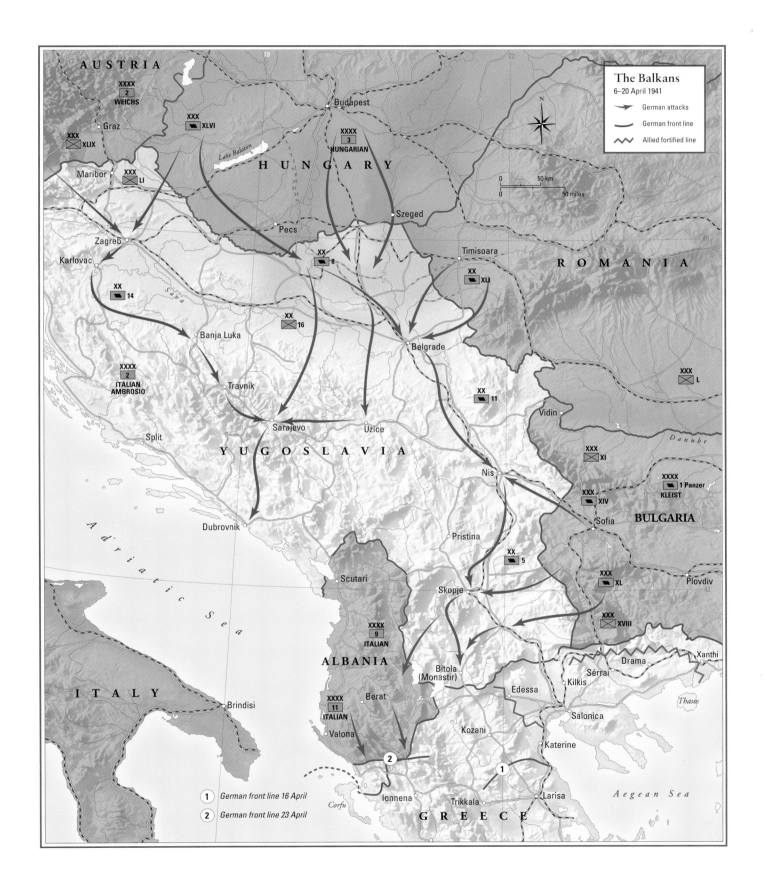

The Balkans
6–20 April 1941

→ German attacks
⌒ German front line
〰 Allied fortified line

AUSTRIA

XXXX 2 WEICHS

Graz

XXX XLIX

XXX XLVI

Budapest

Maribor

XXX LI

Lake Balaton

HUNGARY

XXXX 3 HUNGARIAN

Szeged

Pecs

Zagreb

Karlovac

XX 14

Sava

XX 8

Timisoara

ROMANIA

XX XLI

XX 16

Banja Luka

Belgrade

XXX L

XXXX 2 ITALIAN AMBROSIO

Travnik

XX 11

Vidin

Danube

Split

Sarajevo

Užice

YUGOSLAVIA

Nis

XXX XI

XXXX 1 Panzer KLEIST

XXX XIV

Sofia

BULGARIA

Dubrovnik

Pristina

Adriatic Sea

Scutari

XX 5

Skopje

XXX XL

Plovdiv

XXXX 9 ITALIAN

XXX XVIII

Bitola (Monastir)

Drama

Xanthi

ALBANIA

Sérrai

Kilkis

Thasos

ITALY

XXXX 11 ITALIAN

Berat

Edessa

Salonica

Brindisi

Valona

Kozani

Katerine

Aegean Sea

Corfu

Ionnena

Trikkala

Larisa

GREECE

① Ionnena

② Bitola

① German front line 16 April
② German front line 23 April

87

THE CONQUEST OF GREECE & CRETE 1941

"We have taken a grave and hazardous decision to sustain the Greeks and try to make a Balkan front."

WINSTON CHURCHILL

The planned German attack was preceded by a renewed Italian offensive launched in mid-March. A confident Mussolini was present at the beginning of the offensive but left abruptly when it became bogged down and came to nothing.

The German attack on Yugoslavia began on 6 April, 1941 with the 18th Corps also attacking north-eastern Greece, outflanking Greek defensive positions north-east of Salonika. Within three days German troops were within the city itself. The Metaxas Line, further south, manned by British and Commonwealth troops, was outflanked by the 40th Panzer Corps advancing south from Skopje, in southern Yugoslavia, over "impassable" mountains through the Monastir Gap. They also advanced to the east of the Greek 1st Army facing the Italians, partly cutting off their supply routes. The British forces fell back to an area around Mount Olympus. When these positions became untenable, they again fell back to the Thermopylae Line, protecting the roads leading to Athens. The Greek Army, facing the Italian 11th and 9th Armies now backed up by advancing German units, began to disintegrate. Despite occasional local success, the Greeks held the 40th Corps at Ptolemais and the New Zealanders held part of the 18th Corps advancing near Mount Olympus. The die was cast. By 21 April the British decided to evacuate Greece.

The German invasion of Crete, the first major airborne invasion of World War II, took place on the morning of 20 May 1941 as part of Operation Mercury. Poor intelligence on the German side led them to believe that Crete was badly defended and the civilians would be nothing less than welcoming. This resulted in horrific losses, which determined that they would never again make another large-scale airborne assault. However, it showed to the Allies the potential of paratroop assaults and led them to creating and training units of their own.

The defense of Crete was made up of 9,000 Greeks of the 5th Division plus the Crete Gendarmerie and remnants of the 12th and 20th Divisions. Though these units were poorly armed with little ammunition, they would fight ferociously for their island. There was also an original garrison of some 14,000 British troops that were supplemented by the New Zealand 2nd Division, Australian 9th Division, and the British 14th Infantry Brigade. Commanded by Major-General Freyberg, the defending force lacked any heavy equipment. The initial assault by the Germans was carried out by the Fallschirmjäger of 7th Air Division and the 5th Mountain Division, numbering in all some 25,000 men.

The Germans planned to take the major airfields on the western side of the island, secure these to allow supplies and men to be ferried in, then to advance inland

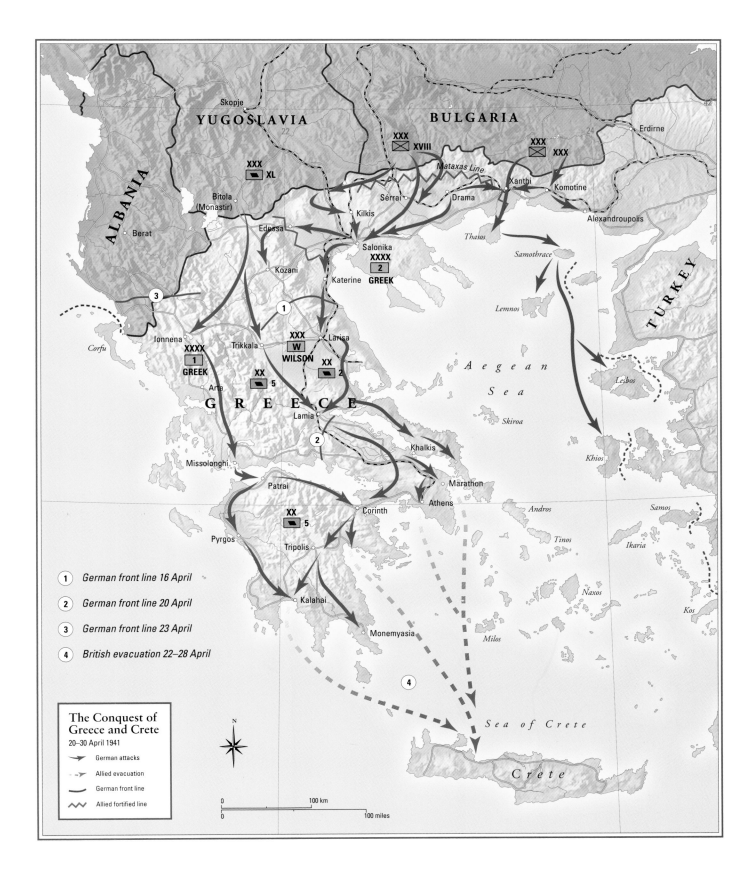

The Conquest of
Greece and Crete
20–30 April 1941

German attacks

Allied evacuation

German front line

Allied fortified line

① German front line 16 April

② German front line 20 April

③ German front line 23 April

④ British evacuation 22–28 April

and take the rest of the island. At 08:00 am paratroops started to descend on the airfields around Maleme and Canea but were severely mauled. Some units straying off the drop zone did, however, manage to set up strong positions off the airfields, which were continually attacked by the defenders and Allied troops, as well as civilians brandishing whatever weapons they could find. In the afternoon a second drop was made around the Rethiminon and Heraklion area, and again the paratroops took many casualties as they fell on units of the 14th Infantry Brigade supported by Australians and Greeks.

The Germans did manage to fight through to the docks of Heraklion but were beaten back by concerted Greek counterattacks. By the end of 20 May none of the German objectives had been seized. On the second day of fighting the Germans succeeded in capturing the airfield near Hill 107 and immediately started landing Ju-52 transports bringing in the 5th Mountain Division, even though the airfield was under continuous artillery fire. An attempt to retake the airfield by a brigade of New Zealanders was beaten back and the Germans could start to establish a bridgehead on the island.

From that point onwards the Allies were fighting a rearguard action as they continued to fall back slowly to avoid flank attacks. The Greek 8th Regiment holding the village of Alikianos in "Prison Valley" successfully held back the Germans for seven days, allowing the Allies to fall back southward and avoid capture. Many brave rearguard actions were fought, including that of the 28th Mauri Battalion that held the road between Souda and Chania long enough for the main force to retreat before retreating themselves with the loss of only two men. Layforce, a Commando unit given the task of covering the withdrawal, were cut-off by the advancing Germans, many of them being captured or killed.

The Royal Navy evacuated many troops from Sphakia and Heraklion before the Germans took the island. By the end of the fighting the Germans had captured 12,250 Allied troops with many of the Greek troops staying behind to blend in and continue the fight as guerrillas. The official German record states that losses were around 6,400 but this was doubtless altered for propaganda purposes, the number being probably nearer 16,000.

THE STUKA

The Ju-87 (Stuka), left, provided almost continuous air support for the hard-pressed airborne forces. It was probably German superiority in the air that tipped the scales in their favor.

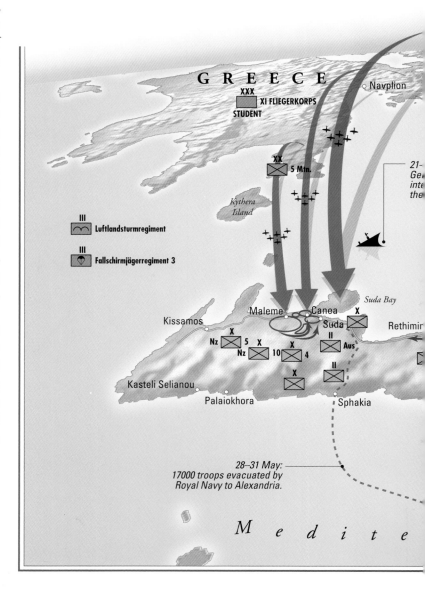

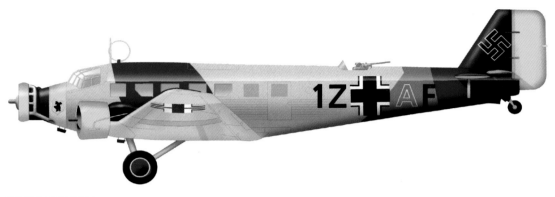

JU-52 TRANSPORT

The Germans deployed almost 1,200 aircraft in operations against Crete. The most numerous were the Ju-52 transport aircraft, above, of which 500 were deployed.

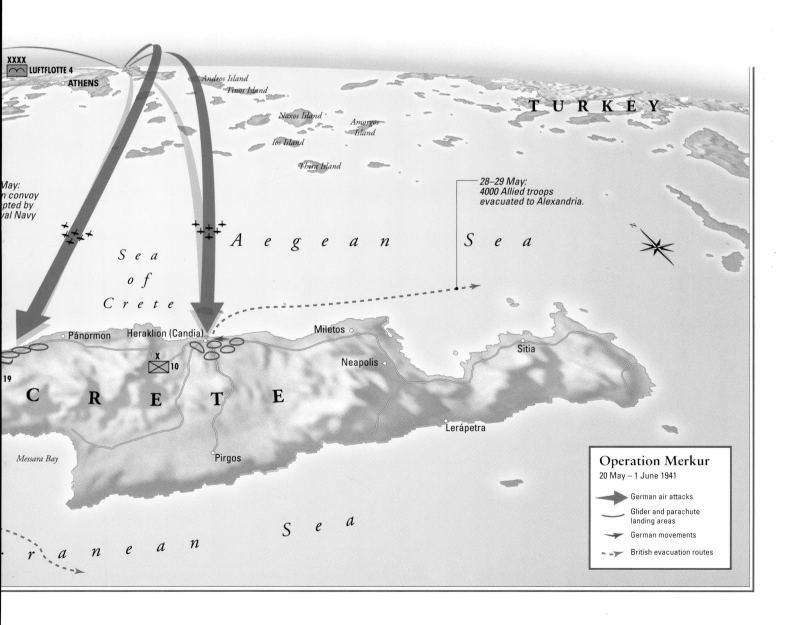

XXXX
LUFTFLOTTE 4

ATHENS

Andros Island

Tinos Island

Naxos Island

Amorgos Island

Ios Island

T U R K E Y

Thira Island

28–29 May:
4000 Allied troops
evacuated to Alexandria.

May:
n convoy
pted by
al Navy

A e g e a n   S e a

S e a
o f
C r e t e

Pánormon   Heraklion (Candia)   Miletos

Sitia

X
10   Neapolis

19

C   R   E   T   E

Lerápetra

Messara Bay   Pirgos

Operation Merkur
20 May – 1 June 1941

→ German air attacks

— Glider and parachute
landing areas

→ German movements

- -► British evacuation routes

S e a

r a n e a n   S e a

OPERATION
BARBAROSSA 1941

"The Red Army and Navy and the whole Soviet people must fight for every inch of Soviet soil, fight to the last drop of blood for our towns and villages ... onward, to Victory!"

STALIN, JULY 1941

On the evening of 21 June, 1941, the largest invasion army in history was assembled on the western border of the Soviet Union. About 10 percent of the adult male population of Germany was armed and waiting for the order to advance. Alongside them stood Finnish, Romanian, and Hungarian units; they would be joined by Italian, Bulgarian, and volunteer units from countries including "neutral" Spain. This gigantic operation was codenamed Barbarossa.

Meanwhile, in Moscow, Stalin refused to believe the domestic and foreign intelligence arriving on his desk. His instructions to forces based along the border were to make no provocative moves that could be misunderstood or misinterpreted by German forces.

Axis strength amounted to almost 3.6 million men with some 3,600 tanks and almost 2,800 aircraft, organized into three army groups: North, Center, and South. These groups were commanded respectively by Field Marshals von Leeb, von Bock, and von Rundstedt. Facing them was the Red Army with 140 Divisions and other brigade-size units numbering around 2.9 million men and 10–19,000 tanks, many of which were obsolete. The Red Air Force with some 8,000 aircraft was in the process of being reequipped.

The invasion began shortly after Hitler's Barbarossa Jurisdiction Decree, which exempted German soldiers from prosecution if they committed crimes against Soviet

FALSE WORDS
Stalin believed totally in his pact with Hitler (being signed, above). When the German invasion began, he was so shocked that he withdrew to his dacha, and did not address the people for two weeks.

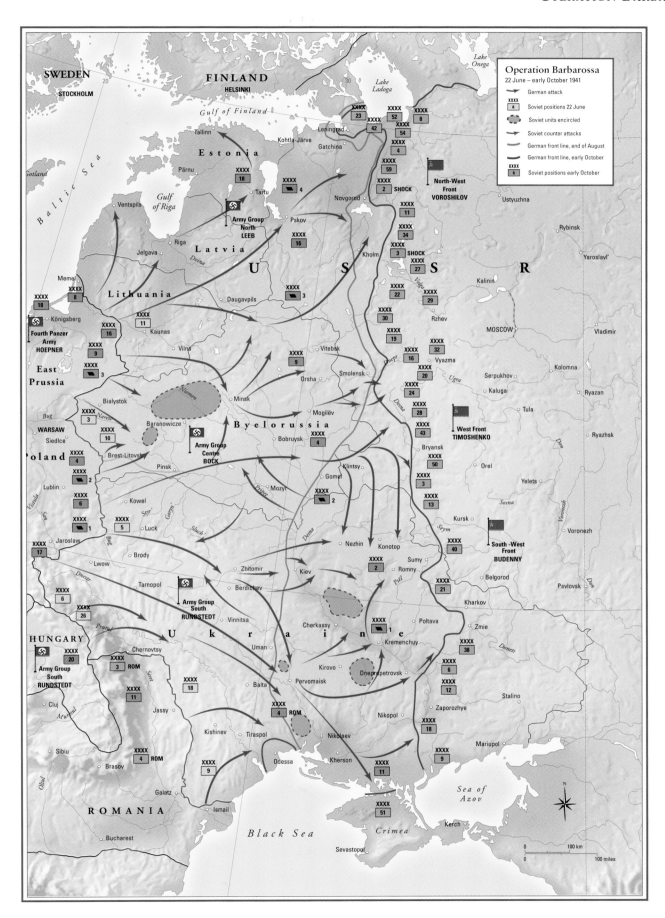

Operation Barbarossa
22 June – early October 1941

→ German attack

6 Soviet positions 22 June

Soviet units encircled

→ Soviet counter attacks

German front line, end of August

German front line, early October

6 Soviet positions early October

SWEDEN
STOCKHOLM

FINLAND
HELSINKI

Gulf of Finland

Lake Onega
Lake Ladoga

Tallinn
Kohtla-Järve

Estonia

Pärnu
Tartu

Leningrad
Gatchina

23
52
8
42
54
4
59
2 SHOCK

Novgorod

North-West Front
VOROSHILOV

Ustyuzhna

Baltic Sea

Gotland

Gulf of Riga

Ventspils
Riga
Jelgava

Latvia

Pskov

Kholm
11
34
3 SHOCK
27

Rybinsk

Yaroslavl'

U   S   S   R

Memel
18
8

Lithuania

Daugavpils

16
3

22
29

Kalinin

MOSCOW

Vladimir

Königsberg

Fourth Panzer Army
HOEPNER

16
9
3

Kaunas
Vilna

Army Group North
LEEB

Vitebsk
Orsha
9

Smolensk

30
19
16
20
24
28
43

32
Vyazma
Ugra

Rzhev

Serpukhov
Kaluga
Tula

Kolomna

Ryazan

East Prussia

Bialystok
3
10
Baranowicze

Minsk

Byelorussia

Mogilëv
Bobruysk
4

Army Group Centre
BOCK

Dnepr

Desna

West Front
TIMOSHENKO

Ryazhsk

WARSAW
Siedlce

Poland
4
2
6
1

Brest-Litovsk
Pinsk

Kowel

Klintsy
Gomel
Mozyr
2

Bryansk
50
3
13

Orel

Yelets

Lublin

Pripet

5
Luck

Brody

Zhitomir

Nezhin
Konotop

Kursk
40

South-West Front
BUDENNY

Voronezh

17
Jaroslaw

Lwow

Dnestr

Tarnopol

Army Group South
RUNDSTEDT

Berdichev

Kiev

2
Sumy
Romny

21

Belgorod

Pavlovsk

Don

6
26

Vinnitsa

Cherkassy
Uman

1
Kremenchuy

Poltava
Kharkov

Zmie

HUNGARY

Army Group South
RUNDSTEDT

20
3 ROM
11

Chernovtsy

18

Balta

Ukraine

Kirovo
Pervomaisk

Dnepropetrovsk

38
6
12

Stalino

Cluj

Jassy

Kishinev
Tiraspol

4 ROM
9

Nikolaev

Nikopol
18

Zaporozhye

Mariupol

Sibiu

4 ROM
Brasov

Ismail

Odessa
Kherson

11

9

Sea of Azov

ROMANIA

Galatz

51

Black Sea

Crimea

Kerch

Bucharest

Sevastopol

N

0   100 km
0   100 miles

SUMMER FIGHTING

German troops invaded in light summer uniforms, and made rapid progress towards Moscow. No-one expected the campaign still to be under way when the bitter Russian winter set in.

ENCIRCLED

Thousands of Soviet troops were captured early on in the campaign, and marched off to prisoner-of-war camps. Few of them survived that ordeal: many prisoners simply starved to death.

citizens. This set the bloody style of what would develop into a brutal campaign. Following the advance of the Wehrmacht came the Einsatzgruppen whose mission was to murder Jewish and any other "undesirable" elements in the conquered population.

After Stalin recovered from the shock of German invasion, he called on all Soviet citizens to commit themselves to a "relentless struggle" against the invaders. On 3 July he called for a scorched-earth policy: nothing of use was to fall into the hands of the invaders and a partisan war must be carried on in occupied territories. What was not destroyed in the fighting was destroyed by retreating Russians. German killing squads were at large and partisan groups began to emerge. Killing on an epic scale spread across western parts of the Soviet Union.

The German advance was met by a confused and disorganized resistance. The Red Army responded slowly to the massive tasks facing it. This was partly down to Stalin's purges of the late 1930s and to his instructions to take no "provocative" action. German High Command knew they had to destroy the bulk of the Red Army before it could fall back into the vast Russian interior, where it would await its greatest friend, General Winter. The early days and weeks of the German campaign witnessed massive advances, led by the four main Panzer groups, sometimes averaging advances of more than 18½ miles per day. It seemed, for a time, like the conquest of France and the Low Countries all over again. But the marching columns of infantry with their horse-drawn transport could not keep up with the Panzers. The Panzer units themselves became increasingly committed to

holding objectives and could no longer push eastward as they had done in the early days of the offensive. They were also outrunning their lines of supply. Destroyed railroads needed repair; the Russian road network was inadequate for German needs. And yet in the first weeks of the war the invaders achieved vast encirclements, capturing hundreds of thousands of Soviet prisoners.

However, there was no Russian collapse. Despite massive losses, they created new replacements. One month after the German attack, the Red Army had grown from 170 to 212 Divisions, although many were under strength. German planners had assumed that the inferior Slav could not withstand the German military machine. Hitler had said to one of his generals, "You just have to give the Russian state a good kick and the whole rotten regime will collapse." His soldiers advancing deeper into Russia were coming to grips with much tougher problems—ones that race and politics would not explain.

The bulk of the German offensive was concentrated north of the Pripet Marshes with the Army Groups North and Center. After crushing Soviet forces in Byelorussia, Army Group Center was to assist Army Group North, driving along the Baltic coast and turning toward Leningrad near Smolensk. Meanwhile, Army Group South would push into the Ukraine.

Army Group North made good progress but still suffered delays waiting for marching columns of infantry

SCORCHED EARTH

The Russians destroyed everything as they retreated. Stalin ordered his people to "blow up bridges and roads, damage telephone and telegraph lines, set fire to forests, stores and transports."

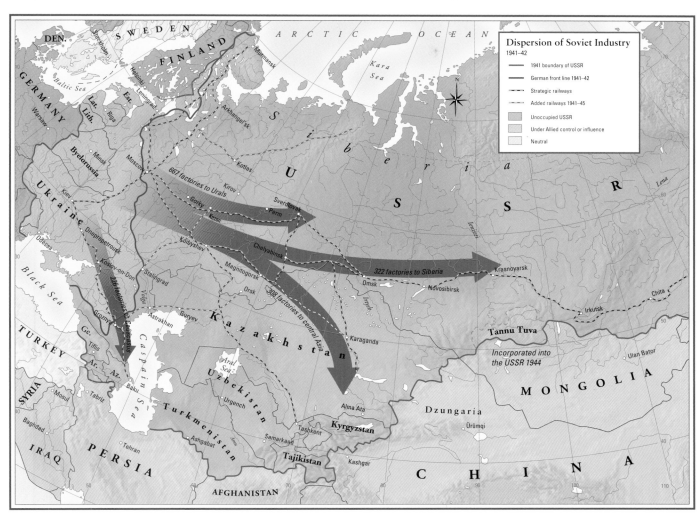

Dispersion of Soviet Industry
1941–42

1941 boundary of USSR
German front line 1941–42
Strategic railways
Added railways 1941–45
Unoccupied USSR
Under Allied control or influence
Neutral

667 factories to Urals
322 factories to Siberia
308 factories to central Asia
226 factories to Caucasus

Incorporated into
the USSR 1944

to catch up. Army Group Center advanced closely to plan, with a massive battle of encirclement at Minsk capturing 280,000 prisoners. This battle delayed the intended advance on Smolensk. However, by 17 July the city was in German hands. At this point Hitler intervened personally, overruling his generals who, according to the second phase of the plan, intended to head for Moscow. Instead he ordered Panzer Group 2 southward to support von Rundstedt's Group South Army. On its way it met with unexpected armored counterattacks and other heavy resistance, causing it to fall behind schedule. Hitler then redirected Panzer Group 3 north to support the advance on Leningrad.

As the Red Army retreated, a massive effort to move industry eastward began. Approximately 50,000 factories and workshops were systematically dismantled, placed on railroad wagons, and sent eastward, whenever possible with their workforce, under the watchful eye of the ruthless People's Commissariat for Internal Affairs, the N.K.V.D. This organization also rounded up any suspected of defeatism, and they were marched into captivity, or simply shot on the spot. Major General Kopets, commander of the Soviet Western Air District, saved the N.K.V.D. the trouble by committing suicide on the first day of the invasion.

The N.K.V.D. was also responsible for labor camps and exercised control over a vast labor force, which was used in the construction of fortifications. They also supplied "elite" forces to support Red Army formations at critical points, similar to the German use of S.S. troops. In July 1941, they were used to defend the approaches to Kiev while the 21st N.K.V.D. Division was used in Leningrad's defense. However, they cast a far more sinister shadow in their apparent willingness to torture and slaughter large numbers of prisoners.

Meanwhile, Army Group North was advancing through the Baltic States and northern Russia, and by 21 August Panzer Group 4 had reached the area of Novgorod. A Soviet counterattack just south of Lake Ilmen temporarily caught Southern Corps off balance, but by 8 September advance elements of Army Group North captured Schlüsselburg, a small town on the shores of Lake Ladoga. With Germany's allies, the Finnish Army moved from the north along the Karelian isthmus, which effectively cut off the city of Leningrad.

Hitler decided not to advance into the city but to reduce it by artillery and air attack. So began one of the greatest sieges of modern times. The Soviets would hold on, defending the city of the October Revolution to the last. Leningrad's long, painful siege had begun.

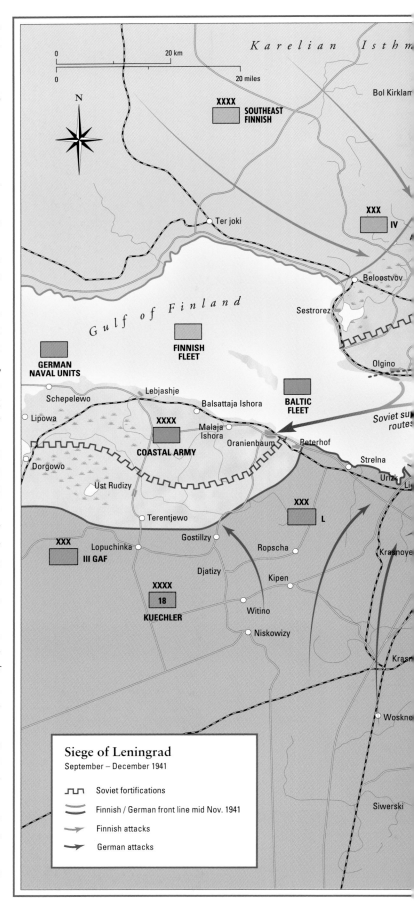

Siege of Leningrad
September – December 1941

⌐⌐ Soviet fortifications

≈ Finnish / German front line mid Nov. 1941

→ Finnish attacks

➤ German attacks

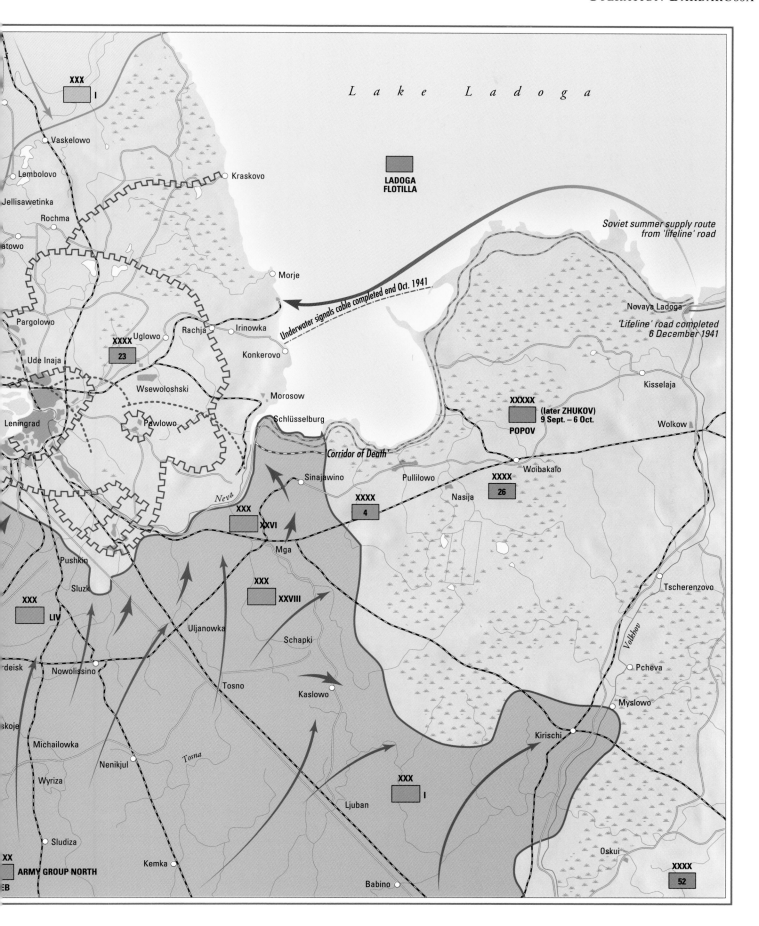

L a k e   L a d o g a

XXX
I

Vaskelowo

Lembolowo

Jellisawetinka

Rochma

atowo

Kraskovo

LADOGA
FLOTILLA

Soviet summer supply route
from 'lifeline' road

Morje

Novaya Ladoga

Pargolowo

Ude Inaja

XXXX
23

Uglowo

Rachja

Irinowka

Underwater signals cable completed end Oct. 1941

'Lifeline' road completed
6 December 1941

Konkerovo

Kisselaja

Wsewoloshski

Morosow

Leningrad

Pawlowo

Schlüsselburg

XXXXX
POPOV

(later ZHUKOV)
9 Sept. – 6 Oct.

Wolkow

Neva

Corridor of Death

Sinajawino

Pullilowo

Nasija

Woibakalo

XXXX
26

XXX
XXVI

XXXX
4

Pushkin

Mga

Sluzk

XXX
XXVIII

Tscherenzovo

XXX
LIV

Uljanowka

Schapki

Volkhov

deisk

Nowolissino

Tosno

Kaslowo

Pcheva

Michailowka

Nenikjul

Tosna

Kirischi

Myslowo

skoje

Wyriza

XXX
I

Ljuban

Sludiza

Kemka

Oskui

XX
ARMY GROUP NORTH

EB

Babino

XXXX
52

OPERATION TYPHOON 1941

"The Russian colossus ... has been underestimated by us ... whenever a dozen divisions are destroyed, the Russians replace them with another dozen."

GENERAL FRANZ HALDER
GERMAN ARMY CHIEF OF STAFF, AUGUST 1941

Intelligence from guerrilla groups around Leningrad spoke of tanks and armored vehicles being loaded onto trains and transported south, away from the city. They were being moved to the area west of Moscow, for an assault on the capital. Georgii Zhukov, commander of the Leningrad Front was summoned to Moscow and ordered by Stalin to oversee the Front. There he found chaos: units had lost touch with each other; stragglers from destroyed units wandered the countryside; and no one seemed to know where the Germans were. Within 48 hours of his arrival Zhukov had assumed personal command of all forces around Moscow.

He inherited 90,000 beaten men, all that remained of the 800,000 who had begun the battle a few weeks earlier. He immediately set about strengthening Moscow's defenses. Ten miles from the city center, hundreds of thousands of forced and volunteer laborers, many of whom were women and children, dug anti-tank ditches, built strongpoints and laid miles of barbed wire. Meanwhile, reinforcements arrived in the form of six Soviet armies, some surviving veterans of earlier battles, and callow youths, fresh from the farm and the factory.

Hitler made the capture of Moscow the primary objective of the 1941 campaign. The assault began on 30 September, as the 2nd Panzer Group broke through the Soviet 13th Army, forcing two Soviet armies—the 50th and the 3rd—to attack eastward to avoid encirclement. Two days later the 3rd and 4th Panzer Groups attacked, shattering Soviet defenses.

On 6 October the first snow fell, earlier than usual. The German advance slowed and, despite the progress made, casualty figures were worryingly high. By the end of September they stood at 551,039, 16 percent of the field army. Replacements, however, were not being sent to the front at the same rate; the German Army on 1 October 1941 was over 200,000 men below strength.

The cities of Kalinin, north of Moscow, and Kaluga, to the south, had been captured by 18 October. It was beginning to look like another battle of encirclement, but only very slow progress was made. The Soviets fought with bravery, driven mercilessly by Zhukov. There were some successes and some disasters but little by little the Soviets were getting to grips with German tactics and finding ways to defeat them.

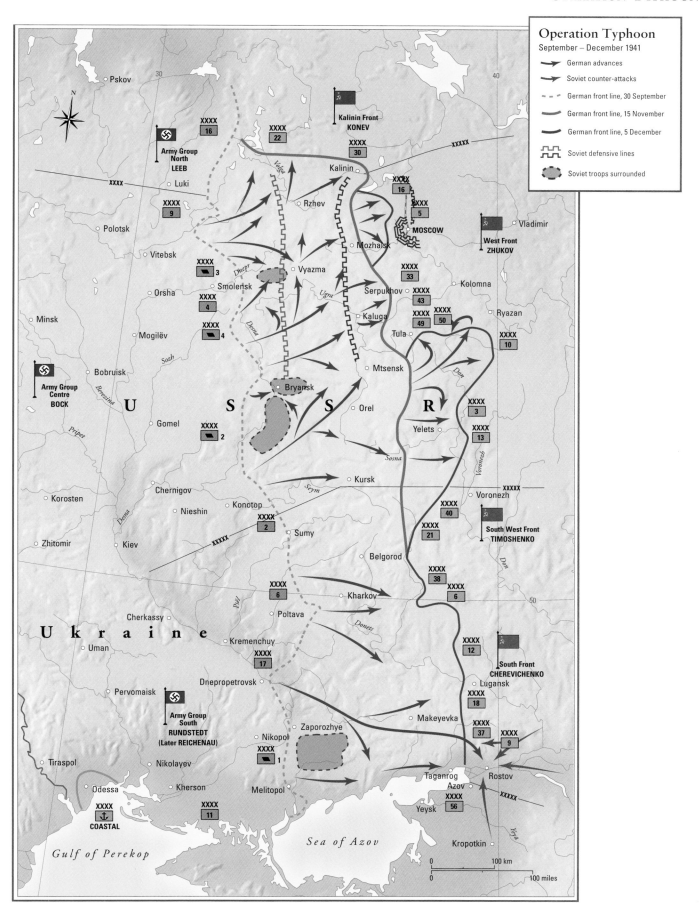

Operation Typhoon
September – December 1941

→ German advances

→ Soviet counter-attacks

- - - German front line, 30 September

⌒ German front line, 15 November

⌒ German front line, 5 December

⊔⊓⊔ Soviet defensive lines

▨ Soviet troops surrounded

THE BATTLE OF MOSCOW 1942

"Oh merciful Lord... crown our effort with victory ... and give us faith in the inevitable power of light over darkness, of justice over evil and brutal force ... of the cross of Christ over the Fascist swastika ... so be it, Amen."

SERGEI, ARCHBISHOP OF MOSCOW, 27 NOVEMBER 1941

On the 24th anniversary of the Great October Socialist Revolution, Stalin made a speech in the bomb-proof depths of Mayakovskaya subway station. "If they want a war of extermination they shall have it!" he said. "Death to the German invaders!" That year, the troops parading through Red Square marched straight from there to the front, only 40 miles away.

To the north, the Germans waited for the fall mud to freeze so that the campaign could resume. On 24 November the 3rd and 4th Panzer Groups took Klin. Reconnaissance units pushed to within 12 miles of Red Square. South of the city, the 2nd Panzer Group attacked toward Tula, but were stalled by determined troops under General Boldin.

At this point, Moscow was defended by 240,000 men plus some 500 tanks, many old and light, and of little use on the battlefield. The bulk of the defenders were survivors of shattered units, men from rear areas, the minimally-trained Moscow militia, and civilians drawn from the streets. It did not look like a battle-winning force, but it held out. By the end of November a quarter of the German army were casualties; their uniforms and equipment were not designed for the Russian winter. Soviet equipment was winter-proof, and the men were mentally ready for extreme cold. The Soviets had survived the worst. Since June almost 2,700,000 of their troops had been killed in action and 3,350,000 taken prisoner. Twenty Soviets had died for every German killed.

At the end of November, Stalin demanded an offensive. Zhukov explained that he did not have the resources to launch an offensive but Stalin would have none of it. Zhukov drew up his plans and presented them to Stalin. His plan was simple: to hit the German pincers around Moscow. Among the forces he aimed to deploy were 58 new division, some drawn from the far east. They were tough Siberians, materially and mentally equipped to fight in the deepest winter.

The offensive began on the morning of 5 December 1941 at 03:00 am. In bitter weather both sides fought to the death, but slowly the Soviets gained more ground, recapturing Klin. In the south Stalinogorsk was liberated and the Soviet attack pushed forward. German Army Group Center was faced with the possibility of encirclement. German commanders asked Hitler for

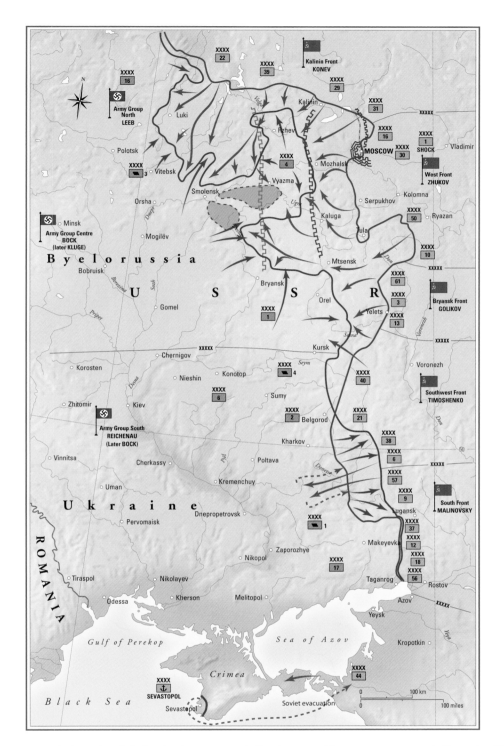

Battle of Moscow
January– June 1942

→ German advances

→ Soviet counterattacks

— German front line end May

— German front line June

⊓⊔ Soviet defensive lines

▨ Soviet Partisans operating behind enemy lines

CIVIL DEFENDERS

As the Germans closed in on Moscow and a street battle looked likely, civilians were taught to shoot.

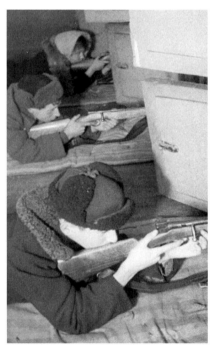

permission to fall back to more defensive positions. Hitler greeted the petition by sacking them all, and on 19 December took over command of the army himself. The battle went on into January, both sides fighting with tenacity and skill. Soviet units infiltrated the German front, while isolated German units were supplied by air or fought their way out.

The sight of Germans on the defensive encouraged Stalin to order offensives along the front. Despite representations by Zhukov that the Red Army was not yet ready, the offensives were forced through. All failed and almost 450,000 Soviet troops were lost. It would be another 18 months before the Red Army would beat the Germans in an all-out summer offensive. Meanwhile, the army fought its dogged battles defending the Caucasus oilfields and in Stalingrad. The isolated Soviet garrison at Sevastopol finally succumbed to the German siege that had lasted from 6 June to 2 July 1942.

PEARL HARBOR 1941

"I continued to watch the sky over the harbor as well as the activities on the ground. None but Japanese planes were in the air, and there were no indications of air combat. Ships in the harbor still appeared to be asleep."

CAPTAIN MITSUO FUCHIDA, COMMANDER FIRST AIR FLEET

As the Japanese empire expanded into China during the 1930s and early 1940s, the U.S. Navy began developing its assets in the Pacific. Japan's Navy and the U.S. Navy were almost identical in size, but Japan could not afford to fight a prolonged war with the U.S., limited by its lack of natural resources, especially oil. Japan looked upon Malaya and the Dutch East Indies as the answer to her fuel crisis. With the European war holding down most of Britain's available forces and with the capitulation of the Dutch and French to Germany, Japan's only threat in the Pacific was the U.S. Navy. A pre-emptive strike on the U.S. fleet would allow the Japanese to grab the assets they so desperately needed and achieve their aims before the U.S. could recover.

The planning of the attack was given to Admiral Yamamoto, even though he thought that making war with America was a grave mistake. Many of the military commanders thought it impossible to attack a fleet at anchor, especially with torpedoes which would simply lodge into the mud of a relatively shallow harbor. This was proven wrong by 21 outmoded British Swordfish biplanes of the Fleet Air Arm, which attacked Taranto harbor on 11 November 1940, sinking many of the Italian fleet and reversing the balance of naval power in the Mediterranean. The Japanese trained its pilots extensively on the attack and modified their torpedoes with wooden fins to

prevent them going below a certain depth. It was to be a massive operation involving the fleet's six best aircraft carriers under the command of Vice-Admiral Nagumo with over 430 aircraft to be deployed in the attack.

After intense training in the Kurile Islands, the fleet left for Hawaii, taking a northern route so as not to be detected by the U.S. Navy. Accompanying the six carriers were two battleships, numerous escort vessels, and eight support ships that would refuel the main force south of the Aleutian Islands. There would also be a force of midget submarines that would infiltrate the harbor and cause as much damage as possible.

American intelligence expected a Japanese attack at some point, but concluded that it would occur in the Philippines. All that was thought possible at Pearl Harbor was minor sabotage. Commander-in-Chief of the Pacific Fleet, Rear-Admiral Kimmel, looked toward the Marshall

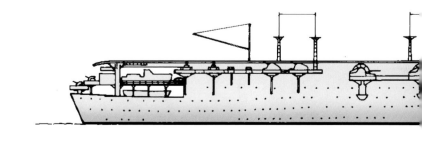

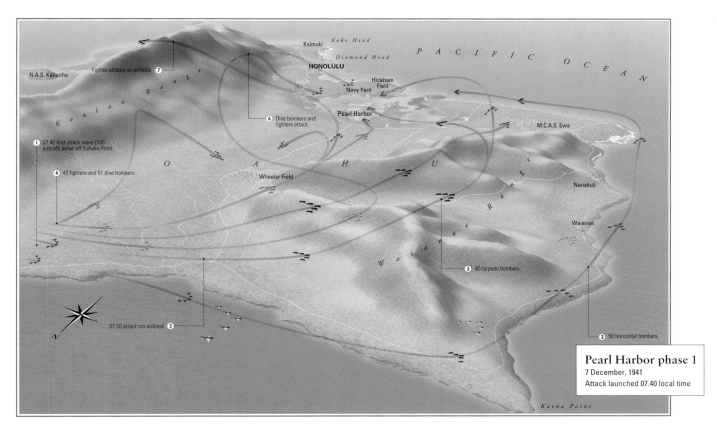

Koko Head
Kaimuki
Diamond Head
HONOLULU
P A C I F I C   O C E A N

Fighter attacks on airfields (7)

N.A.S. Kaneohe

Hickham Field
Navy Yard

Pearl Harbor

(6) Dive bombers and fighters attack.

K o o l a u   R a n g e

(1) 07.40 first attack wave (190 aircraft) arrive off Kahuku Point.

M.C.A.S. Ewa

(4) 43 fighters and 51 dive bombers.

Wheeler Field

O   A   H   U

Nanakuli

W a i a n a e   R a n g e

Waianae

(5) 40 torpedo bombers.

(2) 07.50 attack run ordered.

N

(3) 50 horizontal bombers.

Pearl Harbor phase 1
7 December, 1941
Attack launched 07.40 local time

Kaena Point

Islands, the closest Japanese territory to Hawaii, and it was from here that he expected any operation to be launched. The War Office in Washington, based on best available intelligence assessments, sent a final war warning to all military commanders in the Pacific, including the Army commander Lt-General Walter Short at Oahu. He assumed that this was to prepare for sabotage attacks and did not even authorize the deployment of ammunition to antiaircraft batteries. Aircraft designated to the defense of the islands were not dispersed properly and lined up on the runways like ducks in a shooting gallery.

The Japanese took the decision to attack on a Sunday, since the maximum amount of naval crews would be ashore on leave and would not be able to assist in the defense of their ships or the harbor. With the Japanese strike force now 250 nautical miles north of Hawaii, Nagumo was disappointed to hear from a forward reconnaissance unit that there were no carriers in the harbor. They were in fact delivering aircraft to Midway Island. Nevertheless he gave the order for the first wave to take to the air at 6:00 am. They were in formation and on their way in 15 minutes. The first wave consisted of 51 "Val" dive-bombers, 49 "Kate" level-bombers, 40 "Kate" torpedo-bombers, and 43 "Zero" fighters. This created a serious blip on the radar screens of a training

THE INITIAL WAVE GOES IN

The first air strike deployed at 07:40 am, with the attack run ordered at 07:50 am, as the air group passed just off Keana Point. This first wave of 190 aircraft began their attacks. The primary targets at this point were airfields, the intention being to suppress possible interception by the few American fighters that could be made ready for take-off. Once the airfields had been hit, the next target was the crowded anchorage of Pearl Harbor.

JAPANESE CARRIER ZUIKAKU

The aircraft carrier Zuikaku, launched in November 1939 and weighed in at 32,000 tons, was capable of carrying more than 72 aircraft. She was one of six carriers that took part in the Hawaii Operation.

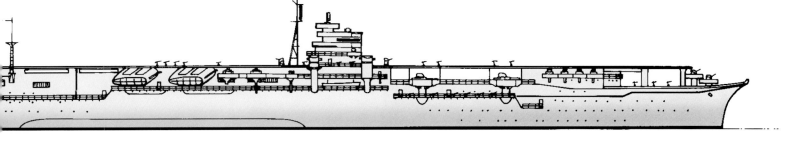

unit on Kahuku Point, but when they reported to the duty officer he shrugged it off as a flight of B-17s expected from the U.S. mainland.

The strike force was guided towards the harbor by local radio broadcasts. First to press home their attack were the dive-bombers, early by five minutes at 7:55 am, then shortly after, the torpedo bombers started their run at battleship row. Meanwhile the Zero fighters were strafing all the nearby airfields and destroying the majority of U.S. aircraft neatly lined up on the ground. With the element of surprise, hardly any anti-aircraft fire and no fighter interceptors to worry about, the Japanese pilots could completely concentrate on the job in hand. Ten minutes after the attack had begun there was an almighty eruption as USS Arizona's ammunition magazine was penetrated by an armor-piercing bomb, immediately

sinking, taking 1,200 sailors down with her. Behind her mangled stern, USS West Virginia and USS California were also torpedoed and sunk. USS Nevada actually got underway and tried in desperation to get to the relative safety of the open sea. The Japanese pilots concentrated fire upon her and she was eventually beached. With the harbor covered in burning oil and stricken and sinking craft, the first wave headed back to the carriers.

There was to be no respite for the servicemen at Pearl Harbor: as soon as the first wave left the second wave of attack planes arrived. However, the defenders by now were starting to get themselves in order and were throwing up a ferocious amount of antiaircraft fire and, with the smoke from fires started in the first attack, the Japanese could not cause as much damage as the initial assault.

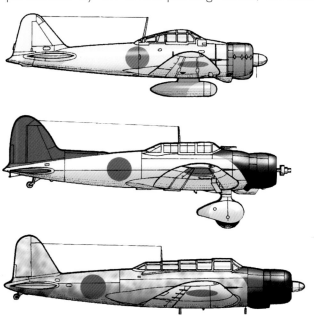

JAPAN'S ATTACK AIRCRAFT
The aircraft taking part in the attacks were, from top to bottom:
Mitsubishi A6M2 "Zero" Fighter
Aichi D3A1 "Val" dive-bomber
Nakajima B5N2 "Kate" Level-bomber.

THE PATH OF THE SECOND WAVE
The second wave to attack consisted of 167 aircraft, arriving off Kahaku Point at 08:40 am. Although the defenses were alerted, they still failed in their efforts to protect their shattered fleet and airfields. Before the Japanese finally withdrew more damage was done at the cost of just 29 Japanese aircraft.

W a i a n a e R a

O   A   H

M.C.A.S. Ewa

Pearl Harbor

Hickham
Field   Navy Yard

HONOLULU

Diamond Head   Kaimuki

N

Pearl Harbor phase 2
7 December, 1941
Second attack ordered 08.54 am.

ARIZONA IN FLAMES

The attack on Pearl Harbor caused massive damage. This image shows three capital ships aflame—the USS West Virginia, the USS Tennessee, and the USS Arizona. But Pearl Harbor was more than its ships, it was also the port itself, and most of the naval installations there remained intact.

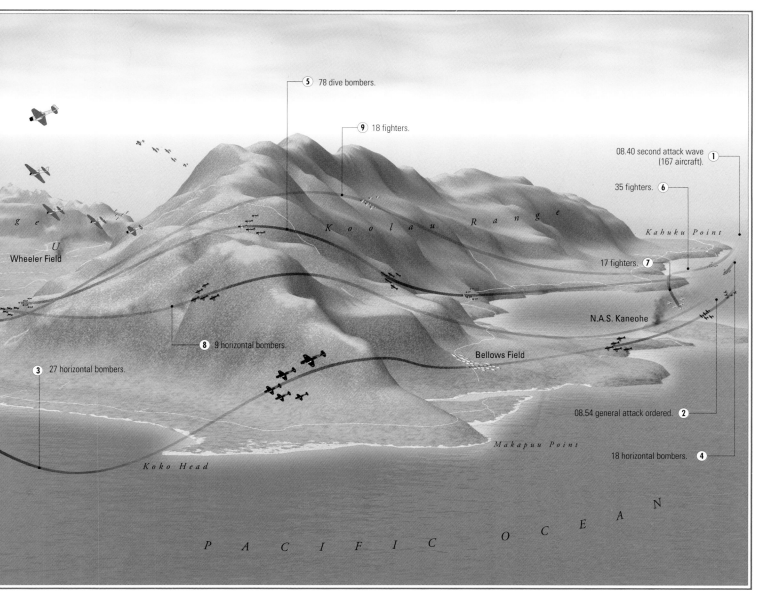

5 78 dive bombers.

9 18 fighters.

08.40 second attack wave (167 aircraft). 1

35 fighters. 6

Koolau Range

Kahuku Point

17 fighters. 7

U
Wheeler Field

N.A.S. Kaneohe

8 9 horizontal bombers.

Bellows Field

3 27 horizontal bombers.

08.54 general attack ordered. 2

Makapuu Point

18 horizontal bombers. 4

Koko Head

P A C I F I C   O C E A N

By the end of the attack, the Japanese forces had lost 29 aircraft but created total havoc below them, sinking six battleships, three destroyers, and three light cruisers, and damaging two. Having received reports, Nagumo decided his luck had been pushed far enough and did not give the order for the third wave to attack. This vital decision was a grave mistake, since none of the harbor installations had been destroyed and Pearl Harbor could still be used as a serviceable base.

The Japanese General Staff considered the air attack on Pearl Harbor to have been about 50 percent successful. Therefore a submarine operation was also launched, involving 18 submarines, five of which carried midget subs to be deployed in Manila Bay and the entrance to Pearl Harbor. The Submarine Force arrived according to plan, before the Task Force. Having time to reconnoiter ships entering and leaving the harbor, it was in a position to attack ships at anchor, or in the immediate area, should the air attack fail.

Below: One of the Japanese midget submarines that was located by the destroyer USS Helms and forced to beach.

Although the attack on Pearl Harbor was a massive blow to the American psyche, the country was united against a deceitful and vicious enemy. Instead of weakening the beast they had only succeeded in making it angry. Nagumo had also missed the opportunity to destroy the U.S. carrier fleet, which was much more important than sinking six outmoded battleships. It may have been a tactical victory for the Japanese but they would soon lose the initiative they needed.

1. Tender *Whitney* and destroyers *Tucker, Conyngham, Reid, Case* and *Selfridge*
2. Destroyer *Blue*
3. Light cruiser *Phoenix*
4. Destroyers *Aylwin, Farragut, Dale* and *Monaghan*
5. Destroyers *Patterson, Ralph, Talbot* and *Henley*
6. Tender *Dobbin* and destroyers *Worden, Hull, Dewey, Phelps* and *Macdough*
7. Hospital Ship *Solace*
8. Destroyer *Allen*
9. Destroyer *Chew*
10. Destroyer-minesweepers *Gamble*, and *Montgomery* and light-minelayer *Ramsey*
11. Destroyer-minesweepers *Trever, Breese, Zane, Perry* and *Wasmuth*
12. Repair vessel *Medusa*
13. Seaplane tender *Curtiss*
14. Light cruiser *Detroit*
15. Light cruiser *Raleigh*
16. Target battleship *Utah*
17. Seaplane tender *Tangier*
18. Battleship *Nevada*
19. Battleship *Arizona*
20. Repair vessel *Vestal*
21. Battleship *Tennessee*
22. Battleship *West Virginia*
23. Battleship *Maryland*
24. Battleship *Oklahoma*
25. Oiler *Neosho*
26. Battleship *California*
27. Seaplane tender *Avocet*
28. Destroyer *Shaw*
29. Destroyer *Downes*
30. Destroyer *Cassin*
31. Battleship *Pennsylvania*
32. Submarine *Cachalot*
33. Minelayer *Oglala*
34. Light cruiser *Helena*
35. Auxiliary vessel *Argonne*
36. Gunboat *Sacramento*
37. Destroyer *Jarvis*
38. Destroyer *Mugford*
39. Seaplane tender *Swan*
40. Repair vessel *Rigel*
41. Oiler *Ramapo*
42. Heavy cruiser *New Orleans*
43. Destroyer *Cummings* and light-minelayers *Preble* and *Tracy*
44. Heavy cruiser *San Francisco*
45. Destroyer-minesweeper *Grebe*, destroyer *Schley* and light-minelayers *Pruitt* and *Sicard*
46. Light cruiser *Honolulu*
47. Light cruiser *St. Louis*
48. Destroyer *Bagley*
49. Submarines *Narwhal, Dolphin* and *Tautog* and tenders *Thornton* and *Hulbert*
50. Submarine tender *Pelias*
51. Auxiliary vessel *Sumner*
52. Auxiliary vessel *Castor*

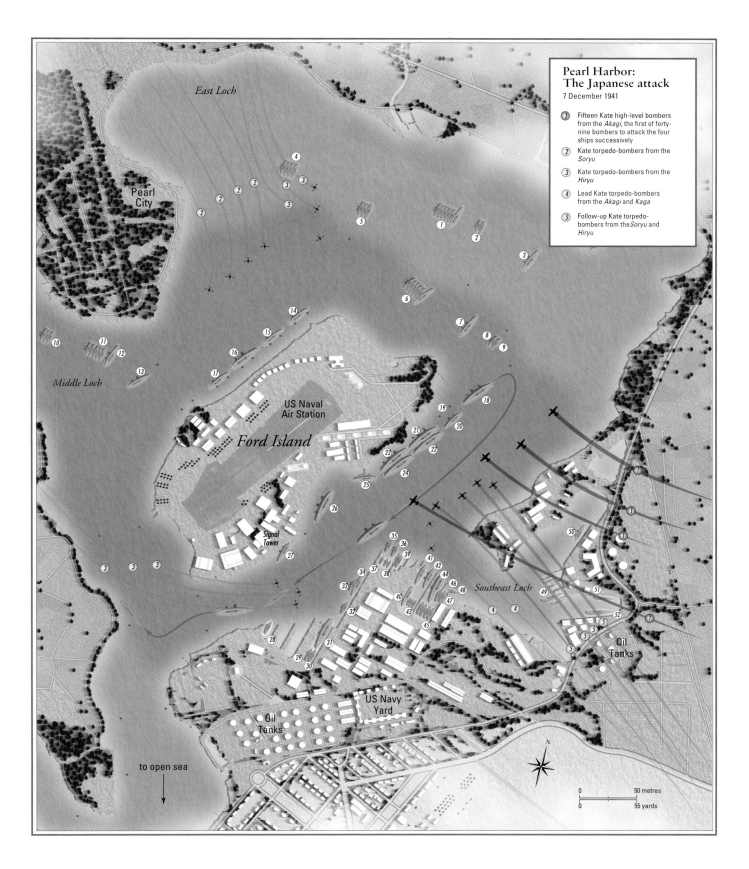

**Pearl Harbor:
The Japanese attack**
7 December 1941

1 Fifteen Kate high-level bombers from the *Akagi*, the first of forty-nine bombers to attack the four ships successively

2 Kate torpedo-bombers from the *Soryu*

3 Kate torpedo-bombers from the *Hiryu*

4 Lead Kate torpedo-bombers from the *Akagi* and *Kaga*

5 Follow-up Kate torpedo-bombers from the *Soryu* and *Hiryu*

East Loch

Pearl City

Middle Loch

US Naval
Air Station

Ford Island

Signal
Tower

Southeast Loch

Oil
Tanks

US Navy
Yard

Oil
Tanks

to open sea

0   50 metres
0   55 yards

CHINA 1942–43

"The Chinese soldier was tough, brave, and experienced. After all he had been fighting on his own without help for years. He was a veteran among the Allies."

GENERAL BILL SLIM

After Japan's attack on Pearl Harbor, the Sino-Japanese War merged into World War II. The Japanese in China had been consolidating their positions and a virtual stalemate existed. Now the war picked up again in an engagement called the Battle of South Shanxi (7–27 May 1941). Later, Japanese forces attempted to take Changsha (6 September–8 October 1941) with over 120,000 troops but were repulsed by Chinese units under General Xue Yue, sustaining casualties of more than 10,000.

Another attempt against Chagsha began at the end of 1941 (24 December 1941–15 January 1942). While marching from Yueyang, four Japanese divisions pushed aside three Chinese divisions, and stormed Changsha on 31 December. The city had been evacuated of civilians while Chinese forces still held on. The Japanese broke the first lines of defense but were held up by the second line when the Chinese launched a counterattack. Meanwhile, the original three divisions returned to assault Japanese supply lines, the combined Chinese onslaught forcing the Japanese to retreat suffering heavy losses. The victory was a much needed boost to Allied morale coming just one month after Pearl Harbor, though little was heard of the battle in the west.

Other major engagements took place during the Battles of the Yunnan–Burma Road. The Chinese intervened under Lt. General Joseph Stilwell to help their British allies in the 1942 Burma campaign. Fourteen engagements took place between 20 March and 23 May 1942, though the British and Chinese were pushed out of Burma. The most publicized battle took place at Yenangyaung (17–19 April 1942) when the Allies lost control of the oilfields there.

On 18 April, the United States launched an attack by B-25 Mitchell bombers from USS Hornet on Tokyo, Nagoya, and Yokohama. The planes were to land in China but crash-landed in Zhejiang and Jiangxi provinces after they ran out of fuel. Sixty-four airmen parachuted into Zhejiang after which the Japanese mounted a huge search operation destroying any settlement thought to be harboring these men. The two provinces were devastated and an estimated 250,000 civilian deaths resulted.

Elsewhere, the Koumintang forces under the command of Chaing Kai-shek established an economic blockade of Communist-held Yan'an. The Communists constantly used small night-time guerrilla actions to attack isolated Japanese positions and communications. These successes resulted in brutal reprisals. During this period, the Communists gained more party members and built up their forces to over 900,000 men and women. Although these forces could not confront heavily-armed Japanese troops in battle, their control of the countryside at night soon tied down some one million Japanese soldiers. Meanwhile, the Nationalists press-ganged the population for military recruits, and this, added to the massive corruption in the political and military elite, created gross inequalities between officers and men. Little fighting against the Japanese took place, Chiang preferred to save his best units for a confrontation against the Communists.

Meanwhile, Major-General Claire Lee Chennault's "Flying Tigers" mercenary force, operating in China, was achieving a superb combat record and later became part of the U.S. 14th Air Force. By 1942, U.S. transport planes were flying supplies over the Himalayas, "the Hump," to help the Nationalists after the Burma Road running between Lashio and Kunming had been cut by the Japanese seizure of Burma.

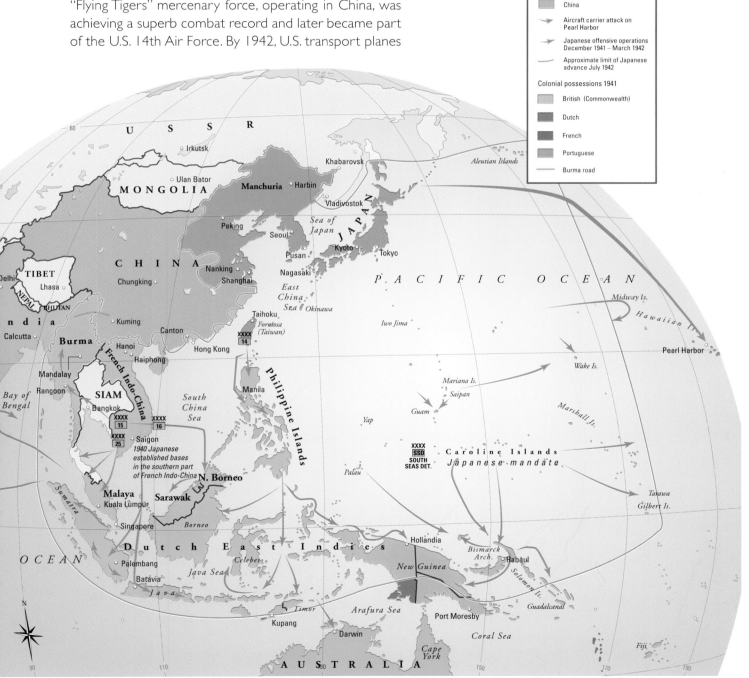

MALAYA, SINGAPORE, THE PHILIPPINES, & THE DUTCH EAST INDIES 1941–42

"In this hour of trial the General Officer Commanding calls upon all ranks of Malaya command for a determined and sustained effort to safeguard Malaya and the adjoining British territories. The eyes of the Empire are upon us."

LT.-GENERAL ARTHUR E. PERCIVAL

The Japanese invasion of Malaya was a decisive blow to British prestige and power in the east. Many of the British units facing the Japanese onslaught were untried, whereas most of the Japanese forces facing the British had been "blooded" in the fighting in Manchuria and China. It was not an equal contest.

On 8 December Japanese forces from the 25th Army, led by Lt-General Tomoyuki Yamashita, invaded northern Malaya and parts of southern Thailand. Yamashita's aim was to take Malaya as quickly as possible and not give the British forces any chance to set up a viable line of defense. He could then attack and capture Singapore from the lightly defended north. Almost all of the British heavy guns faced east, west, and south, covering the seaward approaches to Singapore. After a heavy bombardment from the warships of Vice-Admiral Kondo, Japanese forces swarmed ashore at Koto Bharu in northern Malaya while other forces landed at Singora and Petani in southern Thailand. The defenders on the beach cut down many of the Japanese, but by sheer weight of numbers and determination they were soon overwhelmed.

Yamashita sent his 5th Division heading south toward Singapore, down the west coast of Malaya from Thailand, while elements of 18th Division, known as Koba and Takumi detachments, headed down the east coast. Takumi detachment quickly took the British airbase at Kota Bharu and immediately made use of it as a forward base. The Japanese also began daily bombing raids on Singapore.

The British dispatched two battleships, HMS Prince of Wales and HMS Repulse to attack the Japanese fleet moored off Kota Bharu. However, local commanders failed to provide air cover and they were soon spotted by Japanese aircraft, attacked, and quickly sunk.

The Japanese rapidly advanced to the south. The British set up defensive lines on the west coast but the Japanese simply outflanked them by sea or through the dense jungle. The British forces, thus outflanked, continued falling back. The capital, Kuala Lumpur, was captured by

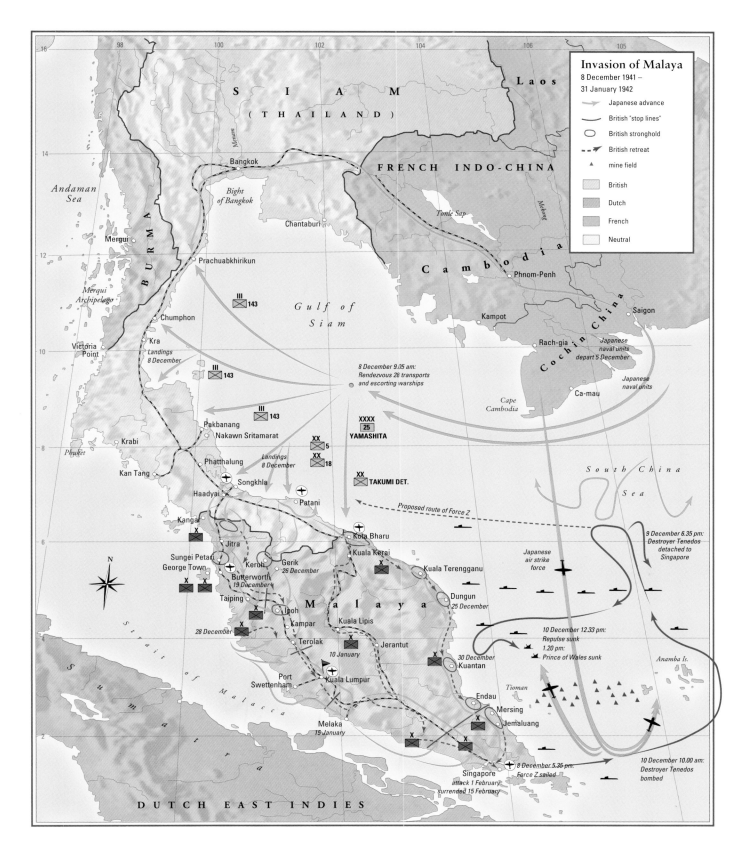

Invasion of Malaya
8 December 1941 –
31 January 1942

→ Japanese advance
⌐ British "stop lines"
◯ British stronghold
- -▶ British retreat
▲ mine field

British
Dutch
French
Neutral

S I A M
(T H A I L A N D)

Andaman
Sea

Mergui
Archipelago

L a o s

FRENCH INDO-CHINA

Bangkok

Bight
of Bangkok

Chantaburi

Tonle Sap

Menam

Mekong

C a m b o d i a

Phnom-Penh

Cochin China

Saigon

Kampot

Rach-gia

Japanese naval units
depart 5 December

Prachuabkhirikun

B U R M A

Chumphon

Kra

⊠ 143

Gulf of
Siam

Cape
Cambodia

Ca-mau

Japanese
naval units

Victoria
Point

Landings
8 December

Pakbanang

Krabi

Nakawn Sritamarat

⊠ 143

8 December 9.05 am:
Rendezvous 26 transports
and escorting warships

Phuket

Kan Tang

Phatthalung

⊠ 143

Landings
8 December

XX ⊠ 5

XX ⊠ 18

XXXX 25
YAMASHITA

XX ⊠ TAKUMI DET.

South China
Sea

Songkhla

Haadyai

Patani

Kota Bharu

Proposed route of Force Z

9 December 6.35 pm:
Destroyer Tenedos
detached to
Singapore

Kangar

Jitra

Kuala Kerai

Japanese
air strike
force

Sungei Petani
George Town

Keroh

Gerik
26 December

Kuala Terengganu

Butterworth
19 December

M a l a y a

Dungun
25 December

10 December 12.33 pm:
Repulse sunk
1.20 pm:
Prince of Wales sunk

Taiping

Ipoh

Kuala Lipis

Anamba Is.

Kampar
28 December

Terolak

Jerantut

30 December
Kuantan

Port
Swettenham

Kuala Lumpur

10 January

Tioman

S
u
m
a
t
r
a

Strait
of
Malacca

Endau

Mersing

Melaka
15 January

Jemaluang

Singapore
attack 1 February
surrendered 15 February

8 December 5.35 pm:
Force Z sailed

10 December 10.00 am:
Destroyer Tenedos
bombed

D U T C H   E A S T   I N D I E S

the Japanese on 11 January. The British set up a holding line north of the Jahore Strait using 8th Australian and 9th Indian Divisions (Westforce) with a similar group (Eastforce) made up from 22nd Australian Brigade. When these failed to stem the Japanese advance, all surviving Allied units were withdrawn to the island of Singapore.

Singapore was the "Gibraltar of the East," but all its defenses were situated to face a seaborne attack and not from the jungle on the mainland to the north. In charge of the defense was Lt-General Percival, who opted to place his forces thinly around the whole perimeter after blowing up the causeway connecting Singapore to the mainland. The forces that would be facing the Japanese onslaught were made up of Indian, Australian, and British troops, totaling about 70,000.

On the night of 8 February Yamashita's 25th Army attacked along the northern shoreline of Singapore with the Allied army putting up a solid defense for a short while. On 12 February Percival ordered the formation of a perimeter around Singapore town. With lack of food and the water supply damaged, the situation went from bad to worse. In desperation, Percival led the surrender of over 62,000 Allied troops, some having just arrived and not even shot at the enemy. This was one of the worst defeats in the history of the British Army.

With the expansion of Japanese influence, including the takeover of French Indochina, the U.S. set about strengthening the Philippines. Roosevelt ordered General MacArthur to make the islands more defensible and to unite the U.S. and Philippine armies under his command.

On the morning of Pearl Harbor, MacArthur received a telegram from Roosevelt ordering him to make war plans. At noon Japanese bombers were sighted near northern Luzon. U.S. bombers and fighters were still on the ground, which made them easy targets, and the U.S. lost much of its air strength in the attack.

Over the next few days the U.S. suffered intense air attacks. The first landings began on 8 December on Bataan Island to the north of the main Philippine archipelago, and they faced little or no resistance. Two days later the Japanese landed on northern Luzon itself, again encountering little opposition and making a rapid advance southward. The Japanese dispatched troops to land on the southern island of Mindinao on 20 December, in order to secure forward airbases ahead of the main invasion, achieving immediate air superiority. The invasion began on 22 December with two divisions landing on the Lingayen Gulf, consolidating their positions, then immediately striking for Manila. A smaller force landed to the east of Manila at Lamon Bay, and these forces

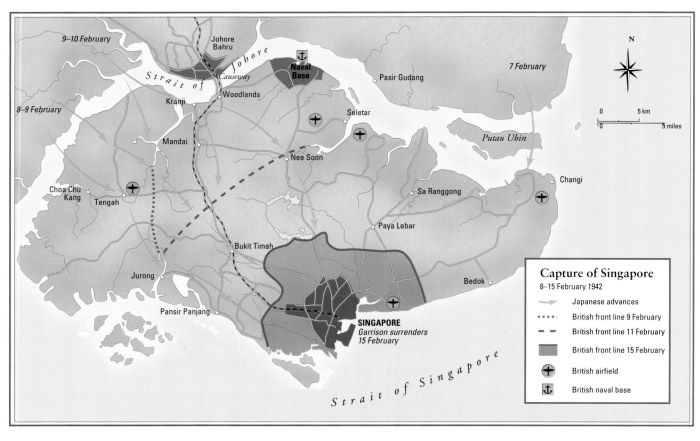

Capture of Singapore
8–15 February 1942

→ Japanese advances
····· British front line 9 February
– – British front line 11 February
▨ British front line 15 February
✛ British airfield
⚓ British naval base

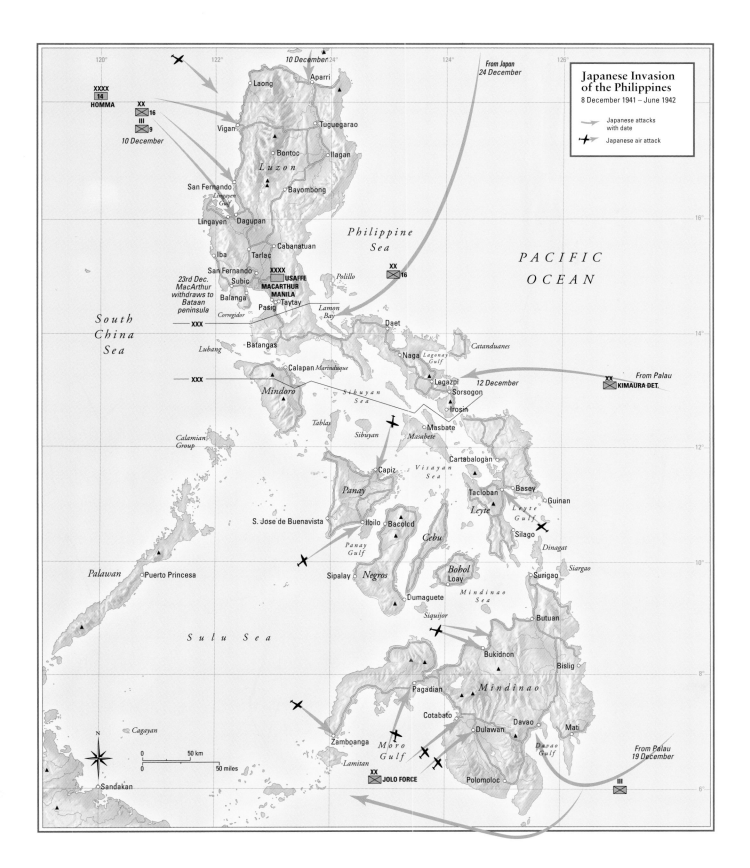

Japanese Invasion
of the Philippines
8 December 1941 – June 1942

→ Japanese attacks
with date

✈ Japanese air attack

immediately began advancing on the capital as well. The Japanese plan was to capture the U.S. forces in a classic pincer movement. On the central Luzon plain were troops under the command of Major General Wainwright. MacArthur soon realized that Wainwright's soldiers were heavily outgunned and gave the order for them to start falling back to the prepared defenses of the Bataan peninsula and the island fortress of Corregidor situated at the mouth of Manila Bay. As this was happening MacArthur gave the command that Manila be declared an open city and then continued with its evacuation.

MacArthur was desperate for Roosevelt to send more troops and equipment to help in the fight against the Japanese advance, but with America's "Germany First" policy this just could not be done. There was embarrassment on the part of the U.S. government that they hadn't defended the islands. They had witnessed the expansion of Imperial Japan and should have prepared for a move aimed at their interests in the Philippines.

The order given to the troops on the Bataan Peninsula and Corregidor was to hold out as long as possible. But there was to be no rescue mission for the troops on the mainland and their outlook was bleak. These forces held on until 9 April at the Bataan garrison and until the 6 May

at Corregidor. MacArthur was ordered to escape via PT boat on 12 March, which took him to an airfield in Mindanao where he boarded a plane to Australia, promising to return.

The Dutch East Indies included Java, Sumatra, Dutch Borneo, Dutch New Guinea, Celebes, Western Timor, and Moluccas. These islands were extremely important to the income of the Dutch Government, which still enjoyed control over the region after the Netherlands had been overrun in 1940. The most vital product was oil, and this is what Japan was most interested in, along with the country's production of rubber, bauxite, and coal, as well as its food production of rice, sugar, and tea. The Dutch Government had stopped the supply of oil to Japan in August 1941, so it was immensely important that the Japanese seize the area.

On 20 December 1941, units of the 16th Army, under the command of Lt-General Imamura Hitoshi, attacked

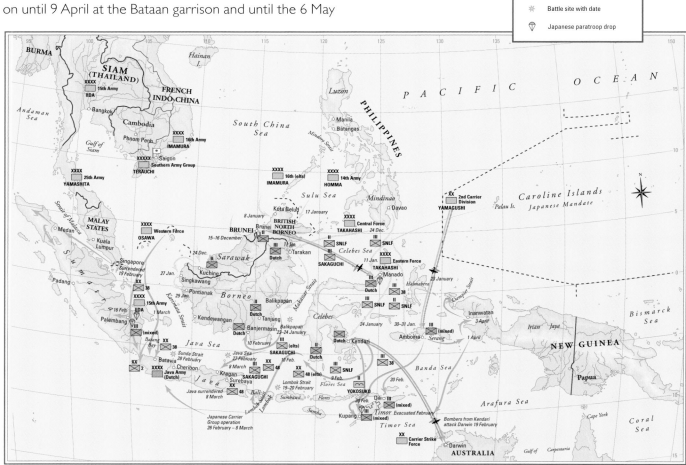

Japanese Invasion of the Dutch East Indies
January – March 1942

⟶ Japanese attack to end January
⟶ Japanese attack to end March
✳ Battle site with date
⛉ Japanese paratroop drop

Dutch Borneo, Celebes, and the Moluccas at the same time, taking the airfields at Kendari and Amboina. On 16 February, Japanese paratroops landed ahead of the amphibious assaults on southern Sumatra in order to secure the massive oil refineries. They then moved on to invade Dutch Timor on the 19th. Initially the advance was contested by the Dutch East Indies Army, assisted by British, American, and Australian troops under the command of General Wavell. However, their air support was virtually wiped out in the attacks on 19 and 27 February, which destroyed many of the Allied aircraft while still on the ground.

As the Japanese approached Java with another invasion force the Allied navies did attempt to take the fight to the enemy in the Battle of Java Sea. The two Japanese invasion forces were attacked by a mixed force of American, British, Australian, and Dutch ships under the overall command of Rear-Admiral Karel Doorman, of the Dutch Navy. His force consisted of five cruisers and nine destroyers, and they fought a night action against Vice-Admiral Tekeo's force of four cruisers and 14 destroyers. Allied communication and control was poor between the multinational fleet that Doorman commanded. This, added to the fact that he had no experience of a fleet action, led to the sinking of two Dutch cruisers and three destroyers. Doorman himself was killed, and the British cruiser Exeter limped off to Surabaya badly damaged. The Royal Australian Navy cruiser Perth and the U.S. cruiser Houston beat a hasty retreat, stumbling upon the transports delivering the Japanese troops onto Java, and proceeding to sink two and damage a further three, before being intercepted and sunk. As the Exeter tried to escape to Ceylon, she was spotted by Japanese reconnaissance planes, attacked by Japanese ships and also sunk. The only surviving ships of the debacle were four U.S. destroyers that sailed through the Bali Straits to Australia.

On 1 March the Japanese troops began landing on Java with the aim of capturing Bandung, and on 8 March the Dutch surrendered, leaving the Japanese to continue their occupation. By the end of the month they were moving on to Dutch New Guinea, having taken Sumatra.

THE ART OF WAR
A Japanese artist depicts aerial combat. Air power was vital to cover the Japanese advance, and in the southeast Asia campaign this was largely provided by capturing airfields and the use of land-based aircraft.

BURMA 1942

"I claim we got a hell of a beating. We got run out of Burma and it is as humiliating as hell. I think we ought to find out what caused it, go back and retake it."

GENERAL JOSEPH W. STILWELL, MAY 1942

Burma was not considered vital in the priorities facing the Allied Command and, as a result, the Japanese swept all before them. Most military personnel and material was sent for the defense of Malaya, Singapore, and the East Indies. However, as soon as it became clear that these could not be saved, Burma became the only area to stop the Japanese driving all the way into India. The Japanese saw Burma as an opportunity to cut lines of communication between China and the Allies in India, and denying the Chinese lines of supply. It would also provide a defensive "buffer zone" for the new Japanese empire. There were few natural resources apart from some agricultural produce that was not of any great importance to the Japanese war effort.

The 15th Japanese Army was to be used for the invasion. In early January they captured the airfields at Tavoy and Mergui, allowing fighters a forward base from which to operate escort missions to the bombers raiding Rangoon and over much of southern Burma. The port at Rangoon became unusable by the end of January.

Facing the Japanese advance was the 17th Division of the Indian Army, which executed a series of holding actions using the rivers Salween, Bilin, and Sittang as natural barriers. The commander of the 17th, Major-General Smyth, took the decision in the chaos created by the rapid Japanese advance to destroy the bridge over the Sittang River while two of his three brigades were still on the eastern side. This caused the Japanese a ten-day

delay in the capture of Rangoon but also led to the dismissal and enforced retirement of Smyth. Rangoon fell to the Japanese 33rd Division on 8 March.

The Chinese 38th Division moved south to assist the 1st Burma Division around Yenangyuang but these forces were soon forced into retreat, marching though Imphal to India. Later in March, General Slim took command of

ROLLING ONWARD INTO BURMA
A Japanese tank moves across the Siamese-Burma border early in January 1942. It is followed close behind by pack horses carrying supplies.

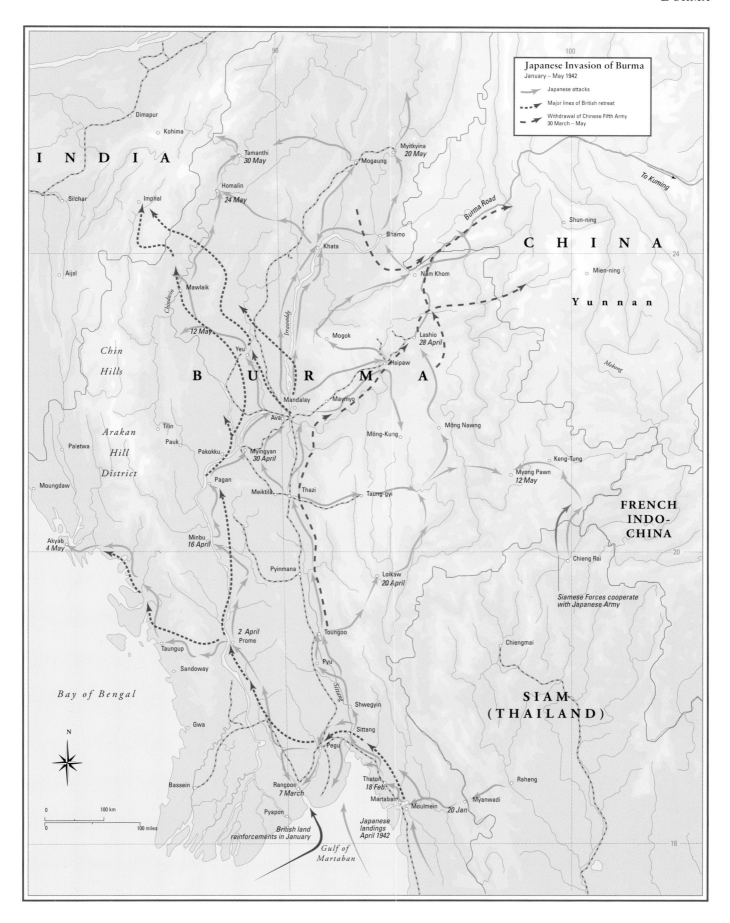

Japanese Invasion of Burma
January – May 1942

⟶ Japanese attacks

⟶ Major lines of British retreat

⟶ Withdrawal of Chinese Fifth Army
30 March – May

INDIA

Dimapur
Kohima
Tamanthi
30 May
Homalin
24 May
Silchar
Imphal
Mawlaik
12 May
Chin
Hills
Aijal
Yeu
BURMA
Paletwa
Tilin
Pauk
Arakan
Hill
District
Pakokku
Myingyan
30 April
Moungdaw
Pagan
Meiktila
Thazi
Akyab
4 May
Minbu
16 April
Pyinmana
Taungup
2 April
Prome
Sandoway
Pyu
Bassein
Gwa
Shwegyin
Bay of Bengal
N
Sittang
Pegu
Rangoon
7 March
Thaton
18 Feb.
Pyapon
British land
reinforcements in January
Martaban
Moulmein
20 Jan
Gulf of
Martaban
Japanese
landings
April 1942

0   100 km
0   100 miles

Mogaung
Myitkyina
20 May
Khata
Bhamo
Nam Khom
Mogok
Lashio
28 April
Mandalay
Ava
Maymyo
Hsipaw
Möng-Kung
Möng Nawng
Taung-gyi
Loikaw
20 April
Toungoo
Sittang

CHINA

Burma Road
To Kuming
Shun-ning
Mien-ning
Yunnan
Mekong
Keng-Tung
Myong Pawn
12 May

FRENCH
INDO-
CHINA

Chieng Rai

Siamese Forces cooperate
with Japanese Army

SIAM
(THAILAND)

Chiengmai

Raheng
Myanwadi

117

1st Burcorps, which consisted of what remained of the British forces left in Burma, and led them in the longest fighting retreat in the history of the British Army, back to the Indian frontier. Of the Chinese forces committed, the 5th, 6th, and 66th Armies were forced back by Thai forces entering the Shan States in early May, Kengtung being captured on 27 May. The Chinese forces then fell back to the Yunnan Province.

Meanwhile Admiral Nagumo had sailed from Staring Bay in the Celebes on 26 March at the head of a fleet consisting of five aircraft carriers, four battleships, two heavy cruisers, one light cruiser, and eight destroyers. His mission was to drive the Royal Navy from the Bay of Bengal. Opposing the Japanese was the Royal Navy's Eastern Fleet, a fast division of one battleship, two carriers, and six destroyers, plus a slow division of four older battleships, three cruisers, and five destroyers. British patrol aircraft spotted the Japanese force approaching Ceylon, giving time to clear the local ports of shipping.

On 5 April Japanese carriers launched a raid on Colombo and on the same day they found and sank two British heavy cruisers: the Dorsetshire and Cornwall. Four days later Nagumo's force raided Tricomalee and also found the carrier Hermes sailing without an escort; she was attacked and sunk. Nagumo failed to find the major part of the British fleet or their anchorage at Addu Atoll. But content with his success, he left the Bay of Bengal. Another Japanese strike force under Admiral Ozawa raided the upper area of the Bay of Bengal during the first week of April, sinking almost 100,000 tons of Allied shipping, with Japanese submarines sinking a further 40,000 tons.

Allied operations in Burma for the rest of 1942 and into 1943 were frustrated by the Government giving priority to the fighting in the Middle East; they could only afford to properly supply one battle front. Matters were not improved by civil disorder in India, a large element of the population protesting for independence from British rule. However, small actions were carried out such as the first Arakan Campaign.

Arakan was a small coastal strip along the Bay of Bengal and crossed by several rivers. An attempt was made, using the 14th Indian Infantry Division, to capture the Mayu Peninsula and Akyab Island, home to an important airfield. After initial success the division was thrown back when Japanese reinforcements arrived over the supposedly impassable ranges on their flank, pushing them back all the way to the Indian frontier.

There was also an operation with the 77th Indian Infantry Brigade led by Major General Orde Wingate, or the "Chindits" as they came to be known, which entailed 3,000 men penetrating deep behind the enemy lines in order to disrupt or sabotage the north–south railroad line. They achieved this objective by putting the railroad out of operation for some two weeks. This was, however, at the cost of a third of the Brigade's men. Many of the survivors were also wracked with disease on their return, although the resourceful exploits of Wingate's Chindits did demonstrate that the Allies could take the war to the Japanese in the jungle.

IN THE JUNGLE
A troop of Japanese soldiers march along a jungle trail. These men were masters of jungle warfare, and always fought with dedication and tenacity.

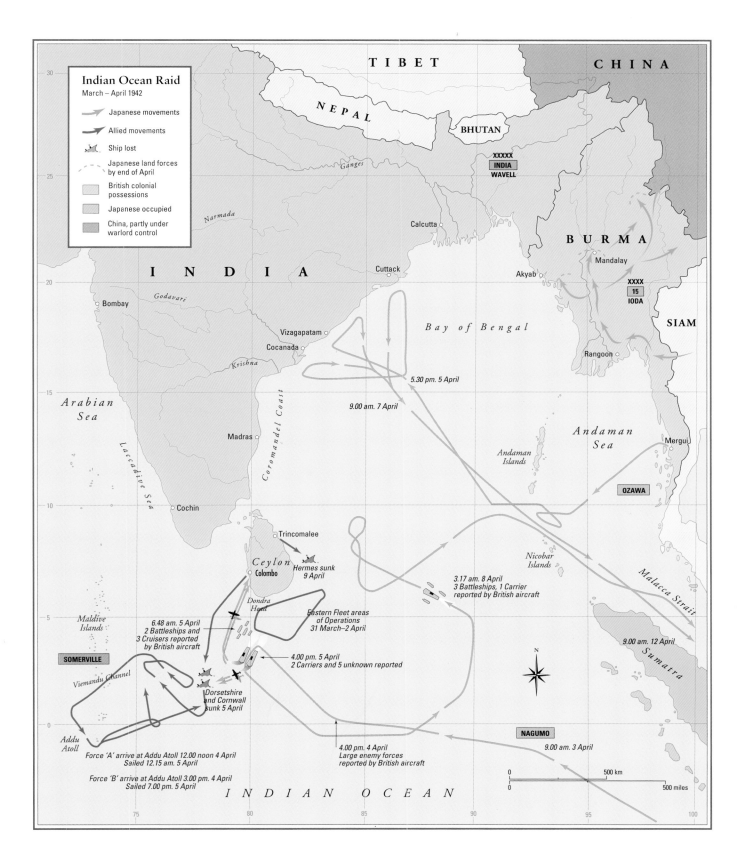

Indian Ocean Raid
March – April 1942

Japanese movements

Allied movements

Ship lost

Japanese land forces
by end of April

British colonial
possessions

Japanese occupied

China, partly under
warlord control

TIBET

CHINA

NEPAL

BHUTAN

XXXXX
INDIA
WAVELL

Ganges

Calcutta

BURMA

Mandalay

Akyab

XXXX
15
IODA

INDIA

Narmada

Godavari

Bombay

Cuttack

Bay of Bengal

SIAM

Rangoon

Vizagapatam

Cocanada

5.30 pm. 5 April

Krishna

*Arabian
Sea*

9.00 am. 7 April

*Andaman
Sea*

Mergui

Madras

Coromandel Coast

*Andaman
Islands*

Laccadive Sea

Cochin

Malacca Strait

Trincomalee

*Nicobar
Islands*

OZAWA

Ceylon

Hermes sunk
9 April

3.17 am. 8 April
3 Battleships, 1 Carrier
reported by British aircraft

Colombo

*Maldive
Islands*

*Dondra
Head*

6.48 am. 5 April
2 Battleships and
3 Cruisers reported
by British aircraft

Eastern Fleet areas
of Operations
31 March–2 April

9.00 am. 12 April

Sumatra

SOMERVILLE

4.00 pm. 5 April
2 Carriers and 5 unknown reported

N

Viemandu Channel

Dorsetshire
and Cornwall
sunk 5 April

*Addu
Atoll*

NAGUMO

9.00 am. 3 April

Force 'A' arrive at Addu Atoll 12.00 noon 4 April
Sailed 12.15 am. 5 April

4.00 pm. 4 April
Large enemy forces
reported by British aircraft

Force 'B' arrive at Addu Atoll 3.00 pm. 4 April
Sailed 7.00 pm. 5 April

INDIAN OCEAN

0   500 km

0   500 miles

CORAL SEA

"Australia and New Zealand are now threatened by the might of the Imperial Japanese forces, and both of them should know that any resistance is futile."

GENERAL HIDEKI TOJO, PRIME MINISTER OF JAPAN

The Battle of the Coral Sea was to be the first sea battle where neither of the combatant fleets saw each other, and was to be one of the first major naval engagements between two carrier forces. The Japanese planned to capture Port Moresby, the capital of New Guinea, in order to provide a forward operating base for attacks aimed at the Australian mainland. Under the command of Vice-Admiral Shigeyoshi were three invasion convoys that were to steam out of Truk and Rabaul, then head to three different locations, the largest heading to Port Moresby and the others to set up sea-plane bases on the island of Tulagi and in the Louisiades.

Protecting these convoys was a covering force commanded by Rear-Admiral Goto Aritomo. Under his command were four heavy cruisers, one destroyer, and one light carrier, the Shoho. There was also a strike force consisting of the two carriers Shokaku and Zuikaku along with two heavy cruisers and a number of destroyers. This force was to be commanded by Vice-Admiral Takagi Takeo. The Japanese expected the Allies to attempt to destroy the invasion convoy, but with this concentration of offensive seapower, the Japanese would strike first.

However, the Commander-in-Chief of the Pacific Fleet was fully aware of the Japanese intent and their strength in the area, thanks to the ULTRA decrypts, and assembled two task forces based around the carriers Yorktown and Lexington, with a third task force under the command of Australian Rear-Admiral John Crace. All these forces were then placed under the command of Rear-Admiral "Black Jack" Fletcher.

The Japanese forces sent to take Tulagi landed without incident on 3 May, but the next day were attacked by aircraft from the Yorktown, which inflicted considerable damage. On 5 May, the U.S. strike forces rendezvoused 400 miles south of Guadalcanal where they then sailed north-west to intercept the main Japanese invasion fleet bound for Port Moresby. Fletcher then ordered Crace to intercept the transports converging on Port Moresby, while his force of carriers went to face Takagi. Fletcher's force themselves then came across the transports, causing the Japanese convoy to retreat until the outcome of the battle had been decided. While this was happening a strike force from Lexington had located the escort carrier Shoho and duly sank her, a promising start for the Allies. When Crace heard that the convoy had been forced to retire, he also waited in reserve.

Fletcher then learned that Takagi's force was somewhere to the stern of him, and on the 8 May the two sides located each other with spotter planes. As soon as the sightings were confirmed they both launched

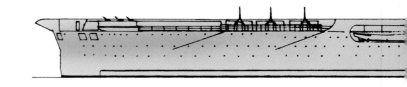

massive airstrikes against each other. Both sides had a similar amount of aircraft but the Japanese were flying superior machines with better training and tactics. The Americans, however, reached the carrier Shokaku first and inflicted enough damage for her to retire north with black smoke trailing from her deck, and therefore unable to land the aircraft she had launched earlier.

Meanwhile the Japanese strike force had sighted Lexington and Yorktown and were beginning to press home their attack. Yorktown took a bomb hit on her flight deck but was still serviceable after the Japanese failed to follow up and finish her off. However, the Lexington took several bombs hits and a torpedo and began burning badly. After an hour fighting the flames, a spark set off the aviation fuel below decks making her beyond saving, and she was scuttled shortly afterwards.

There seemed to be no clear victory in the battle, with the Japanese exacting a vicious blow on U.S. naval power with the sinking of the Lexington and severely damaging Yorktown. But U.S. and Allied forces stopped the invasion convoy reaching Port Moresby and inflicted enough damage on Shokaku and destroyed so many planes from Zuikaku that they were unable to take part later in the Battle of Midway.

THE LEXINGTON ABANDONED...
U.S. sailors leap for their lives from the burning USS Lexington. The ship had been hit by three bombs and one torpedo. The crew fought for over an hour to save the ship but the heat, or perhaps the spreading fires, ignited aviation fuel stored on lower decks.

... THE LEXINGTON DISARMED
The ship, launched in October 1925, was reconstructed from the hull of a battlecruiser. Lexington, along with USS Saratoga, were the first fleet carriers operated by the U.S. Navy. When commissioned, the Lexington was equipped with a main battery of eight 8-inch guns. In 1941, the 8-inch guns were removed. They were supposed to have been replaced with modern 5-inch dual-purpose guns. However, she sailed into action before these new armaments could be fitted.

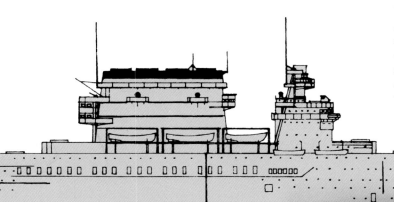
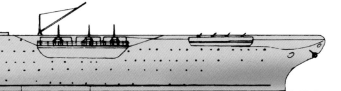

BATTLE OF THE CORAL SEA

This battle was crucial in that it denied the Japanese a forward base at Port Moresby which, in turn, would have threatened Australia and New Zealand.

FRENCH INDO-CHINA

Bangkok

XXXXX
SOUTHERN
TERAUCHI

Camranh Bay

Manila   *Luzon*

PHILIPPINES IS.

Samar

Panay   *Leyte*

Bohol

○ Saigon

Gulf of Siam

XXXX
16
IMAMURA

South China Sea

Palawan

Negros

Mindanao

Davao

Sandakan

XXX
C. FORCE
TAKAHASHI

90

100

110

10

Medan

Malaya

Kuala Lumpur

XXX
W. FORCE
OZAWA

Buguran

Br. North Borneo

Miri

Tarakan

Celebes Sea

Kema

○ Singapore

Kuching   Sarawak

Borneo

Sumatra

Pontianak

Balikpapan

Biak

Celebes

Buru

0

Palembang

Belitung   Bandjermasin

DUTCH EAST INDIES

Java Sea

XXX
E. FORCE
TAKAHASHI

Makassar

Kendari

Batavia

Kragan

Java   Surabaya

Tjilatjap   *Bali*

Jumbawa

Flores Sea

Flores

10

Christmas Is.

Sumba

Dutch Timor

Battle of the Coral Sea
28 April – 11 May 1942

→ Japanese movement

→ Allied movement

✛ Japanese air strikes

✛ Allied air strikes

🐟 Japanese sinking ship

🐟 Allied sinking ship

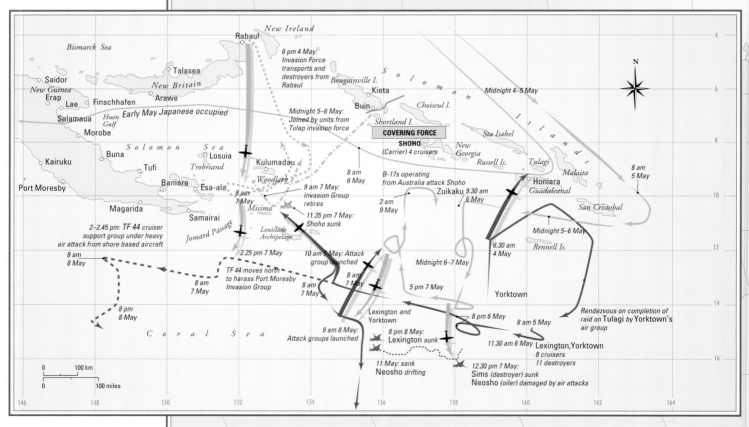

Bismarck Sea

New Ireland

Rabaul

6 pm 4 May: Invasion Force transports and destroyers from Rabaul

Talasea

New Britain

Midnight 4–5 May

Saidor   *New Guinea*   Erap

Bougainville I.

Kieta

Solomon Islands

N

Lae   Finschhafen   Arawe

Huon Gulf

Early May Japanese occupied

Buin

Midnight 5–6 May: Joined by units from Tulap invasion force

Choiseul I.

Salamaua

Morobe

Shortland I.

COVERING FORCE
SHOHO
(Carrier) 4 cruisers

New Georgia

Sta. Isabel

8 am 5 May

Solomon Sea

Losuia

Kulumadau

8 am 6 May

B-17s operating from Australia attack Shoho

Russell Is.

Tulagi   *Malaita*

Buna

Trobriand

Woodlark

Zuikaku 9.30 am 6 May

Honiara   *Guadalcanal*

Kairuku

Tufi

Baniara

Esa-ala

8 am 7 May

9 am 7 May: Invasion Group retires

2 am 9 May

San Cristobal

6.30 am 4 May

Midnight 5–6 May

Port Moresby

Misima

11.35 pm 7 May: Shoho sunk

Rennell Is.

Magarida

Samarai

Jomard Passage

Louisiade Archipelago

2–2.45 pm: TF 44 cruiser support group under heavy air attack from shore based aircraft

2.25 pm 7 May

10 am 7 May: Attack group launched

8 am 7 May

Midnight 6–7 May

8 am 8 May

TF 44 moves north to harass Port Moresby Invasion Group

8 am 7 May

8 am 7 May

5 pm 7 May

Yorktown

8 am 7 May

8 pm 8 May

Lexington and Yorktown

8 pm 6 May

8 am 5 May

Rendezvous on completion of raid on Tulagi *by Yorktown's air group*

Coral Sea

9 am 8 May: Attack groups launched

8 pm 8 May: Lexington sunk

11.30 am 6 May   Lexington, Yorktown
8 cruisers
11 destroyers

0   100 km

0   100 miles

11 May: sank Neosho drifting

12.30 pm 7 May: Sims (destroyer) sunk Neosho (oiler) damaged by air attacks

146   148   150   152   154   156   158   160   162   164

4

6

8

10

12

14

16

122

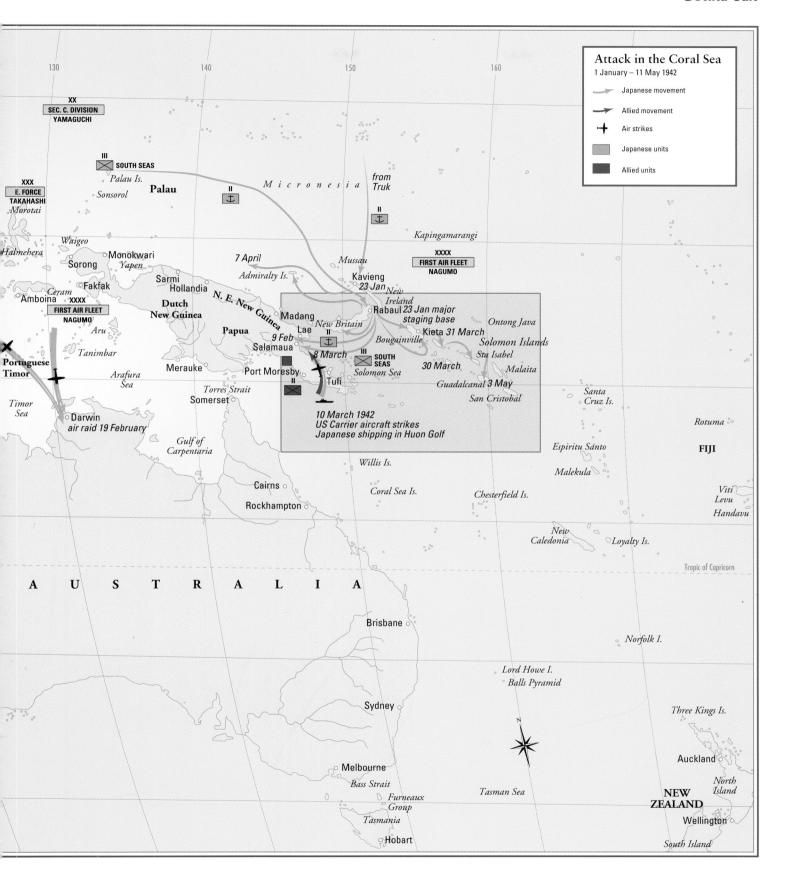

Attack in the Coral Sea
1 January – 11 May 1942

→ Japanese movement

→ Allied movement

✛ Air strikes

Japanese units

Allied units

XX
SEC. C. DIVISION
YAMAGUCHI

III SOUTH SEAS
Palau Is.
Sonsorol
Palau

Micronesia

from Truk

Kapingamarangi

XXX
E. FORCE
TAKAHASHI
Morotai

Waigeo
Monokwari
Sorong   Yapen
Fakfak
Ceram   XXXX
Amboina   FIRST AIR FLEET
           NAGUMO

Halmehera

Sarmi
Hollandia
Dutch
New Guinea

N. E. New Guinea

7 April
Admiralty Is.

Mussau

Kavieng
23 Jan
New
Ireland

XXXX
FIRST AIR FLEET
NAGUMO

Rabaul 23 Jan major
staging base

Ontong Java

Aru
Tanimbar

Papua

Madang
Lae
9 Feb
Salamaua
8 March

New Britain

Bougainville

Kieta 31 March

Solomon Islands
Sta Isabel

Merauke

Port Moresby
Tufi

SOUTH SEAS
Solomon Sea

30 March

Malaita

Portuguese
Timor

Arafura
Sea

Torres Strait
Somerset

10 March 1942
US Carrier aircraft strikes
Japanese shipping in Huon Golf

Guadalcanal 3 May
San Cristobal

Timor
Sea

Darwin
air raid 19 February

Gulf of
Carpentaria

Willis Is.

Santa
Cruz Is.

Rotuma

Espiritu Santo

FIJI

Cairns
Rockhampton

Coral Sea Is.

Chesterfield Is.

Malekula

Viti
Levu
Handavu

New
Caledonia   Loyalty Is.

Tropic of Capricorn

A U S T R A L I A

Brisbane

Norfolk I.

Sydney

Lord Howe I.
Balls Pyramid

Three Kings Is.

Melbourne

Bass Strait

Furneaux
Group

Tasmania

Tasman Sea

Auckland

North
Island

NEW
ZEALAND

Wellington

Hobart

South Island

BATTLE OF MIDWAY

"I was horrified at the destruction that had been wrought in a matter of seconds. There was a huge hole in the flight deck just behind the amidship elevator. The elevator itself, twisted like molten glass, was dropping into the hangar. Deck plates reeled upwards in grotesque configurations. Planes stood tail up, belching livid flame and jet-black smoke."

MITSUO FUCHIDA, AIR COMMANDER, CARRIER ATAGO

In May 1942, Admiral Yamamoto drew up plans to occupy the United States' outpost on the island of Midway, the most westerly point under U.S. command. In order for his plan to work he first needed to lure part of the U.S. fleet away towards the Aleutian Islands. If Yamamoto was successful in this deception he could easily overwhelm the U.S. forces on Midway, then carry on steaming towards Hawaii.

But in order to draw the Americans north toward the Aleutians Yamamoto would have to separate his attack force, therefore already putting himself at a disadvantage. Yamamoto also made the mistake of assuming the USS Yorktown had been sunk in the Coral Sea; this was not the case and the carrier had, in fact, steamed back to Pearl Harbor, where she was repaired and made ready in an amazing 48 hours. If there were any more carriers in Pearl Harbor, Yamamoto planned to deploy a screening force of submarines to ambush any making for Midway.

All Yamamoto's carefully constructed plans were to no avail, thanks to the fact that the Allies had already broken the Japanese code using the ULTRA decrypts.

With this information at his disposal the Pacific Commander-in-Chief, Admiral Nimitz, was able to deploy his sea power in an advantageous position. He sent two carrier groups with a heavy escort comprising the USS Hornet, Enterprise, and the recently repaired Yorktown. This was placed under the overall command of Rear-Admiral Fletcher, who would be aboard the Yorktown with the other carrier group commanded by Rear-Admiral Spruance. Nimitz also placed his own submarine screening force to the west of Midway. All this was achieved and put in place before the Japanese submarines arrived on their planned station to the west of Pearl Harbor.

The Japanese force was separated into three main groups. The first comprised the Invasion Group, supported by a

124

powerful escort, under Yamamoto's command. The strike force was made up of four carriers—Hiryu, Kaga, Akagi, and Soryu—two battleships and other smaller craft, under the command of Vice-Admiral Nagumo. The main group was made up of three battleships and support craft. With all these vessels the Japanese heavily outweighed the U.S. forces.

The invasion force was first sighted on 3 June and was attacked by a force of bombers flying off Midway, although they did little to stop it, or damage it. This highlighted the shortcomings of high-level bombing on naval targets taking evasive action. At dawn the next day Nagumo launched a force of aircraft to attack Midway, and after this successful raid decided to use the aircraft he had held as reserve in case of any U.S. surface vessels intervening as a second wave.

This decision turned out to be a grave mistake, for Spruance's forces spotted Nagumo's carriers and immediately ordered his torpedo and dive-bombers to attack. The torpedo bombers were the first to arrive at the target, but the dive-bombers became lost on the way and suffered horrendous casualties, with only one out of the 41 launched making it back. As this attack faltered and failed, the dive-bombers found the target and, with the torpedo bombers drawing the Japanese fighter cover down to sea level, they were more or less unopposed.

The Japanese carriers' decks were covered in ordnance and aircraft being refuelled were soon set ablaze by the bombs raining down on them. Hiryu managed to escape the attack thanks to a fortuitous squall that hid her from view of the American aircraft. Kaga, Akagi, and Soryu were left as burning hulks and unable to be saved.

Hiryu launched an attack on Yorktown, the only carrier the Japanese thought was in the area; she was hit by three bombs and torpedoed twice, but was still able to stay afloat thanks to the valiant effort of her crew.

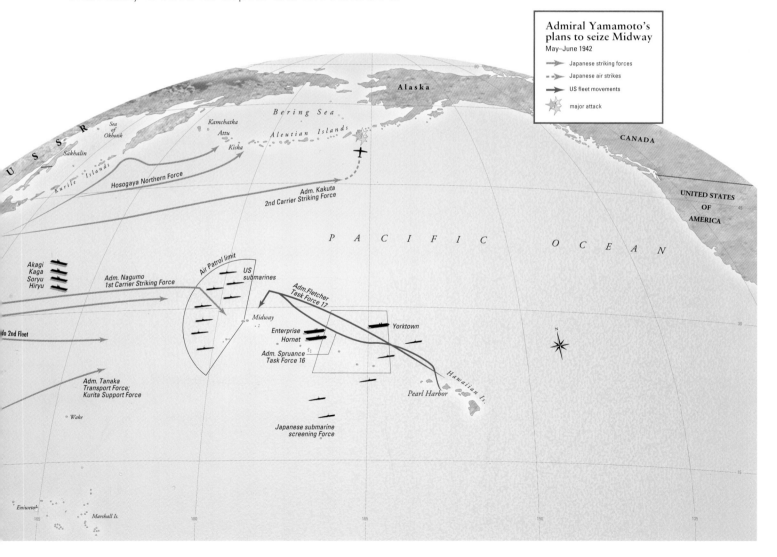

Launching attacks on the Yorktown revealed Hiryu's position and she was severely damaged in the following strike launched by Spruance's aircraft from Enterprise and she would eventually have to be scuttled.

With the loss of four carriers Yamamoto conceded defeat and withdrew east, harassed by U.S. bombers. However, the Japanese did reap revenge when a Japanese submarine sighted Yorktown, torpedoed, and sunk her. Despite this, the battle was a massive defeat for the Japanese and they would never regain their strength in the Pacific. The Americans now held the advantage.

TURNING POINT IN THE PACIFIC

The surviving Japanese aircraft carrier the Hiryu launched two air attacks aimed at the U.S. aircraft carrier Yorktown. Despite putting up a fierce antiaircraft barrage, the Yorktown was heavily damaged by Japanese air attacks and was finally torpedoed by a Japanese submarine. The Japanese lost four aircraft carriers, a cruiser, 332 aircraft and over 3,500 men. Perhaps most significant was the loss of their most experienced carrier pilots. They had failed in their objective of capturing Midway. Meanwhile the Americans lost one aircraft carrier, one destroyer, 150 aircraft, and 307 men. The Battle of Midway marked the turning point in the Pacific War.

JAPANESE CARRIER AKAGI

The Akagi was originally laid down in 1920, as a battle cruiser. However, in 1922 construction was suspended and conversion to an aircraft carrier began in 1923. She entered service in 1927 and was again reconstructed between 1935 and 1938, producing a modern aircraft carrier capable of carrying a maximum of 91 aircraft.

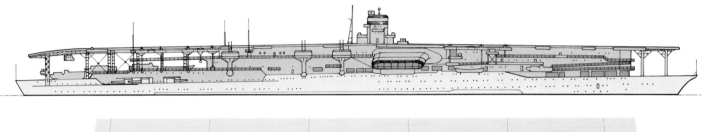

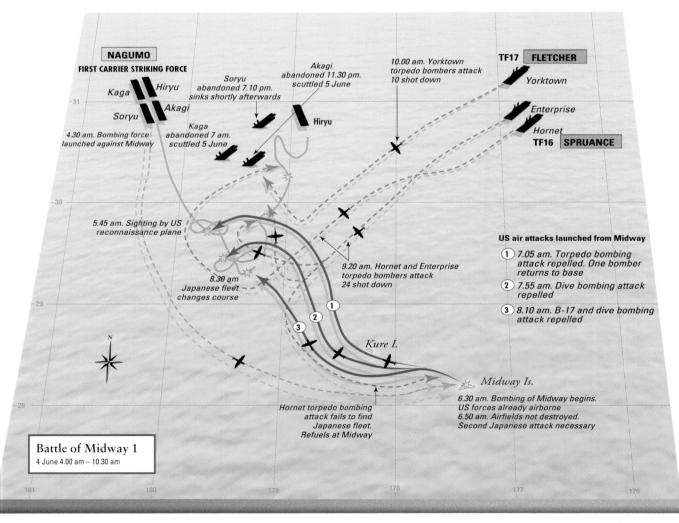

NAGUMO

FIRST CARRIER STRIKING FORCE

Kaga Hiryu
Soryu Akagi

Soryu abandoned 7.10 pm. sinks shortly afterwards

Akagi abandoned 11.30 pm. scuttled 5 June

10.00 am. Yorktown torpedo bombers attack 10 shot down

TF17 **FLETCHER**

Yorktown

Enterprise

Hornet

TF16 **SPRUANCE**

4.30 am. Bombing force launched against Midway

Kaga abandoned 7 am. scuttled 5 June

Hiryu

5.45 am. Sighting by US reconnaissance plane

US air attacks launched from Midway

① *7.05 am. Torpedo bombing attack repelled. One bomber returns to base*

② *7.55 am. Dive bombing attack repelled*

③ *8.10 am. B-17 and dive bombing attack repelled*

8.30 am Japanese fleet changes course

9.20 am. Hornet and Enterprise torpedo bombers attack 24 shot down

N

Kure I.

Midway Is.

Hornet torpedo bombing attack fails to find Japanese fleet. Refuels at Midway

6.30 am. Bombing of Midway begins. US forces already airborne
6.50 am. Airfields not destroyed. Second Japanese attack necessary

Battle of Midway 1
4 June 4.00 am – 10.30 am

181   180   179   178   177   176

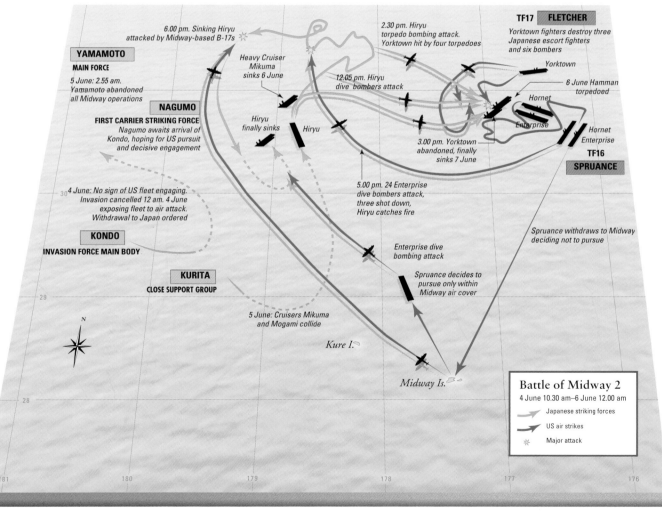

YAMAMOTO

MAIN FORCE

5 June: 2.55 am.
Yamamoto abandoned
all Midway operations

NAGUMO

FIRST CARRIER STRIKING FORCE
Nagumo awaits arrival of
Kondo, hoping for US pursuit
and decisive engagement

6.00 pm. Sinking Hiryu
attacked by Midway-based B-17s

Heavy Cruiser
Mikuma
sinks 6 June

Hiryu
finally sinks   *Hiryu*

2.30 pm. Hiryu
torpedo bombing attack.
Yorktown hit by four torpedoes

12.05 pm. Hiryu
dive bombers attack

TF17 **FLETCHER**

Yorktown fighters destroy three
Japanese escort fighters
and six bombers

Yorktown

6 June Hamman
torpedoed

Hornet

Enterprise

Hornet
Enterprise

TF16

SPRUANCE

3.00 pm. Yorktown
abandoned, finally
sinks 7 June

4 June: No sign of US fleet engaging.
Invasion cancelled 12 am. 4 June
exposing fleet to air attack.
Withdrawal to Japan ordered

KONDO

INVASION FORCE MAIN BODY

KURITA

CLOSE SUPPORT GROUP

5.00 pm. 24 Enterprise
dive bombers attack,
three shot down,
Hiryu catches fire

Spruance withdraws to Midway
deciding not to pursue

Enterprise dive
bombing attack

Spruance decides to
pursue only within
Midway air cover

5 June: Cruisers Mikuma
and Mogami collide

N

Kure I.

Midway Is.

Battle of Midway 2
4 June 10.30 am–6 June 12.00 am

→ Japanese striking forces

→ US air strikes

✳ Major attack

CONVOYS TO RUSSIA 1941–45

"The cold was hardening now, closing on them with steely fingers, feeling for the blood in their veins; it took the wind for an ally and came shrieking down from the North Pole, from the regions of eternal ice. Snow came with it too, and the ships became pale ghosts, moving on under the iron dome of the sky into a world of death and darkness."

JAMES PATTINSON, MERCHANT SEAMAN

The Arctic convoys sailed from August 1941 to the end of the war in Europe. Initially they were of the utmost importance in maintaining Soviet resistance to the German invasion as the Soviets moved most of their surviving industry to the east. Britain and the U.S. supplied vast amounts of fighting vehicles and aircraft as well as the fuel, munitions and clothing for them to remain effective. In order for these supplies to reach the Russian Front, they had to be taken by the only sea route available to the Allies, through the treacherous waters of the Arctic Circle to the northern ports of Murmansk and Archangel. These waters were well within range of land-based German aircraft flying from occupied Norway, as well as being patrolled by U-boats and surface vessels of the Kriegsmarine.

The first convoys sent to the Soviet Union managed to make the ports with little trouble but by mid-July 1942 the Germans were beginning to intercept Allied convoys

COLD SHEFFIELD
A sailor mans a frozen 20-inch signal projector on the HMS Sheffield as it escorts a convoy to Russia in December 1941. The Arctic convoys were surely the coldest field of conflict in the war.

and sinkings rapidly increased. Convoy PQ-17, after suffering losses to Luftwaffe bombers, was forced to scatter when it encountered a large German surface fleet, including Tirpitz and Admiral Hipper, that had been sent to intercept them. The German capital ships were only changing berth however, and the scattered convoy was easy prey for the German U-boats and aircraft, the convoy losing 25 of the 36 ships that had set out for those cold northern ports.

At the end of 1942, Convoy JW51B set sail for the Soviet Union with 14 merchant ships escorted by 6 destroyers, 2 Flower class corvettes, 1 minesweeper, and 2 armed trawlers. Two cruisers, HMS Sheffield and Jamaica which formed Force 'R' were patrolling the Barents Sea and provided cover for the convoy should it meet any trouble. The convoy was duly sighted by U-354 and a report was immediately sent to the German surface fleet to intercept. This fleet included the heavy cruiser Admiral Hipper and the pocket battleship Lutzow along with 6 destroyers. In the early morning of 31 December HMS Obdurate, one of the escort destroyers, spotted a force of German destroyers and moved in order to engage with the other escorts, leaving HMS Achates to lay smoke to cover the convoy. The Germans retreated when faced with the approaching British destroyers, but Hipper returned for another attack, badly damaging the

Onslow before moving to the north of the convoy where it engaged Achates and another escort, sinking Achates.

The firing drew Force "R" into the battle, which immediately started firing on Admiral Hipper causing extensive damage, before both sides broke off the engagement. Force 'R' shadowed the German vessels until it was obvious that they were returning to base as the convoy continued to its destination. The outcome of the raid so incensed Hitler that he ordered the Surface Fleet to be scrapped so the Kriegsmarine could concentrate on U-boat warfare. The head of the Kriegsmarine resigned to be replaced by Admiral Dönitz.

The Arctic convoys' importance was reluctantly recognized by Stalin. It supplied the Soviet armed forces with armaments at its time of greatest need and helped swing the balance in that theater. It also drew German surface and U-boat resources away from other areas where they could have caused more extensive damage to the Atlantic lifeline.

THE PERILOUS NORTHERN PASSAGE

Of the 39 Allied convoys sent to Soviet Russia, made up of a total of 533 escorted ships, 69 were lost to enemy action. Convoy PQ-17 was the most heavily attacked with 22 of its 37 merchant ships sunk.

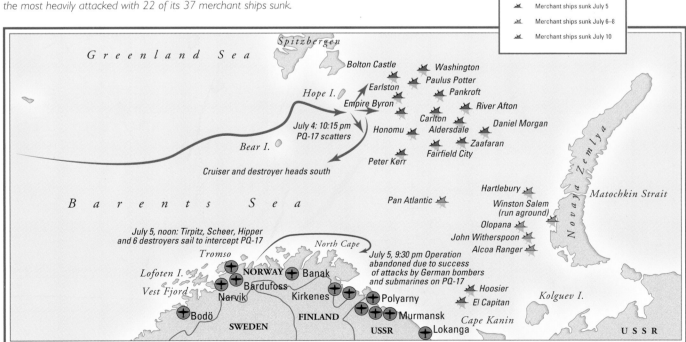

Convoy PQ-17
3–6 July 1942

→ Route of PQ-17
→ Route of German battle group
⊕ German airfield
⊕ Soviet airfield
✦ Merchant ships sunk July 5
✦ Merchant ships sunk July 6–8
✦ Merchant ships sunk July 10

THE CAUCASUS 1942–43

"Wipe out the entire defense potential remaining to the Soviets."

DIRECTIVE NUMBER 41, ADOLF HITLER

Hitler's ambitious plan for the campaign of 1942 was to drive toward Stalingrad and the Caucasus oilfields, then to effect a link up from the Caucasus into the Middle East, and make a massive final sweep northward behind Moscow.

Operation Blue was launched on 28 June. In July German units reached Voronezh then turned south to link up with armies moving through southern Ukraine. As in the summer of 1941, panic seemed to have spread amongst the Red Army. By the end of the month Hitler was so confident of victory that, instead of concentrating his forces on the capture of the oilfields, he split them. Army Group B was sent eastward with orders to capture the city of Stalingrad. Army Group A and the 1st Panzer Army, continued to the oilfields.

The Red Army was, once again, in headlong retreat, Stalin, in some desperation, issued Order 227, Ni Shagu Nazad! (Not a step back!) but this did not stop the Germans advancing between 20 and 30 miles per day. Then progress slowed. By mid-August average progress for Army Group A was a little over one mile per day. On the Soviet side fresh troops and new commanders arrived. Amongst these troops were the internal security N.K.V.D. division.

The German 17th Army, with the Romanian 3rd Army, faced the Soviet Trans-Caucasus Front, struggling to gain control of the coast road running from Novorossiisk to Sukhumi. The 17th Army reached the outskirts of Novorossiisk on 6 September, but stubborn Soviet resistance prevented further progress. Attacks on the coast road also made little further progress before winter set in and made any further meaningful advance

impossible. To the east of the 17th Army, the 1st Panzer Army advanced with ease, skirting the northern foothills of the Caucasus Mountains. The River Terek was crossed at Mozdok on 2 September. Facing Soviet counterattacks the German advance faltered, finally coming to a halt in November on a front from Nalchik to Ordzhonikidze. Snow prevented further advances and the German line of supply was by now at its maximum extent.

The aim of the Soviet winter offensive was to trap Army Group A. This plan required cooperation between various "fronts" (the Russian term for Army groups), in particular the Southern Front and Trans-Caucasus Front. The Trans-Caucasus Front attacked along an axis from Tuapse to Krasnodar; unfortunately they made slow progress in freezing weather. Meanwhile, the 1st Panzer Army managed a fighting withdrawal. The Southern Front, under Yeremenko, failed to close the bottleneck and the German Panzers escaped to rejoin Manstein and the recently formed Army Group Don. At the same time, the German 17th Army were, with the Romanians, left holding the Taman Peninsula.

For most of the summer attention was focused on Rostov-on-Don and northward; the Caucasus Front remained a quiet sector. This changed on 9 September, when a seaborne assault was launched on Novorossiisk, directly into the harbor area. Pressure from the Soviet 58th, 9th, 56th, and the 18th Armies, plus further landings along the coast, cleared the peninsula of German forces by 9 October.

The Soviet liberation of the Caucasus put an end to Hitler's desperate dream of capturing and exploiting the region's valuable oilfields.

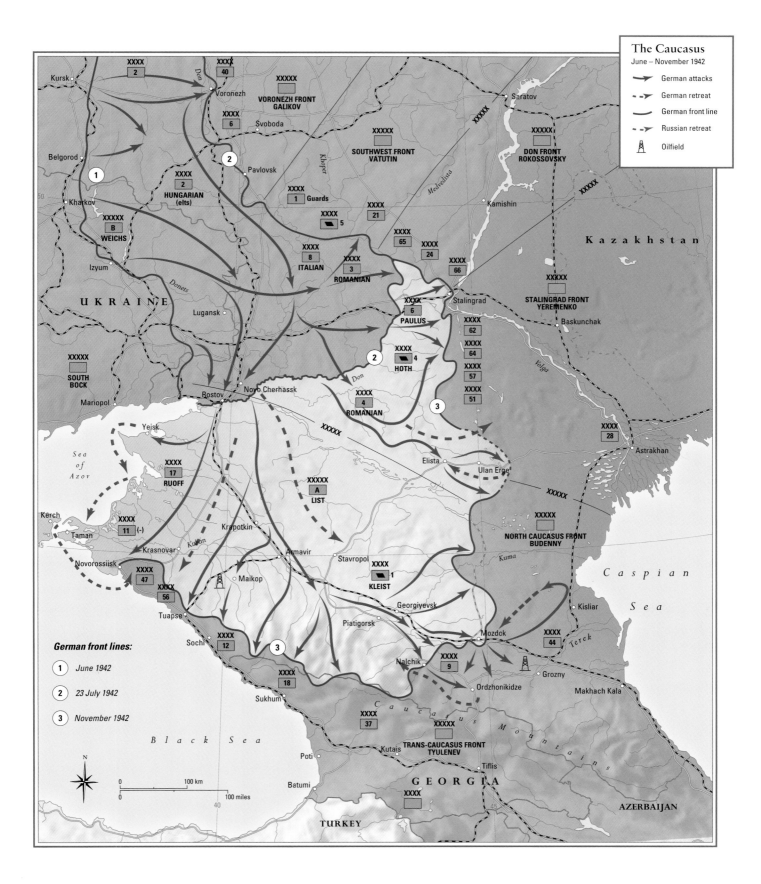

The Caucasus
June – November 1942

→ German attacks
--→ German retreat
⌒ German front line
--→ Russian retreat
⚑ Oilfield

Kursk
XXXX 2
XXXX 40
Don
Voronezh
XXXXX VORONEZH FRONT GALIKOV
Saratov
Belgorod
①
XXXX 6
Svoboda
XXXXX SOUTHWEST FRONT VATUTIN
Khoper
Medvedista
XXXXX DON FRONT ROKOSSOVSKY
②
Pavlovsk
XXXX 2
HUNGARIAN (elts)
Kharkov
XXXX 1 Guards
XXXX 21
XXXX 5
Kamishin
K a z a k h s t a n
XXXXX B WEICHS
Izyum
Donets
XXXX 8 ITALIAN
XXXX 3 ROMANIAN
XXXX 65
XXXX 24
XXXX 66
XXXXX STALINGRAD FRONT YEREMENKO
Baskunchak
U K R A I N E
Lugansk
XXXX 6 PAULUS
Stalingrad
XXXX 62
XXXXX SOUTH BOCK
XXXX 4 HOTH
②
XXXX 64
Volga
Mariopol
Rostov
Novo Cherhassk
XXXX 4 ROMANIAN
Don
③
XXXX 57
XXXX 51
XXXX 28
Astrakhan
Yejsk
XXXXX
S e a o f A z o v
XXXX 17 RUOFF
Elista
Ulan Erge
XXXXX
Kerch
XXXXX A LIST
Krapotkin
XXXXX NORTH CAUCASUS FRONT BUDENNY
C a s p i a n S e a
Taman
XXXX 11 (-)
Kuban
Armavir
Stavropol
Kuma
Krasnovar
XXXX 47
XXXX 1 KLEIST
Kisliar
Novorossiisk
Maikop
Georgiyevsk
Mozdok
XXXX 56
Tuapse
XXXX 44
Terek
Piatigorsk
XXXX 12
③
Sochi
Nalchik
XXXX 9
Grozny
XXXX 18
Ordzhonikidze
Makhach Kala
Sukhum
C a u c a s u s
XXXX 37
XXXXX TRANS-CAUCASUS FRONT TYULENEV
M o u n t a i n s
B l a c k   S e a
Poti
Kutais
Tiflis
German front lines:
① June 1942
② 23 July 1942
③ November 1942
N
0   100 km
0   100 miles
XXXX
G E O R G I A
Batumi
TURKEY
AZERBAIJAN

THE NEW ORDER

"Greater Germany—the dream of our fathers and grandfathers—is finally created."

GUSTAV KRUPP VON BOHLEN, GERMAN ARMAMENTS MAGNATE

Hitler had a vision for Germany: at the head of the European nations, this new Germany would be the political, economic, cultural, and racial hub of the continent. In his vision this power would radiate outward across Europe, eastward to the Ural Mountains, south to the Mediterranean and westward, to the Atlantic Ocean.

By 1941, German rule extended over 15 European states. In Hitler's new racial order the Nordic peoples were accorded the most privileged position, while the Slavic peoples of the east were to be treated as inferior, educated only to the most basic level, fit only to labor for their superiors. The peoples inhabiting the Balkans and the "Latins" of southern Europe held a questionable place in the hierarchy: they were allied to Germany but not quite as equals.

The economic structure for the New Europe matched the racial structure that Germany had started to put into practice following its conquests between 1939 and 1942. Germany planned a compulsory economic union, with the Reichsmark as the reserve or, eventually, the only currency. Berlin was already the emerging financial center of this new system, supported by Vienna extending its traditional trade contacts in central, eastern, and southwestern Europe. These two cities would serve as the financial twins overseeing the commercial and industrial activity of Europe.

German businesses, both state and private, were encouraged to take over European businesses whenever possible. By 1942–43 the German domination and exploitation of Europe's productive capacity became almost complete. Occupied Europe provided huge amounts of materials, labor, and food. Manufactured goods poured into the Greater German Reich amounting to a total of 90 billion Reichsmarks by 1944, a massive contribution toward the German war effort.

The huge, state-owned Reichswerke Holding Company planned industrial development on a massive scale, reaching out from central Germany toward Kiev and beyond in the Ukraine. This giant corporation had already taken over most of the captured heavy industry. All this effort was to be bound together by a vast new continent-wide Autobahn (motorway) system. There would also be a new wide-gauge railroad stretching out from Berlin to Kazan in the east, to Paris in the west, and Istanbul in the south-east. The Führer, always an enthusiast for air travel, planned airports in all major cities, connected, of course, by comfortable German-built aircraft. Hitler's chosen elite, at least, would travel in style.

The political future of this new Europe was less defined, although some kind of sovereignty might be tolerated in the Nordic states of the north and west. The Balkans and the southern countries would be seen as allies, though under some supervision. Only for the east were any concrete plans created, with two main options discussed by Nazi high command. Hitler's preference was to annex to the Reich vast areas of western Russia, parts of the Ukraine, and the Baltic States. These would become areas of settlement, the living space he had written about in *Mein Kampf*. He had stated many times to his acolytes, "the British have India, we shall have the vast spaces of Russia." All the land to the Ural Mountains would be open to settlement and exploitation. The population of the region would be "Germanized," driven eastward beyond the Urals, or exterminated.

There was another view of the east put forward by Alfred Rosenberg, Minister for the Eastern Areas: he wanted to develop national states in the east, the product of German liberation from the Communists. There was enthusiasm for this idea among the nationalist groups in the east, most of whom had suffered woefully under Stalin's rule. However, as the cruel and ruthless rule of the Germans asserted itself, this opportunity was lost. Local identities and interests were summarily swept aside, as conquered areas became part of the Nazi Empire.

The conquest of vast new territories also had a major effect on the Reich's racial policy, as huge numbers of Jews fell under German rule. There was a move from discrimination and brutality to a deliberate policy of genocide. At the dark heart of the Nazi State, it was decided that the extermination of the Jews, and any other "undesirables," should be carried out in a systematic program of annihilation. This was carried out by the

building of a series of special extermination camps under the control of the Reichssicherheitshauptamt (R.S.H.A.). At these camps the majority of victims were gassed on arrival: those incapable of work; children; the elderly; or those deemed to be too weak. The rest were to be worked to death at sites adjacent to these special camps.

The killing went on until the last weeks of the Reich, when trains were used to transport hundreds of thousands of people to the death camps despite the need to move supplies to the front and the wounded back to Germany. The death trains still rolled, given priority by the political hierarchy of the Reich.

Germany had been transformed by the demands of the war. Young Germans had marched off to the battlefields and to police the occupied territories. They, in turn, had been replaced by foreign workers, volunteered, conscripted, and enslaved from across Europe, especially from the east. Germany had become a multiracial slave state, far from the Nordic haven that Hitler and the Nazis originally planned.

The Greater German Reich
1942–44

- Germany 1936
- Territory added 1938-39
- Territory added 1940-41
- Major concentration camps
- Gau borders

BOMBING OF GERMANY
1942–43

"They sowed the wind, and now they are going to reap the whirlwind."

AIR MARSHAL "BOMBER" HARRIS

T he bombing campaign against Germany increased in intensity in the years after 1942, with the introduction of long-range, four-engined bombers that could take an increased bomb load further into enemy territory. The newly-arrived U.S. 8th Air Force also took part in planning a combined bombing offensive. By 1942 the R.A.F., having learned that daylight precision bombing was costly on aircraft and crew, decided on a policy of nighttime area bombing, in the hope of destroying the chosen target and lowering the morale of the enemy.

The U.S. 8th Air Force felt that they could achieve precision bombing with their Norden bomb sights during daylight and be able to defend their more heavily-armed aircraft by flying in mutually-supporting formation. It was

AMERICA'S DAYLIGHT RAIDERS
The Boeing B-17G of the U.S. 8th Airforce in flight. The American policy was precision bombing in daylight, while the British R.A.F. developed area bombing by night. Thus Germany was kept under permanent air attack, forcing it to deploy considerable forces and absorbing a large percentage of the German war effort.

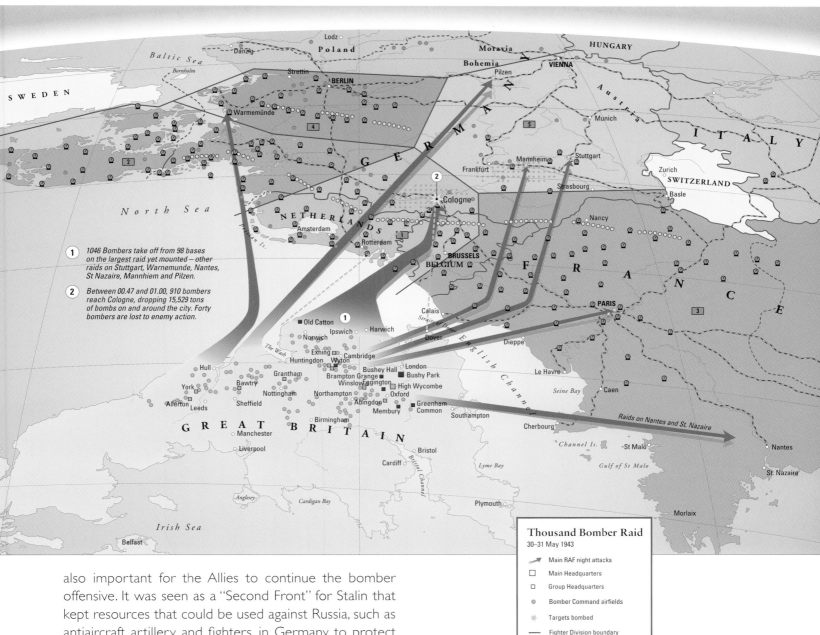

Lodz
Danzig
Poland
Moravia
HUNGARY
Baltic Sea
Bornholm
Bohemia
Pilzen
VIENNA
Stettin
BERLIN
Warnemünde
GERMANY
Austria
Munich
SWEDEN
North Sea
5
ITALY
Mannheim
Stuttgart
Frankfurt
Zurich
SWITZERLAND
Strasbourg
Basle
2
NETHERLANDS
Amsterdam
Cologne
1
Nancy
Rotterdam

1 1046 Bombers take off from 98 bases on the largest raid yet mounted – other raids on Stuttgart, Warnemunde, Nantes, St Nazaire, Mannhiem and Pilzen.

2 Between 00.47 and 01.00, 910 bombers reach Cologne, dropping 15,529 tons of bombs on and around the city. Forty bombers are lost to enemy action.

BRUSSELS
BELGIUM
FRANCE
PARIS
3
Old Catton
1
Ipswich
Harwich
Calais
Norwich
Frisian Is.
The Wash
Dover
Dieppe
Exning
Cambridge
Huntingdon
Wyton
Le Havre
Seine Bay
Bushey Hall
London
Brampton Grange
Bushey Park
Hull
Winslow
Eggington
Caen
York
Bawtry
Grantham
Northampton
High Wycombe
Sheffield
Nottingham
Abingdon
Oxford
Allerton
Leeds
Membury
Greenham
Common
Cherbourg
GREAT BRITAIN
Manchester
Birmingham
Southampton
St Malo
Nantes
Raids on Nantes and St. Nazaire
Liverpool
Bristol
Channel Is.
Gulf of St Malo
Cardiff
Bristol Channel
English Channel
St. Nazaire
Anglesey
Cardigan Bay
Lyme Bay
Plymouth
Morlaix
Irish Sea
Belfast

Thousand Bomber Raid
30–31 May 1943

↗ Main RAF night attacks
□ Main Headquarters
□ Group Headquarters
● Bomber Command airfields
✳ Targets bombed
— Fighter Division boundary
4 Fighter Division
⊘ German radar station
● German night fighter station
∞ Searchlight batteries
Anti-aircraft batteries

also important for the Allies to continue the bomber offensive. It was seen as a "Second Front" for Stalin that kept resources that could be used against Russia, such as antiaircraft artillery and fighters, in Germany to protect its industry.

1942 was a period for the bomber commanders to learn new tactics and train the crews that would be required to fly against the Reich. Time was also spent building up the 8th Air Force in Britain. However, the Germans developed a new and more effective defense system against the Allied bombers that were flying daily and nightly missions into German airspace. They deployed new direction-finding and radar to control fighters and antiaircraft guns as well as improving their tactics.

By May the new Commander-in-Chief of Bomber Command, Sir Arthur Harris, was ready to launch his first "1000 bomber raid" on Cologne. This raid was intended to prove that area-bombing could devastate targets better than attempting precision bombing, and with fewer losses of aircraft. After launching two more raids on a

similar scale, they were discontinued in order to concentrate on the build up of bombers and trained crews. A new tactic was developed with the Pathfinder Force that would be directed to the target using "Oboe," a radio navigation aid, after which they would then mark the target for the following main force.

STALINGRAD 1942–43

"Now we know the Germans are not human. Now the word 'German' has become the most terrible swear word. Let us not speak. Let us not be indignant. Let us kill. If you do not kill the German, he will kill you … if you have killed one German kill another."

ILYA EHRENBURG IN THE "RED STAR"

After continuous campaigning ended in defeat before Moscow, German Army Group Center was totally exhausted, suffering the combined effects of the Soviet counteroffensive and the Russian winter. Hitler's sights turned south toward the vast oilfields and wide agricultural lands that would fuel his country's war machine.

Operation Blue was put into action, an advance using Army Group South that would drive into the Caucasus in two massive groups. The 6th Army, commanded by General Friedrich Paulus, along with General Hoth's 4th Panzer Army, would strike toward Stalingrad. The capture of the city would be a massive propaganda coup for the Nazis as well as denying northern Russia its link to the Caspian Sea and the Caucasus oilfields. The remainder of Army Group South would move southward to the precious oilfields.

By the end of July 1942, the 6th and 4th Armies had reached the banks of the River Don and set about establishing a defensive line using their allies, the Romanian, Hungarian, and Italian troops, while the majority of the German units advanced toward Stalingrad. The battle for the city began with the usual German airstrikes flown by bombers and the Luftwaffe, decimating the city.

Stalin ordered that no civilians were to leave the city. Thousands were employed by the many factories that were now part of a gigantic Soviet industrial effort producing as many tanks and artillery pieces as possible in order to beat off the German invaders. The sight of the population staying in the city would also help to boost the morale of the troops who were defending them. By the height of the air attack some 80 percent of the city was reduced to rubble. Firestorms swept through the city's wooden buildings, leaving many dead and many more homeless.

The initial German advance was met by a mostly female unit, the 1077th Antiaircraft Regiment, who had to level their guns in order to engage the Panzers approaching the city. They only ceased fire when their positions were overrun or destroyed, but they still managed to inflict a heavy toll on the Panzers. As the Germans advanced further into the city, the Russians threw everything in their path. Tanks were rolling off the production lines straight into the thick of battle, sometimes being driven by volunteers from the factory itself. By 23 August, the Germans had advanced to the line of the Volga in the north and south of the city, bringing up their allies to protect their flanks.

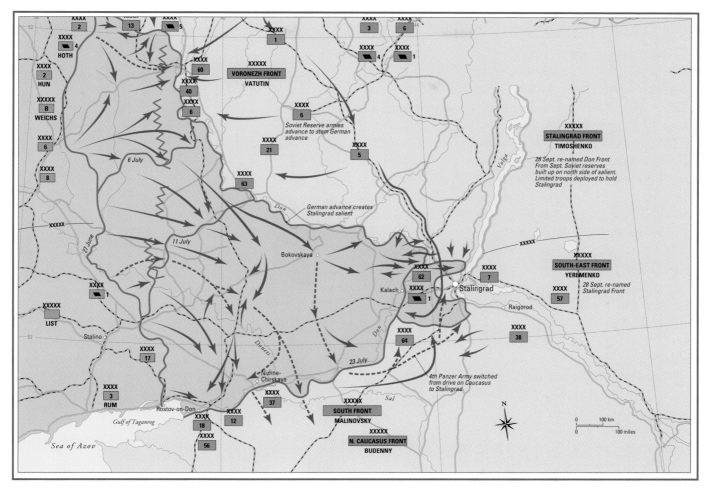

The map labels include:

XXXX 2 | XXXX 13 | XXXX 5 | XXXX 3 | XXXX 6
XXXX 4 HOTH
XXXX 2 HUN
XXXXX B WEICHS
XXXX 1 | XXXX 6
XXXX 60
XXXXX VORONEZH FRONT VATUTIN
XXXX 40
XXXX 6
XXXX 6
Soviet Reserve armies advance to stem German advance
XXXX 21
XXXX 5
XXXXX STALINGRAD FRONT TIMOSHENKO
28 Sept. re-named Don Front From Sept. Soviet reserves built up on north side of salient. Limited troops deployed to hold Stalingrad
6 July
XXXX 63
Don
German advance creates Stalingrad salient
Volga
22 June
11 July
Bokovskaya
XXXXX
XXXX 62
XXXX 1
Kalach
Stalingrad
XXXX 7
XXXXX SOUTH-EAST FRONT YEREMENKO
28 Sept. re-named Stalingrad Front
XXXX 57
Raigorod
XXXX 1
LIST
Stalino
Donets
XXXX 64
XXXX 38
XXXX 17
23 July
Sal
4th Panzer Army switched from drive on Caucasus to Stalingrad.
XXXX 3 RUM
Nizhne-Chirskaya
XXXX 37
Rostov-on-Don
XXXX 12
XXXXX SOUTH FRONT MALINOVSKY
N
XXXX 18
Gulf of Taganrog
XXXX 56
XXXXX N. CAUCASUS FRONT BUDENNY
Sea of Azov
0 100 km
0 100 miles

The Stalingrad Area
June – September 1942

→ Soviet movements
⋀⋀⋀ Soviet defensive lines
→ German movements
— German front lines with dates

The Soviets now clung onto a pocket close by the River Volga. This, their only supply route, came under constant bombardment and strafing attacks from artillery and Stuka dive-bombers. With the city about to fall, Stalin issued his "Not a step back" order, the officers pushing Soviet infantry as close as possible to the Germans to frustrate their artillery and air support. With Soviet troops so close, the Germans could not attack with artillery or air strikes for fear of hitting their own men.

Every street, house, and cellar was now bitterly contested, with vicious hand-to-hand fighting with any lethal object the combatants could lay their hands on, sometimes the Germans winning the living space while the Russians still held the kitchen. On the hill that dominates Stalingrad, Mamayev Kurgan, horrific casualties were incurred by both sides. The hill changed possession several times, the Russians losing almost a division in one counterattack alone. However, the ruined city now favored the defender and was a perfect hunting ground for the talented Russian snipers who stalked the Germans incessantly, notching up hundreds of kills and severely affecting the morale of the German soldier.

The Germans were still stronger in manpower and had succeeded in splitting the pocket on the west bank of the Volga in two, but the Russians stoically held on around the northern district that was home to the Red October and Dzerzhinsky factories. It was here that tanks and heavy weaponry were repaired and sent straight back onto the battlefield. While hand to hand, street by street, struggles had been fought, the Soviets had been building up forces from across the Volga River opposite the Romanian positions to the north and south of Stalingrad. The Romanians were less well equipped and trained than the German army, and were of low morale, especially when their commanders pleaded for reinforcements only to be abruptly turned down. Every available man and machine was being pressed into the capture of the center of Stalingrad. Hitler's obsession with capturing Stalingrad was about to cost him one of the largest and best-equipped German armies deployed in Russia, the 6th. Stalingrad was about to be surrounded by a massive Soviet maneuver that would change the course of the war on the Eastern Front.

On 19 November three Russian armies, under General Vatutin, engaged the Romanians defending the northern flank. This was the start of Operation Uranus. Poorly-equipped Romanians gave a good account of themselves but could not hold the weight of the Russian attack for long, their line broken by the end of the day. In the south the following day, another assault was launched against the Romanians; again this line broke after some initial resistance. The Russians now raced around Stalingrad and met at the small town of Kalach, in a pincer movement that was finally completed two days later. More than 250,000 German troops—along with thousands of Romanian soldiers—were now trapped inside an area that would become known by the men as "Der Kessel," the Cauldron.

The Soviets immediately set about preparing lines facing inward and outward to protect against enemy breakout or a relief force attempting to break in. German command immediately saw the need to plan for a breakout, or else witness the slow destruction of the 6th Army. However, Hitler, after conferring with Goering, commander of the Luftwaffe, agreed that the army could be resupplied by air and ordered the 6th Army to stand fast. This task of resupply was given to Wolfram von Richthofen's 4th Air Fleet. He argued that the entire Luftwaffe did not have enough transports to attempt to resupply the 400-plus tons that they would require each day, let alone the aircraft immediately available to him or within useful range of Stalingrad. Hitler and the German High Command had been encouraged by the Luftwaffe's ability to supply the men that had been trapped in the Demyansk Pocket in early 1942, though this was on a far smaller scale.

Shortly after the air supply mission began its shortcomings were immediately obvious. The Soviet antiaircraft guns and interceptors took a heavy toll of the transports, only a small percentage of the supplies getting through. The troops inside the Kessel were beginning to go hungry and were increasingly short of ammunition, but Hitler reissued the order of "no surrender."

The 4th Panzer Army, with the assistance of the 17th and 23rd Panzer Divisions diverted from the Caucasus

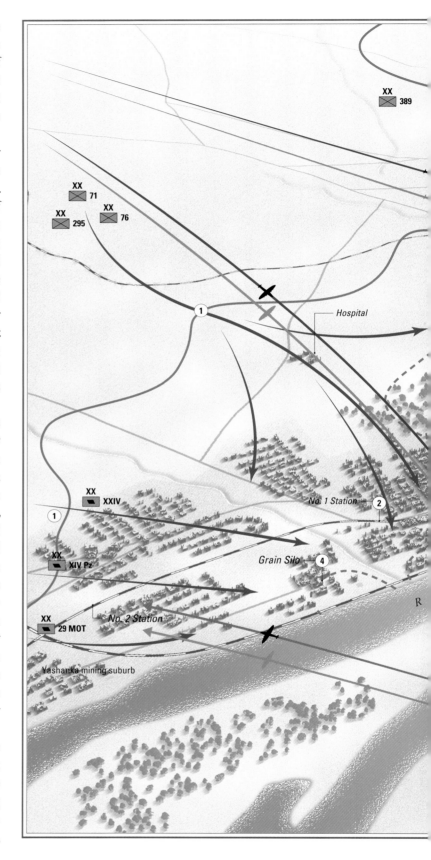

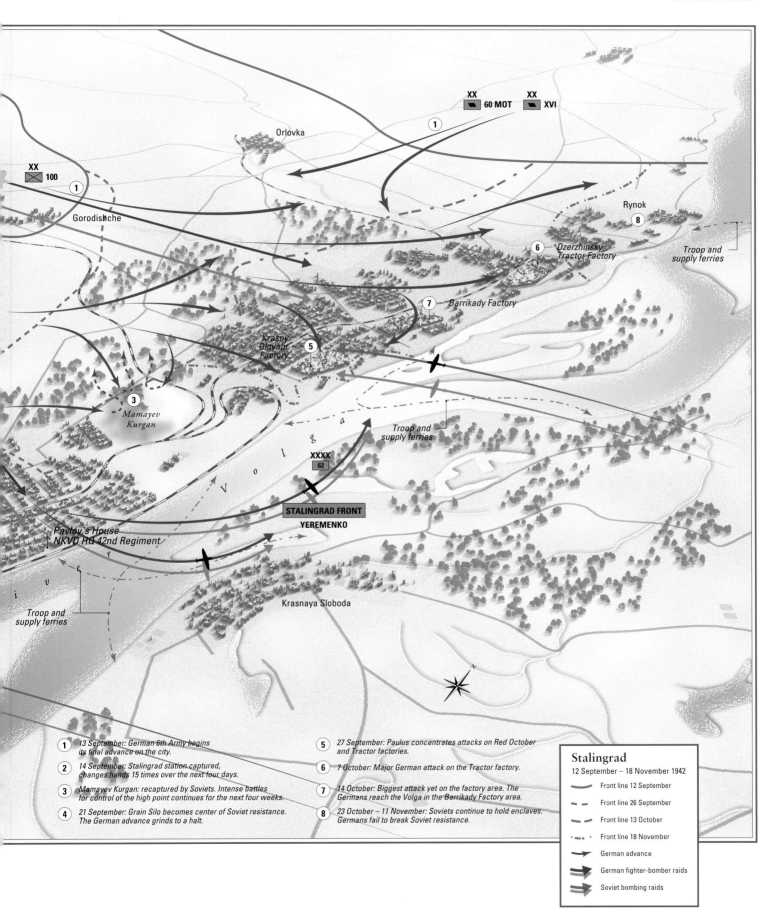

XX 60 MOT   XX XVI

①

Orlovka

XX 100

①

Gorodishche

Rynok

⑧

⑥ Dzerzhinsky Tractor Factory

Troop and supply ferries

⑦ Barrikady Factory

Krasny Oktyabr Factory ⑤

③

Mamayev Kurgan

Troop and supply ferries

V o l g a

XXXX 62

STALINGRAD FRONT
YEREMENKO

Pavlov's House
NKVD HQ 42nd Regiment

r i v e r

Troop and supply ferries

Krasnaya Sloboda

N

① **13 September:** German 6th Army begins its final advance on the city.

② **14 September:** Stalingrad station captured, changes hands 15 times over the next four days.

③ **Mamayev Kurgan:** recaptured by Soviets. Intense battles for control of the high point continues for the next four weeks.

④ **21 September:** Grain Silo becomes center of Soviet resistance. The German advance grinds to a halt.

⑤ **27 September:** Paulus concentrates attacks on Red October and Tractor factories.

⑥ **7 October:** Major German attack on the Tractor factory.

⑦ **14 October:** Biggest attack yet on the factory area. The Germans reach the Volga in the Barrikady Factory area.

⑧ **23 October – 11 November:** Soviets continue to hold enclaves. Germans fail to break Soviet resistance.

Stalingrad
12 September – 18 November 1942

——— Front line 12 September

– – – Front line 26 September

–·–· Front line 13 October

–··–· Front line 18 November

——▶ German advance

━━▶ German fighter-bomber raids

⟹ Soviet bombing raids

Front, attempted to advance into the south of the Russian encirclement around Stalingrad. Operation Winter Tempest, launched on 12 December to aid a planned breakout by Paulus' 6th Army, was beaten back. Hitler personally forbade them to break out. The Führer, thousands of miles away from the front, was adamant that not a single German soldier should retreat. Then the harsh Russian winter really started to hit the trapped Germans, with the frozen Volga helping the supply route to the Russians in the city. As the Russians continued to attack, the Germans inside the pocket fought back doggedly, many of them falling to frostbite and disease rather than enemy action.

January saw the Russians launch a fresh offensive in the Caucasus. Operation Saturn aimed to completely cut off the remainder of the German forces in the south. However, the Germans fought an excellent mobile defense and they fell back to positions 200 miles short of Stalingrad. There was definitely no chance of reprieve and the 6th Army was beyond salvation, although the men were not told of this predicament and they continued to fight in the hope of relief or extraction. The Germans were being pushed up against the banks of the Volga, fighting desperately for every inch. They feared surrender above all else, expecting to be executed on the spot by the vengeful Russians.

On 30 January, Hitler promoted Paulus to Colonel General and then to Field Marshal. This honor was a kind of dark hint because no German Field Marshal had ever surrendered or had been taken prisoner. However, soon afterwards, the new Field Marshal did surrender as Russian troops closed in on his headquarters. All German troops surrendered on 2 February 1943. A total of 91,000 starving and exhausted troops marched into captivity. Only 6,000 would ever see their homeland again; most would succumb to the harsh conditions in Soviet labor camps.

The Battle for Stalingrad was truly horrific in scale and magnitude. Estimates of casualties are hard to compile but it is thought that the Germans and their allies suffered close to 850,000 casualties and the Russians 1,128,000, making it the highest number of casualties in a single battle in human history.

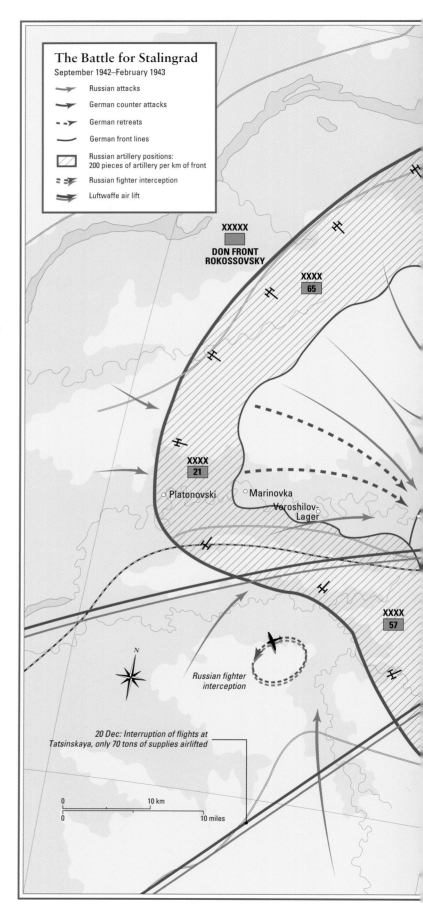

The Battle for Stalingrad
September 1942–February 1943

→ Russian attacks
→ German counter attacks
--→ German retreats
⌒ German front lines
▨ Russian artillery positions: 200 pieces of artillery per km of front
=→ Russian fighter interception
➤ Luftwaffe air lift

XXXXX **DON FRONT ROKOSSOVSKY**

XXXX 65

XXXX 21

Platonovski   Marinovka
                Voroshilov-Lager

XXXX 57

Russian fighter interception

N

20 Dec: Interruption of flights at Tatsinskaya, only 70 tons of supplies airlifted

0   10 km
0   10 miles

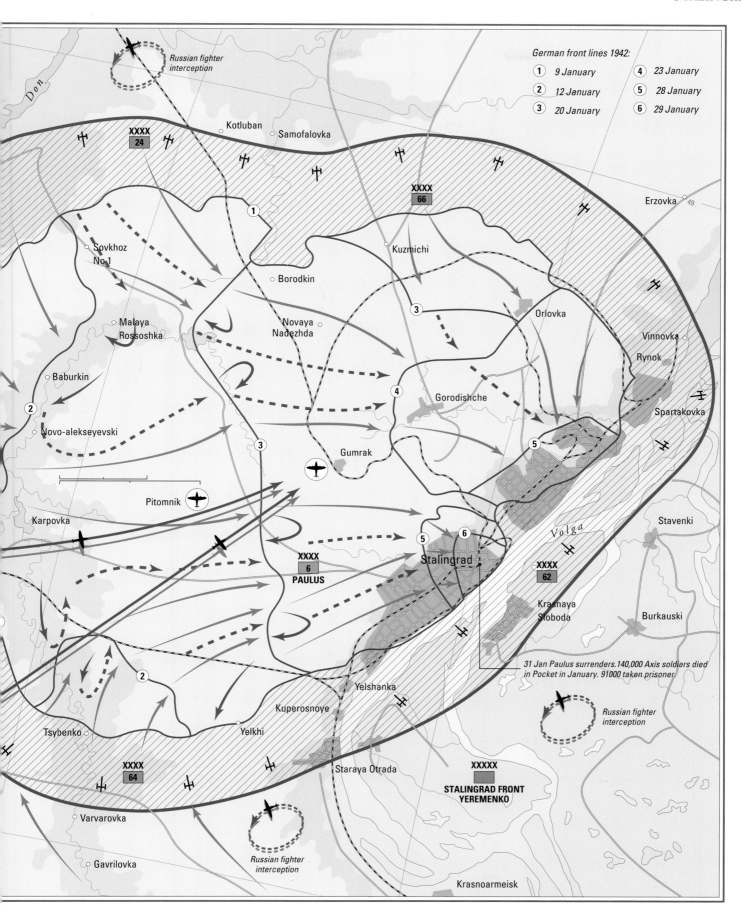

German front lines 1942:
1. 9 January
2. 12 January
3. 20 January
4. 23 January
5. 28 January
6. 29 January

Russian fighter interception

Don

Kotluban
Samofalovka
Erzovka
49

XXXX 24

XXXX 66

Kuzmichi

Sovkhoz No.1

Borodkin

Orlovka

Vinnovka

Rynok

Malaya Rossoshka

Novaya Nadezhda

Spartakovka

Baburkin

Gorodishche

XXXX 62

Novo-alekseyevski

Gumrak

Karpovka

Pitomnik

Stavenki

XXXX 6 PAULUS

Stalingrad

Volga

Krasnaya Sloboda

Burkauski

31 Jan Paulus surrenders. 140,000 Axis soldiers died in Pocket in January. 91000 taken prisoner.

Yelshanka

Russian fighter interception

Kuperosnoye

Tsybenko

Yelkhi

Staraya Otrada

XXXXX STALINGRAD FRONT YEREMENKO

XXXX 64

Varvarovka

Russian fighter interception

Gavrilovka

Krasnoarmeisk

THE SIEGE OF LENINGRAD 1941–44

"The enemy is at the gate. It is a question of life and death."

ANDREI ZHDANOV,
HEAD OF THE LENINGRAD PARTY COMMITTEE

Leningrad stood between the south-western shore of Lake Ladoga and the Gulf of Finland. As St Petersburg, it had been the capital city of the tsars. Now, renamed after Lenin, the city was feted as the "cradle of the revolution." So Leningrad was politically important—militarily too, as it lay across the path of the German's advance into the north of Russia. Until it was captured or isolated, the Germans would be unable to sweep deep into northern Russia and around to the east of Moscow. There were over 200,000 troops stationed in Leningrad, protecting a population of over three million, many of whom stayed in their city as the German war machine approached.

Field Marshal von Leeb's Army Group North cut Leningrad off within weeks of the start of Operation Barbarossa and, with the aid of the Finnish army in the north, was confident of taking this highly-prized city. This was not to be, since the Finnish army refused to advance any further than the prewar boundary with Russia, which was some 40 miles to the north. The Germans assaulted the city from the south but their initial attack faltered on the hastily constructed but stoutly defended anti-tank ditches that covered the approaches to the city, which had been dug by Leningrad's citizens.

With tanks and men needed in other sectors of the Eastern Front, von Leeb decided to lay siege to the beleaguered city. Following this, Hitler issued a directive for the city to be completely destroyed. No surrender was to be accepted. Leningrad's fate was sealed. It now faced ceaseless aerial and artillery bombardments that threatened to reduce the city to dust.

Stalin sent General Zhukov to investigate the crisis developing around Leningrad. The city was under the control of Kliment Voroshilov, regarded by many as militarily incompetent, with the day-to-day work carried out by Andrei Zhdanov. The latter was a competent leader. Stalin ordered Zhukov to replace Voroshilov and defend the city to the last citizen. This he organized with the help of Zhdanov.

The German encirclement of the city had been completed by 8 September 1941, cutting all land communication to the outside world. There was, however, one lifeline left: supply boats across Lake Ladoga. Leningrad was completely dependent on outside sources for fuel, food, and oil, and only held in its warehouses enough food stocks to last a month, maybe two. The prospects were bleak. As winter closed in the population began to die of malnutrition and exposure. There was little water, heating, or electricity for many, and the basic ration for individuals sank to 4.4 ounces (125 grams) of bread a day. Measures were taken as winter set in to try to resupply the city by sending trucks loaded with supplies across the "ice road" built over the frozen Lake Ladoga. This was constantly under artillery bombardment. As the supply trucks returned across the lake they often carried evacuees, especially children, but many still chose to stay

WATCHERS OF THE SKIES

A Soviet anti-aircraft crew mans its gun on a broad square in central Leningrad. In the background can be seen the city's neoclassical facades, as yet relatively undamaged.

amongst the starving and defend their city. Mass graves were dug but many just fell in the street with the snow covering their bodies, remaining unburied.

In January 1942, Stalin, encouraged by the defeat of the German forces before Moscow, gave orders for the siege of Leningrad to be broken, handing the task to General Meretskov, who attacked and achieved a small salient into the German lines north of Lake Ilmen. But this was soon slowed, bogged down into stalemate during the spring thaw as roads and tracks turned to deep mud. When Lake Ladoga's ice melted, the "ice road," which had been so useful to the Russians, vanished. In order to keep supplies running into the city, the Leningrad garrison used any vessel could lay their hands on. These boats, like the trucks on the winter ice, were subject to constant shelling and air attack.

The city's garrison had been slowly gaining strength and, by the early fall of 1942, the Soviets were ready to launch an attack on the Leningrad Front. With General Govorov attacking eastward and Meretskov driving to the west, the two forces met on 19 January near

Schlüsselburg, thus lifting the siege. Soon after, trains were streaming through the small corridor that had been created but the Germans, far from being defeated, kept up a constant artillery barrage.

The situation around Leningrad was static for some considerable time, with neither side making any significant gains. Fighting on other fronts had drained men and material from the Leningrad siege. Despite years of bitter fighting, the city still remained within range of German artillery positions. However, when Meretskov and Govorov were happy that they had a superiority in manpower in early 1944, they gave the order to renew the attack and finally drive the Germans from Leningrad. Hitler, as always, gave the order that no ground was to be given up. This was a battle the Wehrmacht did not really have to fight, with pressure on their limited resources all along the Eastern Front. Soviet forces advanced from the outskirts of Leningrad, liberating Luga and Novgorod during January, and restoring the railroad line to Moscow.

The total numbers lost during the siege will almost certainly never be known. The official total given by the Soviet authorities was 632,253 civilian dead; 16,700 were killed by shelling and bombing and over 1,000,000 were evacuated, leaving a total civilian population by early 1943 of 639,000. From a prewar population of over 3,000,000, this left over 1,000,000 unaccounted for. Some fell into German hands, but most died in the winter of 1941–42. The Leningrad siege remains one of the greatest examples of defiance in the history of World War II.

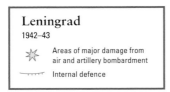

Leningrad
1942–43

✶ Areas of major damage from air and artillery bombardment

⌢⌢⌢ Internal defence

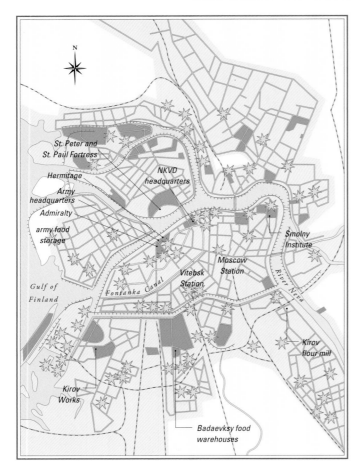

TARGETS IN THE CITY CENTER

The city of Leningrad remained within range of German heavy artillery throughout the siege. As well as targeting the Soviet defenses built around the city, the Germans made every attempt to shell food warehouses, distribution centers, and the limited lines of supply the Soviet commanders could keep open.

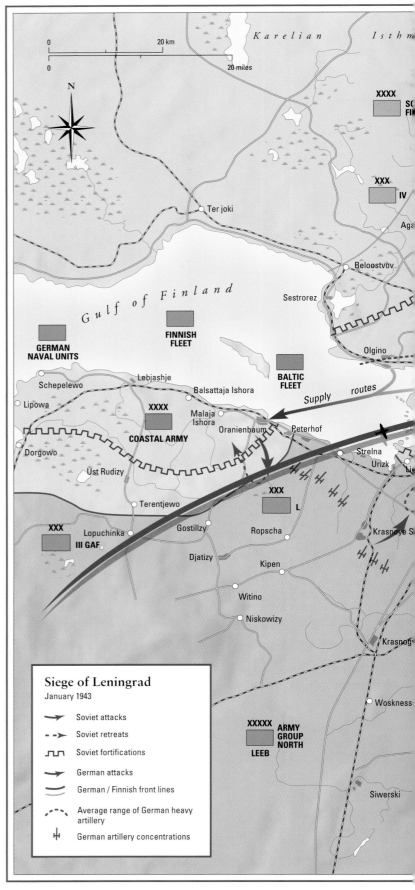

Siege of Leningrad
January 1943

→ Soviet attacks

- ‑ ‑► Soviet retreats

⌐⌐⌐ Soviet fortifications

➤ German attacks

⌒⌒ German / Finnish front lines

- - - Average range of German heavy artillery

╫ German artillery concentrations

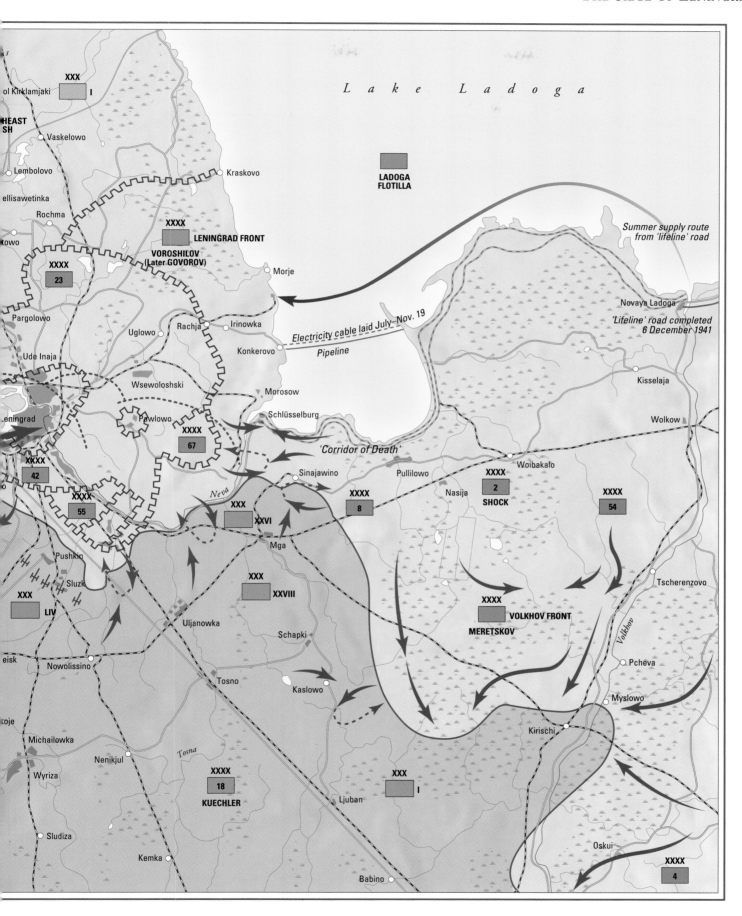

THE BATTLE OF KURSK 1943

"Soldiers of the Reich! This day you are to take part in an offensive of such importance that the whole future of the war may depend on its outcome."

ADOLF HITLER, 5 JULY 1943

The battle for the Kursk salient was to be on a massive scale, involving millions of men from both sides, as well as employing thousands of armored vehicles, aircraft, guns, and mortars. The front line between the Soviets and the Germans ran from Leningrad in the north to Rostov-on-Don in the south, with a salient 120 miles wide and protruding 75 miles into the German sector between Orel in the north and Kharkov in the south. There were three armies in the bulge and the German plan was to attack at each flank and capture these armies, thereby reducing Russian manpower. The "pinching" of this salient would also reduce the length of the front line, allowing the defense to be more heavily manned. This would also mean the capture of the important rail hub at Kursk itself, helping the line of supply.

The German plan was for Model's 9th Army to strike south from the Orel district and Hoth's 4th Panzer Army to strike north from the Kharkov area, meeting in the middle. If all went to plan, they would move east to establish a line along the River Don. This plan was originally intended to be launched at the beginning of May but was postponed to allow time for the delivery of more tanks including Tigers and the new Panther, which was designed

to combat the ubiquitous Russian T-34. Ironically, this delay allowed the Russians to build up their own forces more quickly and soon Russian armament was outstripping that of Germany.

To the Russian commanders it was quite obvious where the next offensive would come. But Stalin, overjoyed with the success at Stalingrad, was keen to push on. Zhukov succeeded in convincing him that it would be to their advantage to prepare a solid defense in depth, and then to allow the Germans to attack. They could then counterattack once the Germans were worn down. Stalin agreed and they immediately set about turning the area around Kursk into a massive fortress lined with thousands of miles of trenches and wire, built by the people of the area as well as the troops that would be defending the salient.

Almost a million antipersonnel and anti-tank mines were laid, with some trenches being almost 100 miles behind the front line. Twenty thousand pieces of artillery were placed, covering the likely German line of approach and carefully camouflaged with dummy gun positions placed to attract German fire away from the real positions. By the time of the attack, the Soviets were fully prepared with 1,300,000 men and 3,600 tanks waiting to meet 800,000 men and 2,700 tanks of the German army, which mirrored the German/Soviet position from two years previously.

The Germans made a few tentative probing attacks on 4 July so as to destroy forward observation posts and preserve the element of surprise. Before the main German advance, Stuka dive-bombers bombarded the area in front of the assaulting forces, followed by artillery fire. The Russians reacted with their own artillery fire. In the north they concentrated on the German artillery positions, which were to support the main assault. In the south, their fire concentrated on the buildup of tank and infantry forces preparing to assault. Both caused enough havoc and confusion to slow up the German advance. With this loss of momentum it was clear that Blitzkrieg was no longer working.

The Soviets also launched preemptive strikes against any known Luftwaffe airfields in the area in an attempt to seize the air over the battlefield. However, many of the Luftwaffe aircraft were already airborne and one of the largest air battles seen in World War II developed as the ground forces were beginning to engage. In the north, the Germans soon ran into a thick minefield and had to call up engineers, who worked under constant shell fire, the mines killing men, disabling tanks, and again slowing advance. The Soviets had correctly identified this as a likely sector where the German attack would come and had prepared defenses accordingly. The numerous anti-tank guns then started to take their toll on the Germans. By the end of the day the attackers had advanced a mere four miles into the Soviet lines.

After the initial Soviet counterstrike was fought off in the south, progress was much better than in the north. The advance frontage was smaller than in the north and was against a much thinner line of defense, but again the Soviets took their toll on the German tanks and, when threatened with being overrun, the Soviets fell back in good order, taking their equipment with them to carry on the fight.

These delaying actions also helped to give the Soviets enough time to push reserves to the threatened areas. At the end of the first day the 4th Panzer had managed to penetrate about 12 miles into the Soviet lines. This penetration was an obvious threat to the whole outcome of the battle. Recognizing this, the 5th Guards Tank Army was rushed to the southern front to help counter the German Panzers.

After heavy fighting and immense losses on both sides, the Germans, losing a particularly high number of

RED FOOTSOLDIERS

Kursk is often seen as a fight in which armadas of tanks roamed the battlefield like ships at sea. But the Soviet plan involved astute use of men armed with tank-busting guns. Close coordination between tanks, infantry and artillery was a key tactic.

tanks, many to breakdowns rather than enemy action, had still not managed to penetrate far into the Soviet lines, the defense in depth working wonders. By the night of 11 July the 5th Tank Army and 5th Guards Army were in place around Prokhorovka to strike at the leading elements of the Panzers—SS Adolf Hitler Panzerkorps—which were trying to drive between the 69th Army and the 1st Tank Army.

On the morning of 12 July, as the German Totenkopf Division was forming up for another assault, they were rushed by the tanks of 5th Tank Army. The Soviets surprised and managed to get up close to the German tanks in order to readdress the balance in firepower, which favored the Germans. Although initially shocked by this attack, the Germans reacted quickly and soon took a heavy toll on the Soviet tanks, which lost two thirds of its strength by midday. By the evening, the Soviets, moved back to the defensive, had lost the ground they had gained in the morning, and had also lost around 300 tanks in the process. Losses on the German side were significant but the Soviets lost more.

After these immense battles, the German commanders had little to show for their sacrifice and started to withdraw forces in order to shorten their defensive lines. While the Battle of Kursk had been raging, an Anglo-American force had landed on Sicily, making Hitler look to other fronts that might require reinforcement, eventually sending the Leibstandarte Adolf Hitler Division. Within two weeks the Soviets had recovered enough to move onto the offensive, starting with Operation Kutuzov in the north that pushed the Germans back to their original start lines. On 3 August Operation Polkovodets Rumyantsev began, pushing the Germans out of Kharkov by 11 August. This was the decisive point where Soviet defense moved to the offensive, and the Germans began their slow retreat to the borders of Germany. Soviet High Command had developed ways of defeating the German war machine and they now held the advantage.

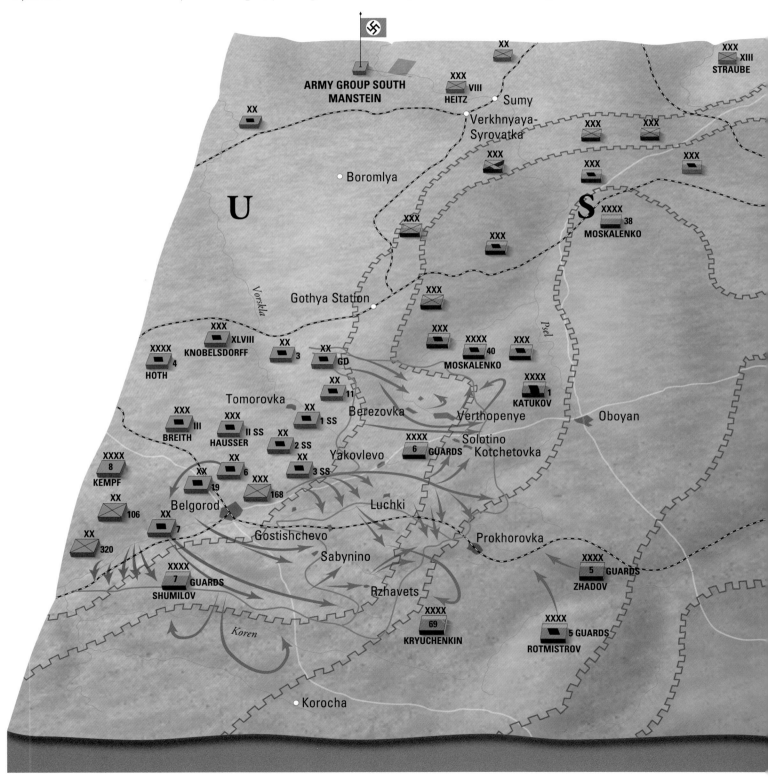

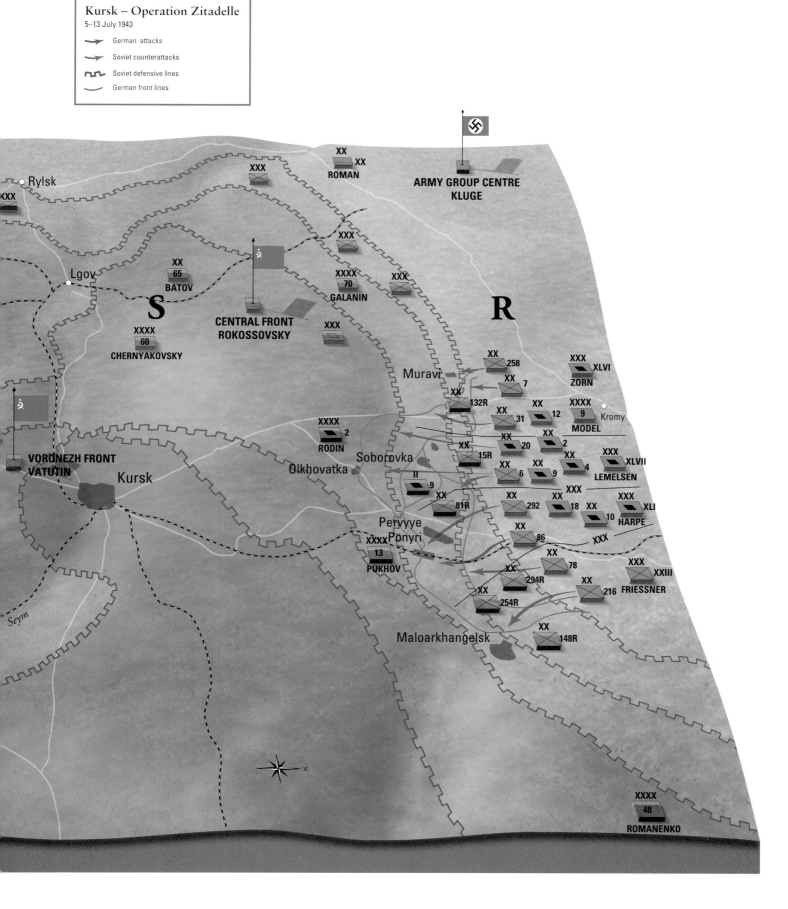

Kursk – Operation Zitadelle
5–13 July 1943

German attacks
Soviet counterattacks
Soviet defensive lines
German front lines

Rylsk

XXX

ARMY GROUP CENTRE
KLUGE

XX
ROMAN
XX

XXX

Lgov

XXX

XX
65
BATOV

XXXX
70
GALANIN

XXX

S

R

CENTRAL FRONT
ROKOSSOVSKY

XXXX
60
CHERNYAKOVSKY

XXX

Muravi

XX
258

XXX
XLVI
ZORN

XX
7

XX
132R

XXXX
2
RODIN

XX
31

XX
12

XXXX
9
MODEL

Kromy

Soborovka

XX
20

XX
2

Olkhovatka

XX
15R

XX
6

XX
9

XX
4

XXX
LEMELSEN

VORONEZH FRONT
VATUTIN

II
9

XX
81R

XXX

XX
292

XX
18

XX
10

XXX
XLVII

Kursk

XXX
XLI
HARPE

Pervyye
Ponyri

XX
86

XXX

XXXX
13
PUKHOV

XX
78

XXX
XXIII
FRIESSNER

XX
294R

XX
216

XX
254R

Seym

Maloarkhangelsk

XX
148R

XXXX
48
ROMANENKO

THE BATTLES FOR KHARKOV

"In Russia the moral comfort of Manstein's latest victory could not obscure the fact that the whole balance of power had changed."

GENERAL VON MELLENTHIN

Kharkov was the most populous city in the Ukraine, the hub of the regional railroad system, and also the administrative center. This meant that it was a highly prized city for both sides and would be the scene of no less than five bloody battles between 1941 and 1943, with the city changing hands four times. The German advance was beginning to meet tougher resistance on the part of the Red Army after their initial successes at the opening stage of Operation Barbarossa. The Germans approached the city limits of Kharkov on 24 October 1941, but this was to be the limit of the 6th Army's advance before the winter closed in and halted any chance of rapid advance. The Germans dug in 40 miles east of the city on the River Donets and prepared for the freezing winter weather.

As General Paulus was preparing his 6th Army for the spring offensive that would take them deeper into Russian territory, Soviet forces attacked his front in a preemptive strike to try to save the city. The Soviet advance achieved a certain amount of surprise but the Germans soon recovered and started throwing in concerted local counterattacks that took a heavy toll on the attackers, so much so that the rear-echelon troops were kept just behind the main line in case they needed to be put in themselves. Within two days General

Timoshenko's troop advance was beginning to falter under the weight of the counterattacks and the increased bombing by the Luftwaffe. But as the attack ground to a halt, the Soviet offensive to the south of the city had taken a reasonable amount of land, creating a massive bulge on the German front.

On 17 May Kleist's 1st Panzer Army plunged into the Soviets in a pincer movement on the Barvenkovo area. With this Kleist was trying to catch as many Russians as possible in a pocket. By the 24 May the Russian forces that had made the attack were completely surrounded, after Stalin had stalled the order for the retreat. Nearly a quarter of a million men were trapped in the salient along with nearly a thousand tanks. What had started off as a possible Russian victory in its time of need, had finished as yet another German victory. What was highlighted most here was the lack of experience of the newly conscripted Soviet army and the serious problems in supplying them. It also showed the need for more concentrated planning of such offensives.

After the defeat, the Russians waited for nearly a year to attack Kharkov again; this came in mid-February 1943. Defending the city against the Russian onslaught was the veteran II SS Panzer Corps, having been recently equipped with the new, heavy Tiger tank. When the Soviets attacked,

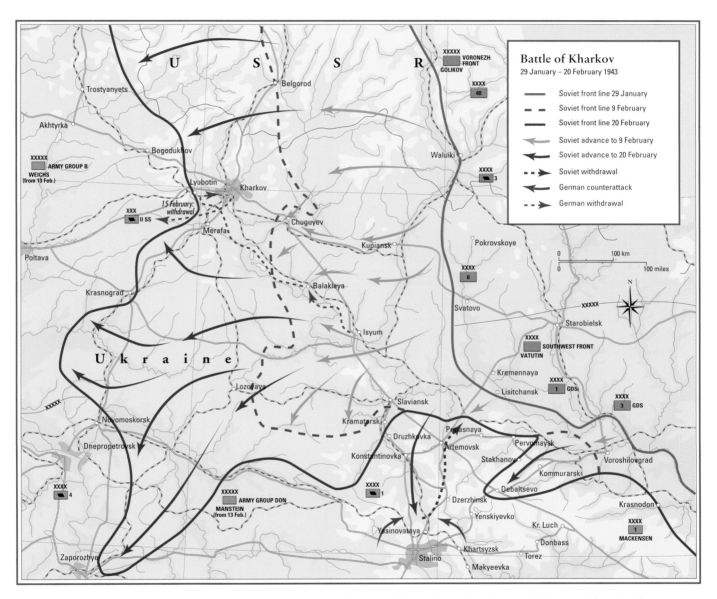

Battle of Kharkov
29 January – 20 February 1943

———	Soviet front line 29 January
- - -	Soviet front line 9 February
———	Soviet front line 20 February
←	Soviet advance to 9 February
←	Soviet advance to 20 February
⇢	Soviet withdrawal
←	German counterattack
⇠	German withdrawal

the Germans were heavily outnumbered but still managed to hold on for a time. However, the sheer numbers involved in the Soviet attack became too much and the commander, Hausser, was refused the chance to retreat and ordered to make the city a fortress and fight to the death. This order, straight from the Führer himself, Hausser chose to disregard and ordered his troops to pull back. These units were later attached to Manstein's counterattack and Kharkov was quickly retaken in a masterful example of mobile warfare.

Soon after, the city would be used by the Germans as the springboard for their offensive on the Kursk salient to the north. This offensive would be beaten back by a massive Russian force of over one and a half million men, and Kharkov would be their first objective. On the morning of 23 August, the Russians approached the city and engaged the Germans. By midday the Germans were given the order to retreat from the city. The battered ruins of Kharkov now belonged to the Soviets once more—this time for good.

GUADALCANAL 1942

"It is a sorry thing that we must leave the bodies of our comrades and the ground we have won so dearly. Sleep peacefully, my friends. Farewell! We shall meet again in heaven!"

LIEUTENANT SAKAMOTO, OFFICER AT GUADALCANAL

Guadalcanal was the first major offensive against the Imperial Japanese forces in the Pacific war. The plan for the attack involved Marines assaulting the two islands of Florida and Tulagi, while the main part of the force landed on Guadalcanal itself, where the Japanese were building an airfield. Overall command of the campaign would be given to Vice-Admiral Robert Ghormley while the Marines would be led by Major-General Alexander Vandegrift.

The landings took place on 7 August, 1942. Two battalions of Marines landed on Tulagi unopposed. They met resistance inland, but had taken the island by the end of 8 August. As the minor islands were being cleared, the main force landed on Guadalcanal unopposed. The next day Marines captured the airfield. Meanwhile on the beaches, the transport and accompanying escort was under attack by land-based bombers flying from Rabaul. This led the carrier force and transports to withdraw, having first attempted to land as much material as possible. While this was in hand, a Japanese naval force struck, sinking three U.S. cruisers and one Australian before quickly withdrawing.

Having set up a perimeter around the airfield, Vandegrift now set about moving supplies from the beaches. On 20 August, the first squadrons of fighters arrived on the island. They immediately got to work intercepting the Japanese bombers that constantly bombed the strip. On 21 August the Japanese attempted to assault the perimeter at night but had underestimated the Marines' strength. The attackers were annihilated. They tried again in mid-September, this time using a force of 6,000 troops, but after savage fighting they were again beaten back.

After this attack, U.S. forces attempted to expand the perimeter and push the Japanese artillery out of range of the newly-named Henderson Field, but it was still subject to bombardment by Japanese battleships. While the struggle for the airfield played out, naval actions were fought for the control of the sea approaches.

An action on 24 and 25 August ended in a stalemate, but the Americans succeeded in interfering with Japanese troop reinforcements. On the night of 11/12 October the U.S. Navy successfully intercepted a force on the way to bombard Henderson Field and the resulting engagement ended as a tactical victory for the Americans. Even though they lost a destroyer, they managed to prevent the bombardment of the vital airfield.

Despite heavy American casualties, all these naval actions meant that they were able to outnumber the Japanese troops on the island. By November, the Japanese made a concerted attempt to land the 38th Division on Guadalcanal. The transports were heavily escorted and met a quick but terrible engagement on the night of 12/13 November. The U.S. Navy lost six ships and the Japanese three in just half an hour. While the Japanese Navy was attempting to unload the Division, fighter

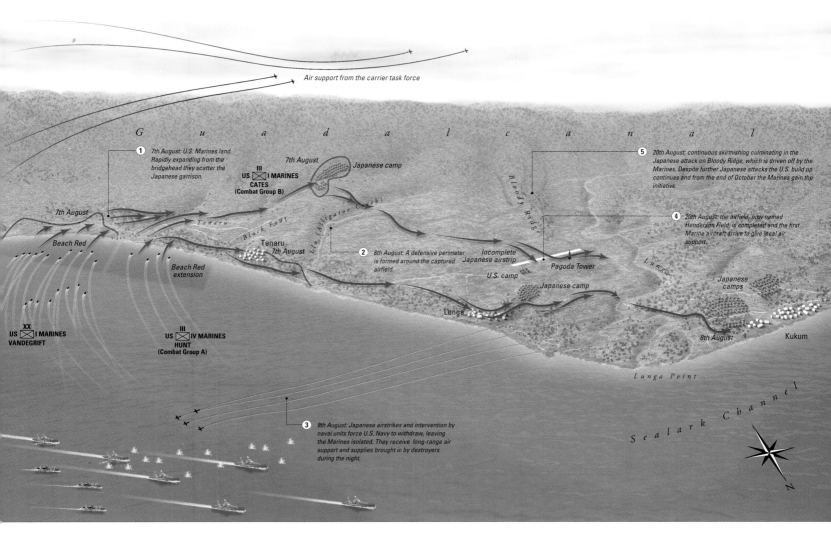

Air support from the carrier task force

Guadalcanal

① 7th August: U.S. Marines land. Rapidly expanding from the bridgehead they scatter the Japanese garrison.

III
US ☒ I MARINES
CATES
(Combat Group B)

7th August

Japanese camp

⑤ 20th August: continuous skirmishing culminating in the Japanese attack on Bloody Ridge, which is driven off by the Marines. Despite further Japanese attacks the U.S. build up continues and from the end of October the Marines gain the initiative.

Bloody Ridge

④ 20th August: the airfield, now named Henderson Field, is completed and the first Marine aircraft arrive to give local air support.

7th August

Beach Red

Tenaru

Block Four

Tenaru
7th August

Lin (Alligator Creek)

Beach Red extension

② 8th August: A defensive perimeter is formed around the captured airfield.

Incomplete Japanese airstrip

U.S. camp

Pagoda Tower

Lunga

Japanese camps

XX
US ☒ I MARINES
VANDEGRIFT

III
US ☒ IV MARINES
HUNT
(Combat Group A)

Japanese camp

Lunga

8th August

Kukum

Lunga Point

③ 9th August: Japanese airstrikes and intervention by naval units force U.S. Navy to withdraw, leaving the Marines isolated. They receive long-range air support and supplies brought in by destroyers during the night.

Sealark Channel

N

Guadalcanal
August 1942 – February 1943

→ U.S. movements
→ Japanese advance
∿∿∿ Japanese defence line
⌒ U.S. front line 7th August

UNOPPOSED LANDING
U.S. Marines (top) storm ashore at the island of Guadalcanal. This was their first major action of the Pacific war, but the real fighting began once they left the beach and headed inland.

SITUATION REPORT
From left to right, Major General Alex Vandegrift, Colonel Gerald Thomas, and Colonel Merrit Edson discuss the situation just after the Japanese had been driven from their positions.

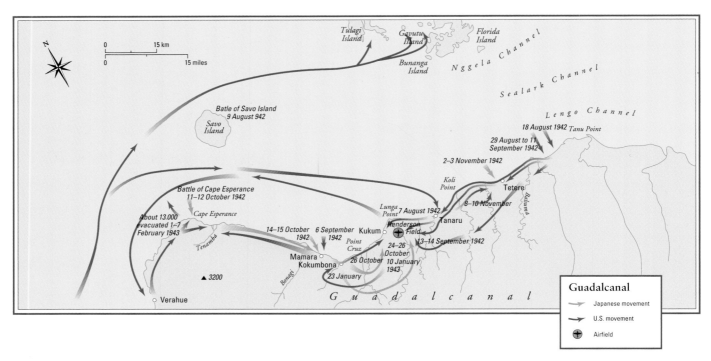

Guadalcanal

- Japanese movement
- U.S. movement
- ⊕ Airfield

Tulagi Island

Gavutu Island

Florida Island

Bunanga Island

Nggela Channel

Sealark Channel

Battle of Savo Island
9 August 942

Savo Island

Lengo Channel

18 August 1942 *Tanu Point*

29 August to 11
September 1942

2–3 November 1942

Battle of Cape Esperance
11–12 October 1942

Cape Esperance

Koli Point

Tetere

About 13.000
evacuated 1–7
February 1943

14–15 October
1942

6 September
1942

Kukum

Lunga Point 7 August 1942

Henderson Field

8–10 November

Tanaru

Tenambia

Point Cruz

24–26
October
10 January
1943

13–14 September 1942

Mamara
Kokumbona

26 October

23 January

▲ 3200

Bonugi

Balsuma

o Verahue

G u a d a l c a n a l

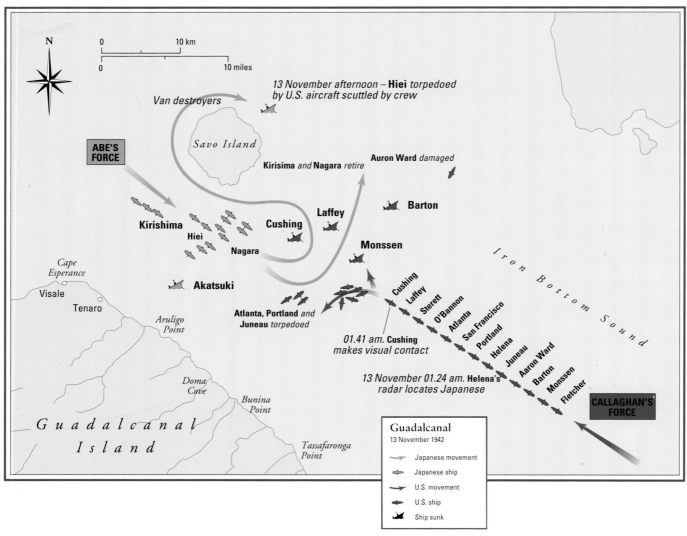

N

0 ____ 10 km ____ 10 miles

13 November afternoon – **Hiei** *torpedoed
by U.S. aircraft scuttled by crew*

Van destroyers

Savo Island

ABE'S FORCE

Kirisima *and* **Nagara** *retire*

Auron Ward *damaged*

Barton

Kirishima

Hiei

Cushing

Laffey

Nagara

Monssen

Cape Esperance

Akatsuki

Visale

Tenaro

Aruligo Point

Atlanta, Portland and
Juneau *torpedoed*

I r o n   B o t t o m   S o u n d

Cushing
Laffey
Sterett
O'Bannon
Atlanta
San Francisco
Portland
Helena
Juneau
Aaron Ward
Barton
Monssen
Fletcher

01.41 am. **Cushing**
makes visual contact

Doma Cove

Bunina Point

13 November 01.24 am. **Helena's**
radar locates Japanese

CALLAGHAN'S FORCE

*G u a d a l c a n a l
I s l a n d*

Tassafaronga Point

Guadalcanal
13 November 1942

- Japanese movement
- Japanese ship
- U.S. movement
- U.S. ship
- Ship sunk

bombers from Henderson sank six out of seven of the transports and a cruiser. By this time essential supplies were not getting through to the Japanese soldiers on the island, who were already on starvation rations. This caused the turn of the tide as the U.S. forces slowly took the tactical and numerical advantage, and after the Marines had been replaced by the 25th Army Division, the Japanese were forced to retreat to Cape Esperance.

As the Americans pushed forward, the Japanese evacuated their remaining troops in a nighttime operation that succeeded in getting more than 13,000 soldiers off the island. This would be a defeat from which the Japanese would never recover, although they felt far from defeated at this time.

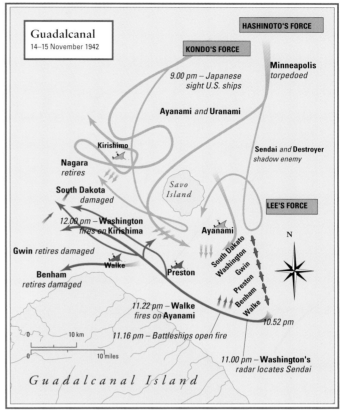

Guadalcanal
14–15 November 1942

HASHINOTO'S FORCE

KONDO'S FORCE

9.00 pm – Japanese sight U.S. ships

Minneapolis *torpedoed*

Ayanami *and* **Uranami**

Kirishimo

Sendai *and* **Destroyer** *shadow enemy*

Savo Island

Nagara *retires*

LEE'S FORCE

South Dakota *damaged*

12.00 pm – **Washington** *fires on* **Kirishima**

Ayanami

N

Gwin *retires damaged*

South Dakota
Washington
Gwin
Preston
Benham
Walke

Walke

Preston

Benham *retires damaged*

11.22 pm – **Walke** *fires on* **Ayanami**

10.52 pm

0   10 km
0   10 miles

11.16 pm – *Battleships open fire*

11.00 pm – **Washington's** *radar locates Sendai*

Guadalcanal Island

FALLEN AVENGER

The wreckage of a downed US Grumman TBF Avenger. These torpedo bombers were a powerful weapon against Japanese ships at Guadalcanal and elsewhere in the Pacific theater.

New Guinea & Cartwheel 1942–43

"In times of peace a package of used razor blades might be —in terms of barter—a reasonable price to pay for a native hut in Buna village. But Buna cost dearly in war, because possession of the north coast of New Guinea was vital to future Allied operations."

LT.–GENERAL ROBERT L. EICHELBERGER

On 8 March 1942, two Japanese battalions landed at Lae and Salamaua on the Houn Gulf with the aim of striking south to capture Port Moresby, from where they could launch further attacks on the Australian mainland. Opposing these troops were two small Australian units, one at Wae—which was known as Kanga Force—and the other based at Kokoda. These units were severely depleted because of the overseas commitments of the Australian Army. Many troops were fighting in the Western Desert and many more had been captured in Singapore.

After the Battle of Midway MacArthur authorized limited operations on Papua New Guinea to assist the Australians in forcing the Japanese back. But before any reinforcements for the Australians arrived, Major-General Horii Tomitaro's South Seas Detachment landed on the north coast of Papua. The Japanese force intended to advance down the Kokoda Trail over the Owen Stanley Range and capture Port Moresby. The Australians moved up the trail to meet them but were badly mauled.

By 14 August the Japanese detachment was at Isurava. The Australians surviving the Kokoda engagement fell back on positions at Ioribaiwa, with the chances of the Allies holding on to Papua New Guinea looking slim. Thanks to ULTRA decrypts the Allies secured information about the Japanese submarine screen that was being prepared off Milne Bay to the southeast of the island. This meant the Allies had time to prepare defensive positions, using the 18th Australian Brigade supplemented by a contingent of U.S. engineers and two squadrons of Australian fighters. On the night of 25/26 August, 2,000 Japanese troops landed and were immediately engaged by the Australians. During the course of the action a further 600 troops were landed but by 4 September the Japanese force withdrew with only 1,200 survivors.

By 17 September, on the Kokoda Trail, the Australians had been beaten back to their final defensive positions at Imata Ridge. MacArthur, losing faith in the Australians and not realizing the conditions they were fighting under, sacked the commander and put General Blamey, another

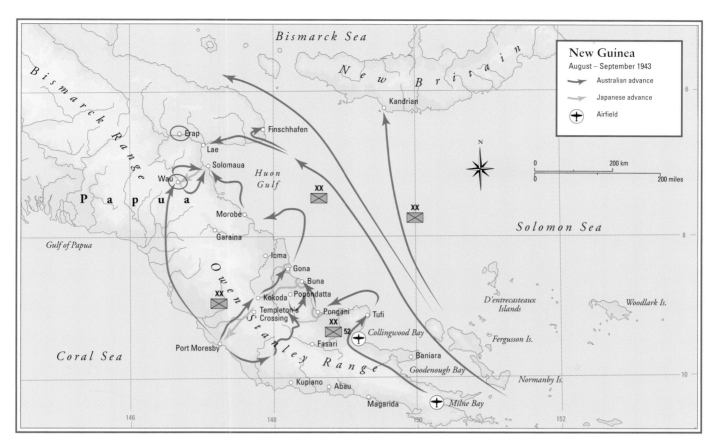

Australian staff officer, in charge. By the time this was implemented Horii's troops had overextended their supply line and were now under constant air attack by the 5th USAAF. This all conspired, along with Japanese troops being transferred to the fighting on Guadalcanal, to cause Horii to withdraw to his original beachhead on the northern coast. In doing so, Horii ordered the fortification of this beachhead with an 11-mile perimeter that would be hard to break.

During this time the U.S. 32nd Division landed on the island. It was sent into the offensive without proper equipment or jungle training. On 19 November, they were thrown into an attack on Buna and Cape Endaiadere while the Australians advanced up the Kokoda Trail to Gona and Sanananda. Casualties were enormous for the Americans, while the Australians were suffering through exhaustion and disease. When the Australians captured Gona after terrible fighting, the Americans entered Buna on 2 January 1943, eventually pushing the Japanese from the area three weeks later.

The fighting now moved to the Australian-mandated New Guinea, where the Allies now faced a force of Japanese that had been recently reinforced by Lt-General Adachi's 18th Army. Again the Japanese aim was to secure Port Moresby and send 2,500 troops down the Bulolo

Valley with the aim of destroying Kanga Force and capturing the airbase at Wau. This force was held back on the perimeter of the airbase until an additional brigade of Australian troops could be flown in to push the Japanese back to Mubo. By this time, the situation on Guadalcanal had become worse for the Japanese, so holding onto New Guinea was imperative. The 4th Air Army was moved to the area to reinforce the ground troops and a new Japanese offensive was planned.

Adachi continued to build up his forces. To oppose this threat, MacArthur created two new groups: Alamo Force, which consisted of U.S. troops; and New Guinea Force, which was made up of Australian troops. These troops were to be used as part of Operation Cartwheel with the aim of isolating the forward base of Rabaul on New Britain.

The Allies also set about constructing a forward airbase for its fighters, which were until now out of range of the Japanese bomber bases around Wewak. On 17 August, raids were launched against these strips, which succeeded in decimating Japanese air power in the theater, leaving only 40 serviceable aircraft at their disposal and only one out of four airstrips in use. This attack meant that the Allied ground forces could continue their advance almost unhindered by air attack. The

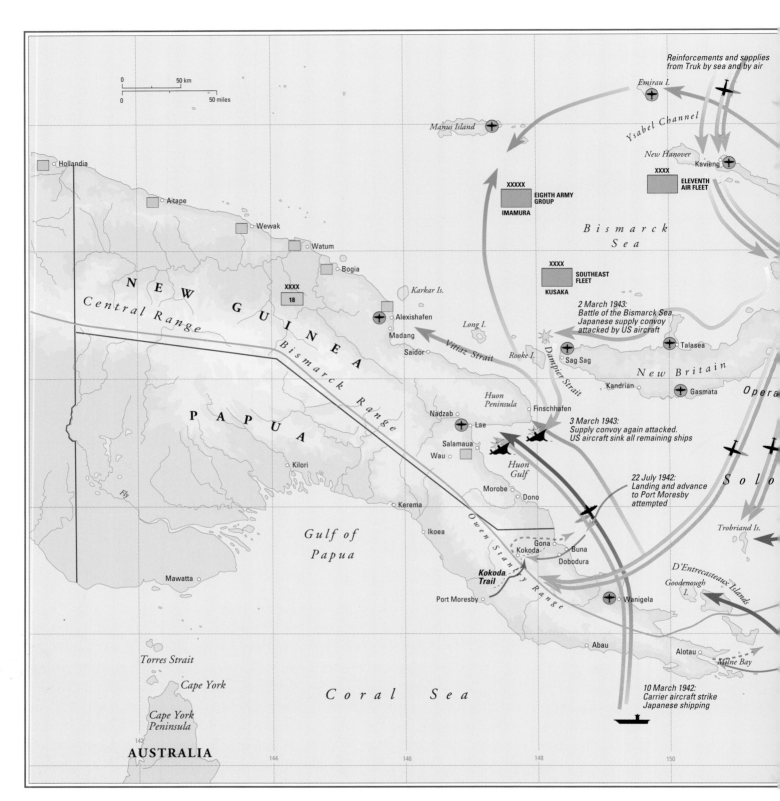

Australian 7th Division was then moved by air to the areas of Nadzab and a feint was launched to draw the Japanese from Lae to Salamaua. Once this had succeeded, the 7th advanced northward while the 9th Division landed, via the sea, east of Lae. The Japanese were being forced from the area by mid-September, but not before evacuating over 7,000 troops from the peninsula. The 7th Division proceeded to advance up the Dompu Valley and another amphibious assault allowed the Australians to capture Finschhafen by early October. Fighting also continued in the Huon Peninsula until all resistance was cleared by mid-December.

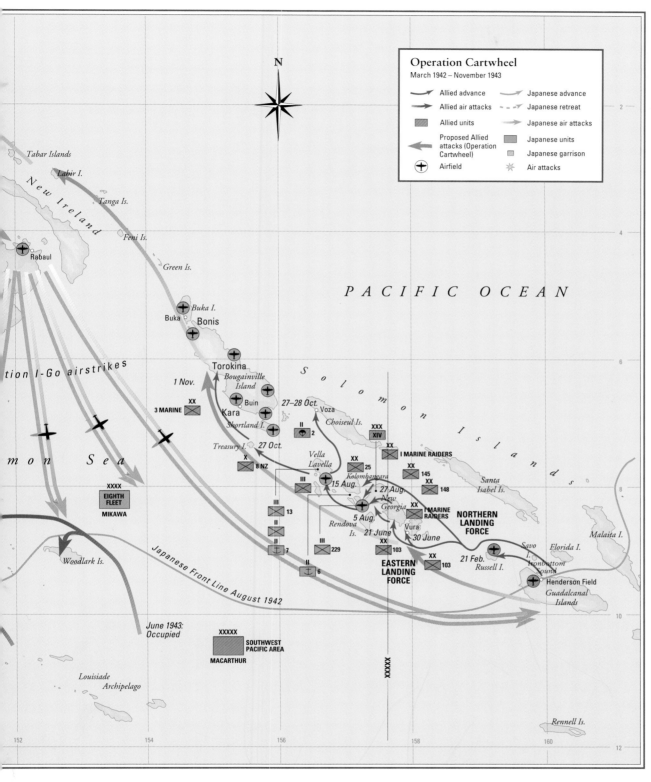

Operation Cartwheel
March 1942 – November 1943

Allied advance — Japanese advance
Allied air attacks — Japanese retreat
Allied units — Japanese air attacks
Proposed Allied attacks (Operation Cartwheel) — Japanese units
Japanese garrison
Airfield — Air attacks

Attempts were made to cut the line of retreat of the Japanese 20th and 51st Divisions by the U.S. 32nd Division as they landed at Saidor, but this failed. A landing at Hollandia and Ataipe on 22 April 1944 cut Adachi's retreat. In October, after Wakde and Baik Islands had been cleared, U.S. troops handed over responsibility for

the New Guinea campaign to the Australians, because they were needed in the upcoming invasion of the Philippines. The Australians pursued the Japanese up the coast, and eventually took Wewak in May 1945. After this, the Japanese withdrew into the Prince Alexander Ranges, where they fought on until the end of the war.

THE ITALIAN CAMPAIGN— SICILY TO ROME 1943

"Better to fight for something than live for nothing."

GENERAL GEORGE SMITH PATTON

The invasion of Sicily was to be the largest amphibious assault to date, incorporating two armies, Lt-General Patton's U.S. 7th Army and Montgomery's British 8th Army. The operation was planned to bring the war in the Mediterranean to a swift conclusion but caused many interservice problems and rivalries later on in the campaign, particularly between "Monty" and some of the American generals. This was partly Montgomery's fault for not working closely enough with the U.S. forces.

The amphibious landings were preceded by parachute and glider landings by men of the U.S. 82nd Airborne Division and the British 1st Airlanding Brigade. The airborne units were severely compromised by the adverse weather on the night of 9/10 July and many came down in the sea, or else were forced to turn back to their bases in Tunisia.

Those units that did manage to land safely caused chaos behind the lines, ambushing convoys, and holding onto strategic objectives. One such occurrence was successfully achieved by troops of the British Brigade (although only numbering 100 when there should have been 1,500). They managed to hold the bridge to Siracusa at Ponte Grande against overwhelming odds. They were eventually beaten off the bridge with only eight men escaping. While two men fired at the enemy engineers who were trying to lay demolition charges, the other men went in search of reinforcements and found the newly-landed British 5th Division and were duly able to win back the bridge.

The amphibious landings, although again affected by the adverse weather, went relatively well against little opposition. The British landed to the east between Pozallo and Siracusa with the aim of advancing north towards Messina, while the Americans landed between Cape Scaramia and Licata and would cover the left flank of the 8th Army's advance. The British made a swift advance and took control of Siracusa on the day of the landings, whereas the Americans faced a strong counterattack by elements of the Hermann Goering Division. The Germans were eventually beaten back, however, with the aid of naval gunfire from the invasion fleet offshore.

After this setback the advance continued well. Within two weeks Patton's 7th Army had reached Palermo on the northern coast, but the British hit a strong line of defense in the rugged terrain of eastern Sicily. A problem lay in the fact that General Omar Bradley, commander of the 2nd U.S. Corps, had to safeguard Monty's flank rather than dashing north, trapping the 15th Panzer Division on the west of the island and denying them an escape route to the Italian mainland. Monty's troops made slow progress advancing north, faced by a capable enemy in excellent defensible positions and, because of the rugged terrain, their tanks had to keep to the small mountain roads; this soon

SICILY BOUND

At a French naval base in Tunisia, American tanks and their crews stand in line, waiting to be loaded aboard L.S.T. landing craft and transported to Sicily. The invasion was two days away.

caused bottlenecks and they then became easy prey for the German anti-tank gunners. Patton, frustrated by Monty's slow advance, suggested he go for Messina in a big push along the north coast but this was held back by General Alexander.

Hitler did not want any plan to be made for the evacuation of his troops, although the situation changed when Mussolini fell from power on 25 July. Hitler now authorized an evacuation. The Allies tried to outflank the defenders by launching small amphibious assaults, but these failed; the Germans had already retreated to another line of defense. Hube, commander of the German forces, managed to hold open the Messina Strait with little air and naval support. He pulled back his troops to a shorter defensive line and thinned out his men, doing this several times before the total evacuation on the night of 11/12 August, when the last troops crossed unimpeded by any Allied attacks. Hube took with him nearly all the garrison of Sicily, along with their supplies and vehicles. Patton won the race to Messina when he entered the city on 16 August.

The next step for the Allies was to assault the Italian mainland. The Italian campaign was marred by tactical difficulties from the start. Being a mountainous country it would be unsuitable for massed armored advances yet perfect for the Germans to defend. On learning of Mussolini's downfall, the German High Command wasted no time, disarming the Italian army and reinforcing their own positions.

A plan was drawn up for the British 8th Army to land at the toe of the Italian peninsula. This was to be followed by an amphibious landing by the 5th Army at the Bay of Salerno. The first landing incurred relatively few casualties and achieved its aim, if a little slowly and cautiously. The second landing, on the other hand, was to be a near disaster for the Allies, but they learned from their mistakes, and later applied that knowledge to the invasion of western Europe.

The 8th Army crossed the Strait of Messina on 3 September with some elements sailing to the port of Taranto, which fell with ease on 9 September. The landings on Salerno began the morning after the official surrender of Italy, and the troops were expecting few problems. However, the Germans had been quick to take over the old Italian positions and were prepared for the assault. The British landed to the north of the bay and initially faced little opposition, since the German units were still digging in. This was not to last as the 14th Panzer Division soon began to assault the initial advance.

The American part of the invasion force landed further south in the bay and was soon pinned down and unable to break out from the beachhead. The German commander, General Heinrich von Vietinghoff, quickly coordinated a strong counterattack, achieving enough success to panic the Allied commanders into almost evacuating their beachhead. This attack was eventually beaten back but only after every available person who could fire a weapon was thrown into the line, and elements of the 82nd Airborne Division were dropped onto the beachhead as reinforcements. By 16 September, the Germans had begun a steady withdrawal to a defensive line north of Naples. This same day the leading units of the 8th Army joined up with the Salerno beachhead, the Allies eventually entering Naples on 1 October, almost a month after arriving on the mainland.

The campaign reached a stalemate as the Italian countryside and mountains were perfect defensive positions and the Allies could not sweep forward because their armor was confined to the small mountain roads.

Supplies were blighted by the winter rains, which soon caused everything to be clogged in mud. The only route for an advance on Rome was through the Gustav Line, which involved fighting through the Liri Valley, dominated by Monte Cassino. Any movement could be seen clearly by German observers and artillery directed onto any

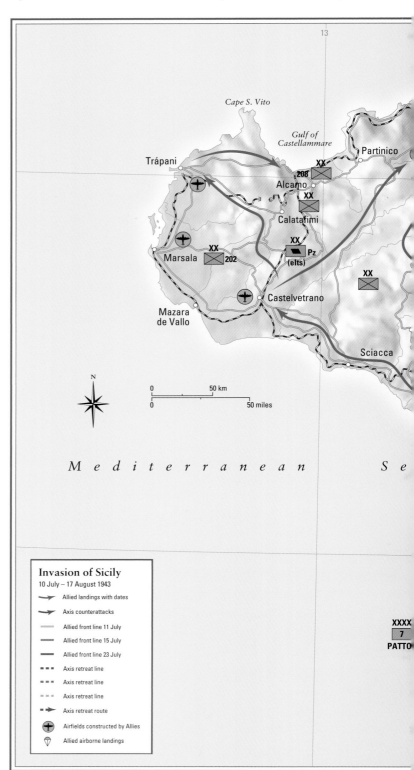

Invasion of Sicily
10 July – 17 August 1943

→ Allied landings with dates
→ Axis counterattacks
— Allied front line 11 July
— Allied front line 15 July
— Allied front line 23 July
- - - Axis retreat line
- - - Axis retreat line
- - - Axis retreat line
- ➤ Axis retreat route
✈ Airfields constructed by Allies
☂ Allied airborne landings

FEARLESS LEADER
George Patton (center, foreground) wades ashore in Sicily. He was an erratic general, but unfailingly aggressive to the enemy. "Courage," he once remarked, "is fear holding on a minute longer."

Supplies were blighted by the winter rains, which soon caused everything to be clogged in mud. The only route for an advance on Rome was through the Gustav Line, which involved fighting through the Liri Valley, dominated by Monte Cassino. Any movement could be seen clearly by German observers and artillery directed onto any assault. General Mark Clark, in command of the U.S. 5th Army gave the task of taking Monte Cassino to 2nd U.S. Corps. This attack was beaten off with appalling losses. Clark decided on an improvised amphibious assault with the aim of outflanking the defenders and catching them in a pincer movement.

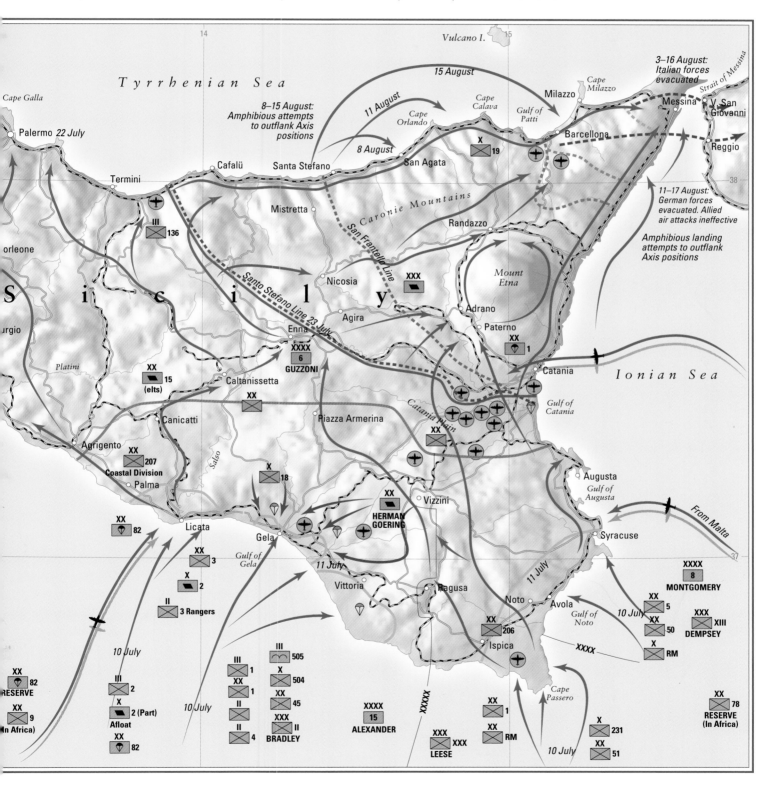

END OF THE LINE

German prisoners of war, captured at Anzio, await transfer. The traffic was not all one way: Allied soldiers also got taken prisoner in the battle, and saw out the war in Bavarian P.O.W. camps.

Major-General Lucas' 6th Corps landed on the Anzio beachhead on 22 January and, rather than break out quickly, he decided to consolidate his beachhead position. Even though the landing had achieved complete surprise, Lucas was wary of advancing until he felt he had adequate reserves. This hesitation allowed the German Field Marshal Albert Kesselring to organize and move six divisions, under the command of General von Mackensen, to surround the beachhead. When Lucas' troops were ready to advance from his line they suffered heavy losses and immediately went back onto the defensive. A German counterattack came on 16 February, but was beaten back, thanks to ULTRA decrypts enabling the Allies to coordinate air, naval, and artillery bombardments. Shortly after this attack, Lucas was replaced by Major-General Truscott, who had formerly been his deputy commander.

Several more assaults on Monte Cassino using the New Zealand Corps had failed, again with appalling losses and few lessons being learned. Preceding these attacks had been enormous aerial and artillery bombardments, reducing the ancient monastery on the mountaintop to rubble. This, ironically, created a much more defensive position for the German paratroopers defending the mountain. The fourth attack, which was part of Alexander's spring offensive, involved both the 5th and 8th Armies. Its aim was for the 13th Corps of 8th Army and 2nd Polish Division to advance on Cassino, along with the Free French Corps advancing to the east down the Liri Valley, while the bridgehead at Anzio broke out in the direction of Valmontone. On 11 May the artillery laid down a massive barrage which, when lifted, enabled the 13th

Corps and the Poles, who had suffered enormous losses, to break through and eventually capture Monte Cassino from the crack German paratroopers. The French also made a rapid advance and breached the Hitler Line, behind the Gustav Line, with relative ease.

The 23 May saw the breakout of the Anzio beachhead and the encirclement of the German forces seemed inevitable. But before this movement could be successfully concluded, Mark Clark's gaze fell on Rome. He was adamant that he and his 5th Army would be the ones to liberate the city, and he did not want to share the glory. He ordered Truscott to alter his advance even before his objective was complete, much to Truscott's annoyance. This change of advance opened up a salient big enough for the German army to slip through yet again and fight another day. A great decisive maneuver was lost. Rome fell on 4 June to Clark's 5th Army, as planned, with no shots fired. There were, however, to be many more months of fighting left in Italy and Clark's "glory" was to be eclipsed by the great undertaking that unfolded on the shores of northern France two days later.

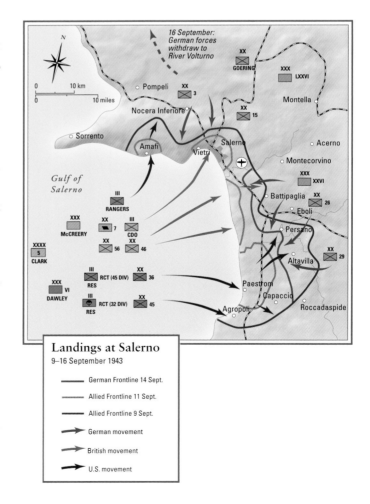

Landings at Salerno
9–16 September 1943

——— German Frontline 14 Sept.
- - - Allied Frontline 11 Sept.
——— Allied Frontline 9 Sept.
——→ German movement
——→ British movement
——→ U.S. movement

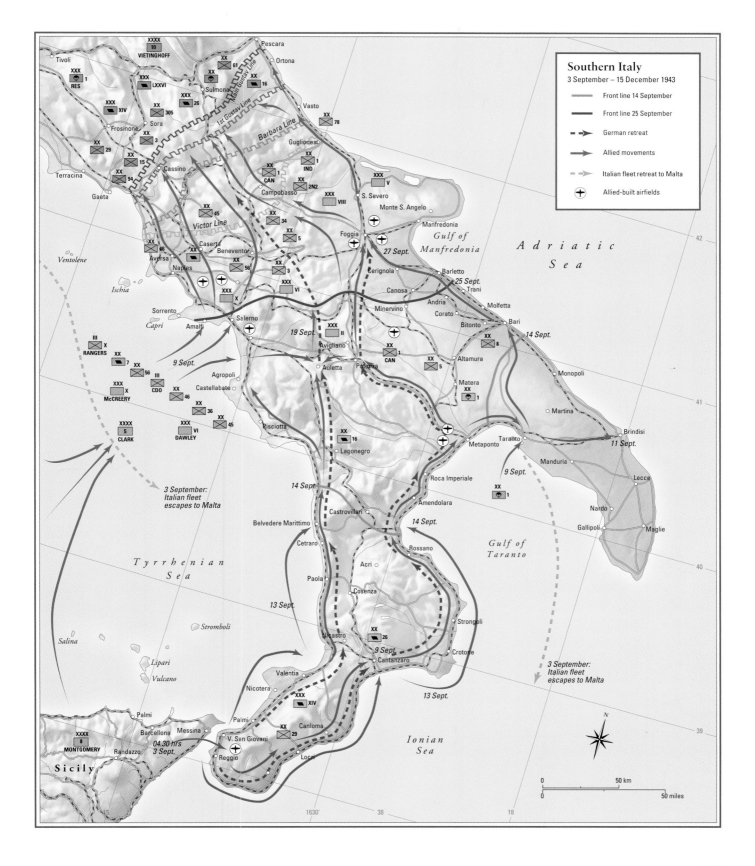

Southern Italy
3 September – 15 December 1943

Front line 14 September
Front line 25 September
German retreat
Allied movements
Italian fleet retreat to Malta
Allied-built airfields

THE UKRAINE 1943–44

"To a distant land is our comrade departing,

His native winds a sad farewell are piping,

His beloved town, his home, his lover's tender gaze,

Vanish with his native fields in a deep blue haze."

POPULAR RUSSIAN WARTIME SONG

The five months from August to December 1944 witnessed one of the great battles of the Soviet–German war: the Battle of the River Dnieper. The Soviet plan involved five fronts or army groups, over 2,600,000 men, 50,000 heavy mortars and guns, 2,400 tanks (and mobile assault guns) supported by almost 2,800 aircraft. Facing this huge force was the German 2nd Army, part of the Army Group Center commanded by Field Marshal von Kluge; the 4th Panzer; and the 1st, 6th and 8th Armies from Army Group South, commanded by von Manstein. Total German forces available were 1,240,000 men, 12,600 guns, 2,100 tanks and assault guns, and 2,100 aircraft. The Soviets enjoyed an advantage in men and guns but the balance was about even in tanks and aircraft.

Planning and implementation for this huge campaign began as the Battle for Kursk developed in July 1943, and finally ended in defeat for the German offensive, Operation Citadel. The initial aim was to liberate the eastern Ukraine, with its valuable industrial areas of the Donbass, then to advance and liberate Kiev. This would take place on a 400-mile front, involving many separate operations. The distinctive feature of these would be numerous river crossings. As usual, the Red Army soldiers were driven hard by their commanders. At river crossings they were sent over on anything that could float: timbers

lashed together, oil drums, or whatever came to hand to gain a bridgehead, before engineers came to build a sturdy structure capable of supporting tanks and trucks.

On 13 August, the right wing of the Soviet Steppe Front, under General Ivan Konev, launched its attack in the direction of Krasnograd. Three days later another attack began from a bridgehead on the northern Donets River, all as part of the Donbass Offensive that lasted until 22 September. The Southwest Front, supported by the 17th Air Army, attacked German Army Group South and Luftflotte (Airfleet) 4. By December they had reached the Dnieper River just south of the city of Dnepropetrovsk.

Meanwhile, on 26 August in the north, the Soviet Center Front had attacked German Army Group Center, under the command of von Kluge, who had appealed to Hitler for permission to fall back to a more defensible line along the Dnieper River. Hitler refused, and ordered the Germans to hold their ground at all costs. Hitler did give permission, however, for General von Manstein's Army Group South to fall back to a line between the city of Melitopol and the Dnieper. The Führer also sent four divisions of reinforcements from the hard-pressed Army Group Center.

Army Group South's withdrawal to its new line was, in the face of massive odds, a bold maneuver. Three armies withdrew, fighting to keep the enemy at bay each

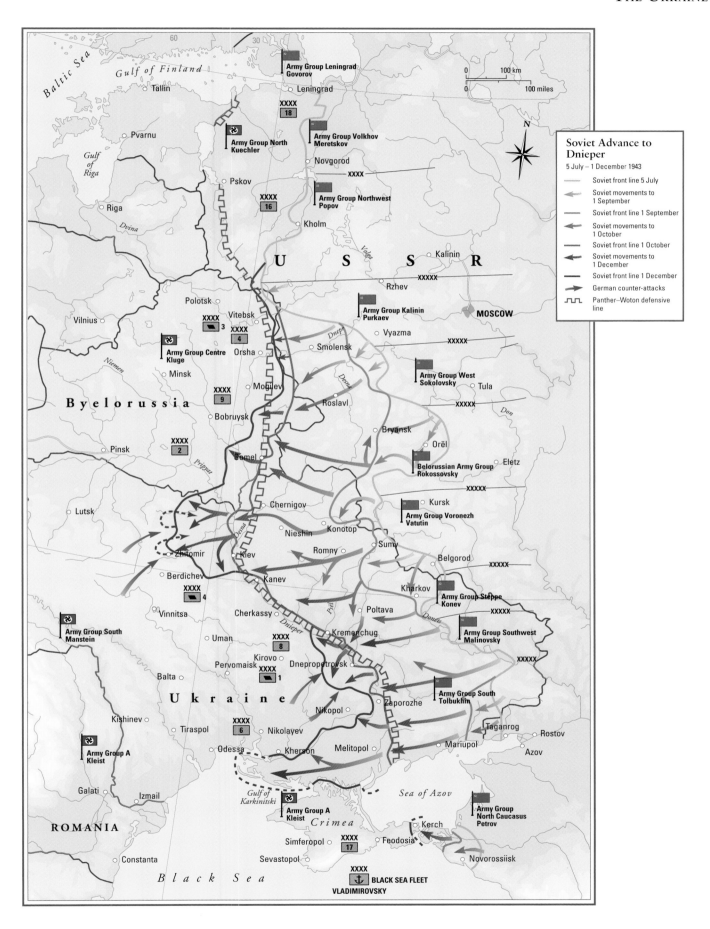

Soviet Advance to Dnieper
5 July – 1 December 1943

Soviet front line 5 July
Soviet movements to 1 September
Soviet front line 1 September
Soviet movements to 1 October
Soviet front line 1 October
Soviet movements to 1 December
Soviet front line 1 December
German counter-attacks
Panther–Woton defensive line

step of the way, and converging on just five crossing points of the Dnieper. Safely across, they fanned out to redeploy west of the river, all accomplished without the pursuing Soviets gaining a foothold.

There was no let up for the Germans, however, since the Soviets immediately ordered men across the river and successfully seized small bridgeheads on the west bank at Bukrin and Rzhishchev. On the night of 24/25 September they attempted an airborne landing in support, which was not entirely successful. However, the surviving airborne troops from this operation fought on behind German lines. The main Soviet group of fronts now approached the Dnieper line on a front of almost 500 miles. Early in October, Soviet forces reached Zaporozhye, and once there they found abandoned river barges, which they used to cross the river. Two weeks later, another bridgehead was established to the north, at Lyutezh. Kiev was finally liberated after fierce fighting on 6 November. By that time there were numerous bridgeheads across the river and Hitler's defense line, although stubbornly defended, did not hold. In the north, Smolensk had also been liberated. In the south a massive group of Soviet forces attacked out of the Zaporozhye bridgehead and along the northern shore of the Sea of Azov, trapping the German 17th Army, part of Army Group A, in the Crimea.

By the end of 1943, the Soviet forces on the Southern Front had consolidated their gains and were ready for further offensive operations. The German hope that winter would slow them down, giving time for replacements and new equipment to arrive, was dashed. On 24 December attacks were launched toward Zhitomir and Korosten by the 1st Ukrainian Front, and on 5 January 1944, Kirovgrad was captured by Konev's 2nd Ukrainian Front. The advances threatened the positions of the German 8th and 1st Panzer Armies, but as usual, Hitler forbade withdrawal: they were encircled, trapping 60,000 Germans at Zvenigorodka. Von Manstein counterattacked, almost reaching the surrounded troops, then, after bitter fighting on the night of 16/17 February, the cut-off troops attempted a breakout. Some 20,000–30,000 escaped, although Soviet sources claim that a lot less survived.

On 4 March, the 1st Ukrainian Front, commanded by Zhukov, attacked through the mud of an early spring thaw, then was joined 24 hours later by the 3rd Ukrainian Front. In the face of this massive onslaught, there was little the German commanders could do; it seemed likely that the 2nd Ukrainian Front, in the north, would meet up with the 1st Ukrainian Front from the southwest of Vinnitsa. This time they could trap the remains of the 1st Panzer Army at Kamenets-Podolsky. Meanwhile, the 2nd Ukrainian Front moved into Moldavia, threatening Army Group A and forcing the Germans to fall back to the line of the River Bug.

Von Manstein pleaded with Hitler for reinforcements and the Führer gave way, sending the 2nd Panzer Corps from France. This newly-arrived Corps launched an attack linking up with 1st Panzer Army near Ternopol. After all his efforts von Manstein lost his command. It was renamed Army Group North Ukraine and given to Field Marshal Walter Model. Further south, Army Group A was renamed Army Group South Ukraine, von Kleist dismissed and replaced by General Ferdinand Schörner. By the time these changes were made, the River Bug Line was breached and Odessa liberated. Soviet troops crossed the border into Romania on 10 April. The Ukraine was free, or at least in Soviet hands.

Further east, in the Crimea, the German 17th Army was still cut off. Hitler, following his usual approach, refused any suggestion of withdrawal. Instead he had dispatched reinforcements and, by April 1944, there were 76,000 German and 46,000 Romanian troops facing three Soviet armies of 500,000 men. The Soviets attacked on 8 April and in 18 days the Germans and Romanians had been pushed back into the fortress city of Sevastopol. This, in turn, fell on 5 May, with less than 1,000 survivors escaping by sea to Romania. The Crimea was Soviet again.

PUSHING ONWARD
Russian troops set off across the Dnieper River as they advance in the Ukraine. By now, their forward momentum through Soviet territory was unstoppable.

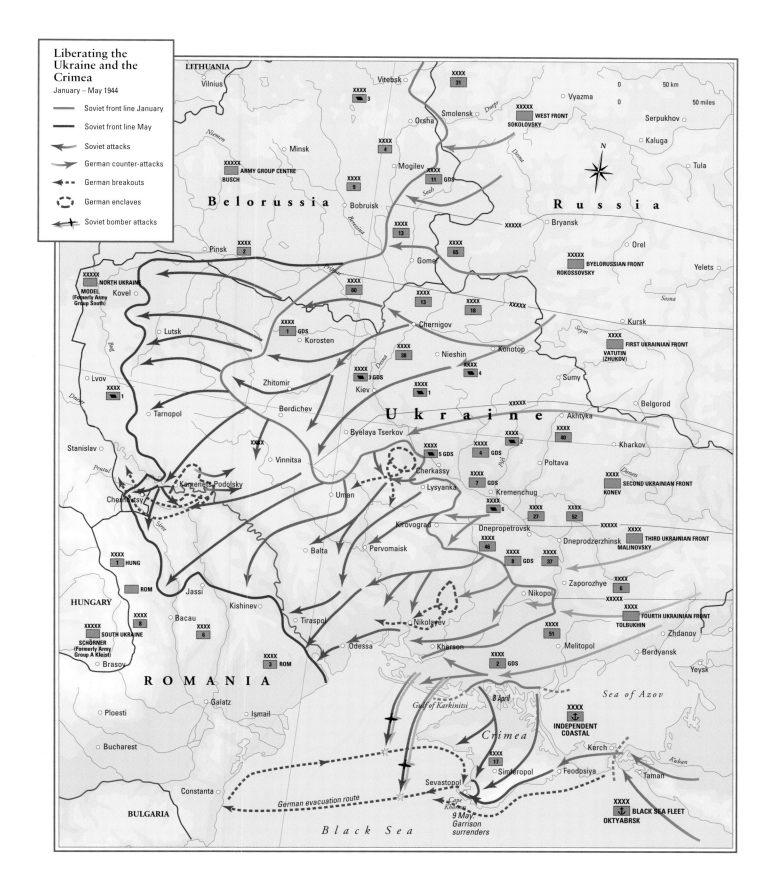

Liberating the Ukraine and the Crimea
January – May 1944

- ▬▬ Soviet front line January
- ▬▬ Soviet front line May
- ➤ Soviet attacks
- ➤ German counter-attacks
- ◄┅┅ German breakouts
- ◌ German enclaves
- ◄┼ Soviet bomber attacks

LITHUANIA
Vilnius
Niemen
Minsk

Belorussia

XXXXX ARMY GROUP CENTRE BUSCH
Pinsk
XXXX 2
XXXXX NORTH UKRAINE MODEL (Formerly Army Group South)
Kovel
Bug
Lutsk
XXXX 1 GDS
Korosten
Lvov
XXXX 1
Zhitomir
Tarnopol
Dnestr
Stanislav
Prutul
XXXX
Vinnitsa
Kamenets Podolsky
Chernovtsy
Siret
XXXX 1 HUNG
ROM
Jassi
HUNGARY
XXXX 8
XXXXX SOUTH UKRAINE SCHÖRNER (Formerly Army Group A Kleist)
Bacau
XXXX 6
Brasov
XXXX 3 ROM
ROMANIA
Galatz
Ismail
Ploesti
Bucharest
Constanta
German evacuation route
BULGARIA

Vitebsk
XXXX 31
XXXX 3
Orsha
Smolensk
Dnepr
Mogilev
XXXX 4
XXXX 9
XXXX 11 GDS
Bobruisk
Berezina
XXXX 13
Sozh
Gomel
XXXX 65
Pripet
XXXX 60
Chernigov
XXXX 13
XXXX 18
Desna
XXXX 38
Nieshin
Konotop
XXXX 3 GDS
XXXX 4
Kiev
XXXX 1
Ukraine
Berdichev
Byelaya Tserkov
XXXX 5 GDS
XXXX 4 GDS
XXXX 2
Cherkassy
Uman
Lysyanka
XXXX 7 GDS
Kremenchug
Psel
XXXX 6
Kirovograd
XXXX 27
XXXX 52
Pervomaisk
Balta
XXXX 46
Dnepropetrovsk
Dneprodzerzhinsk
XXXX 8 GDS
XXXX 37
Nikopol
Zaporozhye
XXXX 6
Kishinev
XXXX 6
Tiraspol
Nikolayev
Odessa
Kherson
XXXX 51
XXXX 2 GDS
Melitopol
Berdyansk

Vyazma
Serpukhov
XXXXX WEST FRONT SOKOLOVSKY
Kaluga
Tula
Russia
Bryansk
Orel
Yelets
XXXXX BYELORUSSIAN FRONT ROKOSSOVSKY
Sosna
Kursk
Seym
XXXXX FIRST UKRAINIAN FRONT VATUTIN (ZHUKOV)
Sumy
Belgorod
Akhtyka
XXXX 40
Kharkov
Poltava
XXXX SECOND UKRAINIAN FRONT KONEV
Donets
XXXXX THIRD UKRAINIAN FRONT MALINOVSKY
XXXXX FOURTH UKRAINIAN FRONT TOLBUKHIN
Zhdanov
Yeysk

N

0   50 km
0   50 miles

Sea of Azov
8 April
XXXX ⚓ INDEPENDENT COASTAL
Kerch
Kuban
Taman
Crimea
XXXX 17
Simferopol
Feodosiya
Sevastopol
Cape Khorson
9 May: Garrison surrenders
XXXX ⚓ BLACK SEA FLEET OKTYABRSK
Gulf of Karkinitsi
Black Sea

RESISTANCE 1941–44

"Whatever happens, the flame of French resistance must not be extinguished and will not be extinguished."

GENERAL CHARLES DE GAULLE

Resistance networks were set up in all occupied territories to some degree, with each country reacting in their own unique way to counter Axis occupation, although these forces never unified to form a single national force. The majority of occupied countries aided resistance in some form or other, be it passively or actively. Resistance also helped the morale and self-respect of the occupied countries and helped them feel they were contributing to the war effort and to retain some national pride.

Active resistance involved gathering intelligence, which could be used locally and then sent via radio messages to Britain and other Allied countries, the aiding of escaped prisoners of war, sabotage of enemy installations, or ambush of enemy troops. Passive resistance could include strikes at important war production facilities, working at a slower rate, or demonstrating against the occupiers.

In order to resist effectively secrecy had to be complete; those who bragged, or were loose with their tongues, were soon found, arrested and, quite often, turned against their own side. Churchill, recognizing that Britain might need a resistance network should she be invaded, gave a directive for the Special Operations Executive (S.O.E.) to be set up. This agency set about recruiting and training men and women, especially those who had escaped from occupied countries. They would then be returned to their native country to raise and lead resistance movements, as well as sending back vital information. The S.O.E. also equipped these resistance

groups and armies, which ranged from the Maquis in France to the partisans in Yugoslavia. The United States also saw the need to create a clandestine operations unit and set up the Office of Strategic Services (O.S.S.). This unit operated, like its British counterpart, all over the globe and particularly aided the forces of Chiang Kai-shek in China, as well as forces in northern France before and after the Normandy landings.

During the period between May 1941 and August 1944 over 400 S.O.E. agents were dropped into occupied France, setting up many new networks and planning attacks so that the operations of the resistance were coordinated with the overall Allied plan. The most effective of these attacks was staged before D-Day in the sabotage of railroad lines and communications, severely disrupting German lines of supply. As well as direct sabotage, railroad workers either worked extremely slowly or not at all, effectively bringing the rail system to a halt. But reprisals could be harsh, as witnessed when the population of the French village of Oradour-sur-Glane were massacred.

The S.O.E. supported resistance movements in south-eastern Europe, particularly Greece and Yugoslavia. In Yugoslavia, the Republican Chetnik movement was at first supported with arms and radios, but when they were found to be ineffective and often collaborated with the enemy, S.O.E. aided the pro-Communist partisan movement led by Josip Broz, known as "Tito." His partisans, located deep in the mountains and well hidden from the enemy, formed an effective resistance force and

UNITED KINGDOM

LONDON

North Sea

French Resistance:
Industrial Sabotage
1942–44

☀ Sabotage location

Targets

F Fuel
P Power
A Aviation
M Military
I Industrial
T Transport
E Electrical
C Metals and chemicals

Date of Operation

● 1942
● 1943
● 1944

English Channel

50

Roubaix I

BELGIUM

I Lille
Willems F
T Fives-Lille
F Liéven
Douai
(Corbehem) F

Montataire T

Rouen
(Dieppedalle) E
I Déville-les-Rouen
Beaumont-sur-Oise I
I Asnières
Choisy-au-Bac T
Bar P
St. Georges P
Luneville T
Levallois-Perret M
Sevran T
A Courbevoie
Aubervilliers I
Ivry-sur-Seine I
Boulogne-sur-Seine I M
T Mantes
C Mantes-Gassicourt

Orléans (Chaigny) E
E Blois

F R A N C E

Belfort

A Bourges
Prémery C
Fourchambault A
M Monbéliard (Sochaux)

SWITZERLAND

Le Creusot P

46

*Bay of
Biscay*

Montluçon M T

Limoges (St. Marc) P

Ussel I
Clermont-Ferrand
A T
Lyons
(St. Fonds)
Lyons Villeurbanne I
Annecy I

N

Limoges
(Des Cassaux)
M Tulle
A Lyons
Lyons Venissieux
A T
Ugine P

Tulle (Virevialle) P
St. Etienne I
P Mauzac
Brive-la-Gaillarde E

Figeac A

Grenoble
C I

ITALY

Decazeville F

P Briançon

Garonne

Lot

Salindres C

Carmaux I
Montbartier C
Teillet (Argenty) E

Rhône

I Pau
Tarbes A M
Béziers
T
St. Marcel
L'Estaque C
Gardanne C
MONACO

M Bagnières de Bigorre
Lannemezan C
P Laruns
P Gripp
Sarrancolin
St. Lary P
Lavelanet P
Gulf of Lion

I
C

Bordères-
Louron
C

Tarascon-sur-Ariège C
Escouloubre P

SPAIN

Usson P

ANDORRA

Adour

Saône

0 ____ 50 km
0 ____ 50 miles

Tito soon became a target of the German occupying forces, narrowly avoiding capture and death several times. Although mainly supplied by the western Allies, Tito often fell out with U.S. and British liaison officers because of his close links to Stalin and the Communist cause. After the war Tito was to rise to become the Prime Minister of the country but later broke his links with the Stalinist regimes of eastern Europe.

In Norway there were many active resistance groups but perhaps the most famous was the group that attacked the German heavy-water plant, essential to Nazi ambitions to produce an atomic weapon. The operation entailed dropping S.O.E.-trained Norwegians with detailed knowledge of the area by parachute, to make a reconnaissance of the plant at Vemork. After this was completed they were to be joined by Royal Engineers landing in two gliders on a frozen lake. However, poor weather caused the gliders to crash land and the survivors were captured, tortured, and shot. The Norwegians managed to survive the horrific winter in hiding, living on lichen and moss, and eventually, on the point of starvation, killing a reindeer. As spring approached the S.O.E. dropped in more Norwegian commandos, who succeeded in breaking into the plant, setting explosive charges and making their escape. The heavy-water stocks were destroyed in the explosion and all ten of the commandos successfully escaped, without having fired a shot. Six skied to neutral Sweden; four stayed to continue the fight alongside the local resistance.

The German occupation of the Soviet Union was brutal in the extreme with villagers hanged, entire village populations exterminated, and arbitrary machine-gunning of men, women, and children. As the Germans advanced, many villagers fled into the forests, often becoming partisans engaged in guerrilla warfare against the invaders. The experience of this cruelty and suffering motivated ordinary people to fight back, even though German army orders were to shoot captured partisans or bury them alive to increase their agony and as an example to the local population. The story of partisan schoolgirl, Zoya Kosmodemyanskaya, who was tortured and hanged, became widely known. Elsewhere in Russia a woman partisan pretending to be a housemaid blew up a German commander known as the "Butcher of Byelorussia."

The partisans were especially effective operating out of the vast Pripet Marshes near Pinsk. The partisan group, the Young Guard of the Donbass—teenagers and students—sabotaged army positions around the German garrisons until they were all eventually captured, tortured,

and buried alive in their local coal mines. The courageous stand of the partisan movement generated hope, but the Soviet military did little to support them because they were suspicious of armed locals.

Large-scale resistance took place in Poland, occupied since September 1939 by both Germany and the U.S.S.R., and after 1941 by Germany alone. The country became a center for repression and extermination. The Polish resistance collected information to send to London and attacked German supply lines and garrisons. Perhaps, therefore, it is no surprise that the greatest uprising in occupied Europe happened in Poland.

The Warsaw Uprising began in August 1944, lasting until 2 October, after 63 days of combat. By 1944, Warsaw was the center of Polish resistance carried out by the Polish Home Army. This force was supported by and was loyal to the anti-Communist Polish government in exile. Led by General Tadeusz Komorowski, known as General Bor, the Home Army sought to expel the German army before Soviet forces reached Warsaw.

During the German siege, Red Army General Rokossovsky reached the outskirts of the city but failed to cross the River Vistula. The Russians refused to aid the Home Army and sat back watching German air raids pulverizing the city, while Stalin refused to let U.S. airplanes use Soviet airstrips as bases to parachute supplies to the Polish resistance fighters. Finally, on 18 September, one flight was allowed. It consisted of 110 B-17s, but it was too little too late.

Between 150,000 and 180,000 citizens of Warsaw died in the uprising and its aftermath, with the Germans sending many surrendered resistance fighters to concentration camps and then systematically destroying the city. Now, with all independent Polish resistance having been eradicated by the Germans, the Red Army entered Warsaw and established a Soviet-sponsored Committee of National Liberation, which imposed a Communist provisional government on Poland on 1 January 1945. Soviet control of Poland was recognized by the Allies at the 1945 Potsdam Conference.

In the Far East there were many resistance units. The most significant were the Hukbalap, or "The People's Army Against the Japanese," based in the Philippines. They grew to 20,000 active combatants, who often fought the Americans as well as the Japanese in order to throw out any occupying power. In Malaya and Burma there were also active guerrilla movements, but these were not as well supported by the Allies, mainly because of their Communist leanings.

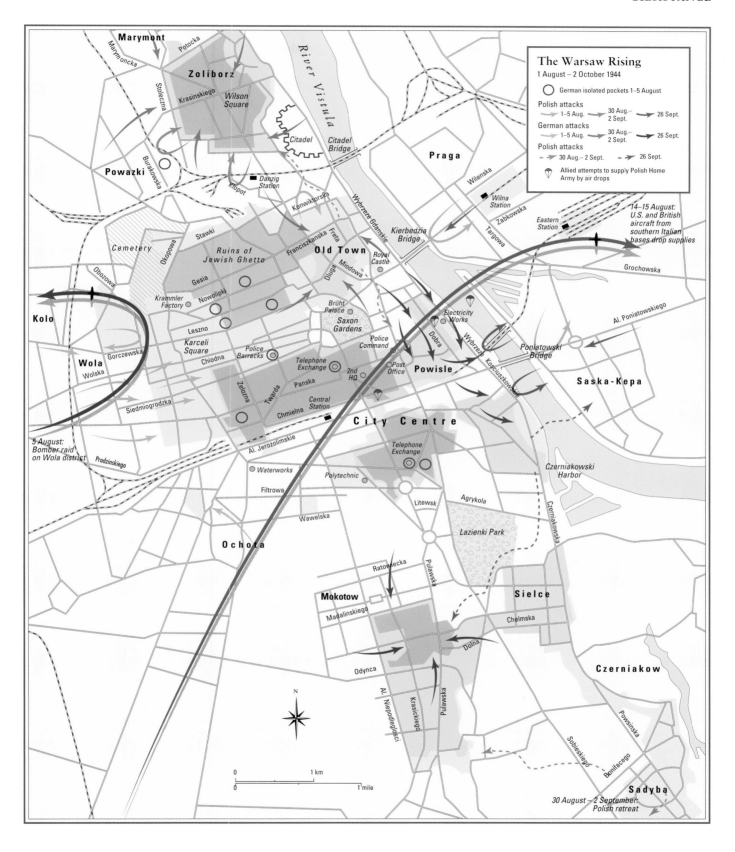

The Warsaw Rising
1 August – 2 October 1944

○ German isolated pockets 1–5 August

Polish attacks
→ 1–5 Aug.   → 30 Aug.–   → 26 Sept.
                   2 Sept.
German attacks
→ 1–5 Aug.   → 30 Aug.–   → 26 Sept.
                   2 Sept.
Polish attacks
---→ 30 Aug. – 2 Sept.   ---→ 26 Sept.

⊽ Allied attempts to supply Polish Home
   Army by air drops

14–15 August:
U.S. and British
aircraft from
southern Italian
bases drop supplies

5 August:
Bomber raid
on Wola district

30 August – 2 September.
Polish retreat

THE BALKANS 1941–44

"Into battle against the Fascist occupation hordes who are striving to dominate the whole world."

TITO, PARTISAN LEADER
CALLING ON THE PEOPLE OF YUGOSLAVIA, 4 JULY 1941

After his invasion of the Balkans, Hitler reorganized the region, mostly along national lines. The following states were established: Croatia, largely pro-German; Serbia, occupied by Germany; Bosnia, occupied by Germany; Herzegovina, occupied by Italy; Montenegro, under Italian administration; Kosovo and western Macedonia, under Italian control and joined administratively to Albania. The rest of Macedonia was administered by Bulgaria. Other smaller areas were transferred to Hungary. In Greece, Thrace was administered by Bulgaria while the area immediately adjacent to the Turkish border, Demotila, was occupied by Germany, as were the areas around Salonika, Athens, and some of the major Greek islands. The rest came under Italian occupation

In Yugoslavia, after the German conquest, remnants of the army took to the mountains, led mostly by Serb officers, who became known as the Chetniks, under the command of Drage Mihailovich. His plan was to restore the monarchy, then, when the Allies returned, to take revenge on the Communists. In Croatia, however, under the Ustaša resistance group, a campaign of genocide was launched against the region's Serbs, with the Jews, gypsies, and Communists also marked out for extermination.

Amongst all of this developing situation emerged Josip Broz Tito, who took his Communist partisans to war. Firstly, he contested western Serbia with Mihailovich and his Chetniks, before moving into any area he could extend his influence. Mihailovich appealed to the Germans for arms in order to crush the Communists, but they refused. He then went to war with the partisans, almost throwing them out of Serbia. A civil war broke out in Serbia, spreading to the rest of the country, but the Communist partisans still held on, surviving until the German-led offensives of Weiss and Schwarz in the first half of 1943.

By April, Tito's forces were also receiving aid from the British. With the Italian surrender, Tito claimed the right to recognition as the future ruler of post-war Yugoslavia. He also stated that his forces—300,000-strong—were tying down as many Axis forces as the western Allies were in Italy. He was also busy destroying his Chetnik rivals in Serbia. To help toward this end, he asked Stalin to divert part of the advancing Red Army. Stalin agreed and Belgrade fell on 20 October 1944. The partisans were left to chase the Germans out of Yugoslavia.

Albania had organized a Communist-led liberation movement in 1942. They faced a pro-Axis republican movement, the Balli Kombëtar. When Axis forces withdrew, the Communists overcame their republican rivals, forming a government in the fall of 1944.

In Greece, Communists were the first to form an effective resistance movement, and by 1943 the National Popular Liberation Army (E.L.A.S.) was well-organized. As the Germans withdrew E.L.A.S. failed to fill the vacuum quickly enough, allowing the British-backed government to assume control. They did not know that Stalin had abandoned them under a deal with Churchill, in which Greece came under the British sphere of influence.

Vienna • Bratislava

GREATER GERMANY

Graz

Varazdin

Zagreb
Karlovac
Blagaj • Prekopa • Gudovac
Jasenovac
• Stara Gradiska
Banja Luka

CROATIA
• Jajce
Travnik

Sarajevo

Dubrovnik

MONT.

Adriatic Sea

HUNGARY

Budapest

Subotica

Szegek Arad

Nyiregyhaza

Debrecen

Oradea Dej
Cluj

Carpathians

Botosani

Jassy Chisinau

Bocau

Sibiu Brasov

ROMANIA

Buzau

Galati
Tulcea

Banjika
Belgrade

Turnu-Severin

Uzice

SERBIA

Nis

Mitrovica
Pristina

Kyustendil

Skopje

MACEDONIA

ALBANIA

Monastir

Berat

Edessa

Pitesti Ploesti

Craiova Bucharest

Vidin
Giurgiu
Ruse

Sofia

BULGARIA

Stara Zagora

Plovdiv
Khaskovo Erdirne

Xanthi Komotine
Drama
Serrai Alexandroupolis
Kilkis
Salonica *Thasos*
Kozani
Katerine *Samothrace*

Black Sea

Varna

Burgas

Constanta

Istanbul

Sea of Marmara

ITALY
Allied to Germany until September 1943

Brindisi

Ionian Sea

Corfu
Ionnena
Trikkala

Arta

GREECE
Lamia

Missolonghi
Patrai

Pyrgos
Tripolis

Larisa

Lemnos

Aegean Sea

Khalkis
Marathon
Corinth Athens
Andros

Kalahai

Monemyasia

Khios

Lesvos

Izmir

TURKEY

Tinos

Naxos

Balkans
1941–44

▮ Massacre sites

● Concentration camps

▤ Occupied by Germany

☐ Allied to Germany

▨ Pro Axis. Occupied by Italy and Germany

▨ Occupied by Italy, with limited German support

N

0   100 km

0   100 miles

BOMBING OF GERMANY 1943–44

"After Hamburg in the wide circle of political and military high command could be heard the words 'the war is lost.'"

COLONEL ADOLF GALLAND, LUFTWAFFE

Air Chief Marshal "Bomber" Harris inaugurated his area-bombing strategy with the Battle of the Ruhr, a six-week assault on Germany's industrial heart. This battle also included the Dambusters raid against the Möhne and Eder dams. Crews flying modified Lancasters dropped "bouncing bombs," mines that skimmed across the reservoir then sank to the base of the dam before exploding. Next came the bombing of

Hamburg with Operation Gomorrah, four raids that decimated 60 percent of the city with firestorms, killing nearly 50,000 people.

FLYING FORTRESSES
American B-17s dropping bombs over Bremen in 1943. By now they were equipped with radar, meaning that they could locate targets accurately from above a blanket of cloud.

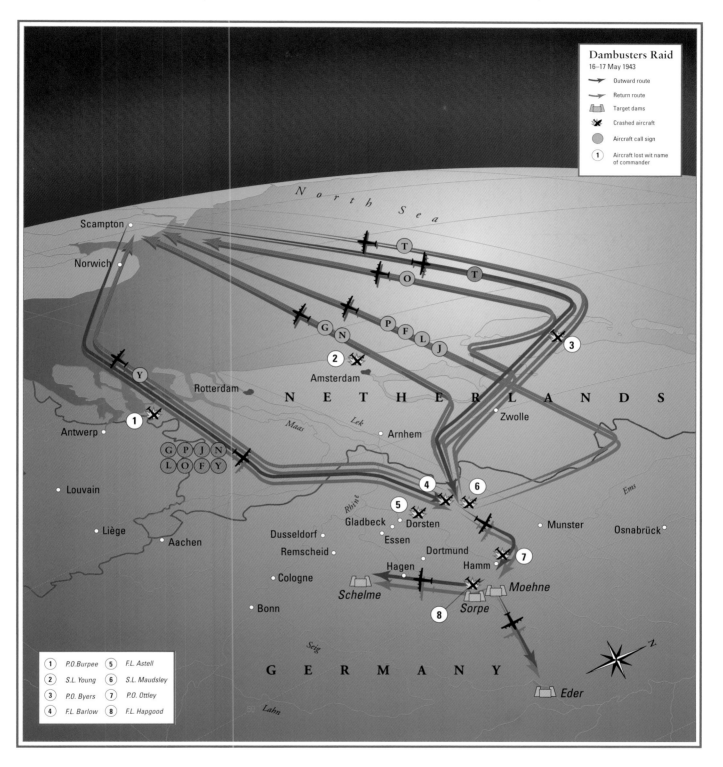

Dambusters Raid
16–17 May 1943

→ Outward route

→ Return route

⬯ Target dams

✕ Crashed aircraft

⬤ Aircraft call sign

① Aircraft lost wit name of commander

①	P.O.Burpee	⑤	F.L. Astell
②	S.L. Young	⑥	S.L. Maudsley
③	P.O. Byers	⑦	P.O. Ottley
④	F.L. Barlow	⑧	F.L. Hapgood

CRACKING THE DAMS *Operation Chastise, the Dambusters' raid, was carried out by 617 Squadron under the command of Guy Gibson. The crews flew in three formations, and took routes that were carefully planned to avoid concentrations of flak. They also flew at extremely low altitude whenever possible, so as to avoid radar detection. At one point, one of the Lancaster bombers passed along a firebreak in a forest, below the level of the treetops. The final approach to the dams also required expert low-level flying. Unless the aircraft were at precisely the right height, the bombs would not bounce properly over the torpedo nets in the dams' reservoir.*

By this time the U.S. 8th Air Force was well into its offensive against the Reich, flying "box" formations in which each aircraft provided cover for those around it. Despite this tactic, the Luftwaffe still managed to shoot down large numbers of bombers.

By mid-May the intensity of the raids had increased and the 8th Air Force started to penetrate deeper into the Reich. They attacked the Messerschmitt factory at Regensberg and the ball-bearing plant at Schweinfurt, but as these targets were out of range for the protecting fighters losses were heavy. By early 1944, the range of the escort fighters had been increased with the introduction of drop fuel-tanks that allowed the fighters to fly all the way to the targets and back. The Mustang proved to be the best all-round fighter of World War II. For the first time U.S. bombers enjoyed real protection.

The R.A.F.'s Bomber Command was also making attacks deep into enemy territory, flying a series of raids on Berlin in a campaign running from November 1943 to March 1944. These raids had a high price for the relatively small damage incurred, with 587 aircraft being lost and most of the crews killed or taken prisoner. To Harris's annoyance the Allied air offensive against Germany was called to a halt as the combined resources of Bomber Command and the U.S. 8th Air Force were required to help in the D-Day invasion of France and to attack the new German terror weapon, the VI flying bomb, or "Doodlebug," being launched from northern France against the south of England.

BOMBER HARRIS *Arthur Harris pores over a map. His stated aim was "the destruction of German cities, the killing of German workers, and the disruption of civilised life throughout Germany." Below, a U.S. B-24D.*

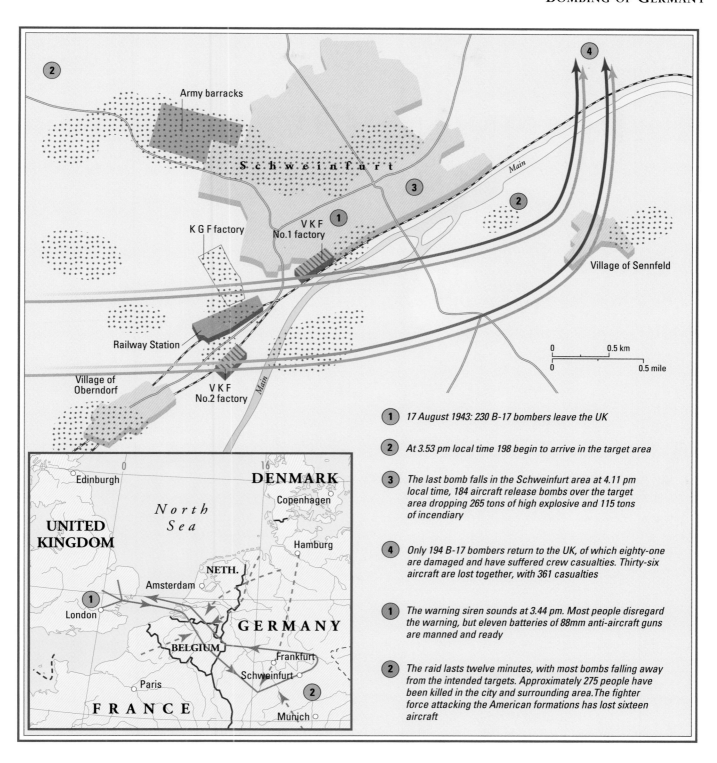

1. 17 August 1943: 230 B-17 bombers leave the UK

2. At 3.53 pm local time 198 begin to arrive in the target area

3. The last bomb falls in the Schweinfurt area at 4.11 pm local time, 184 aircraft release bombs over the target area dropping 265 tons of high explosive and 115 tons of incendiary

4. Only 194 B-17 bombers return to the UK, of which eighty-one are damaged and have suffered crew casualties. Thirty-six aircraft are lost together, with 361 casualties

1. The warning siren sounds at 3.44 pm. Most people disregard the warning, but eleven batteries of 88mm anti-aircraft guns are manned and ready

2. The raid lasts twelve minutes, with most bombs falling away from the intended targets. Approximately 275 people have been killed in the city and surrounding area. The fighter force attacking the American formations has lost sixteen aircraft

Schweinfurt Bombing Results

- Bombing areas
- Ball-bearing factories
- Planned approach flights

Inset
- Major German interceptions
- Bombers route

COSTLY MISSION *The ball-bearings produced in Schweinfurt were key components in all kinds of vehicles and armaments. And so in theory, destroying the factories would have a crippling effect on the entire German war machine. But 60 aircraft were lost in the mission, more than double the total of any previous raid. This was too high a price to pay. The heavy losses also made it impossible to follow up with a swift second strike, to prevent repairs being made to the factories. And, as it turned out, Germany held large stockpiles of ball-bearings elsewhere, so the effects of the August raid, and of the second raid in October, were minimal.*

PLANNING OVERLORD 1943–44

"The Enemy must be annihilated before he reaches our main battlefield… we must stop him in the water."

FIELD MARSHAL ERWIN ROMMEL, APRIL 1944

An ambitious plan for the invasion of Europe was presented at the Quebec conference in August 1943. The plan—Operation Overlord—had been devised by C.O.S.S.A.C., an organization headed by Lt.-General Frederick Morgan, the Chief of Staff to the Supreme Allied Commander. The object was to utilize forces and equipment in the UK to secure a lodgement area on the Continent, from which further offensive operations would be developed. The operation would be part of a concerted assault upon German-occupied Europe from the UK, the Mediterranean, and Russia.

Overlord depended upon resources that were not readily available at the time; the Sicily landings had taken place the month before the conference and, with Italy near to collapse, it was decided that landings should take place on the Italian mainland. This meant that landing craft that would need to be returned to Britain for the proposed invasion of France, and others that were to be redeployed to Burma, would be retained in the Mediterranean. The conference also accepted a U.S. proposal for landings in the south of France, as a diversion and an adjunct to Overlord. C.O.S.S.A.C. was instructed to proceed with detailed preparations for the invasion.

Ground forces, in the shape of the British 21st Army Group and U.S. 1st Army Group, were allocated to the operation. Two commanders had been appointed. The Overlord air commander was to be Sir Trafford Leigh-Mallory, whose Allied Expeditionary Air Force (A.E.A.F.) of fighters and day bombers was made up of the U.S. 9th Air Force and British 2nd Tactical Air Force, together with transport aircraft. The naval commander was to have been Admiral Sir Charles Little, but Churchill felt that he lacked the necessary capacity to deal with such a major undertaking. Instead, he proposed Sir Bertram Ramsay, the man who had masterminded the evacuation from Dunkirk, and had then been the deputy naval commander for the "Torch" landings in north Africa and in charge of the naval forces supporting the British landings on Sicily. Ramsay had also served as a member of the Combined Command. This proposal was accepted by the Combined Chiefs of Staff, although Ramsay would not return to Britain until December 1943. A land commander had yet to be chosen.

Meanwhile, other Allied landings went ahead. The British made virtually unopposed landings on the toe of Italy on 3 September 1943. In Lisbon, Portugal, on the same day, an Italian representative signed an armistice agreement with the Allies, kept secret until the second landing. This took place at Salerno on 8 September in the face of fierce and unexpected German opposition. There was also a serious flaw in the planning in that the beachhead was too wide for the available amphibious

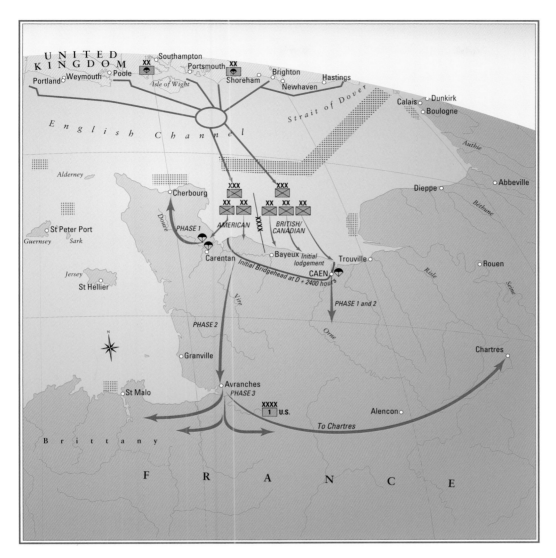

C.O.S.S.A.C.
Invasion Plan

April 1944

→ Assault divisions and follow up

Airborne landings

Initial bridgehead at 24.00 hrs

British minefields

German minefields

landing force, making it difficult to defend. Even so, the Germans eventually withdrew, enabling the Allies to break out. The Germans reacted quickly, pouring in reinforcements through northern Italy and taking advantage of the hilly and mountainous terrain. The fall rains slowed the Allied progress still further, and by the end of the year they were held up by the formidable Gustav Line in the mountains south of Rome.

The situation in Italy was to have a bearing on Overlord, as Allied relations became strained. In the aftermath of the Italian surrender, Churchill gave orders for the Greek Dodecanese islands in the Aegean to be occupied. It was part of his desire to bring Turkey into the war on the Allied side, and develop a campaign in the Balkans. The problem was that the British garrisons on the islands lacked air support and the Americans were not prepared to divert any from Italy. The German forces in Greece took advantage of this and overran the British garrison on the Dodecanese islands in October.

Meanwhile, the question over who would be the overall commander for Overlord was finally resolved. It had been agreed that he should be an American, while his subordinate single-service commanders were to be British. After some discussion in Washington, President Roosevelt appointed Eisenhower, who now had over a year's experience as an Allied coalition commander and the diplomatic skills to bind the Allies together, even if he had no combat experience at lower level. As for the ground commander, Montgomery was the obvious choice. In spite of his bumptious character, which did, at times, irritate the Americans, he had clarity of mind and drive, and had proved himself the most successful British general of the war so far.

At the beginning of January, Montgomery arrived back in Britain, while Eisenhower flew back to the States for a short break. Eisenhower had already seen a copy of the C.O.S.SA.C. plan for Overlord at the end of October 1943, well before he was given overall command of it,

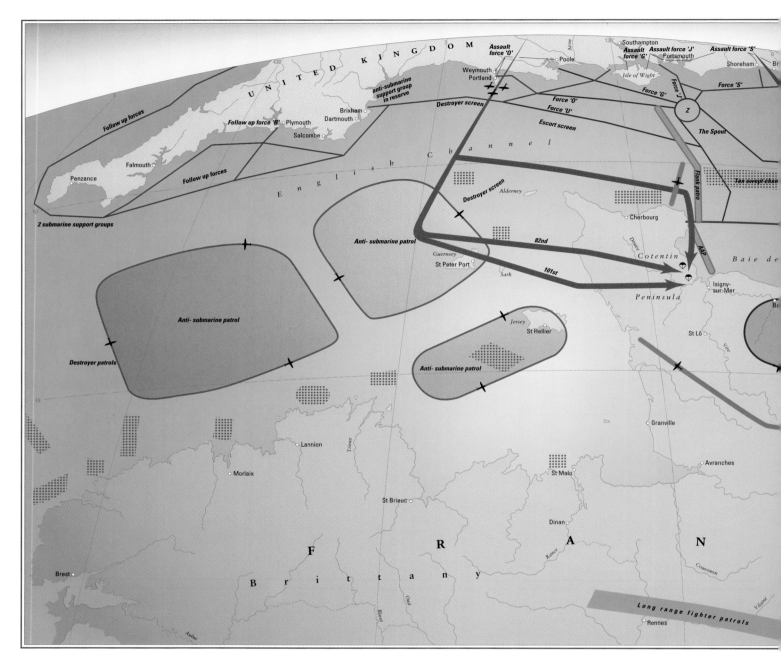

and commented that there was insufficient "punch" in the initial attack. Montgomery had his first sight of the plan when he was shown a copy by Churchill during a stopover at Marrakesh, on his way back to Britain. Montgomery agreed with Eisenhower's view, and also stated that the proposed landing front was too narrow, which would inevitably lead to congestion on the beaches as follow-up forces were landed. He wanted each corps to have a dedicated group of beaches so that its follow-up divisions could land on them.

On 3 January 1944, Montgomery convened the first of many meetings at St Paul's School, London. The C.O.S.S.A.C. staff presented their revised plan, which

Montgomery immediately criticized, pointing out all of its shortcomings. Four days later, he produced his own plan. The landing frontage had been greatly extended and now stretched from the east coast of the Cotentin peninsula to the west bank of the River Orne. Five divisions would now make the initial assault, two from the U.S. 1st Army in the west, and three from the British 2nd Army in the east. The task of the Americans would be to seize Cherbourg and then advance south and west into Brittany, and east towards Paris, while the British provided a shield for them. It was, in many ways, remarkably similar to the C.O.S.S.A.C. version of August 1943. But General Morgan's plan had been constrained by likely amphibious

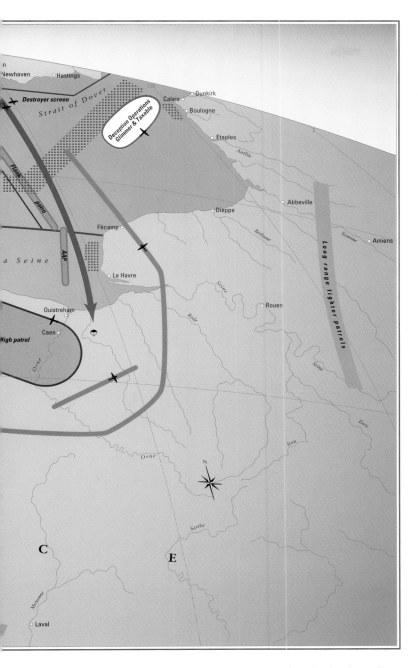

Air Plan for D-Day
June 1944

——— Swept channels
——— Neptune channels
::::::: British minefields
::::::: German minefields
⬭ Patrols (AAP-assault area patrols)
⬯ High air patrol
▬ Night fighter patrol lines
☂ Drop zones
↘ Air assault routes

held his first conference and approved Montgomery's plan. He was, however, very conscious of the shipping problem. In order to ensure that there was enough for the revised Overlord, he asked the Combined Chiefs of Staff if the invasion could be postponed until June. They eventually agreed, grudgingly, stipulating that D-Day—the date for the Normandy landings—must now be 31 May or a few days either side. There was also the question of the simultaneous landings in the south of France, codenamed "Anvil." The British, who had never really been in favor of them, pointed out that this operation merely served to aggravate the shipping problems and pressed for its cancellation.

Detailed beach reconnaissance was carried out by specialist teams. There was particular concern over the types of obstacle that the Germans were placing on the beaches. It would also be necessary to find beaches in Britain which were similar to those that would be encountered in Normandy, so that the assaulting troops could train on them. The U.S. assault divisions were the 1st Infantry Division, veterans of Tunisia and Sicily, and the unblooded 4th Infantry Division, which arrived in Britain in January 1944. The British contribution was much the same in terms of experience. The 50th (Northumbrian) Division had fought in North Africa from 1941 onwards, while the 3rd Infantry Division had not seen combat since France in 1940. The 3rd Canadian Division had been in Britain since arriving from Canada in July 1941. Of the airborne divisions, the U.S. 82nd had served in North Africa and Sicily, but the 101st was without combat experience, as was the British 6th Airborne Division. The divisions that had not seen recent combat did, however, have some veterans posted in. The ground forces trained intensively through the first months of 1944, while in secret offices around Britain, the minutiae of the largest invasion in human history were teased out.

shipping availability, and doubts remained whether there would be sufficient to support a five-division landing.

Eisenhower arrived in Britain on 12 January. Two days later, Morgan held his last weekly staff meeting, and on 17 January Eisenhower took over, with the H.Q. becoming Supreme Headquarters, Allied Expeditionary Force (S.H.A.E.F.). He had brought his own Chief of Staff, Walter Bedell Smith, and Morgan stepped into the background, although he remained on the S.H.A.E.F. staff.

At the same time, a Deputy Supreme Allied Commander was appointed, the British Air Marshal Arthur Tedder, with whom Eisenhower had worked closely in the Mediterranean. On 21 January, Eisenhower

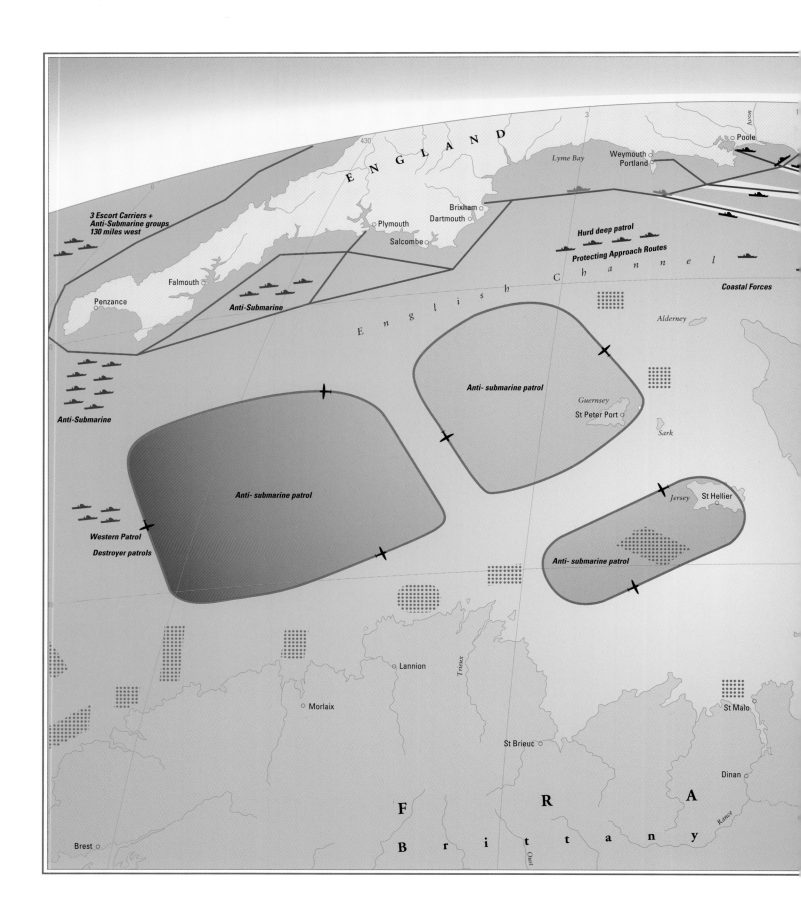

3 Escort Carriers +
Anti-Submarine groups
130 miles west

ENGLAND

430

Lyme Bay

Weymouth
Portland

Poole

Brixham
Dartmouth

Plymouth

Salcombe

Hurd deep patrol

Protecting Approach Routes

Falmouth

C   h   a   n   n   e   l

Coastal Forces

Penzance

Anti-Submarine

E   n   g   l   i   s   h

Alderney

Anti- submarine patrol

Guernsey

St Peter Port

Sark

Anti-Submarine

Anti- submarine patrol

St Hellier

Jersey

Anti- submarine patrol

Western Patrol

Destroyer patrols

Anti- submarine patrol

Lannion

Trieux

St Malo

Morlaix

St Brieuc

Dinan

F   R   A

B   r   i   t   t   a   n   y

Brest

Oust

Rance

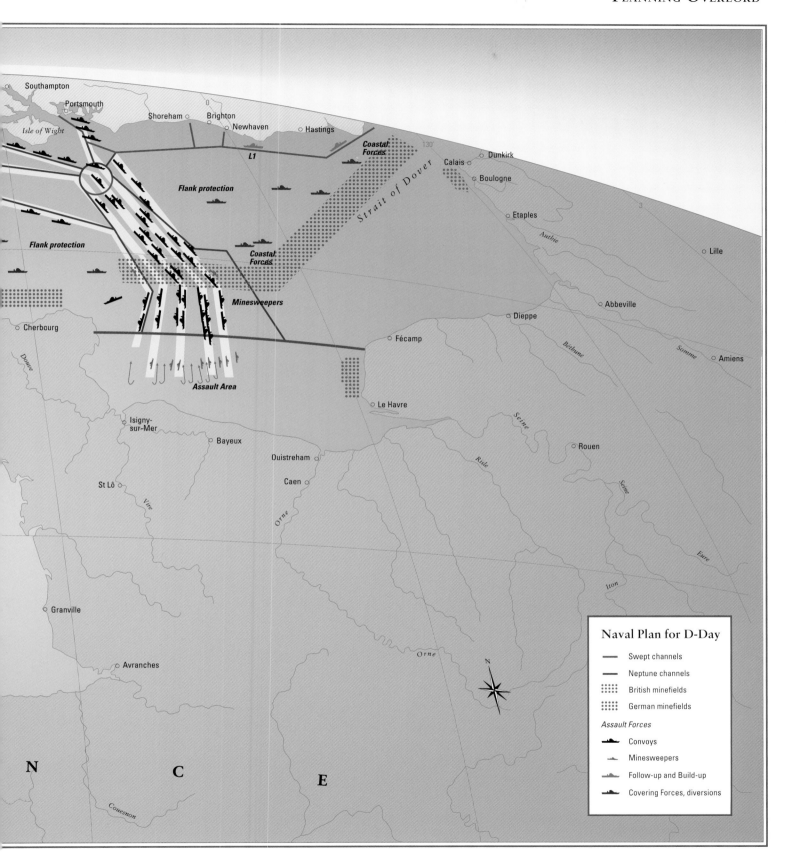

Southampton
Portsmouth
Shoreham
Brighton
Newhaven
Hastings
Isle of Wight
0
Coastal Forces
130'
L1
Dunkirk
Calais
Boulogne
Flank protection
Etaples
3
Strait of Dover
Authie
Lille
Flank protection
Coastal Forces
Minesweepers
Abbeville
Béthune
Dieppe
Somme
Cherbourg
Fécamp
Amiens
Assault Area
Le Havre
Donne
Isigny-sur-Mer
Seine
Bayeux
Ouistreham
Rouen
St Lô
Caen
Risle
Vire
Orne
Seine
Granville
Eure
Orne
Iton
N
Avranches
C
E
Couesnon

Naval Plan for D-Day

— Swept channels
— Neptune channels
⠿ British minefields
⠿ German minefields

Assault Forces

🚢 Convoys
🚢 Minesweepers
🚢 Follow-up and Build-up
🚢 Covering Forces, diversions

D-Day and the Battle of Normandy 1944

"Your task will not be an easy one ... your enemy is well-trained, well-equipped, and battle-hardened. He will fight savagely."

GENERAL DWIGHT D. EISENHOWER

On 6 June 1944, after months of meticulous planning, Allied forces mounted a full-scale invasion of German-occupied northern France. A prelude to "D-Day" had taken place at dusk on 5 June, when a series of airborne deception operations were mounted by Lancaster bombers of 617 Squadron, the "Dambusters." They overflew the Straits of Dover in an elliptical course, dropping strips of aluminium foil known as "Window." This metal snowstorm was intended to be picked up by German radar, on which it would be indistinguishable from a seaborne fleet of ships heading towards the Pas-de-Calais. Stirling aircraft of 218 Squadron carried out a similar exercise off Boulogne, while other Stirlings and Halifaxes dropped dummy parachutes and various firecracker devices designed to simulate rifle fire. These measures created the impression that airborne landings were taking place well away from the true drop zones (D.Z.s) of the two U.S. airborne divisions, whose vital task was to block the approaches to the landing beach that had been codenamed "Utah."

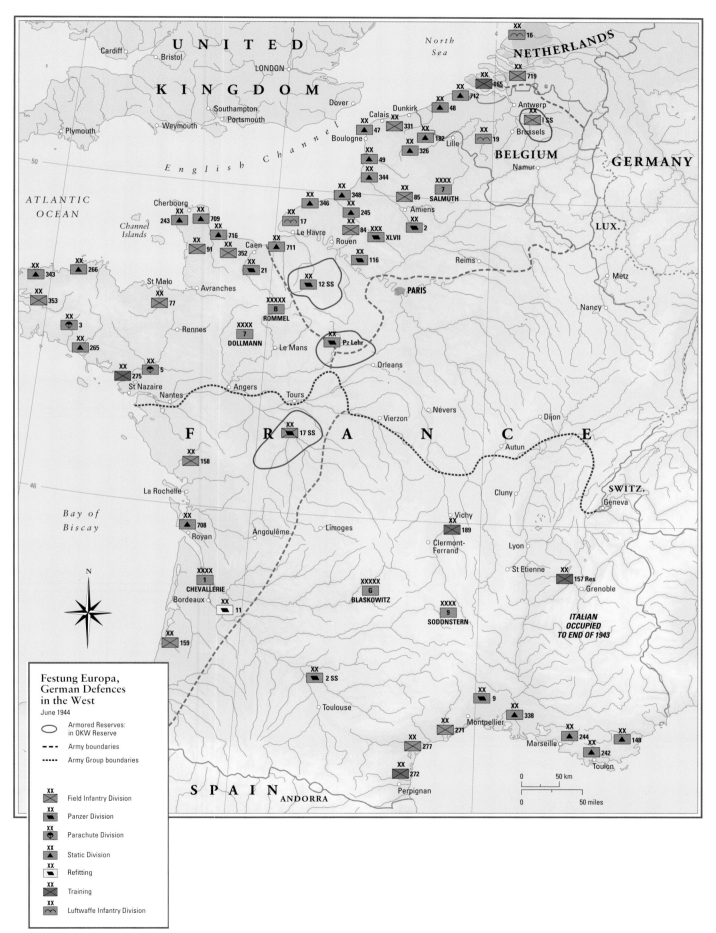

Festung Europa,
German Defences
in the West
June 1944

Armored Reserves:
in OKW Reserve

Army boundaries

Army Group boundaries

Field Infantry Division

Panzer Division

Parachute Division

Static Division

Refitting

Training

Luftwaffe Infantry Division

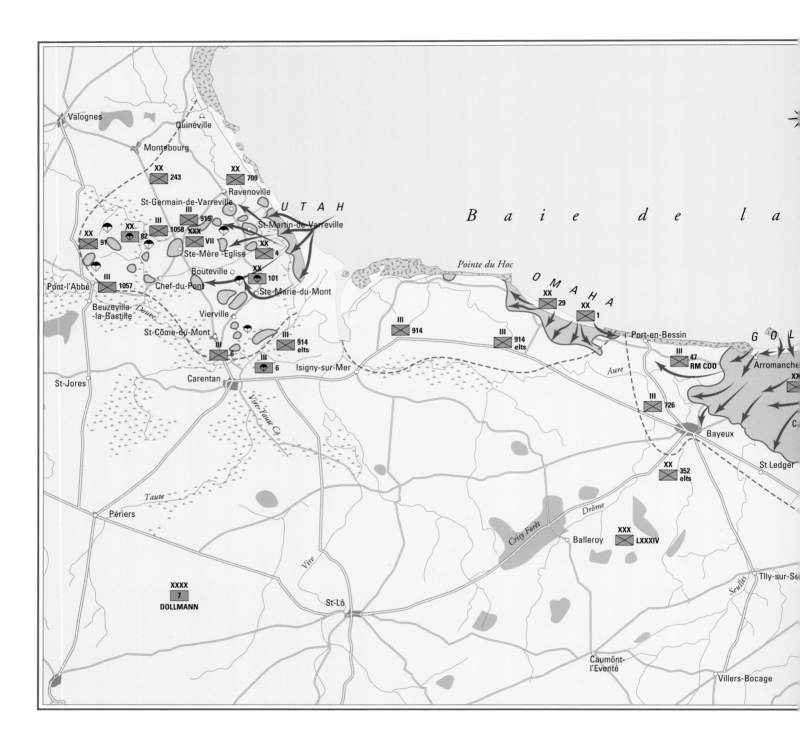

Valognes
Quinéville
Montebourg
XX 243
XX 709
Ravenoville
St-Germain-de-Varreville
III 919
III 1058
XXX
St-Martin-de-Varreville
XX 91
XX 82
VII
Ste-Mère-Eglise
XX 4
III 1057
Bouteville
XX 101
Pont-l'Abbé
Chef-du-Pont
Ste-Marie-du-Mont
Beuzeville
-la-Bastille
Douve
Vierville
St-Côme-du-Mont
III 6
III 914 elts
III 6
St-Jores
Carentan
Isigny-sur-Mer
Vire-Taute C4
UTAH
Baie de la
Pointe du Hoc
OMAHA
XX 29
XX 1
Port-en-Bessin
GOL
III 47 RM CDO
Arromanche
III 914
III 914 elts
Aure
III 726
Bayeux
St Ledger
Taute
XX 352 elts
Périers
Drôme
Crisy Forêt
Balleroy
XXX LXXXIV
Seulles
Tlly-sur-Se
Vire
XXXX 7 DOLLMANN
St-Lô
Caumont-l'Eventé
Villers-Bocage

THE USS ARKANSAS

Launched in 1911, the USS Arkanas was the oldest U.S. battleship to serve in World War II. Her primary armament was twelve 12-inch guns and she supported the Omaha landings and the assault on Cherbourg.

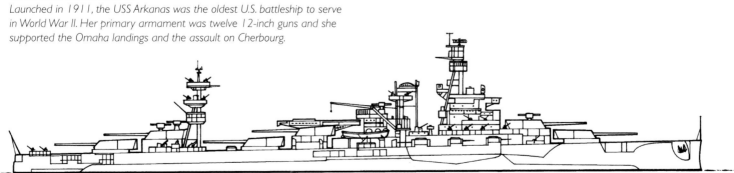

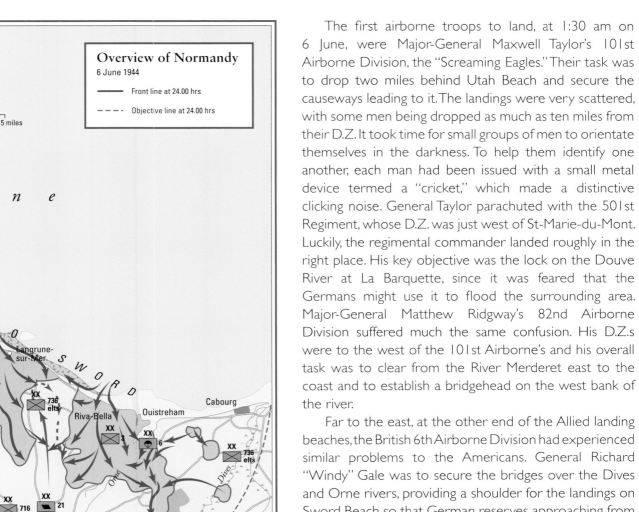

Overview of Normandy
6 June 1944

—————— Front line at 24.00 hrs

- - - - - - Objective line at 24.00 hrs

0   5 km

0   5 miles

Seine

JUNO

SWORD

Courseulles-sur-Mer

Langrune-sur-Mer

50

XX 51

XX 736 elts

XX 736 elts

Riva-Bella

Ouistreham

Cabourg

XX 3

XX 6

XX 736 elts

Orne

Dives

XX 716

XX 21

Carpiquet

Caen

Troarn

XXX 1 SS

Odon

XX 12 SS

o Bourguébus

Vimont

The first airborne troops to land, at 1:30 am on 6 June, were Major-General Maxwell Taylor's 101st Airborne Division, the "Screaming Eagles." Their task was to drop two miles behind Utah Beach and secure the causeways leading to it. The landings were very scattered, with some men being dropped as much as ten miles from their D.Z. It took time for small groups of men to orientate themselves in the darkness. To help them identify one another, each man had been issued with a small metal device termed a "cricket," which made a distinctive clicking noise. General Taylor parachuted with the 501st Regiment, whose D.Z. was just west of St-Marie-du-Mont. Luckily, the regimental commander landed roughly in the right place. His key objective was the lock on the Douve River at La Barquette, since it was feared that the Germans might use it to flood the surrounding area. Major-General Matthew Ridgway's 82nd Airborne Division suffered much the same confusion. His D.Z.s were to the west of the 101st Airborne's and his overall task was to clear from the River Merderet east to the coast and to establish a bridgehead on the west bank of the river.

Far to the east, at the other end of the Allied landing beaches, the British 6th Airborne Division had experienced similar problems to the Americans. General Richard "Windy" Gale was to secure the bridges over the Dives and Orne rivers, providing a shoulder for the landings on Sword Beach so that German reserves approaching from the east and south-east could be blocked. He also had to capture and destroy a coastal battery at Merville, which would otherwise be able to fire into the flank of the Sword landing. The next phase of the plan was a daring glider operation. A company of the 2nd Oxfordshire and Buckinghamshire Light Infantry, under the command of Major John Howard, took off in six gliders, their objective the bridges over the River Orne and Caen Canal at Bénouville. Three gliders had been allocated to each bridge and all would land on the narrow strip between the two waterways.

THE HMS WARSPITE

A veteran of Jutland in May 1916, she also saw extensive service in World War II, including Norway in 1940 and the Mediterranean. On D-Day her eight 15-inch guns were used to silence German batteries at Villerville.

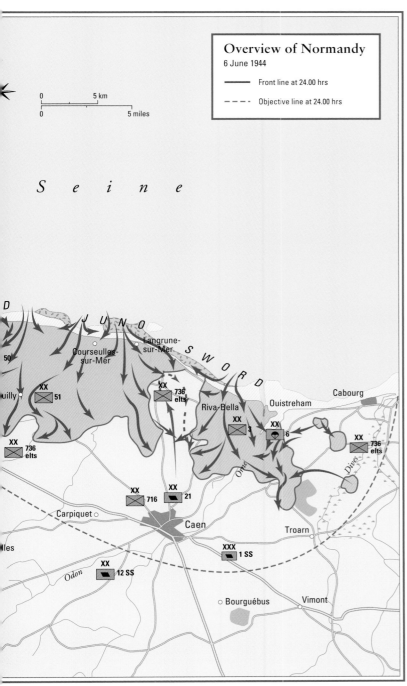

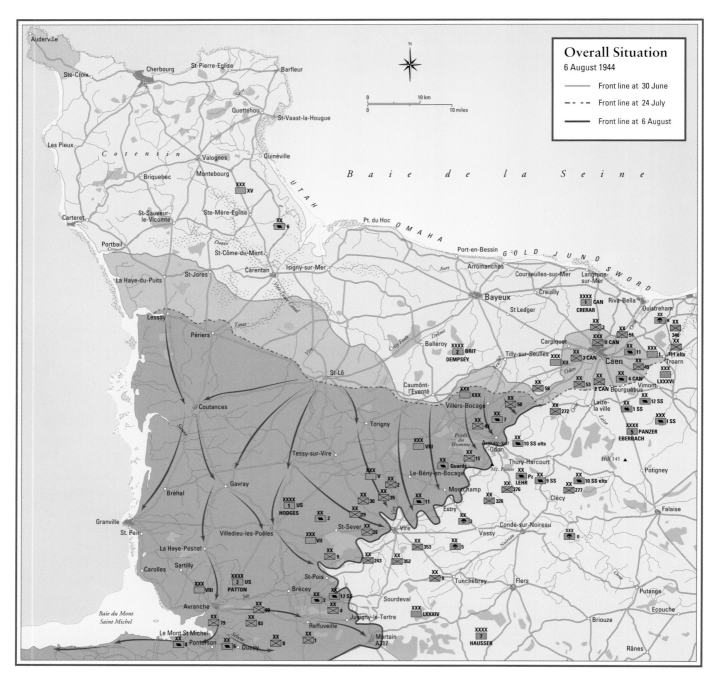

There were other necessary preliminaries to the actual beach landings. First, Bomber Command attacked the coastal batteries, dropping almost 5,000 tons of bombs, mostly through heavy cloud. The bombers partly overcame the poor visibility by using "Oboe," a radar system fitted to Mosquitoes, the fast, light bombers that would mark the target for the heavier bombers. With the coming of daylight, the U.S. 8th and 9th Air Forces would join in, together with medium bombers, fighter-bombers, and fighters of the British 2nd Allies Tactical Air Force. On D-Day the Allies flew almost 15,000 air sorties, while the Germans were able to manage only 319.

It was now the turn of the Allied navies. Each of the five task forces was preceded by minesweepers. Such was the success of their operations that only two vessels were sunk in the Channel on D-Day. By 2:00 am on 6 June the minesweepers were off the beaches. They had two tasks: to clear the approaches of mines and also the lanes that the bombarding ships would use. They faced a problem in that the Germans had laid several delayed-action mines, which remained on the sea bottom until activated. Consequently no stretch of water could be guaranteed totally free of mines. This was, in fact, the major cause of loss of Allied ships off Normandy.

The bombarding ships' task was to silence the German coastal batteries and they were organized in three groups. The heavier vessels in each task force—battleships, monitors, and cruisers—were positioned some 11,000 yards from the coast and operated in lanes parallel to the shoreline, in which they could maneuver. The destroyers, on the other hand, had to approach within 5,500 yards and then anchor. Although this made them more vulnerable to German fire, they would be less prone to falling victim to the delayed-action mines.

It was the Germans who opened fire first. With the coming of dawn, they began to spot ships through the murk. At 5:05 am a battery opened fire on the destroyers USS Fitch and USS Corry off Utah Beach.

Utah was the responsibility of General J. Lawton Collins' U.S. 7th Corps. A veteran of the Pacific campaigns on Guadalcanal and New Georgia, he was now tasked with cutting off the Cotentin peninsula and securing Cherbourg. Utah itself was less than a mile and a half long and characterized by gently sloping sand backed by a sea wall, between four and twelve feet high. Behind the beach there was some flooding, which made the causeways leading inland from the beach vital.

Because the beach was relatively narrow, Collins decided that the initial landing would be made by just one reinforced Regimental Combat Team (R.C.T.) of the 4th Infantry Division. This unit was to advance off the beach to the River Merderet and link up with the airborne troops. Eighty-five minutes after H-hour (the time of the first attack), a second R.C.T. would land and move north to secure Quinéville. The 4th Division's final R.C.T. would land at H+4 hours, advance northwest and seize a crossing over the Merderet. Finally, a Reserve R.C.T., from 90th Division, would also land. Amphibious Sherman D.D. tanks would also float ashore to support the first wave of troops landing.

The landings on Omaha began at 6:30 am, with the amphibious tanks supporting 116th R.C.T. launched. Almost immediately, some tanks began to founder in the rough sea and only five out of thirty-two reached the shore. Three survived only thanks to the L.C.T. commander pulling up his ramp when the first of the tanks he was carrying sank. Those carrying the tanks to support the other R.C.T. also ran into the shore and landed them one minute before H-hour.

Some of the landing craft in the leading waves were swamped during the run-in and as a result, almost all their supporting field artillery was lost. Poor visibility and the current played its part, as on Utah, with troops landing in the wrong place and being disorientated. Many landed shoulder-deep in water and struggled to carry their equipment ashore.

Under intense German fire, many fell. Those who did make it onto dry land sought shelter under the sea wall or among the beach obstacles, but many found that their radios did not work. Officers running between groups to

MISSION OF MERCY
British medical orderlies tend a badly wounded German officer on the Normandy battlefield.

try to restore some semblance of cohesion were shot down, and total confusion reigned.

Some six miles east of Omaha was the westernmost of the British beaches, Gold. The terrain here was somewhat different to Omaha. The beach was fringed merely by low sand dunes and behind it lay somewhat boggy ground intersected by dykes.

One problem was that much of the foreshore was made up of blue clay, which made it difficult for vehicles to traverse. Gold Beach lay in the eastern part of 352nd Division's sector and was covered by two battalions, supported by the Division's mobile reserve, which consisted of a further three battalions. The beaches had both underwater and exposed obstacles, which included mines attached to posts. There were also plenty of strongpoints overlooking the beach and the villages were well fortified.

The Royal Marine Commando was tasked with landing on the right flank of 231st Brigade and then advancing west to seize Port-en-Bessin and link up with the Americans who were battling their way up Omaha. Sword Beach presented many of the same problems as the adjacent Canadian sector, codenamed Juno. Shoals meant that the landing area was restricted. Behind the beaches the ground was generally low-lying, apart from the high ground that ran to Caen on the east flank.

The Allies had fought their way ashore in reasonable order, except for Omaha where bloody fighting had taken place. The U.S. 1st and 29th Divisions, despite all odds, had fought through terrible obstacles and intense small arms fire to seize the heights beyond the beach. While they had failed to secure many of their objectives, the Allies could feel content. They had succeeded in landing 150,000 men in Normandy at a cost of 9,000 casualties, less than many had feared. The experience gained in previous amphibious operations had proved invaluable.

But much still needed to be done. The five beachheads had to be linked up and expanded. Follow-up forces needed to be landed quickly so that the initial success could be exploited. At the same time, while a major German counterattack had not materialized on D-Day itself, it was certain to come soon. As for the Germans, the day had been bewildering, catching many by surprise. Yet they were still unconvinced that the landings in Normandy were a full-scale invasion, and not a feint. An assault elsewhere was still possible. With a significant armored force now gathering, there was still time to defeat the Allies before they advanced far inland.

The main concern was still Omaha Beach, one that General Omar Bradley, commanding the U.S. 1st Army, shared. Apart from the fact that its beachhead was the shallowest of the five, there was a yawning gap between it and the British 2nd Army, which could be easily exploited by Rommel. Montgomery therefore decided that he would have to postpone U.S. 7th Corps' advance to Cherbourg from Utah Beach. Instead, it was to link up with Omaha. To keep the Germans distracted, the British and Canadians were to continue to advance inland. To Rommel, sitting in his headquarters at the La Roche Guyon château, on a loop in the Seine near Bonnières, Caen and Cherbourg were the two principal areas of interest. As long as both were held, the Allies would have neither a firm left flank nor a useful port. Meanwhile, the Allies continued to grind on. West of Caen, the Canadians attacked on 3 July, their objective Carpiquet airfield. They managed to secure the village of the same name but their old adversary, 12th S.S. Panzer Division, denied them the airfield. This, however, was a mere preliminary to the main assault on Caen.

General Miles Dempsey, commanding the British 2nd Army, decided that maximum firepower was the key that would unlock the door. That night 450 heavy bombers blasted the northern outskirts. At 11:00 pm the artillery opened fire, pounding the German positions. At 4:20 am on 8 June, 90 minutes before sunrise, the D-Day veterans of 3rd Infantry Division and the newly-arrived 59th Division attacked. Numbed by the ferocity of the preparatory bombardment, the Germans in the forward defenses succumbed quickly.

The 3rd Canadian Division now began to attack from the west. By the end of the day it and the British 3rd Division had advanced two and a half miles, but 59th Division's progress was not as good, resulting in a two-mile gap between the former two formations. But the pressure on 12th S.S. Panzer Division had become almost unbearable and that night General Heinrich Eberbach agreed that all German forces around and in the city could withdraw to the south bank of the Odon.

The Americans, too, had begun to press south. Montgomery's concept was for them to now swing south and east from Caumont and then attack into Brittany as well as breaking out eastward. To Bradley the crucial first objective to enable all this to happen was the road communications center at Saint-Lô. With his 14 divisions now in place, outnumbering the Germans opposite 1st Army by at least three to one, it appeared straightforward. The terrain, however, was against him. Along the 50 miles of American front there were no open areas where he could deploy armor en masse. In the east the deep valley of the River Vire and the tenacious German hold on Saint-Lô itself gave him few options. The center of the sector was dominated by flooding with just one decent road, running from Carentan to Périers, while the west was covered with thickly-wooded hills and ridges.

Nevertheless, to Bradley the right flank seemed to offer the best prospects, and it was here that the U.S. 8th Corps kicked off the offensive on 3 July. Its opponent was the German 84th Corps, formerly commanded by one-legged General Erich Marcks, who had been killed by a U.S. fighter-bomber on 12 June, and now under General Dietrich von Choltitz. The new commander took maximum advantage of the terrain to make the American advance slow and costly. The U.S. 19th and 7th Corps experienced much the same frustration and by 10 July Bradley was forced to call a halt, even though Saint-Lô was still firmly in German hands. But the attrition was having its effect. The German 88th Corps warned: "The struggle cannot be maintained with the present forces for any length of time."

The American forces broke through by launching Operation Cobra, sweeping south and west into Brittany. Other elements of the U.S. forces headed to Rennes, then turned east, heading first for Le Mans and then turning north to Alençon and Argentan. Here they were to meet the British and Canadians heading south from the battles around Caen. Despite disagreements, the Allies closed in on the retreating Germans at Falaise. The annihilation of the Falaise pocket marked the end of the Battle for Normandy.

ON THE ALERT

U.S. paratroops moving towards their rendezvous in Normandy. They had numerous minor clashes with Germans on D-Day and had to be always on the lookout for surprise attack.

Assault of Southern France

"Where are we going? We are going to hold till hell freezes over or we are relieved, which ever comes first."

LT.–COLONEL WILLIAM P. YARBOROUGH,
COMMANDER OF 509TH PARACHUTE BATTALION

The planning for the invasion of southern France went through many drafts before the final concept was born. Churchill was keen for a landing to be made in the Balkan region so as to place British troops on the eastern front and achieve a presence there before Stalin could bring the region under his own control. But it looked to U.S. commanders like Churchill was trying to stake a colonial claim under a pretext of strategic necessity, and they dismissed the plan. At one point the plan had been to make a landing in the south of France that coincided with Operation Overlord, the invasion of Normandy. But this was ruled out, as the Allies did not have enough landing craft to support both ventures simultaneously.

The plan, as finally approved, was to land three divisions of the U.S. 6th Corps on the French Riviera, between the Golfe de Napoule and the Baie de Cavalaire. This force, under the command of General Lucian Truscott, was transferred from Italy for the task. It was to be flanked by French commandos and the U.S. 1st Special Service Force. There was also to be an airborne landing made up of Anglo-American forces, combining to form the 1st Airborne Task Force, which was to be dropped near Le Muy in order to cause havoc behind the lines. Following up these assaulting Corps was French Army B,

comprising seven divisions under the command of General de Lattre de Tassigny. The air support was to be supplied by the 12th Tactical Army Air Force flying from bases on Corsica and Sardinia, which itself was to be supplemented by fighter aircraft from seven Royal Navy and two U.S. carriers.

FIGHTING THE CHAMPAGNE CAMPAIGN
U.S troops arrive in the old port of Marseilles at the beginning of Operation Dragoon. As the invasion developed it became clear that the Germans would offer less resistance than anticipated and, indeed, they began a fighting withdrawal to the north. The operation became known to the men as the "Champagne Campaign."

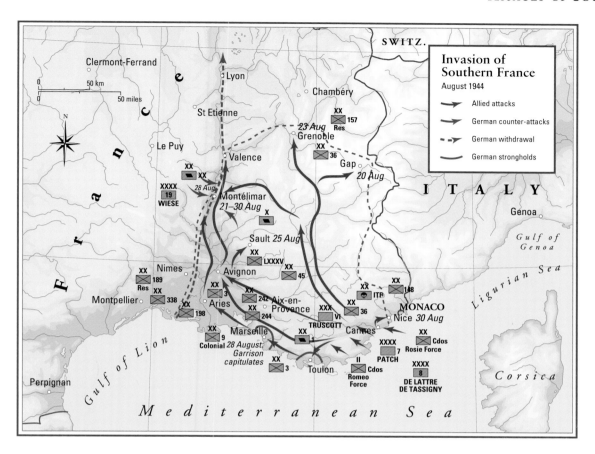

Opposing the Allied Task Force were around ten German divisions under the command of General Blaskowitz with only three divisions in the immediate area of the assault beaches. Air superiority was enjoyed by the Allies, since the Germans could only muster 200 aircraft to the 2,000 Allied.

The landings were, as usual, preceded by a massive aerial and naval bombardment. Underwater demolition teams of sappers were also sent in to clear paths through the extensive underwater obstacles. The 3rd Division landed with relative ease on the western beach known as Alpha Beach, thanks to the bombardment neutralizing the defenders, with a similar landing for the 45th Division on Delta Beach. On Camel Beach, where the 36th Division landed, they encountered thick enemy minefields as well as dug in machine-gun posts that took a serious toll on the soldiers assaulting. By the end of the day a strong bridgehead had been achieved. The following day saw the link up of troops moving inland from the beach with the airborne units.

Once through the main line of defense on and around the shoreline, the strategy was one of pursuit and entrapment, so Truscott struck northwest toward Avignon and north toward Sisteron. The French II Corps turned toward the two ports of Toulon and Marseilles

and expected a strong fight as Hitler had given the order for them to become "fortresses" and hold out in order to deprive the Allies of any useful port. The French attacked to the rear of Toulon, which was protected by three fortified hills, with the port protected from the sea by massive guns taken from a scuttled French battleship La Provence. The hills were taken by 23 August and the French began to assault the port itself, with bombardments from the sea aiding them. These bombardments took a heavy toll on the German defenders and Allied ships sailed into the harbor on the 26th, with the formal surrender of the German defenders on 28 August.

By the beginning of September the American forces had swept northward, giving chase to the German division past Grenoble and Valence, though the strong resistance of 11th Panzer Division aided in Blaskowitz's army's escape north before it could be trapped. Lyon fell on 3 September shortly followed by Dijon on 11 September, only a day after Truscott's forces had joined up with elements of Patton's 3rd Army. Then on 15 September all the Dragoon forces were placed under the command of Eisenhower, with their advance slowing because it was outstretching its supply columns coming up from the south. The Dragoon forces had managed to advance some 400 miles in 40 days.

LIBERATION OF PARIS & BRUSSELS

"Attended a thanksgiving service ... for the liberation of Paris ... hearing the Marseillaise gave me a great thrill. France seemed to wake again."

GENERAL SIR ALAN BROOKE, CHIEF OF IMPERIAL GENERAL STAFF

As Allied forces broke out of Normandy, the population of Paris began to feel that liberation was almost upon them. Railroad workers in the French capital went on strike on 10 August in order to make difficulties for the Germans, and the police followed suit five days later. These actions were to be followed by a general strike of all the capital's workers on 18 August.

The joyful anticipation of Parisians notwithstanding, Eisenhower wanted to delay the liberation of Paris for as long as possible. It would divert vital supplies that were still coming ashore through the beachheads to feeding the population of a major city instead of feeding and fueling his troops in the headlong pursuit of the Germans. But as the civil population grew bolder and began to build barricades in the streets and attack the German garrison, Eisenhower had no choice but to divert forces for the liberation.

De Gaulle insisted that the forces to liberate Paris were to be French and for this task he chose elements of General Leclerc's 2nd Armored Division. This unit was fighting with the U.S. 5th Corps under General Gerow at the time, and he was ordered to send a force of ten armored cars and a similar number of tanks to drive for the capital immediately. Fighting in the capital between the Germans and the civilian population had reached a

critical point by the time the French force entered Paris. General Choltitz, the commander of the German garrison, had been given explicit orders from the Führer to fight for every brick and stone of Paris. This was one order he was not to carry out: no one would want to be known in history as the destroyer of such art and architecture. Choltitz signed the surrender document on the afternoon of 25 August. Many of his troops did put down their arms, although not immediately, for fear of attacks of retribution from the population of the city, eager for revenge after years of exploitation and occupation.

A victory parade was organized hastily for the next day. Troops marched down the Champs Elysées, with the crowd still under occasional sniper attack. Another parade was held for the U.S. liberators a few days later.

Meanwhile, the Allied forces were flooding across the Seine and any useable bridge, with pontoon bridges being built at any appropriate point. The Allied pursuit gained momentum, fighting only small skirmishes, trying not to let the enemy use any of the rivers on the line of its retreat as a defensive position. Montgomery's 21st Army Group advanced on the left, the Canadians captured the ports of Le Havre, Dieppe, Boulogne, and Calais, while British 2nd Army drove onto Amiens and Lille. South of Montgomery's group was Hodge's 1st Army, which had

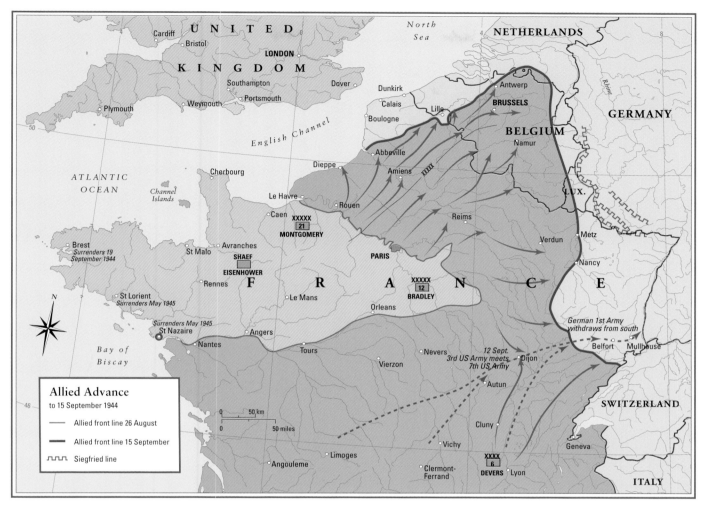

Allied Advance
to 15 September 1944

——— Allied front line 26 August

━━━ Allied front line 15 September

⊓⊔⊓⊔ Siegfried line

taken Mons and Tournai on 2 September, and was now heading toward the Meuse and the German border. Further south was Patton's 3rd Army, which was advancing at an astonishing rate. However, by the end of August, the enemy was not to be the Germans but a severe lack of fuel, and the Allied advance came to a standstill.

When the British heard of the capture of Tournai they felt confident that nearby Brussels could be taken with just as much ease. The Guards Armored Division, which was in the vanguard of the British advance, was ordered to race ahead and capture the city. This they did within 24 hours of receipt of the order, to be greeted not by the enemy, the last of whom had left that morning, but by a throng of joyous Belgians, lining the streets in their thousands. Yet another city had been liberated from the dying Nazi empire.

FREE PARIS

Hitler's order that Paris be defended was disobeyed by General Choltitz, who later claimed that his courageous insubordination had saved the city from ruin. Whatever his motives, the street-fighting was almost over by the time that Free French forces entered the city.

OPERATION MARKET GARDEN

"Hand grenades flew in every direction. Each house had to be taken this way. Some of the British offered resistance to their last breath."

GERMAN SOLDIER, ARNHEM

Operation Market Garden was a plan conceived by Montgomery as a means of flanking the German defensive line known as the West Wall, or Siegfried Line, and driving down into the Ruhr from the Netherlands, bringing the war in the west to a close. It would also secure a crossing point for the River Rhine, which the Germans regarded as their strongest defensive line. The mission was to use the First Allied Airborne Army under the tactical command of Lt-General Browning. This was made up of two American divisions, the veteran 82nd and 101st, and the British 1st. These divisions were to be dropped behind the lines to seize the bridges over eight waterways in Holland. The 30th Corps would use the bridges as it broke through the lines to meet up with the 1st Division dropped around Arnhem. Flanking attacks were to be contained by the 43rd and 50th Division.

The "Market" part of the plan involved the airborne forces, the 101st Division, which would drop nearest to the 30th Corps start line at Eindhoven. To the north would be the 82nd Division, under Major-General Gavin, taking the bridges at Grave and Nijmegen. Just to the northeast would be the 1st Airborne Division, taking the final bridge at Arnhem over the Lower Rhine, under

General Roy Urquart. This massive undertaking was to be the largest airborne operation of the war, eclipsing even Overlord. Nearly 35,000 men were to be parachuted in, but due to lack of air transport for them all they would have to be dropped over several days.

The "Garden" part of the plan would concern the 30th Corps' rapid advance up the single narrow highway, through all towns and bridges captured by the airborne troops for an eventual link up with the 1st Airborne at Arnhem. To cover the 60-odd miles to Arnhem, General Horrocks, commander of 30th Corps, said they would have three days. Battles, however, tend not to run to strict timetables. Intelligence from the Dutch Resistance also indicated that there were two German Panzer divisions refitting in the area north of Arnhem, although these were deemed not to be strong enough to pose a real threat. In fact, these forces were full of veteran soldiers who had spent time on the Eastern Front, as well as being augmented by the crack troops of 1st Parachute Army under the command of General Kurt Student.

In the early afternoon of 17 September the 2,800 troop-carrying aircraft and 1,600 gliders also packed with troops, jeeps, and artillery, made their way over the Dutch countryside, protected by over 1,200 fighter escorts. All

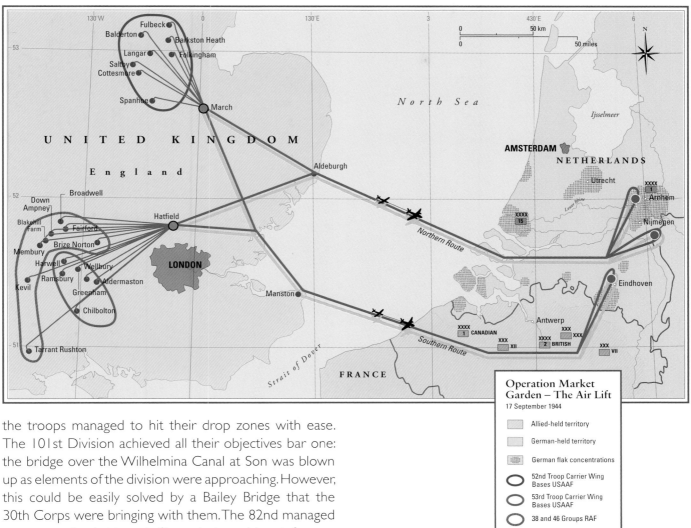

Operation Market
Garden – The Air Lift
17 September 1944

- Allied-held territory
- German-held territory
- German flak concentrations
- ⬤ 52nd Troop Carrier Wing Bases USAAF
- ⬭ 53rd Troop Carrier Wing Bases USAAF
- ⬭ 38 and 46 Groups RAF

the troops managed to hit their drop zones with ease. The 101st Division achieved all their objectives bar one: the bridge over the Wilhelmina Canal at Son was blown up as elements of the division were approaching. However, this could be easily solved by a Bailey Bridge that the 30th Corps were bringing with them. The 82nd managed to secure the bridge at Grave but could not force a crossing of the two main spans in Nijmegen.

In the British drop zone, the troops had landed safely but were over seven miles from the bridge at Arnhem. This, coupled with the loss of the majority of their jeep transportation in crashed gliders, meant that only the leading battalion, the 2nd Battalion under Lt-Colonel John Frost, reached the northern end of the bridge by the end of the day and consolidated their positions. However, because only half the British force had been flown in, the other half already in Holland had to stay and defend the drop zones. This meant that Frost's battalion would not be reinforced for a further 24 hours. Frost's men did attempt a crossing of the bridge twice that afternoon but were repelled both times. With the 2nd Battalion on the northern end of the bridge and the other two battalions of the brigade fighting in the outskirts and Oosterbeek, problems arose with communication. The radio sets that had been issued were not working well, or at all, and others were destroyed in the fighting. This meant that commanders could not keep in contact with each other. Urquart could not, therefore, have a clear view of the outcome of the battle and the division could not communicate with fighter bombers for support. This led Urquart to try and reach the bridge himself. Having to dodge German patrols and hiding in a Dutch loft for many hours, he was out of touch with his troops, while the German defense was getting stronger and more organized.

The 30th Corps advance did not begin until after the paratroops had landed, their advance soon ran into anti-tank positions on either side of the road. The armored column made an easy target for the German gunners. The next day, three more battalions of paratroops

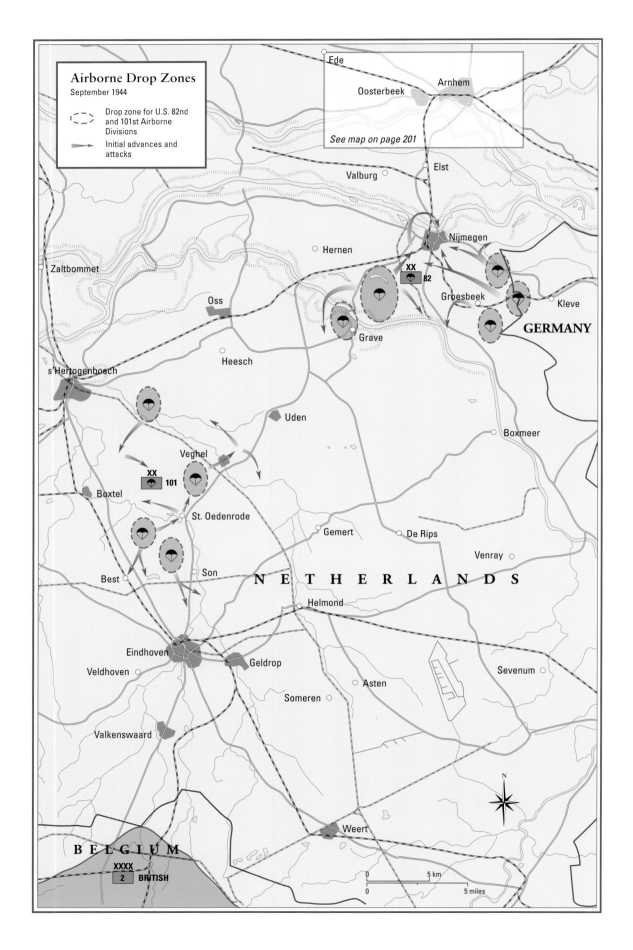

Airborne Drop Zones
September 1944

Drop zone for U.S. 82nd
and 101st Airborne
Divisions

Initial advances and
attacks

See map on page 201

Ede

Oosterbeek

Arnhem

Elst

Valburg

Nijmegen

Hernen

XX 82

Groesbeek

Kleve

Zaltbommet

GERMANY

Oss

Grave

Heesch

s'Hertogenbosch

Uden

Boxmeer

XX 101

Veghel

Boxtel

St. Oedenrode

Gemert

De Rips

Venray

Best

Son

N E T H E R L A N D S

Helmond

Eindhoven

Veldhoven

Geldrop

Sevenum

Asten

Someren

Valkenswaard

Weert

B E L G I U M

XXXX
2 BRITISH

0   5 km

0   5 miles

N

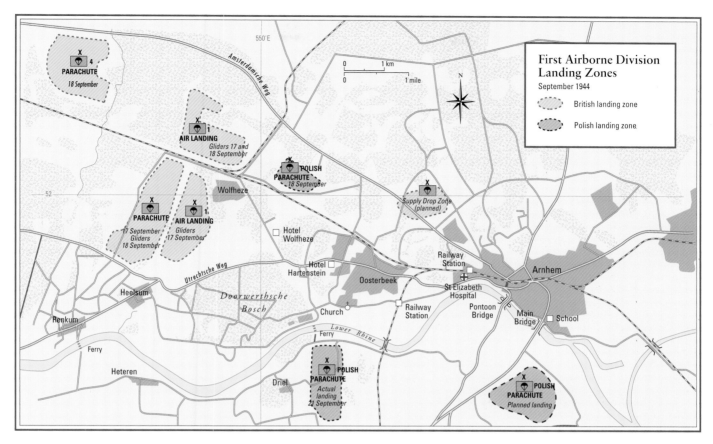

First Airborne Division
Landing Zones

September 1944

British landing zone

Polish landing zone

dropped into the Arnhem area. On the third day, paras again attempted to break through to the bridge, where Frost's men were being heavily shelled. They had no anti-tank ammunition, so the German tanks could approach and open fire at point-blank range. The men defending the bridge had no choice but to surrender. In Nijmegen a hasty attack was laid on using the 3rd Battalion of the 504th Paratroop Infantry Regiment, who crossed the river in boats. This costly attack was to become known by the men as "Little Omaha" in reference to the high losses suffered on that beach on D-Day. About half the battalion made it across and then had to fight over 218 yards of ground with no cover, eventually forcing the Germans off the bridge. The 101st Division was having problems with repeated attacks by German Panther tanks attempting to cut the road, denying any supplies to the forward elements, but these attacks were beaten back.

The men in the Oosterbeek pocket continued to wait for the 30th Corps to arrive but to no avail. Lt-General Brian Horrocks, Commander of 30th Corps, although across the Waal at Nijmegen, refused to go forward while his troops were in such a confused state, as over half the Guards Armored Division were engaged elsewhere. The Polish 1st Parachute Infantry were dropped opposite the British at Dreil, but could not find

a place to cross. The 101st also continued to fend off attempts to cut the road southeast of Arnhem.

The next day the British Airborne Division was being constantly pounded by artillery. The Germans had pulled some men out to face the Poles on the other side of the river, fearing they would try to assault the southern end of the bridge, cutting off the 10th S.S. Panzer facing 30th Corps. Attempts were made to cross troops over to the north bank of the Rhine, but heavy casualties were incurred and the attempt was called off.

Over the weekend, fighting continued, with the Germans again trying to cut off the British paras from the Rhine with heavy losses on both sides. Also an attempt to put across a battalion of the Dorset Regiment ended in disaster when only 75 of the 315 that crossed managed to reach the paras. After this attempt the decision was made to evacuate the paras from the north shore and establish the new front line south of Nijmegen.

Having managed to hold off a major attack by the German S.S. (Schutzstaffel) on Monday, that same night the remnants of the 1st Airborne were ferried over by engineers under the cover of darkness. Out of the 10,000 men sent into Arnhem about 2,500 made it back across the Rhine. Nearly 1,500 had died and the rest were captured. Half of those prisoners had been wounded.

CARRIERS IN THE PACIFIC 1941–45

"The United States possesses today control of the sea more absolute than was possessed by the British. Our interest in this control is not riches and power as such. It is first the assurance of our national security, and, second, the creation and perpetuation of that balance and stability among nations which will insure to each the right of self-determination under the framework of the United Nations Organization."

FLEET ADMIRAL CHESTER W. NIMITZ, U.S. NAVY

Only four of the nations that took part in the war possessed aircraft carriers: the United States, Great Britain, Japan, and France. And only two of these—the United States and Japan—had developed the role of these ships beyond supporting the heavy guns of the battle fleet. Before the war the Japanese had evolved an aircraft-carrier force that was designed to protect its battle fleet. The U.S. regarded Japan as its major threat in the Pacific, and responded by developing seaborne air power. Capital ship hulls that would otherwise have been scrapped were converted into aircraft carriers. Both the U.S. and Japan therefore acquired large carriers with well-equipped air groups and quickly gained an understanding of their potential.

In the early phases of the war, British fleet carriers were in short supply and were equipped with low performance aircraft. They were seen as the "eyes" of the fleet and to some extent its air defense. The strike role, while understood, never received the investment required to create a meaningful attack force. Despite this failure, in 1940 the Royal Navy managed to attack the Italian fleet anchored in the Italian harbor of Taranto, sinking two and damaging one battleship, an engagement carefully studied by both Japan and the U.S.

By 1941 the Japanese had ten carriers at their disposal. With six of these ships, they perfected and carried out the Pearl Harbor attack. Ironically, they failed to sink the American carriers, which were absent from Pearl Harbor on maneuvers.

These very ships became the core of the American fight back in the Pacific. In 1941, the U.S. Navy had seven fleet carriers and one escort carrier in service. With

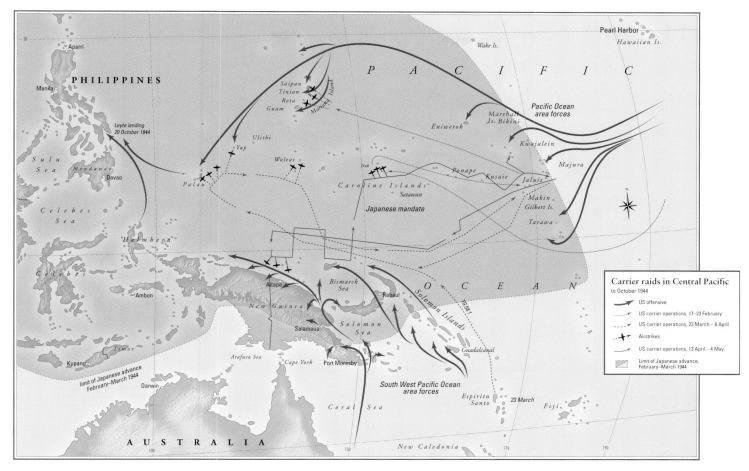

these ships the vital battles of the Coral Sea and Midway were fought and won. As American industry got into gear major new warships, especially the Essex-class carriers, were added to the U.S. Navy. With the delivery of these new ships, the U.S. fleet was able to launch carrier raids deep into enemy territory to attack Japanese island bases across the central Pacific, and this paved the way for the great seaborne offensives that followed.

By the end of 1944, the U.S. Navy could count on 18 fleet carriers and 76 other light and escort carriers giving an immense offensive air power equipped with some 3,800 aircraft. All this power was carefully backed up with an immense fleet "train" of supply ships reaching from the supply centers of the U.S. west coast to the theater of operations. This was a feat unequalled before or since.

The epitome of American carrier design incorporating all the lessons of the Pacific War was the immense USS Midway, laid down in October 1943, launched in March 1945 and commissioned on 10 September 1945, just missing involvement in the war. She could carry over 130 aircraft, with a displacement of 60,000 tons and a crew of 4,104 men. She served for almost five decades, being decommissioned at last in April 1992.

THE NEW CARRIER CLASS

Epitomizing the "New Order" in the U.S. Navy, carriers lead a line of battleships and cruisers. In the foreground is a C.V.L., converted from a cruiser hull and with funnels characteristically cranked out to starboard. Next in line is an Essex-class C.V. The large aircraft "deck-parks" were typical of American ships.

The Gilbert & Marshall Islands 1943

"The 2nd Marine Division has been especially chosen by the High Command for the assault on Tarawa ... What you do here will set the standard for all future operations in the central Pacific area."

MAJOR-GENERAL JULIAN C. SMITH, COMMANDER 2ND MARINE DIVISION

On 10 November 1943, U.S. Task Force 52 set sail for the Gilbert Islands in the Pacific, where it split in two. A northern force steamed towards the Makin Atoll where the Japanese garrison numbered only 800 men. The 27th Division landed on 20 November, suffering few losses. Resistance was cleared in two days. The southern force headed for Tarawa, an atoll of 38 tiny islands, with one airfield on Betio. This was much more strongly defended than Makin, with 5,000 men under the command of Rear-Admiral Shibasaki Keiji. He had at his disposal 14 coastal defense guns captured in Singapore in 1942. U.S. bombardment did little to affect the defenses—and it lasted too long, delaying the assault until low tide. Assault boats became stranded on the reef, leaving the soldiers to wade through 700 yards of surf under heavy fire to get to the beach. There they were obliged to wait for support. This arrived in the form of a lone tank, behind which came men armed with flamethrowers, to deal with bunkers. The Marines succeeded in splitting the defenders into two groups. After Keiji was killed, the last group of 150 Japanese soldiers staged a last-ditch bayonet charge. The only Japanese survivors were 17 wounded.

The next target, the Marshall Islands, was bombed continuously for seven weeks before the landings. The 7th Infantry Division headed for Kwajalien, and the 4th Marine Division to the atoll of Roi-Namur. The Marines were first in. Resistance was light and the island was taken with ease. On Kwajalien the attacking troops faced a tougher defense. The Japanese commander of the island personally led several charges in an attempt to dislodge the Americans' bridgehead. The defenders then fell back on a strong line of trenches supported by concrete bunkers. However, after six days of hard fighting the island was in U.S. hands.

The last island series to be taken was Eniwetok, which was defended by about 4,000 Japanese troops. Invaded by 8,000 U.S. Marines and 2,000 Army personnel, the island was taken again with relative ease and with almost total annihilation of the defenders, most of whom preferred death to surrender.

With the Gilbert and Marshall Islands in U.S. hands, they could look to the next strategic group of islands to invade. They were ahead of schedule, but there were lessons to be learned from the recent campaign. There was a need for better organization in getting troops and stores off the beach, and the attackers had to allow for the fierce resistance of the Japanese, who would not surrender while any remained alive. This could only mean that the job would not get any easier as the Americans closed in on the Japanese home islands.

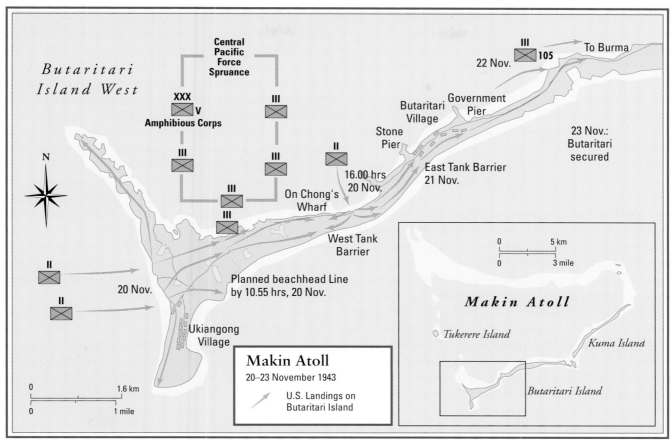

Butaritari Island West

Central
Pacific
Force
Spruance

XXX
V
Amphibious Corps

III

III

III

III

III

III

II

II

N

20 Nov.

On Chong's
Wharf

West Tank
Barrier

16.00 hrs
20 Nov.

Planned beachhead Line
by 10.55 hrs, 20 Nov.

Ukiangong
Village

Stone
Pier

Butaritari
Village

Government
Pier

East Tank Barrier
21 Nov.

III
105

22 Nov.

To Burma

23 Nov.:
Butaritari
secured

0   1.6 km
0   1 mile

Makin Atoll

20–23 November 1943

↗ U.S. Landings on
Butaritari Island

0   5 km
0   3 mile

Makin Atoll

○ *Tukerere Island*

Kuma Island

Butaritari Island

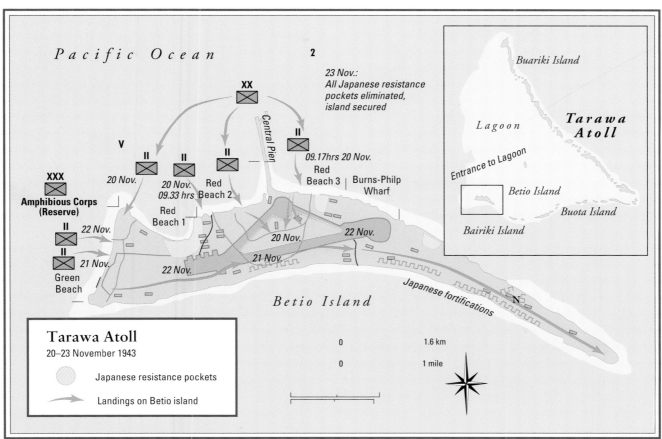

Pacific Ocean

2

XX

V

XXX
Amphibious Corps
(Reserve)

II

II

II

II

Central Pier

20 Nov.

20 Nov.
09.33 hrs

Red
Beach 2

Red
Beach 1

22 Nov.

II

II

22 Nov.

21 Nov.

Green
Beach

21 Nov.

22 Nov.

20 Nov.

22 Nov.

09.17hrs 20 Nov.
Red
Beach 3   Burns-Philp
           Wharf

23 Nov.:
All Japanese resistance
pockets eliminated,
island secured

Betio Island

Japanese fortifications

N

Tarawa Atoll

20–23 November 1943

◯ Japanese resistance pockets

→ Landings on Betio island

0   1.6 km
0   1 mile

Buariki Island

*Tarawa
Atoll*

Lagoon

Entrance to Lagoon

Betio Island

Buota Island

Bairiki Island

N

THE MARIANA & PALAU ISLANDS 1944

"I have always considered Saipan the decisive battle of the Pacific offensive ... it was the naval and military heart and brain of the Japanese defense strategy."

LT.-GENERAL HOLLAND–SMITH, JULY 1944

The Mariana Islands had been occupied by the Japanese since the end of World War I, so were heavily defended and garrisoned, especially as they formed part of the main defensive line in the Pacific. Saipan, Tinian, and Guam had to be taken by U.S. forces, since the islands would provide the airfields required for the new B-29 Superfortress that would bring the Japanese homeland within bombing range.

The first of the islands to be assaulted was Saipan, using the 2nd and 4th Marine Divisions on the first day, and the 27th Infantry Division on the second day. Defending the island was the Japanese 43rd Division commanded by Lt-General Yoshitsugu Saito. U.S. aerial and naval bombardment continued for three days before the assault was launched, but when the Marines came ashore on 15 June the Japanese artillery had carefully zeroed in on the beach and took a terrible toll on the landing forces. However, a beachhead some seven miles wide was established and all Japanese counterattacks were successfully beaten off. The 27th Division advanced on Aslito Airfield and, after initial fighting, this valuable real estate was abandoned by Saito and his men on 18 June. When Saito realized that the Japanese fleet was not going to arrive and attack the U.S. fleet, he ordered his men to fall back into the mountainous central region of the island around Mount Tapotchau and stall the Americans for as long as possible. The U.S. 27th Division was ordered to attack this rugged area, which became known as "Purple Heart Ridge" because of the number of casualties incurred. But the division failed to take the ridge, which led the Marine commander, General Holland Smith, to replace the division's leadership. On 7 July, with nowhere to go, Saito ordered his men to make an all-out infantry charge. This was to be the war's largest banzai attack. Some 3,000 Japanese troops were killed in a desperate and reckless gesture, at the conclusion of which Saito committed suicide. A wider consequence of the battle was that the Japanese Prime Minister, Hideki Tojo, was relieved of his post as head of the Army. He resigned along with all his Cabinet.

Tinian was assaulted on 24 July, after a successful feint drew the defenders away from the actual landing site on the north coast. The 2nd and 4th Marine divisions came ashore with relative ease, but at night their positions would be counterattacked and Japanese soldiers would infiltrate the lines and attack from the flanks and rear. Again the Japanese retreated into the central part of the island in an attempt to forestall the Americans. However,

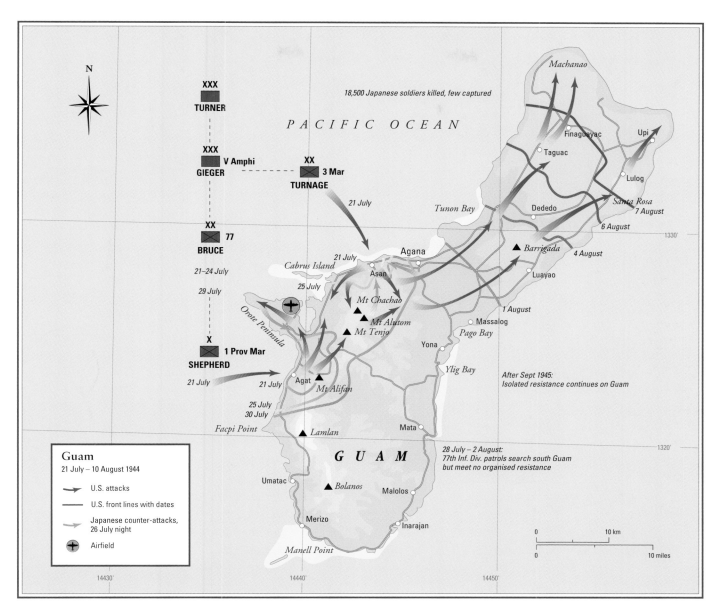

the terrain on Tinian was more conducive to tank warfare and the island was made secure within nine days of the assault. Construction battalions soon got to work on the airfields, which would be used to support further planned landings, as well as air attacks on the Japanese mainland.

Guam was the largest of the Mariana Islands and was assaulted on 21 July by 3rd Marine Division and 77th Infantry Division, who landed on both sides of the Orote Peninsula. The Marines made good progress, but the Infantry Division, which was short of amphibious vehicles, had to wade in over the coral while under heavy fire. Again the Japanese used the tactic of counterattack and infiltrating troops behind the U.S. advance to fire from the rear; the frontal attacks were always driven off with heavy losses. Orote Airfield was captured on 30 July, shortly after the death of the Japanese commanding officer, Takashima, with Lt-General Obata taking over command. The constant counterattacks by the Japanese soon exhausted even the hardiest of the soldiers, and they fell back into the interior of the island, retreating to an area around Mount Barrigada. Eventually the U.S. forces broke this final line and pursued the last of the enemy to the north of the island, where a few surrendered.

Finally, the 1st Marine Division and the 81st Infantry Division assaulted Peleliu, where the Japanese had made use of the many caves on the island, this time defended against flamethrower and explosive attack, which made the U.S. advance far more difficult. The Americans had to develop different tactics to defeat the enemy's new methods. After immensely difficult fighting and intense attacks led by tanks, the Marines and Infantry overcame all of these difficulties.

CHINA 1944–45

"Every Communist must grasp the truth that political power grows out of the barrel of a gun."

MAO TSE–TUNG

The war gathered momentum in China in 1944, when the Japanese attempt to invade India was stopped at the Battle of Kohima-Imphal. In northern Burma, U.S. General Stilwell's Chinese troops approached Mogaung and Myitkyina. Chiang Kai-Shek was threatened by the U.S. that Lend-Lease would be suspended if he failed to use the 12 divisions of his Yunnan Army in Burma. These subsequently began crossing the Salween River, moving on Myitkyina, Bhamo, and Lashio. Myitkyina Airfield was seized by Stilwell's forces, with Merrill's Marauders on 17 May, while Mogaung was taken by Britain's Chindits. Myitkyina fell to Stilwell's Chinese forces on 3 August.

By 1944, U.S. 14th Air Force bombers operating from Chinese bases were pulverizing Japanese supply lines in the northeast and plans were almost complete for deploying B-29 Superfortress bombers to airfields around Chengdu in Sichuan. These aircraft would be capable of striking at Japan from the new bases.

This air campaign caused the Japanese to launch a series of attacks known as Ichi-go, "the last throw." This Japanese strategy sought to control the railroad from Beijing, through Hankou, to Guangzhou, and to Indo-China, together with an attempt to capture the American airbases around Chungqing on the River Chang Jiang (River Yangtze). This offensive began in April, when 150,000 Japanese marched towards Zhengzhou from the east and south. The city fell on 22 April, allowing the advance to push westward taking Lo-yang in May, and Lingbau in June. Simultaneously, more Japanese forces moved south from Zhengzhou, attempting to link with a thrust north from Xinyang. By mid-June, the Japanese held the railroad from Beijing to Hangzhou, leaving the Chinese to retreat.

Elsewhere, a southward assault from Hangzhou moved toward the city of Chang-sha where the Chinese put up a stiff defense. Despite losing Chang-sha on 5 June and Hengyang (where the railroad forked towards Indo-China) in August, Chiang Kai-shek's forces, supported by the U.S. 14th Air Force, inflicted heavy casualties and bought valuable time. Nevertheless, when another Japanese advance commenced in late August, attempting to clear the railroad down to Guangzhou, huge areas of territory were abandoned to the Japanese. By November, Guilin, Liuzhou, and Yongning, plus the neighboring airfields, were captured and Chungqing was threatened. In December, a Japanese force moved out of northern Indo-China, making contact with other forces near Longzhou. The railroad was now clear along the entire length from Hanoi to Beijing.

Throughout their campaigns, the Chinese Nationalist Army adopted a tactic termed "magnetic warfare" in which Japanese troops would be offered a target, such as Chang-sha, then ambushed, outflanked, and encircled. During the subsequent major engagements the Japanese would suffer from attrition. This offensive-defensive tactic worked successfully. Out of about 57 major engagements between 1931 and 1945, the Chinese were victorious in 20 and even when suffering defeat they inflicted severe casualties on the enemy.

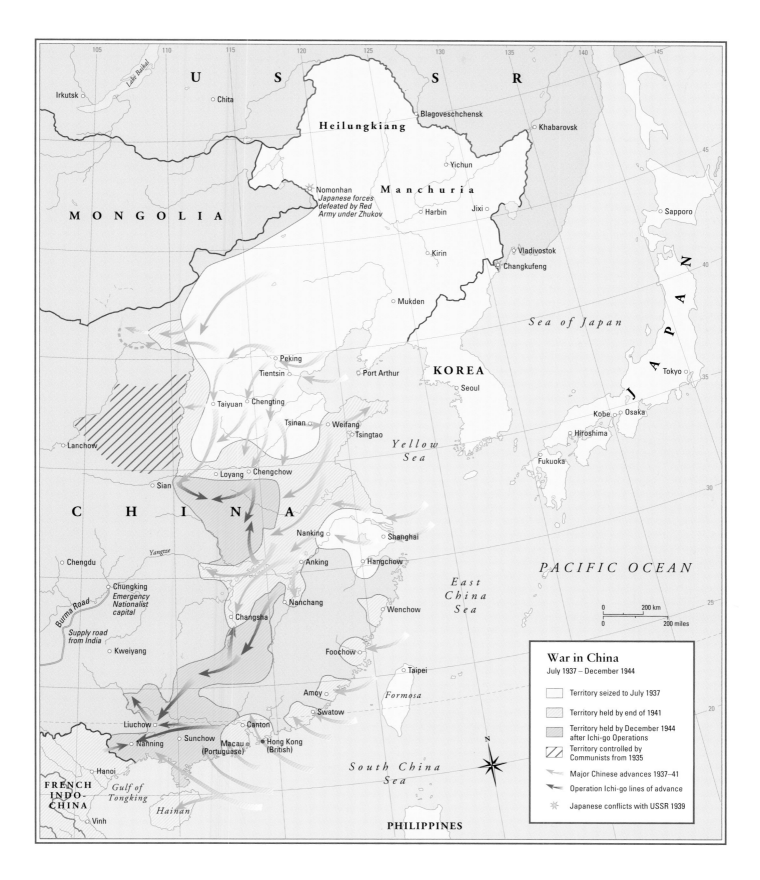

Irkutsk

Lake Baikal

U S S R

Chita

Blagoveschchensk

Khabarovsk

Heilungkiang

Yichun

Nomonhan
*Japanese forces
defeated by Red
Army under Zhukov*

M a n c h u r i a

Harbin   Jixi

Sapporo

M O N G O L I A

Kirin

Vladivostok

Changkufeng

Mukden

Sea of Japan

K O R E A

Peking

Tientsin

Port Arthur

Seoul

J A P A N

Tokyo

Taiyuan   Chengting

Lanchow

Tsinan   Weifang
Tsingtao

Kobe   Osaka

Hiroshima

*Yellow
Sea*

Fukuoka

Loyang   Chengchow

Sian

C H I N A

Chengdu

Yangtze

Nanking   Shanghai

Anking   Hangchow

PACIFIC OCEAN

Chungking
*Emergency
Nationalist
capital*

Nanchang

*East
China
Sea*

Burma Road

*Supply road
from India*

Changsha

Wenchow

Kweiyang

Foochow

Taipei

Amoy

Formosa

Liuchow   Swatow

Nanning   Sunchow   Canton
Macau
(Portuguese)   Hong Kong
(British)

Hanoi

**FRENCH
INDO-
CHINA**

*Gulf of
Tongking*

Hainan

*South China
Sea*

N

PHILIPPINES

Vinh

War in China
July 1937 – December 1944

Territory seized to July 1937

Territory held by end of 1941

Territory held by December 1944
after Ichi-go Operations

Territory controlled by
Communists from 1935

Major Chinese advances 1937–41

Operation Ichi-go lines of advance

Japanese conflicts with USSR 1939

0   200 km
0   200 miles

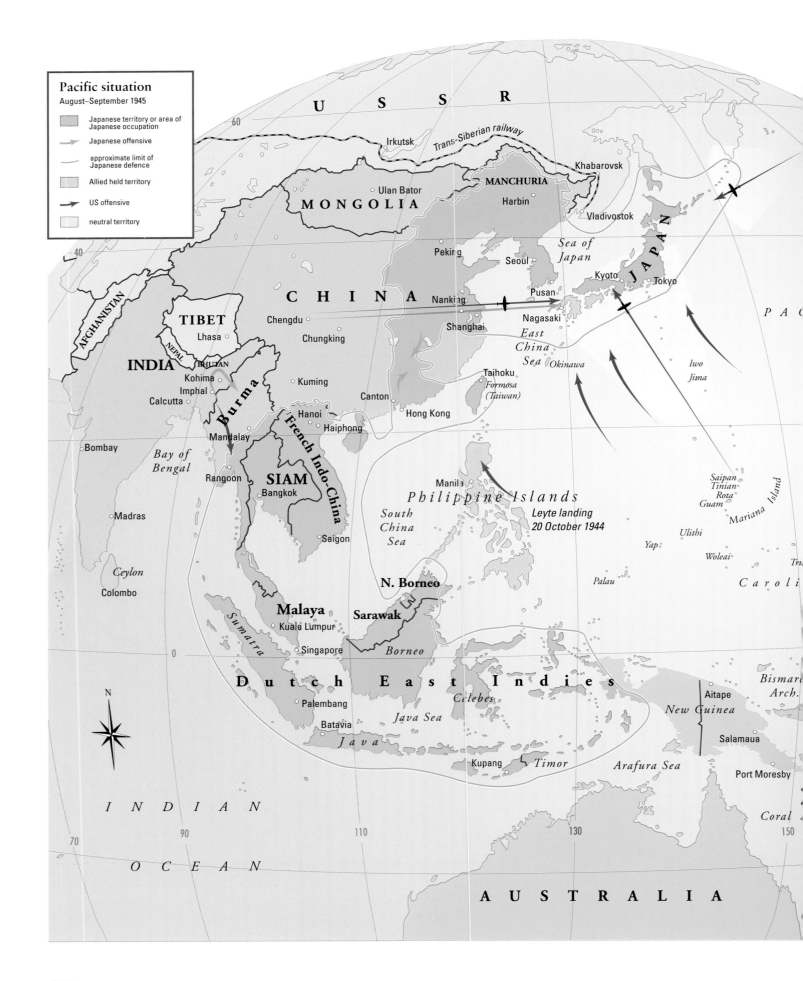

Pacific situation
August–September 1945

Japanese territory or area of Japanese occupation

Japanese offensive

approximate limit of Japanese defence

Allied held territory

US offensive

neutral territory

U S S R

Irkutsk

Trans-Siberian railway

Khabarovsk

MANCHURIA

Ulan Bator

Harbin

MONGOLIA

Vladivostok

JAPAN

Sea of Japan

Peking

Seoul

Kyoto

Tokyo

C H I N A

Nanking

Pusan

Chengdu

Nagasaki

Shanghai

East China Sea

TIBET

Chungking

Okinawa

Lhasa

Taihoku

Formosa (Taiwan)

Iwo Jima

INDIA

BHUTAN

Kuming

Canton

NEPAL

Burma

Kohima

Hong Kong

Imphal

Hanoi

Calcutta

Mandalay

Haiphong

French Indo-China

AFGHANISTAN

Bombay

Bay of Bengal

Manila

Saipan
Tinian
Rota

Rangoon

SIAM

Philippine Islands

Guam

Bangkok

South China Sea

Leyte landing
20 October 1944

Mariana Island

Madras

Saigon

Ulithi

Yap

Ceylon

Woleai

Colombo

Palau

Caroli

N. Borneo

P A C

Malaya

Sarawak

Tru

Kuala Lumpur

Sumatra

Singapore

Borneo

Bismar
Arch.

D u t c h   E a s t   I n d i e s

Aitape

Palembang

Celebes

New Guinea

Batavia

Java Sea

Salamaua

J a v a

Kupang

Timor

Arafura Sea

Port Moresby

N

I N D I A N

Coral

O C E A N

A U S T R A L I A

60

40

0

70

90

110

130

150

The Japanese were severely stretched and their supply lines were very thin; the Ichi-go campaigns had incurred tremendous casualties, leaving reduced numbers to hold the newly-captured territories. The link between Indo-China and Hengyang could not be held for long, especially after Chiang Kai-shek's forces began to rebuild themselves, with American aid, after the recent losses. By November 1944, he was reequipping and training, this campaign being masterminded by his new American advisor, Major-General Wedemeyer, Stilwell having been recalled. Thirty-nine new divisions were planned and although they were not fully effective by the end of the war in nine months time, their threat tied up more than 500,000 Japanese, some of whom could have been used elsewhere in the Pacific theater.

The conflict in China caused divisions between China, the U.S., and Britain. Churchill did not want to commit his defeated troops to re-open the Burma Road, while General Stilwell saw that target as being a prime concern. Chiang Kai-shek also distrusted the British, who he thought were using Chinese troops in their Burma campaign to bolster Britain's imperial holdings in Asia. Chiang wanted to use his forces in eastern China to protect U.S. airbases, a ploy which delighted Claire Lee Chennault and his "Flying Tigers" mercenary force. A further complication was Chiang's vocal support for Indian independence, including a meeting with Gandhi. Britain was not happy. However, on 6 and 9 August respectively, Hiroshima and Nagasaki were atom-bombed, while the Soviets entered Manchuria. The Japanese surrendered on 2 September 1945.

Chinese Communist Party propaganda expressed the view that Mao Tse-Tung's armies, which grew from nothing to 1.7 million soldiers, were the victors. The view of many in the West was that they seemed more intent on planning for events after the war than in hard campaigning against Japan. General Chiang's Kuomintang forces fought in 24 major battles involving more than 100,000 men on each side, 1,171 minor engagements (most of which with 50,000 men on each side), and nearly 39,000 skirmishes. They lost some 3.22 million troops while the Japanese losses were at least 1.1 million. The generally held view is that Chiang's Kuomintang, which included many warlords who fought the enemy under the Kuomintang banner, made the major contribution against the Japanese in China.

BATTLE OF THE BULGE 1944

"That whole Ardennes fight was a battle for road junctions, because in that wooded country in deep snows, armies do not move off roads."

GENERAL MATTHEW B. RIDGWAY, 101ST AIRBORNE DIVISION

The Ardennes Offensive, known as the "Battle of the Bulge" (referring to the bulge in the Allied line), was Hitler's last major offensive in World War II. Its aim was to cut in two the Allied advance on the West Wall (a prewar defensive line on the western borders of Germany) and destroy the U.S. divisions caught in the resulting pocket, then capture the port of Antwerp, splitting the Allied armies. Antwerp was strategically important to the Allies, as most of their supplies still came via the road network all the way from the Mulberry Harbor at Arromanches and from Cherbourg on the Normandy coast. This, Hitler hoped, would catch the Allies napping. For the Germans the Ardennes—heavily forested with few major roads—was the best place to strike, as this was the weakest area where recuperating or new Allied units were placed.

The plan for the offensive was much like the one used for the summer offensive against France in 1940, except that, instead of passing through the Ardennes before attacking, the battle lines would be within the forest. The plan called for a bridgehead to be secured over the Meuse River, then for the major part of the force to swing north west toward Antwerp. For this attack there would be four armies: the newly-formed 6th S.S. Panzer Army commanded by Josef 'Sepp' Dietrich in the north; the 5th Panzer under Hasso von Manteuffel in the center; and Erich Brandenberger's 7th Army in the south. The 15th Army would be kept in reserve toward the northern sector. These forces would be overseen by Field Marshals Walter Model and Gerd von Rundstedt, who strongly disagreed with the plan and tried to seek a less ambitious one. This was seen as defeatist by Hitler.

For the plan to work the Germans would need complete surprise, and security was tight. Von Rundstedt did not even hear of the plan until the attack was close. In addition, poor weather would be required to stave off any chance of Allied air attack. Most important would be a rapid advance to overwhelm the defenders and capture as much enemy fuel as possible to feed the thirsty Panzers. In order to create as much panic and uncertainty as possible in the U.S. ranks, teams of English-speaking troops were infiltrated behind the American lines wearing U.S. uniforms in order to disrupt troop movements and spread rumors.

At 05:30 on 16 December the German artillery opened fire and blasted the U.S. troop positions for nearly an hour before all the three assaulting armies moved off their start lines. The 6th S.S. drove on toward

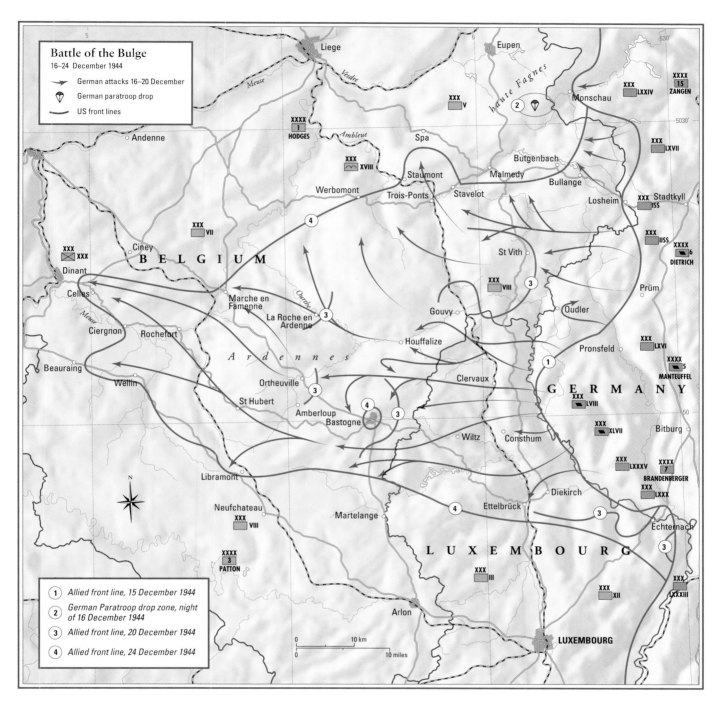

Battle of the Bulge
16–24 December 1944

→ German attacks 16–20 December

⊗ German paratroop drop

⌒ US front lines

1 Allied front line, 15 December 1944

2 German Paratroop drop zone, night of 16 December 1944

3 Allied front line, 20 December 1944

4 Allied front line, 24 December 1944

Liege while 5th Panzer drove to secure the vital road junctions at St. Vith and Bastogne. The 7th Army would push on steadily across the border into Luxembourg in order to establish a strong flank defense. Surprise was total, with some entire U.S. regiments surrendering to the sudden German assault. Stout defense did hold the attackers in some places. The 6th S.S. in the north were held up by the 2nd Infantry Division, and the 99th Division. The Allied High Command was caught by surprise, both Montgomery and General Omar Bradley believing that the Germans were all but finished and

definitely not capable of a major offensive. The German advance slowed by the end of the day as the weather got steadily worse, creating the mixed blessing of keeping the Allied airforces on the ground, but also causing major traffic jams on the narrow woodland roads. As part of the offensive, there was also an airborne operation, codenamed Auk, which involved dropping over a thousand paratroopers behind the lines just north of Malmedy to secure an important crossroads 'Baraque Michel.' Due to poor weather the drop was delayed until the early hours of 17 December and even this was affected by bad conditions, low clouds causing the paratroops to be badly scattered. Only 300 paras made the rallying point. The commander, Friedrich von der Heydte, who won the Iron Cross leading a battalion during the invasion of Crete, realized that the small force would not be able to hold the junction, and decided instead, to use his troops as a harassing force. This created enough chaos that U.S. commanders redirected troops on the way to the front to secure rear areas.

By the end of the day, General Eisenhower had taken the decision to send the 101st Airborne Division to Bastogne, to be joined by a combat team from the 10th Armored Division. This movement was carried out with incredible speed and would prove to be a vital course of action. The 82nd Airborne Division was also thrown into the fray, taking up positions defending the approach to Liege.

The spearhead of the 6th Panzer Army, Kampfgruppe Peiper—commanded by Joachim Peiper— struck out for Stavelot and reached it on 18 December. On the journey the day before, elements of Peiper's force captured 150 U.S. troops, who had surrendered when taken by surprise. The prisoners were then herded into a field and, according to eyewitness reports, an S.S. officer began to indiscriminately shoot them, his men following suit with machine guns. Some men managed to escape but 84 were murdered in scenes common on the Eastern Front,

but rarely seen on the Western. As reports started to spread of the 'Malmedy Massacre' U.S. troops took revenge on German prisoners and no quarter would be given in the fighting for the bulge from then on. Peiper was faced by strong defense at Stavelot and decided to reach the bridge at Trois Ponts, only to find that it had been blown earlier by U.S. engineers. Peiper moved his force on to Stoumont, where again the bridge had been blown and was heavily defended. Stavelot was completely retaken by U.S. soldiers on 19 December, cutting off Peiper. He had no choice but to give the order to abandon his tanks and half-tracks so his men could break through to the main German force. This he achieved with most of his men.

In the 5th Panzer sector, advance was severely hampered by the defenders of Bastogne. This was a major road junction with seven roads leading to it and was essential to the speedy advance of the German plan. The defenders, 101st Airborne Division and a combat command of 10th Armored Division, held onto the perimeter even though they were critically short of ammunition and winter clothing. Conditions inside the perimeter were harsh, with medical supplies very short, but the troops held and, when offered a chance to surrender, the commander of the besieged town, General McAuliffe, simply answered "Nuts!" By 23 December the weather was breaking enough for aircraft to fly sorties to

SCREAMING EAGLE

An exhausted trooper of General Matthew "Bunker" Ridgway's 101st Airborne Division—known as the Screaming Eagles—reflects on the heroic defense of Bastogne.

TAKEN PRISONER

A young soldier of the Waffen S.S. is taken prisoner by the U.S. 82nd Airborne Division. The Waffen S.S. gave no quarter in the Battle of the Bulge, and received little mercy in return.

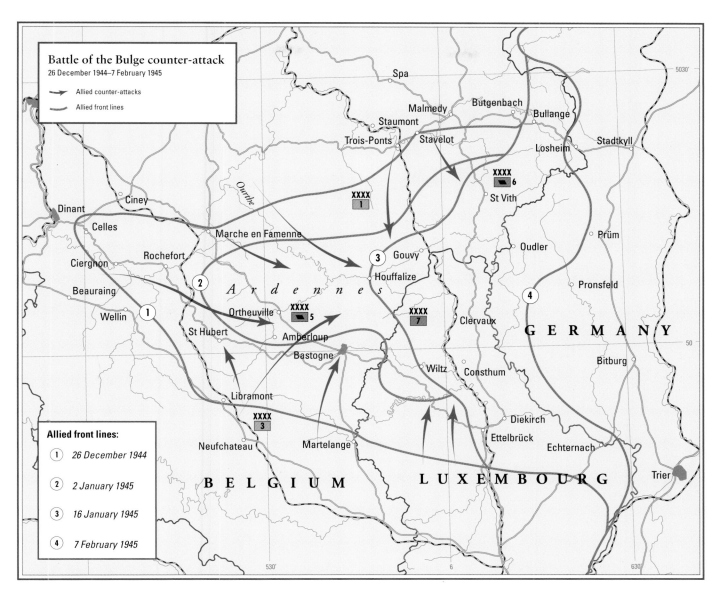

attack the long columns of German tanks confined to the narrow woodland roads, and to destroy their supplies in the rear. This caused an even worse shortage of fuel for the leading Panzers and the advance effectively ground to a halt, the Germans not even managing to reach the Meuse. On 26 December elements of Patton's 3rd Army broke through the perimeter of Bastogne and lifted the siege, bringing in much needed support and firepower.

On 1 January 1945, the Germans launched two simultaneous attacks. The first was launched by the Luftwaffe with the aim of destroying Allied aircraft on the ground in Belgium and the Netherlands. This it succeeded in doing but caused heavy loss to itself in the process, partly from antiaircraft flak from both sides (German antiaircraft batteries not being told about the operation) and Allied interceptors. The Luftwaffe lost 300 aircraft, from which it would never recover. In the south opposite

the U.S. 7th Army, German Army Group B launched an attack into the Alsace. This achieved initial success pushing the Americans back to the south bank of the Moder River. Again this attack failed due to lack of supplies and another determined defense by U.S. forces.

While this was happening, Eisenhower had ordered Montgomery in the north, and Patton, into the Bastogne area, toward the south of the bulge to advance toward each other and pinch out the salient. Patton proceeded immediately and took heavy casualties in a slow advance. Monty stalled for three days waiting out heavy snowstorms. The Germans put up a dogged rear guard action, and was able to save many of its troops at the cost of most of its heavy equipment, which had to be left behind because of a shortage of fuel. The two Allied forces eventually met on 15 January, effectively bringing to an end the last major offensive by the Germans in the West.

BOMBING OF GERMANY 1944–45

"...We walked toward the Grosse Garten. I felt rain trickling out of the sky, thin and cold, and then I heard the hum of aircraft engines ..."

BRUNO WERNER, CITIZEN OF DRESDEN

By the beginning of 1944 Bomber Command and the U.S.A.A.F. had built up a massive bomber force. Their task was aided by new radio-detection equipment that allowed the bombers to identify their targets more accurately, and by the introduction of long-range P-51 Mustang and P-47 Thunderbolt fighters that could escort the bombers all the way to the target and back.

In February of 1944, the Allied bomber offensive targeted the German aircraft industry in what was known as "Big Week," which resulted in German factories having to be moved into more dispersed areas, slowing down production and allowing the airforces a freer reign over the skies of Germany. The bombers were then thrown into the tactical role of bombing targets in aid of Operation Overlord. These raids over northern France concentrated on railroad yards and bridges, so as to slow or halt the movement of reinforcements. The R.A.F. was also called upon to soften up targets before the army attacked, such as the aerial bombardment of Caen, although this proved to be of little use as the enemy was well dug in. The damage to the city inhibited armored advance as well as causing a high civilian casualty rate.

The next targets for the combined bombing offensive, when it returned to its original duty, was to bomb oil refineries and transportation with the aim of again undermining enemy production. The 15th Air Force of the U.S.A.A.F., based in the Mediterranean, carried out raids continuously on the Romanian oil refineries until the sites were overrun by the advancing Soviet Army. In Germany the rail yards were targeted to hamper troop movement from the different fronts that Germany was

IN CONTROL OF THE SKIES
In the last months of the war, B-17 bombers, along with their P-51 fighter escorts, had complete dominance of the airspace over Nazi Germany.

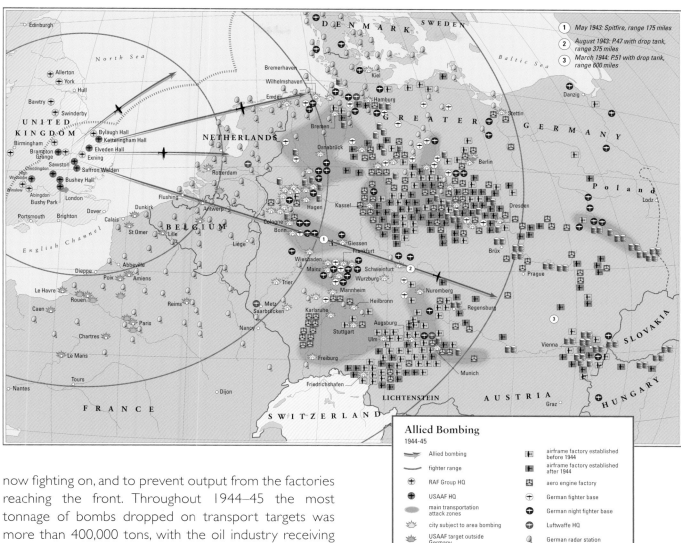

Allied Bombing
1944–45

✈ Allied bombing	⊞ airframe factory established before 1944
⌒ fighter range	⊞ airframe factory established after 1944
⊕ RAF Group HQ	⬢ aero engine factory
⊕ USAAF HQ	⊕ German fighter base
main transportation attack zones	⊕ German night fighter base
city subject to area bombing	⊕ Luftwaffe HQ
USAAF target outside Germany	German radar station
oil targets attacked by Bomber Command	┄ limit of German radar
oil targets attacked by USAAF	neutral territories

① May 1943: Spitfire, range 175 miles
② August 1943: P.47 with drop tank, range 375 miles
③ March 1944: P.51 with drop tank, range 600 miles

now fighting on, and to prevent output from the factories reaching the front. Throughout 1944–45 the most tonnage of bombs dropped on transport targets was more than 400,000 tons, with the oil industry receiving more than 220,000 tons of bombs.

One of the most controversial targets was the bombing of cities, brought to the fore with the bombing of Dresden during 13–15 February 1945. In order to aid the Russian offensive in the east that was now closing in on the borders of Germany, the R.A.F. and U.S.A.A.F. suggested bombing targets that would cause the maximum amount of disruption to German infrastructure and communication, and to destroy transport hubs that would be used by the enemy to move troops from the west to the Eastern Front. These cities included Berlin, Leipzig, Chemnitz, and Dresden. On the night of 13 February, nearly 1,000 Lancaster bombers, aided by pathfinder Mosquitoes, flew to Dresden in two waves and dropped a total of 1,400 tons of high explosive and 1,100 tons of incendiaries. The aim of this technique was to blow the roof off the buildings and set alight the wooden beams that were now exposed. This resulted in a terrible firestorm that reached temperatures of over

2,764°F, killing more than 30,000 inhabitants, with 70 percent of the city being damaged. This raid was again followed up by aircraft from the 8th Air Force on 14 and 15 February. The impact of the raid was used by the Nazis for propaganda purposes and made many people on the Allied side feel uncomfortable because of the moral questions that it raised.

The bombing of the Reich by the R.A.F. and the U.S.A.A.F. did not beat Germany into submission on its own, like many of its proponents had promised, but it played a decisive role in holding down resources such as antiaircraft artillery and aircraft, which could be have been used elsewhere. It never broke the will of the Germans, but it did slow down production, and created fear in the workforce with the constant threat of attack.

THE FALL OF ITALY 1945

"We were thrust out …, if not like the proverbial sore thumb, certainly like an aggressive forefinger, reaching out for the enemy's throat along the line of the Santerno."

GEOFFREY COX, NEW ZEALAND INTELLIGENCE OFFICER

After the capture of Rome, the Italian campaign became something of a sideshow in the eyes of Allied commanders. General Mark Clark, obsessed with the capture of Rome, lost the chance of capturing the German 10th Army when the U.S. 5th Army broke out of the Anzio beachhead and, as the Allies advanced, they faced yet another line of prepared defense. This would prove just as difficult and as expensive in lives as previous German lines. The Allied armies had also been severely depleted, with experienced units being pulled out of the line in order to take part in Operation Dragoon, the invasion of southern France, these units being replaced by untested troops.

The next line the Allies had to break was the Gothic Line, later changed by Hitler to the "Green Line" in order to downplay its importance. This defensive line stretched from Persaro on the Adriatic coast, to just south of La Spezia, on the western coast, incorporating thousands of machine-gun nests, anti-tank guns, and ditches. Progress was slow once the Allies had moved up to the Gothic Line, with attacks achieving little. On the 5th Army front, which was now separated from the British and Canadians by the Apennine Mountains, a limited advance was achieved around Mount Fogarito. These hills guarded the entrance to the Po Valley, and all previous frontal assaults had failed. Soldiers of the 442nd Regimental Combat Team climbed up the steep slopes of the mountain and managed to take the German positions by surprise, but this was one small victory on a massive front.

The British and Canadians, together with elements of the Polish Army, also attacked on the eastern side of the Apennines. At Rimini, on the night of 25/26 August, an attack succeeded after four days of bitter fighting in breaching the Gothic Line. This was not fully appreciated immediately by the Allies, allowing the Germans to reorganize, and it took a further three weeks of fighting before the breakthrough could be exploited. By this time the fall weather had set in, which turned the dust into an impassable muddy quagmire. General Alexander, now Allied Supreme Commander in the Mediterranean, halted all offensives until the spring.

With these two breaches of the Gothic Line, Kesselring was becoming increasingly worried: if the Allies broke out onto the wide, flat Po Valley they could annihilate the German 10th Army, which was already suffering partisan attacks and was, because of constant bombing of the Alpine passes and the Italian rail network, almost cut off from the rest of Europe.

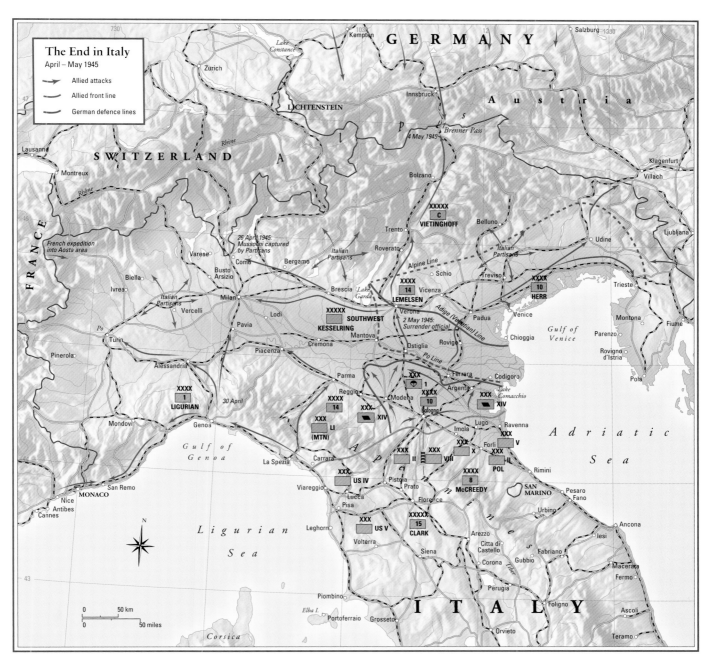

During the winter months the Americans received some reinforcements in the form of the first African-American combat unit—the 92nd, the 10th Mountain Division, and a Brazilian brigade. These units would have to wait until spring, however, to enter the offensive.

At the start of April, the Allies eventually broke out of their winter positions and took the Germans by complete surprise. By mid-April they had broken onto the Po Valley and were beginning to move at speed, trapping many Germans against the Po River itself since all the bridges had been destroyed by air attack. Many Germans escaped by swimming across the river, although at the cost of their heavy equipment. The Po was quickly bridged and the pursuit continued all the way to the Alps, where all the passes were in Allied hands by the close of April. By then, Kesselring had been replaced by General Vietinghoff, who later would surrender his troops on 2 May 1945.

With that surrender the fighting on the Italian peninsula, which had been extremely costly in resources and lives, was finally at an end. Without this theater of operations many lessons may not have been learned, particularly about amphibious assaults against a prepared enemy. The Italian campaign also held down enemy divisions that could have been used elsewhere. But Italy was far from being the "soft underbelly of Europe," as Churchill had so hopefully described it.

THE SOVIET ADVANCE 1944

"There was no doubt that at this stage of the war the Russians collared for their infantry divisions anyone, regardless of training, age, or health—and sometimes of sex—and pushed them ruthlessly into battle."

GENERAL FRIEDRICH VON MELLENTHIN

At long last, as a result of the hard-won victories in the Ukraine, the Soviets were ready to launch an offensive that would drive the German troops from their positions around Leningrad. The city had been under siege continuously since September 1941. The offensive, launched on 14 January 1944, involved the Leningrad, Volkov, and Second Baltic Fronts, supported by long-range aviation (the equivalent of the American and British Strategic Bomber Force). More than 35,000 partisans were also involved, their function to disrupt German lines of supply. By 1 March the Soviets had reached the border of Latvia, and Leningrad's 900-day siege was over.

In the spring of 1944, Soviet planning for the Byelorussia operation began. The High Command had come to the conclusion that the next area for liberation was Byelorussia itself. The northern part of the German front line in Russia still appeared close to the Russian heartlands. The operation to remove this salient was called Bagration, named after one of the Russian heroes of the Napoleonic invasion of 1812. The operational plan was extended in May to take the advance well clear of the Pripet Marshes and to liberate the area between the Dvina and Neman Rivers. This would mean an advance of 400 miles along a front of 360 miles.

The offensive would involve 1,400,000 men, 31,000 guns and mortars, 5,200 tanks and assault guns, with over 5,000 aircraft in support. The main objective was the destruction of German Army Group Center. This army group could still muster 1,200,000 men, 9,500 guns and heavy mortars, 900 tanks, and 1,350 aircraft in its defense.

German radio operators picked up increasing traffic, and on 10 June intercepted an order from Moscow to Soviet partisans to increase attacks on rail communications. These were carried out over the next 12 days. On the night of 22/23 June—three years to the day since the German invasion—the Soviet airforce attacked German rear areas and lines of supply. In the early morning of 23 June, the first part of the offensive began. Meanwhile, on 6 June, the western Allies had landed in Normandy and the Second Front became a reality. Germany was now fighting in the west as well as the east.

On 23 June, the first attacks were launched, made up of operations heading towards Bobrinsk, Vitebsk, Orsha, Mogilev, and Polotsk. There was a determined plan to surround the concentration of German forces at Minsk.

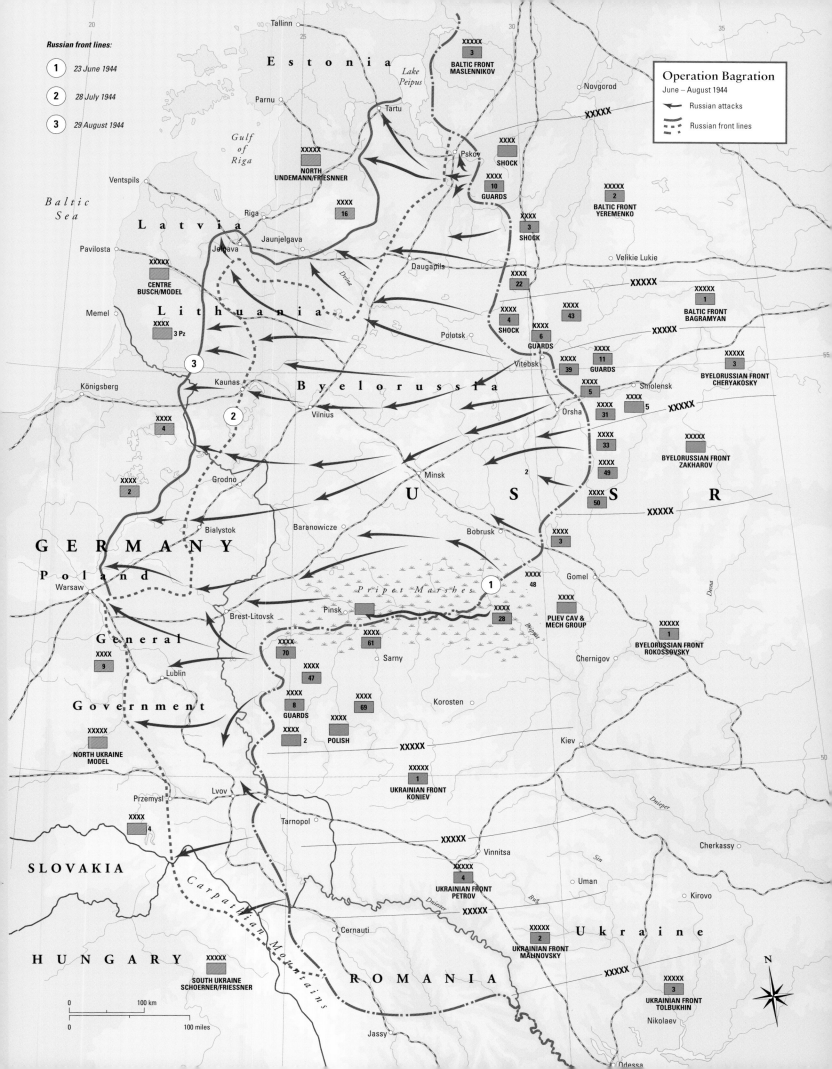

Russian front lines:
1 23 June 1944
2 28 July 1944
3 29 August 1944

Operation Bagration
June – August 1944
→ Russian attacks
⌇⌇ Russian front lines

Tallinn

Estonia

Lake Peipus

Novgorod

XXXXX 3 BALTIC FRONT MASLENNIKOV

Parnu

Tartu

XXXXX

Gulf of Riga

Pskov

XXXX SHOCK

XXXX 10 GUARDS

Novgorod

XXXXX 2 BALTIC FRONT YEREMENKO

Ventspils

Baltic Sea

Latvia

Riga

XXXXX 16 NORTH UNDEMANN/FRIESNNER

Jaunjelgava

XXXX 3 SHOCK

Velikie Lukie

Pavilosta

Jelgava

Daugapils

XXXX 22

XXXXX

XXXXX 1 BALTIC FRONT BAGRAMYAN

Lithuania

Dvina

Polotsk

XXXX 4 SHOCK

XXXX 43

XXXXX

XXXXX CENTRE BUSCH/MODEL

Memel

XXXX 3 Pz

XXXX 6 GUARDS

Vitebsk

XXXX 39

XXXX 11 GUARDS

XXXXX 3 BYELORUSSIAN FRONT CHERYAKOSKY

3

Königsberg

Kaunas

Byelorussia

XXXX 5

Smolensk

Vilnius

XXXX 31

XXXX 5

XXXXX

2

XXXX 4

Orsha

XXXX 33

XXXXX BYELORUSSIAN FRONT ZAKHAROV

Minsk

U   S   S   R

XXXX 49

Grodno

XXXX 2

Baranowicze

Bobrusk

XXXX 50

Gomel

Bialystok

XXXX 3

Denia

GERMANY

Warsaw

Poland

Pripet Marshes

XXXX 48

XXXX PLIEV CAV & MECH GROUP

General

Brest-Litovsk

Pinsk

XXXX 28

Pripet

XXXXX 1 BYELORUSSIAN FRONT ROKOSSOVSKY

Chernigov

Lublin

XXXX 9

XXXX 70

XXXX 61

Sarny

XXXX 47

Korosten

Government

XXXX 8 GUARDS

XXXX 69

North Ukraine Model

XXXXX NORTH UKRAINE MODEL

XXXX 2

POLISH

Kiev

XXXXX

Przemysl

Lvov

XXXXX 1 UKRAINIAN FRONT KONIEV

XXXX 4

Tarnopol

XXXXX

SLOVAKIA

Carpathian Mountains

Vinnitsa

Sin

Bug

Cherkassy

Kirovo

XXXXX 4 UKRAINIAN FRONT PETROV

Uman

HUNGARY

Cernauti

Dniester

XXXXX 2 UKRAINIAN FRONT MALINOVSKY

Ukraine

XXXXX

XXXXX SOUTH UKRAINE SCHOERNER/FRIESSNER

ROMANIA

XXXXX 3 UKRAINIAN FRONT TOLBUKHIN

Dnieper

N

0   100 km
0   100 miles

Jassy

Nikolaev

Odessa

20   25   30   35

55

50

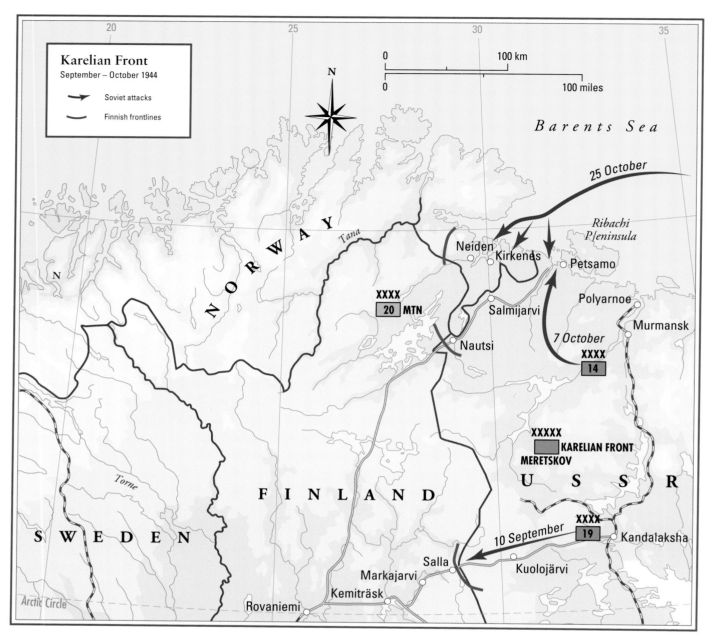

Barents Sea

0   100 km

0   100 miles

N

25 October

Neiden

Kirkenes

Ribachi Peninsula

Petsamo

Tana

NORWAY

N

XXXX
20 MTN

Salmijarvi

Polyarnoe

Murmansk

Nautsi

7 October

XXXX
14

XXXXX
KARELIAN FRONT
MERETSKOV

U   S   S   R

Torne

FINLAND

SWEDEN

XXXX
19

10 September

Kandalaksha

Salla

Kuolojärvi

Markajarvi

Kemiträsk

Arctic Circle

Rovaniemi

Hitler, again, ordered that a defense line be somehow created, with "feste Plätze," or strongpoints, to be held to the last man. By 3 July the Germans, consisting of the 27th Panzer Corps, 110th Division, and other elements at Minsk, were surrounded. These forces were destroyed between 5 and 11 July. The rest of Army Group Center fell back westward from Minsk.

General Walter Model was now in command of Army Group Center. He requested a meeting with Hitler asking to withdraw the garrison at Vilna. Hitler said "No, hold out at all costs." But Model did get some reinforcements from Army Group North to strengthen his remaining resources. While this was happening Vilna fell on 13 July, followed by Pinsk on 14 July, and Grodno

THE KARELIAN FRONT

As well as the gigantic offensive to retake the western parts of the U.S.S.R., the Soviets launched a series of attacks in the far north, protecting their ports and installations along the White Sea coast.

on 16 July. Then on 20 July, the Red Army finally destroyed Army Group Center as a fighting force. Of its 67 Divisions, 17 had been annihilated and the remaining 50 lost at least 50 percent of their strength.

After this massive achievement, the Soviet advance began to lose momentum, reaching just short of Bialystok and Kaunas. Over the next four weeks, the Soviets captured Kaunas and advanced to the old prewar borders of East Prussia. To the south they managed to advance a further 60 miles almost to the eastern suburbs of Warsaw.

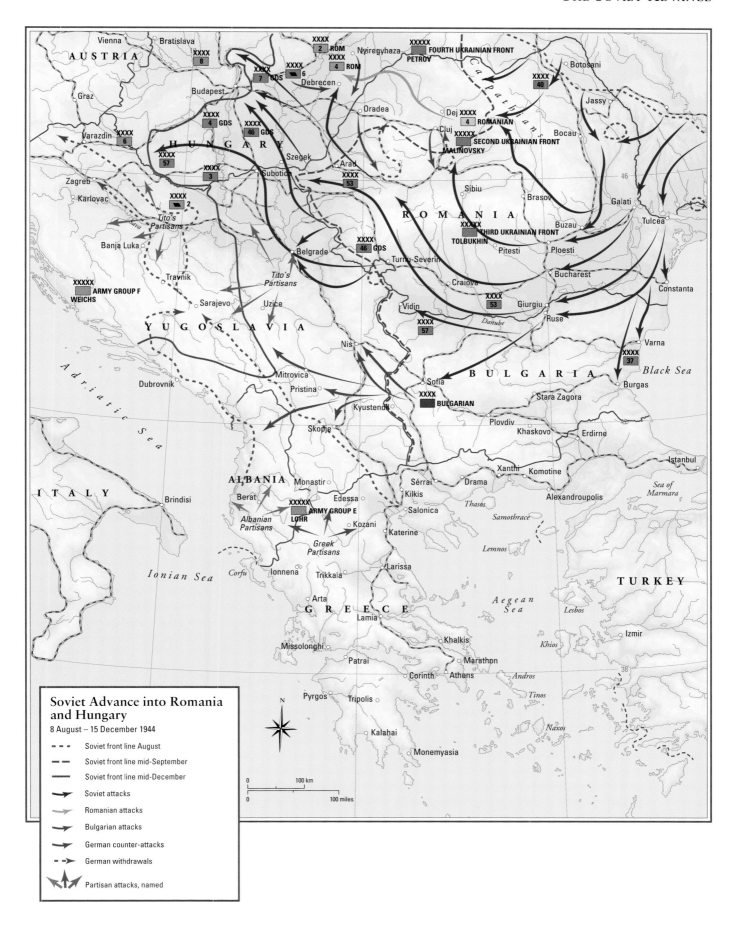

Soviet Advance into Romania and Hungary

8 August – 15 December 1944

- - - - Soviet front line August
- - - Soviet front line mid-September
───── Soviet front line mid-December
➤ Soviet attacks
➤ Romanian attacks
➤ Bulgarian attacks
➤ German counter-attacks
- ➤ German withdrawals
↟ Partisan attacks, named

0   100 km
0   100 miles

ADVANCE INTO GERMANY 1945

"Excuse me, mate, is this the road to Berlin?"

BRITISH TANK DRIVER TO GERMAN CITIZEN WHILE CROSSING THE BORDER

With the last German offensive defeated, Eisenhower looked to advance into Germany. He decided to keep his "broad front" strategy, with Montgomery's 21st Army Group, still incorporating U.S. 9th Army, in the north; Bradley's 12th Army Group in the center; and Dever's 6th Army Group, with Patton's 3rd Army and the French 1st Army, in the south.

First to strike would be 21st Army Group in the north. The Canadian 1st Army was to attack from the Nijmegen area in conjunction with the U.S. 9th Army to its south to pinch off the area between the Ruhr and the Rhine. The Germans, anticipating the attack, blew the largest dam on the Ruhr, flooding the plain . Von Rundstedt hoped the time gained would allow him to withdraw his troops east of the Rhine, but Hitler refused to allow it. When the U.S. 9th Army advanced on 23 February, these German forces were trapped.

The Rhine was now the last remaining obstacle before Germany. Simpson's 9th Army arrived at its banks near Düsseldorf, only to find that all the bridges had been blown. On 7 March an armored reconnaissance patrol of Hodge's 1st Army came across the Ludendorf bridge, still intact. More than five divisions crossed under aerial bombardment before the bridge collapsed into the river. By that time pontoon bridges had been assembled allowing the bridgehead to be expanded. The failure to blow the bridge led Hitler to dismiss von Rundstedt. He was replaced by Kesselring.

A surprise crossing was made by the men of Patton's 3rd Army at Oppenheim, south of Mainz, establishing a bridgehead to the south, just before Montgomery's massive attack in the north. Operation Plunder was launched on 24 March. The assault deployed the British 30th and 12th Corps between Rees and Wesel, and the U.S. 16th Corps to the south. The British crossed the river but soon ran into a concerted defense on the eastern bank. The American units faced lighter defense and soon constructed a pontoon bridge, which was complete by the evening of the 24th. The river crossing was supported by an airborne drop codenamed "Varsity," utilizing the British 6th Airborne Division and the U.S. 17th Airborne Division. This secured the high ground overlooking the River Issel. These troops were then to join up with the 21st Army and continue with them in their advance to Germany's Baltic coast.

The 21st Army Group advanced northeast toward Hamburg, losing the U.S. 9th Army as it encircled the Ruhr from the north, heading south to eventually meet up with the U.S. 1st Army, and capturing 300,000 German soldiers in the pocket. The 12th Army Group headed east toward the River Elbe and southward into Bavaria and Czechoslovakia. In the south, 6th Army Group headed to the southeast of Germany to enter Austria and northern Italy. Germany, which had so ruthlessly invaded most of Europe, was now overrun with invading troops. The fall of the thousand-year Reich was just days away.

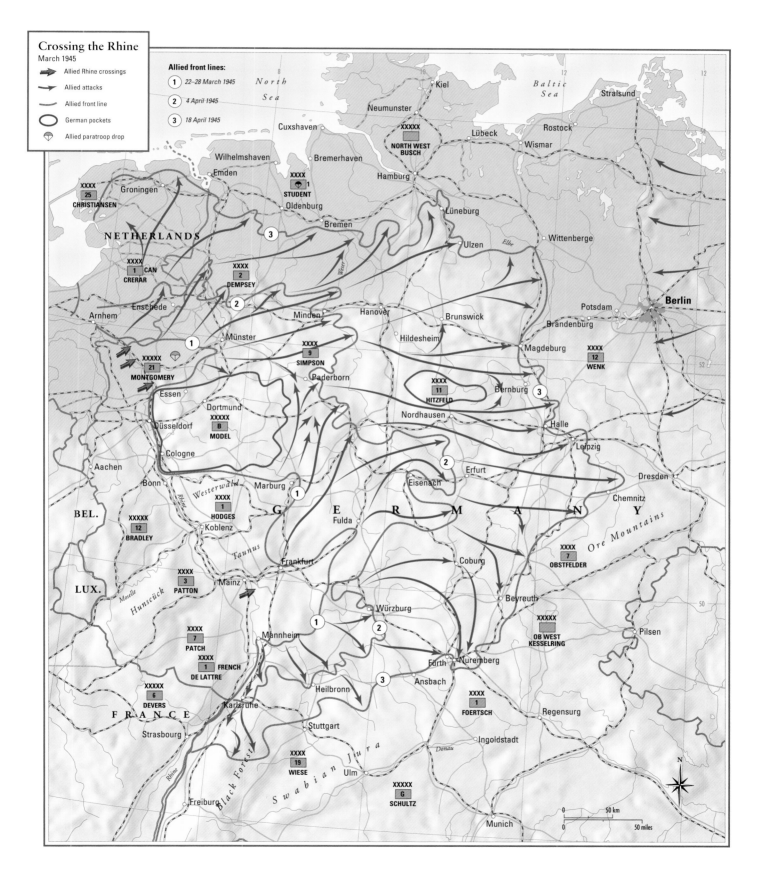

Crossing the Rhine
March 1945

Allied Rhine crossings
Allied attacks
Allied front line
German pockets
Allied paratroop drop

Allied front lines:
① 22–28 March 1945
② 4 April 1945
③ 18 April 1945

North Sea
Baltic Sea

Kiel
Neumunster
Stralsund
Cuxshaven
Lübeck
Rostock
Wilhelmshaven
Bremerhaven
Wismar
Hamburg
Emden

XXXX 25 CHRISTIANSEN
Groningen
XXXXX NORTH WEST BUSCH

XXXX 1 STUDENT
Oldenburg
Lüneburg

NETHERLANDS
Bremen
Ulzen
Elbe
Wittenberge

XXXX 1 CAN CRERAR
Enschede
Minden
Hanover
Brunswick
Potsdam
Berlin
Brandenburg

Arnhem
XXXX 2 DEMPSEY
Münster
Hildesheim
Magdeburg
XXXX 12 WENK

XXXXX 21 MONTGOMERY
XXXX 9 SIMPSON
Paderborn
XXXX 11 HITZFELD
Bernburg

Essen
Dortmund
Nordhausen
Halle

Düsseldorf
XXXXX B MODEL
Leipzig
Cologne
Erfurt
Dresden

Aachen
Bonn
Westerwald
Marburg
Eisenach
Chemnitz

BEL.
XXXXX 12 BRADLEY
XXXX 1 HODGES
Koblenz
G E R M A N Y
Fulda
Ore Mountains
XXXX 7 OBSTFELDER

LUX.
Moselle
Taunus
Frankfurt
Coburg
Beyreuth
XXXXX OB WEST KESSELRING

Hunsrück
XXXX 3 PATTON
Mainz
Würzburg
Pilsen

XXXX 7 PATCH
Mannheim
Fürth
Nuremberg
XXXX 1 FOERTSCH
Regensurg

XXXX 1 FRENCH DE LATTRE
Heilbronn
Ansbach

XXXXX 6 DEVERS
Karlsruhe
Stuttgart
Donau
Ingoldstadt

F R A N C E
Strasbourg
XXXX 19 WIESE
Swabian Jura
Ulm

XXXXX G SCHULTZ
Black Forest
Freiburg
Munich

0 — 50 km
0 — 50 miles

225

THE FALL OF BERLIN 1945

"If the war is lost, the German nation will also perish… There is no need to take into consideration the basic requirements of the people… those who will remain after the battle are those who are inferior; for the good will have fallen."

ADOLF HITLER TO ALBERT SPEER

The fall of Berlin was one of the last major battles in the European war. Here two massive Soviet army groups, with the support of another, encircled the city and finally destroyed the capital of the Third Reich. By the end of a huge series of Soviet offensives, Romania and Bulgaria had been overrun and most of Hungary, including its capital Budapest, was in the hands of the Red Army.

After waiting for the Warsaw uprising to be crushed by the Germans, the Red Army had pushed across Poland, taking the Baltic coast around East Prussia and Danzig. The Russians were poised on the eastern bank of the Oder, having beaten back a counterattack by Himmler's newly-formed Army Group Vistula. It was at this point that Stalin gave the order for Berlin to be captured by 1 May—which was Workers' Day, an important political holiday in the Soviet Union.

Before the final push, Russia had to redeploy its armies in line with this operation. This it did with great speed and efficiency, something that would have been unachievable four years earlier, at the start of the conflict. Zhukov's 1st Byelorussian Front was positioned due east

of Berlin for the main advance, flanked in the north by Rokossovsky's 2nd Byelorussian Front with Konev's 1st Ukraine Front to the south. The total number of men reached almost 2.5 million, with 6,250 tanks, 41,600 guns and mortars and 7,500 aircraft. Facing this enormous force were the remnants of the German army, made up of 33 severely depleted divisions, with 12th Army to the west of Berlin on the east bank of the River Elbe facing the Americans and British.

General Gotthard Heinrici had been placed in command of Army Group Vistula and set about creating a workable defensive line. Anticipating that the main Russian advance would come across the Oder and along the autobahn heading straight into Berlin, he created three defensive lines around the Seelow Heights, incorporating anti-tank ditches, guns, and bunkers overlooking the river some 70 miles west of Berlin, leaving only a delaying force on the west bank.

The Russian assault went in before dawn on 16 April, following a bombardment that did little to the German defense. Progress was slow against the Germans and the advance began to stall, Zhukov throwing in his reserves in

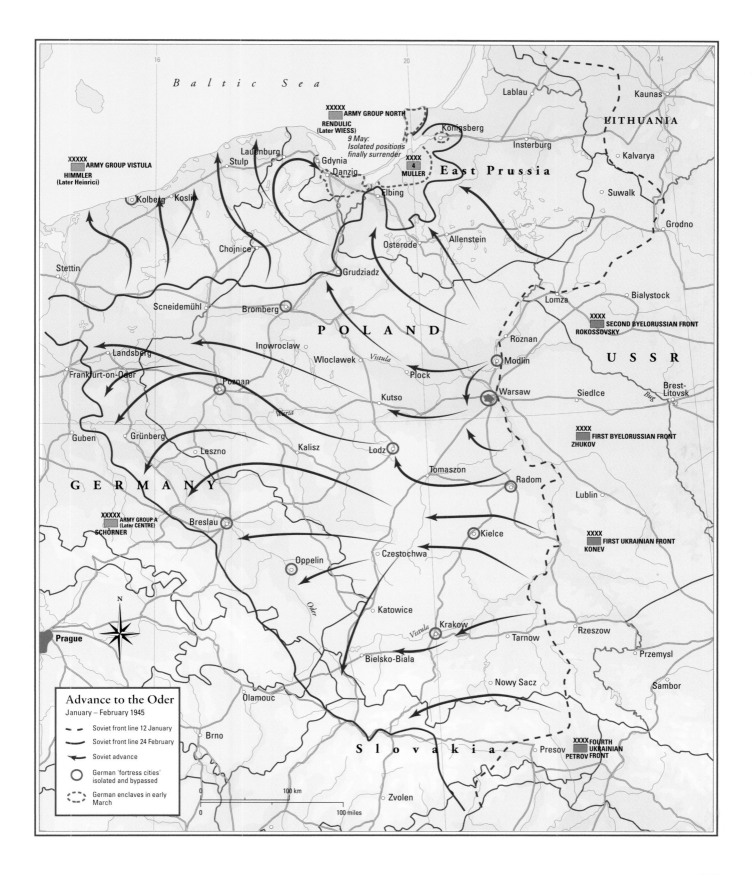

Baltic Sea

Lablau

Kaunas

XXXXX
ARMY GROUP NORTH
RENDULIC
(Later WIESS)

LITHUANIA

Königsberg

Insterburg

Kalvarya

9 May:
Isolated positions
finally surrender

Lauenburg

Stulp

Gdynia

Danzig

XXXXX
ARMY GROUP VISTULA
HIMMLER
(Later Heinrici)

Kolberg

Koslin

XXXX
4
MULLER

East Prussia

Suwalk

Elbing

Grodno

Chojnice

Osterode

Allenstein

Stettin

Grudziadz

Scneidemühl

Bromberg

P O L A N D

Lomza

Bialystock

XXXX
SECOND BYELORUSSIAN FRONT
ROKOSSOVSKY

Landsberg

Inowroclaw

Wloclawek

Vistula

Plock

Roznan

Modlin

U S S R

Frankfurt-on-Oder

Poznan

Kutso

Warsaw

Siedlce

Brest-
Litovsk

Bug

Guben

Grünberg

Leszno

Kalisz

Lodz

XXXX
FIRST BYELORUSSIAN FRONT
ZHUKOV

G E R M A N Y

Tomaszon

Radom

Lublin

XXXXX
ARMY GROUP A
(Later CENTRE)
SCHÖRNER

Breslau

Kielce

XXXX
FIRST UKRAINIAN FRONT
KONEV

Oppelin

Czestochwa

Oder

Katowice

Krakow

Vistula

Tarnow

Rzeszow

Prague

Bielsko-Biala

Przemysl

Nowy Sacz

Sambor

Olamouc

Advance to the Oder
January – February 1945

- – – – – Soviet front line 12 January
- ‿‿‿‿ Soviet front line 24 February
- ◄——— Soviet advance
- ◯ German 'fortress cities' isolated and bypassed
- ⬭ German enclaves in early March

Brno

S l o v a k i a

Presov

XXXX
FOURTH
UKRAINIAN
FRONT
PETROV

100 km

100 miles

Zvolen

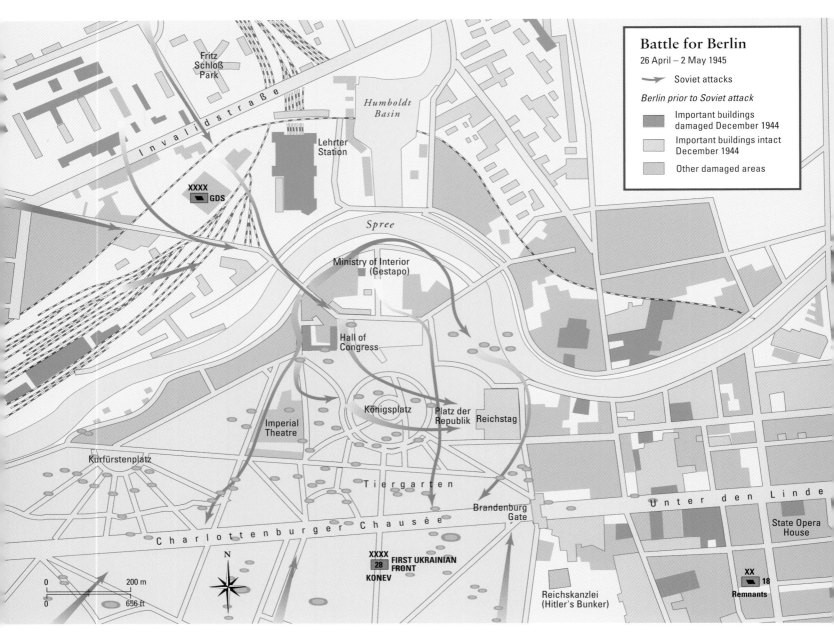

Battle for Berlin

26 April – 2 May 1945

→ Soviet attacks

Berlin prior to Soviet attack

Important buildings
damaged December 1944

Important buildings intact
December 1944

Other damaged areas

Fritz
Schloß
Park

Invalidstraße

*Humboldt
Basin*

Lehrter
Station

XXXX GDS

Spree

Ministry of Interior
(Gestapo)

Hall of
Congress

Königsplatz

Platz der
Republik   Reichstag

Imperial
Theatre

Kurfürstenplatz

Tiergarten

Brandenburg
Gate

Charlottenburger Chausée

Unter den Linde

State Opera
House

N

0   200 m
0   656 ft

XXXX
28   FIRST UKRAINIAN
      FRONT
KONEV

XX
18
Remnants

Reichskanzlei
(Hitler's Bunker)

the hope of achieving a breakthrough. To the south Konev's forces were enjoying greater success, especially against 4th Panzer Corps, which was being forced back. Stalin ordered Konev to exploit their gap and, once through it, to swing north for Berlin. With the threat of encirclement Heinrici had to fall back with his divisions. By 18 April the 1st Byelorussian Front was at the third defensive line about to burst through, and 1st Ukraine Front had reached Forst. Then the 2nd Byelorussian Front launched their attack in the north, holding 3rd Panzer Army on the northern flank, unable to fall back to Berlin. On 19 April the 1st Ukraine Front had beaten its way through 4th Panzer Corps and were now heading north to meet up with the 1st Byelorussian Front and west to meet U.S. forces on the River Elbe.

On 20 April, Hitler's birthday, Berlin was greeted by Russian artillery shells raining down on the city center. The Soviets would not stop the shelling until the German garrison surrendered. They moved north and south of Berlin, encircling the city. On 22 April Alfred Jodl, Chief of Staff of German High Command, suggested to an increasingly deranged Hitler that they should move 12th Army away from the Elbe to link up with 9th Army in defense of Berlin. However, on 23 April 12th Army was stopped in its tracks by the advancing 1st Ukraine Front. Hitler appointed General Helmuth Weidling as defense commandant of Berlin. On 25 April Zhukov's and Konev's forces linked up, encircling the city, with Konev's men linking with the U.S. 69th Division near Torgau on the River Elbe.

Inside Berlin, the severely depleted men of the S.S., the Wehrmacht, and the police—alongside boys of the Hitler Youth and old men of the Volksturm home guard—prepared for the final onslaught. The Russians advanced from all sides and vicious house-to-house fighting continued, many German soldiers fighting on for fear that if they surrender they would simply be shot on the spot. Hitler ordered General Heinrici to hold the city at all costs. He refused this order and was replaced by General Kurt Student.

On 30 April, Hitler married his long-time partner, Eva Braun. Shortly after the wedding both of them killed themselves. Many of Hitler's inner circle followed suit. Goebbels and his wife killed themselves in the bunker, having first fed poison to their six children.

General Weidling surrendered Berlin on 2 May but many pockets of resistance held out for some days after. Berlin had fallen, and the end of the war in Europe was within sight. In accordance with Hitler's last will and testament, Grand Admiral Karl Dönitz was appointed the new Reichspresident. The same day, 1 May, the 10th Army, fighting in northern Italy, under the command of General von Vietinghoff, ordered his forces to cease hostilities in the region. The order came into effect on 2 May, the same day that Berlin surrendered.

On 4 May, Montgomery took the surrender of all German forces in the Dutch, North-west German and Danish regions from Grand Admiral Hans-Georg von Friedburg and General Hans Linzel on Luneburg Heath.

The following day, Dönitz ordered all submarines to cease operations and return to base.

Alfred Jodl, representing German High Command and Reichspresident Dönitz, arrived in Rheims on 6 May and on the following day signed the total and unconditional surrender in the presence of General Eisenhower. The news soon broke and Victory in Europe was announced to the western Allies.

Soon after, the Reich was partitioned, East Prussia being divided between Poland and Russia, as well as the land east of the Oder. The remainder of Germany was partitioned into four zones, occupied by the United States, Great Britain, France, and the U.S.S.R. Austria, now politically separated from Germany, was also occupied and divided into four zones. Five years of war had left Europe in ruins. Many fine cities had been obliterated, their cultural heritage lost forever. And more than 43 million people had died, leaving behind them hundreds of millions more who were ravaged, scarred, and grieving.

VICTORY IN EUROPE

Below left, Field Marshall Wilhelm Keitel signs the ratified surrender terms at Russian headquarters in Berlin. This dour and humiliating moment for the German armed forces contrasts with the scenes of joy taking place, more or less at that moment, elsewhere in Europe. Below, jubilant American soldiers and sailors share their victory celebration with an Englishwoman at Piccadilly Circus in London.

BURMA 1944–45

"We had no ammo, no food, no clothes, no guns. The men were barefoot and ragged and threw away everything except canes to help them walk. At Kohima we were starved then crushed."

SHIZUO MARUYAMA, JAPANESE FOOTSOLDIER

With the creation of South East Asia Command, in August 1943 the Allies were ready to take the initiative in Burma. There were three active fronts. In the north, Stilwell's forces advanced on Shinbwiyang with the road being constructed directly behind the advance. If a stronghold or Japanese force impeded their progress, Merrill's Marauders, a U.S. commando unit adept at jungle fighting, would plunge headlong into the jungle, outflank the Japanese, and destroy their positions. Also helping the advance, the Chindits launched attacks on the Japanese supply lines. They were then moved further north nearer to the advancing Chinese 38th Division and took heavy casualties defending the captured airfield at Myitkyina. The Chinese, by this time, had started a new offensive from Yunnan on a 200-mile front and the Japanese now had to fight a two-front campaign in the north.

On the Southern Front, the Indian 15th Corps advanced on the Mayu Peninsula along the coast and captured the small port of Maungdaw in January 1944, which aided the supply of the advance as overland routes were still not navigable during the monsoon season. They then went on to capture the rail tunnels leading through the mountains linking Maungdaw with the Kalapanzin Valley. However, this move was foreseen by the Japanese 55th Division, which got around the rear of the attacking Indian Division, the 7th, and cut them off from the rest of

15th Corps. Thanks to air supply the troops managed to hold out in what became known as the Battle of the Admin Box and were relieved when the 5th Division broke through to lift the siege. They then went on to capture the rail tunnels before halting the advance when the monsoon season closed in.

Meanwhile, on the Central Front, the Japanese launched an offensive that aimed to isolate the forward divisions of 4th Corps, go on to capture Imphal, then move to Dimapur. This attack came on 8 March 1944, and the Indian 20th Division fell back to the Imphal Plain on 13 March. The 17th Division was cut off by the Japanese advance, but managed to fight through the Japanese positions and arrive on the plain in early April. General Slim then decided to reinforce the Central Front by flying in the 5th Indian Division from the south and sending two Brigades to Imphal and one to the Dimapur and Kohima area. On 5 April the Japanese launched a series of vicious attacks against the defenders of the small town of Kohima, the defenders fighting from positions around the District Commissioner's tennis court. The men were relieved by an Indian Brigade on 18 April.

The Allies now went on the offensive. By mid-May they had managed to drive the Japanese off the Kohima Ridge. After this the Imphal offensive collapsed. By July the Japanese had fallen back behind the line of the Chindwin River. The Japanese 15th Army pulled back

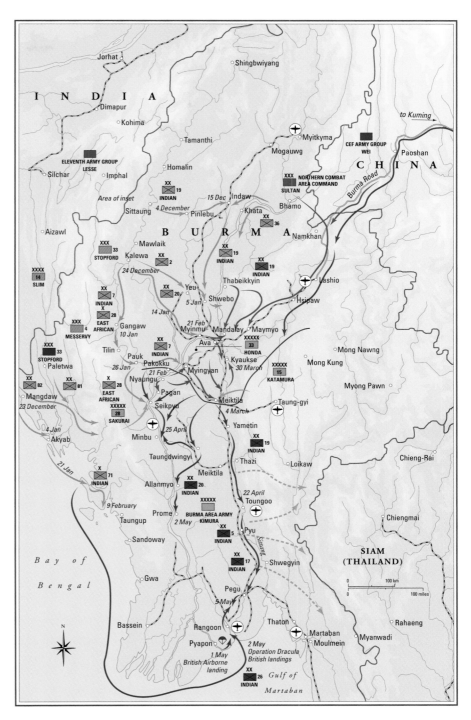

behind the Irrawaddy River, while the 28th Army was to defend the Arakan district in the south. The 33rd Army would continue to harass Stilwell's northern forces On 21 January 1945, the Chinese Yunnan forces linked up with Stilwell. In the south the advance restarted after the monsoon as the Indian 25th Division advanced on Foul Point and Rathedaung, and the West African 81st and 82nd Divisions advanced on Myohaung. With the aid of amphibious commando assaults the Myebon Peninsula was cleared by mid-January. Commandos then landed on Daingbon Chaung and linked up with 82nd Division coming overland.

In January and February the 33rd Corps successfully captured crossings over the Irrawaddy near Mandalay while, in late February, 4th Corps captured the crossing at Nyuangu. They captured Meiktila on 5 March after a rapid motorized advance. The Japanese attempted to recapture the town but the 4th Corps was now being constantly reinforced and the Japanese suffered heavy losses, breaking off the attack at the end of March. While the main concentration of Japanese forces had been attacking Meiktila, Mandalay had fallen to 33rd Corps on 20 March, much of the city being destroyed in the process. This cut communications with the 33rd Army in the north, and the 15th Army was reduced to small units that were forced to retreat into the

Shan States. The 33rd and 4th Corps then turned to advance down the Irrawaddy and Sittang valleys toward Rangoon.

The Japanese evacuation of the port began on 22 April. By 30 April all that was left in the Rangoon area was the rearguard and stragglers that had been left behind in the withdrawal, leaving the Allies to take the port by 2 May. The Japanese attempted another counteroffensive in July across the Sittang River but the plans for this operation were captured and the Allies had time to set up artillery concentrations and ambushes that completely decimated the Japanese attack. Now all that was left to do in Burma was to round up the remnants of the Japanese forces.

BOMBING OF JAPAN 1944–45

"United States commanders … stated their belief that, by the coordinated impact of blockade and direct air attack, Japan could be forced to surrender without invasion."

UNITED STATES STRATEGIC BOMBING SURVEY

The first raid on the Japanese home islands was carried out by 16 modified B-25 Mitchell bombers in a sortie flown from the U.S. carrier Hornet in 1942 and led by Lt-Colonel Jimmy Doolittle. This mission achieved very little damage but was a massive propaganda boost for the United States, also showing the Japanese people that, despite their leaders' claims, their islands could be bombed. The next raids on Japan would not be for another two years, after the introduction of the new Boeing B-29 Superfortress with a 1,500-mile range. Missions could be flown from new airfields constructed on mainland China to attack targets as distant as Tokyo. By the end of the war in the Pacific over 90 percent of the bombs dropped on the Japanese mainland would be delivered by these immense four-engined, long-range bombers.

Raids were carried out from Chengdu in China by aircraft from the U.S. 20th Air Force under the command of General Henry "Hap" Arnold, later replaced by Major General Curtis LeMay, who had personal experience of leading raids over occupied Germany. The aircraft flying from these Chinese bases had to have extra fuel tanks fitted in order to make the return journey, which in turn reduced the bomb load carried and therefore the effectiveness of the raids. The supply route to the new force was flown in over the "Hump" (the Himalayas) from India, so resources were extremely limited. Not until the island-hopping campaign and the capture of the Marianas, would bases be brought into service that were close enough for the B-29s to fly with a full bomb load.

The first of these new bases was on Saipan, and its first mission was launched in late October 1944. The Marianas were ideal bases for the B-29s and their needs were easily supplied by sea from Tinian, Guam, and Saipan. The Marianas were the main hub for all B-29 missions for the rest of the war. The 20th Air Force adopted, as in Europe, a policy of high-level, daylight bombing. But European methods were soon recognized as untenable due to factors such as the weather over mainland Japan. It was often cloudy, which hampered aiming. Even in clear weather, high winds tended to make the bombs drift off target as they fell.

The Japanese air defense system, though woefully inadequate when the U.S. campaign began, started to gain experience and equipment, such as more antiaircraft artillery and high level interceptors. All this convinced LeMay to follow the example of the R.A.F. against German targets, one of slightly lower level night attacks, often

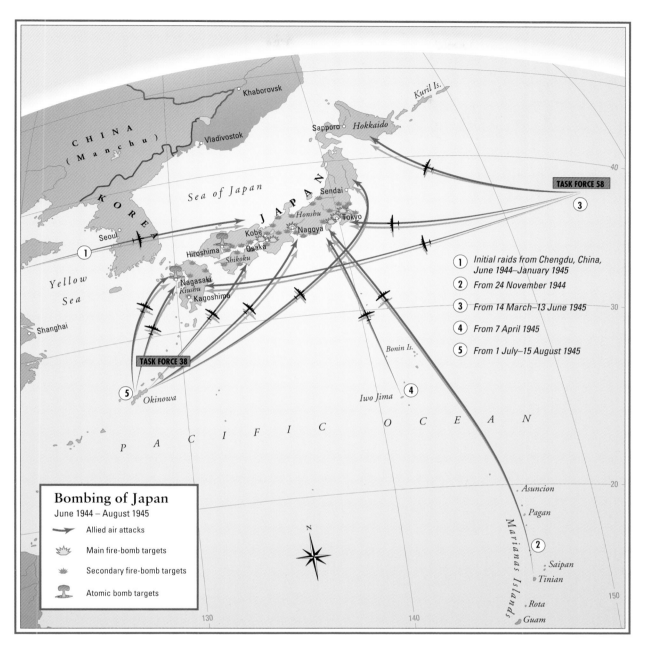

Bombing of Japan
June 1944 – August 1945

→ Allied air attacks

🌼 Main fire-bomb targets

🌸 Secondary fire-bomb targets

☁ Atomic bomb targets

① Initial raids from Chengdu, China, June 1944–January 1945

② From 24 November 1944

③ From 14 March–13 June 1945

④ From 7 April 1945

⑤ From 1 July–15 August 1945

TASK FORCE 58

TASK FORCE 38

using incendiaries. The major targets chosen for this campaign were to be Tokyo, Nagoya, Osaka, and Kobe, although most Japanese cities would be hit in some way. They were all susceptible to incendiary attack, since many of their buildings were made of wood and paper, resulting in massive firestorms. The first raid was on Kobe on 3 February 1945, which caused massive destruction in civilian areas of the city but also reduced manufacturing production by 50 percent and extensively damaged its shipyards. These successful attacks proved LeMay's theory a viable option and they were continued.

A mission flown on the night of 23/24 February to Tokyo using 174 aircraft succeeded in destroying a square mile of the city. A further raid on the night of 9/10 March,

after American pathfinders had marked the target, involved 1,665 tons of incendiaries being dropped. Sixteen square miles of the city were engulfed in an enormous firestorm that resulted in the deaths of over 100,000 people, which was the most destructive and deadly conventional raid ever carried out.

Concerned by the civilian deaths that these raids were causing, the 20th Air Force began dropping leaflets prior to major raids warning the civilians to leave the city, but these were seen by the Japanese as a form of psychological warfare so were played down by their own officials. By the end of the campaign the 20th Air Force destroyed nearly half the built-up areas of all the major cities in Japan, and hundreds of thousands had died.

THE BATTLE FOR THE PHILIPPINES

"The fate of the Empire rests on this one battle. Every man is expected to do his utmost."

MESSAGE TO ALL JAPANESE SHIPS

When the U.S. forces launched the invasion of Saipan on 15 June 1944, Japanese Vice-Admiral Jisaburo Ozawa saw this as his opportunity to strike at the enemy in the Philippine Sea. Under his command was a force consisting of five fleet carriers, four light carriers, five battleships, and an accompanying escort of cruisers, destroyers, and oilers.

Early on the morning of 19 June both fleets had air patrols out searching for enemy ships. A Japanese aircraft spotted Task Force 58 and immediately relayed its position to Ozawa, who ordered aircraft based on Guam to attack. These aircraft were picked up on radar and a squadron of Hellcat fighters was launched from USS Belleau Wood. They caught the Japanese planes still forming up and shot down 35 of 50 before being ordered back to their carrier. More enemy aircraft were approaching from the west. They were engaged before they reached the Task Force and 41 of 68 were shot down. Later in the morning, the Japanese launched another strike. Again, thanks to radar, the U.S. fighters could engage the Japanese before they reached the main carrier group. Some slipped through and attacked the carrier USS Enterprise. Almost all these were shot down, and Enterprise was undamaged. Of the 109 fighters launched by the Japanese, 97 were destroyed. Two more raids were made that day. They were not so costly to

the Japanese as the morning engagements, but were just as futile, as they caused no significant damage to the American fleet.

During the air battles U.S. submarine Albacore sighted Ozawa's carrier group and proceeded to attack the Taiho, disabling her. Ozawa moved his command to a destroyer while his men fought the fires on board. She eventually succumbed, exploded, and sank in the late afternoon. Another U.S. submarine, the Caralla, sighted Shokaku and fired three torpedoes into her. The fires created by the hits finally reached her bomb store, causing her to blow.

U.S. Task Force 58 then took the initiative on 20 June and started to sail west in search of the Japanese, but failed to find them until mid-afternoon. Admiral Mitscher immediately ordered a strike, even though his bombers would have to return in the dark. Two hundred and sixteen aircraft were launched from the U.S. carriers and the attack went in at 6:30 that evening. The Japanese carrier Hiyo was attacked by torpedo bombers and damaged, eventually sinking despite her crew valiantly trying to save her. Three other Japanese carriers were also badly damaged. The U.S. aircraft returning to the Task Force had trouble finding it, even when Mitscher ordered the fleet to operate all its landing lights and for the escort to fire starshell bursts. Eighty aircraft were eventually lost—some from heavy landings on the decks of the

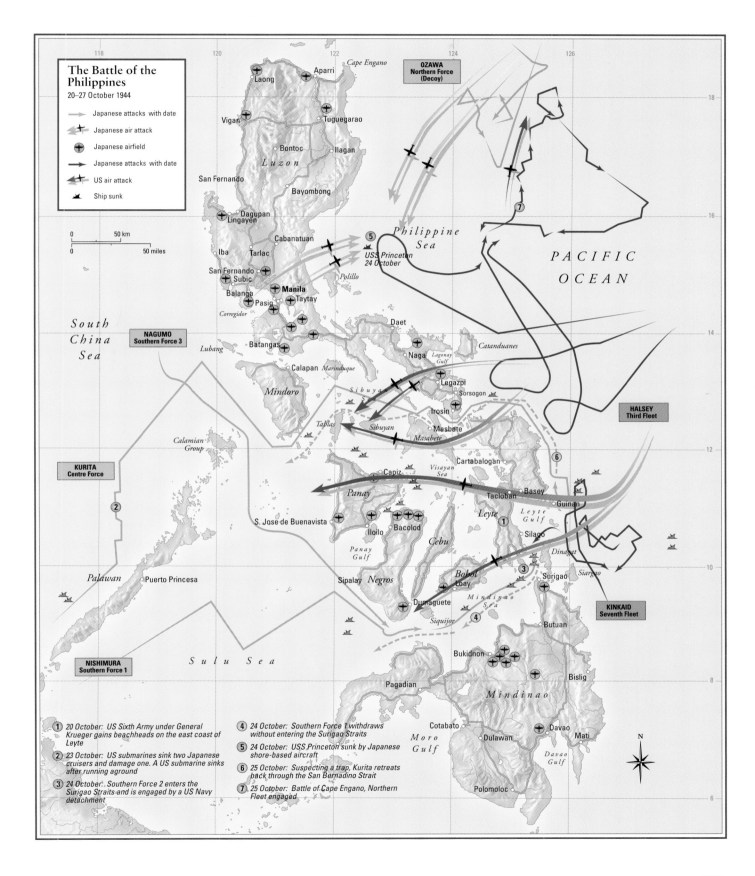

The Battle of the Philippines
20–27 October 1944

→ Japanese attacks with date

✈ Japanese air attack

⊕ Japanese airfield

→ Japanese attacks with date

✈ US air attack

⚓ Ship sunk

0   50 km
0   50 miles

Luzon

Philippine Sea

PACIFIC OCEAN

South China Sea

OZAWA
Northern Force
(Decoy)

NAGUMO
Southern Force 3

KURITA
Centre Force

NISHIMURA
Southern Force 1

HALSEY
Third Fleet

KINKAID
Seventh Fleet

Cape Engano

Laong   Aparri

Vigan   Tuguegarao

Bontoc   Ilagan

San Fernando

Bayombong

Dagupan
Lingayen

Cabanatuan

Iba   Tarlac

San Fernando
Subic

Balanga   **Manila**   Taytay
Pasig
Corregidor

Daet

Batangas

Lubang   Calapan   *Marinduque*   Naga   *Lagonay Gulf*   *Catanduanes*

Mindoro   *Sibuyan*   Legazpi
Sorsogon

Tablas   Sibuyan   Irosin

Calamian Group   *Masbate*   Masbate

Capiz   *Visayan Sea*   Cartabalogan

Panay   Tacloban   Basey
Guinan

S. Jose de Buenavista   *Leyte Gulf*

Iloilo   Bacolod   *Cebu*   *Leyte*   Silago

Panay Gulf   Dinagat

Palawan   Puerto Princesa   Sipalay   *Negros*   *Bohol*   Surigao   *Siargao*
Loay

Dumaguete   *Mindanao Sea*   Surigao

Siquijor

Sulu Sea   Butuan

Bukidnon

Bislig

Pagadian   *Mindanao*

Cotabato   Davao
Moro Gulf   Dulawan   *Davao Gulf*   Mati

Polomoloc

USS Princeton
24 October

N

① 20 October: US Sixth Army under General Krueger gains beachheads on the east coast of Leyte

② 23 October: US submarines sink two Japanese cruisers and damage one. A US submarine sinks after running aground

③ 24 October: Southern Force 2 enters the Surigao Straits and is engaged by a US Navy detachment

④ 24 October: Southern Force 1 withdraws without entering the Surigao Straits

⑤ 24 October: USS Princeton sunk by Japanese shore-based aircraft

⑥ 25 October: Suspecting a trap, Kurita retreats back through the San Bernadino Strait

⑦ 25 October: Battle of Cape Engano, Northern Fleet engaged

EMBATTLED ZUIKAKU

The carrier Zuikaku under aerial attack. She managed to escape damage, the only remaining survivor of the attack on Pearl Harbor. She was later sunk during the Battle of Leyte Gulf.

MANILA BURNING

American troops make their way through the smouldering suburbs of Manila, the location of the majority of the street fighting that took place in the Pacific campaign.

carriers and battle damage and some overflying the deck and crashing into the sea, although many of the crew were rescued. The Japanese force was ordered to withdraw. Mitscher desperately wanted to give chase, but was overruled.

Before the invasion of Luzon—the main island in the Philippines—could take place, General MacArthur was keen to establish airfields closer to the northern island. For this he would have to capture Mindoro Island. Defenses on Mindoro were minimal, with about 1,000 troops stationed there. The 24th and 19th Infantry Divisions supported by a combat team of 11th Airborne overwhelmed the island within two days. However, there were more assaults on the invasion fleet using the new, unnerving kamikaze tactics (suicide attacks from the air), damaging the cruiser USS Nashville and several landing ship tanks (LSTs). Within days of the assault on the island, engineers were at work on the airfields and just 17 days later they were ready to receive U.S. aircraft.

Before the invasion of Luzon, the American forces put in place a deception plan, flying reconnaissance and bombing missions over the southern part of Luzon, even dropping dummy paratroops to lure the Japanese to the south. This deception plan worked so well that when Krueger's 6th Army landed at Linguyan Bay on 9 January 1945 there was no opposition. Within a few days a beachhead of some 20 miles had been established and the coastal town of San Fabian captured, by which time some 175,000 troops were ashore. Again the kamikaze attacks came, sinking the escort carrier USS Ommany Bay and sinking a destroyer, as well as heavily damaging many more transports and LSTs.

General Yamashita, in charge of the defense of Luzon, could do very little to halt the rapid advance of the U.S. forces and decided to opt for a battle on two fronts. He split his forces into two, one retreating into the interior of the island and the other to the defense of Manila, hoping to draw out the fighting for as long as possible. Although his forces outnumbered the Americans, he could do little without the all-important air support now almost unavailable to him.

Clark Field airfield was captured on 23 January and the race to capture Manila was on. The U.S. 11th Airborne and 1st Cavalry Divisions, along with 37th Division, advanced from the north with 12th Cavalry being the first to enter the city on 1 February. Two days of hard fighting saw them in the city center but street fighting was set to continue. As the 1st Cavalry entered the city, Yamashita gave orders to Vice-Admiral Denshichi Okochi to destroy all port installations and then declare Manila an open city.

Okochi openly defied this idea, and sent his men about the city committing terrible atrocities on the local population, and destroying hospitals while patients were still inside. More than 100,000 Filipinos would die in this cruel Japanese retribution. House-to-house fighting continued throughout February, and by the time Manila was declared secure it had been reduced to rubble.

With Mindanao assaulted by men of the 8th Army on 10 March, where fighting in the jungles would continue until the end of hostilities, the entire Philippines was declared secure on 30 June 1945. Twenty-five Japanese divisions had been all but wiped out. U.S. losses amounted to just 820 men.

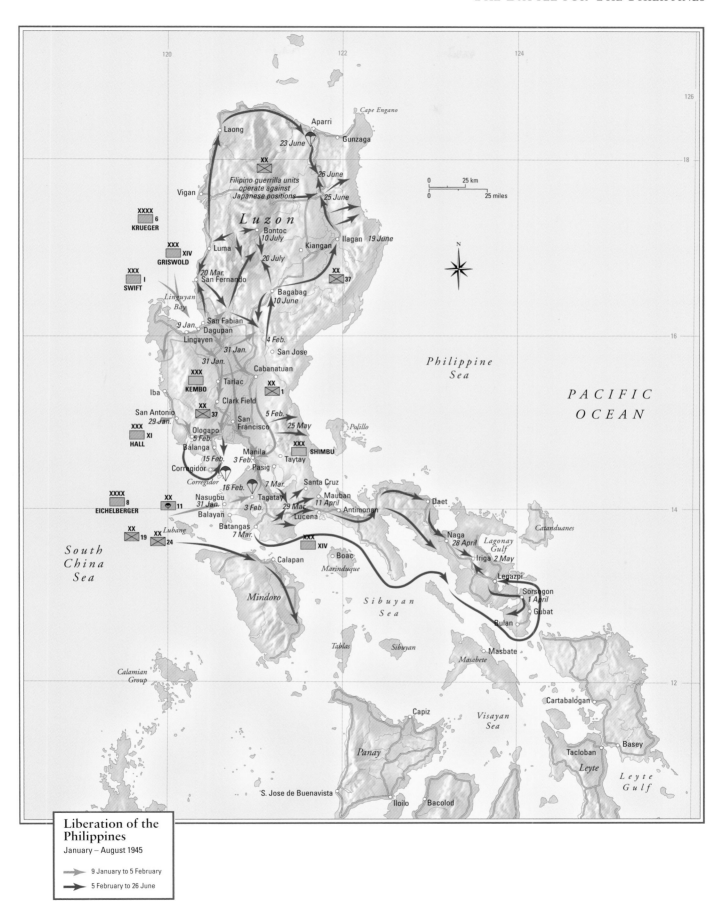

Liberation of the
Philippines
January – August 1945

9 January to 5 February
5 February to 26 June

LEYTE & LEYTE GULF

"I will break into Leyte Gulf and fight to the last man ... Would it not be shameful to have the fleet remaining intact while our nation perishes?"

VICE-ADMIRAL TAKEO KURITA

The Battle of Leyte Gulf, in October 1944, was one of the largest sea battles ever fought. Japanese Admiral Toyoda planned to draw the U.S. Third Fleet northward with a decoy force led by Admiral Ozawa, while a pincer movement was executed by the forces of Vice-Admiral Kurita, approaching via the Straits of San Bernardino, and of Vice-Admiral Nishimura, approaching through the Surigao Strait.

Kurita's force was attacked by two U.S. submarines on the night of 23/24 October. Two cruisers were sunk,

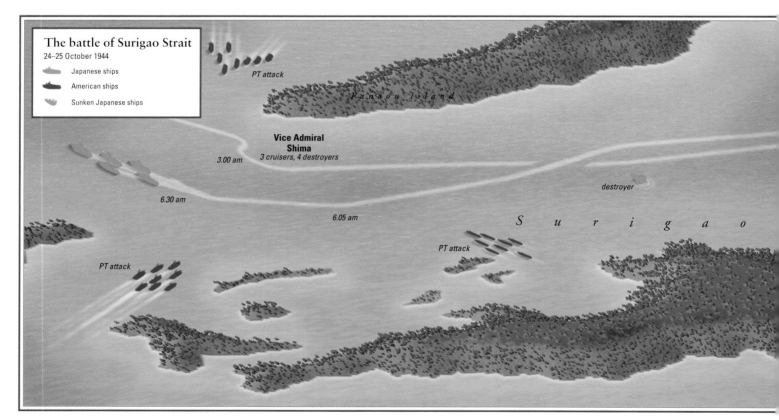

The battle of Surigao Strait
24–25 October 1944

Japanese ships
American ships
Sunken Japanese ships

Panaon Island

PT attack

Vice Admiral Shima
3 cruisers, 4 destroyers

3.00 am

6.30 am

6.05 am

destroyer

PT attack

PT attack

S   u   r   i   g   a   o

and one cruiser damaged. As Kurita entered the narrow Sibuyan Sea, his force was spotted by aircraft from Task Force 38. Over 200 U.S. aircraft attacked the Japanese ships and forced Kurita to withdraw. Nishimura's force entered the Surigao Strait on 24 October, and ran into the 7th U.S. Fleet Support Force, under Admiral Thomas Kinkaid. The U.S. battleships opened fire with their radar-controlled main armament. Only one ship from Nishimura's force survived. The Americans succeeded in "crossing the T" of the Japanese forces so that they could bring all the U.S. guns to bear on the enemy. This was the last time this naval maneuver would occur.

Meanwhile, Ozawa's Northern Force was spotted in the afternoon of 24 October. Admiral Halsey could not resist the opportunity to destroy the last of the Japanese Navy. Believing Kurita to be out of the fight, Halsey took the bait offered by Ozawa and headed north with nine carriers, eight light carriers and numerous other fighting craft. The next morning Ozawa launched 75 planes to attack the pursuing Americans, but few returned. The U.S. carriers launched 500 sorties, sinking the carrier Zuikaku, the only surviving carrier of the Pearl Harbor attack, Three other carriers—Zuiho, Chiyoda, and Chitose—were also destroyed. As Halsey was about to press home final victory, he heard of the plight of a task group off the coast of Samur and broke off the pursuit.

Kurita had steamed down the San Bernardino Strait and was now sailing along the coast of Samur. In his way were three groups from the U.S. 7th Fleet, commanded by Admiral Kinkaid. Each Task Group, or "Taffy" 1, 2, and 3, consisted of six escort carriers and six destroyers. Being lightly armored, they were susceptible to a battleship's heavy guns. Kinkaid thought he had the protection of a Task Force of battleships that had, in reality, gone with Halsey in pursuit of Ozawa. Kurita stumbled upon Taffy 3, surprised to see the Japanese battleships moving toward them. The commander, Clifton Sprague, sent in his destroyers as a distraction while his carriers beat a retreat. The destroyers broke up the Japanese formation with incredible skill and bravery, as they avoided the torpedoes fired on them, gaining enough time to launch the aircraft from the escort carriers, which then attacked the Japanese ships. But as the carriers retreated, the Japanese continued to fire on them and succeeded in sinking the carrier Gambier Bay.

Kurita continued his pursuit of the carriers and came within range of the other Taffys before disengaging after the loss of three cruisers. By the time Kurita arrived back in Japan, only Yamato was serviceable. The fighting to secure the beachheads had moved in the Americans' favor, but while the sea battle had been raging, the land battle had only just begun.

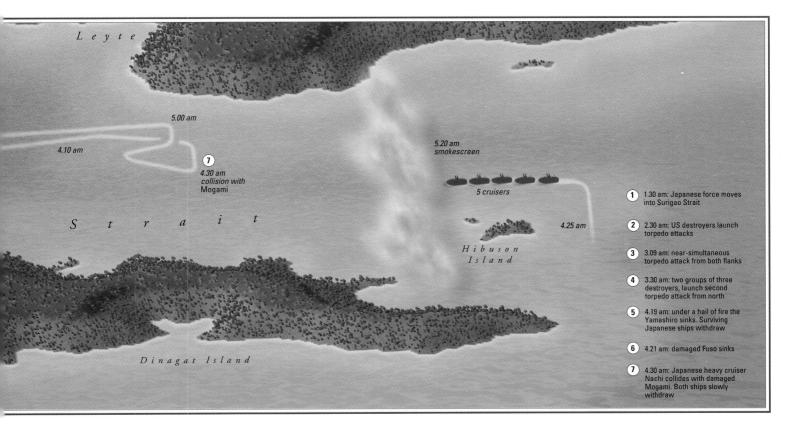

Leyte

5.00 am

4.10 am

⑦
4.30 am
collision with
Mogami

S t r a i t

5.20 am
smokescreen

5 cruisers

4.25 am

*Hibuson
Island*

Dinagat Island

① 1.30 am: Japanese force moves into Surigao Strait

② 2.30 am: US destroyers launch torpedo attacks

③ 3.09 am: near-simultaneous torpedo attack from both flanks

④ 3.30 am: two groups of three destroyers, launch second torpedo attack from north

⑤ 4.19 am: under a hail of fire the Yamashiro sinks. Surviving Japanese ships withdraw

⑥ 4.21 am: damaged Fuso sinks

⑦ 4.30 am: Japanese heavy cruiser Nachi collides with damaged Mogami. Both ships slowly withdraw

Iwo Jima & Okinawa

"Among the men who fought on Iwo Jima, uncommon valor was a common virtue."

ADMIRAL NIMITZ, 16 MARCH 1945

The battles for the islands of Iwo Jima and Okinawa were among the largest and most costly fought in the Pacific area of operations. As the Japanese were retreating nearer to the home islands, they became even more fanatical in their defense, frequently fighting to the death rather than face the shame of surrender.

Iwo Jima, 650 miles south of Tokyo but inside its prefecture, was a volcanic island only five miles in length. However it was the home of three airfields that Japanese interceptors set out from to attack B-29s as they flew missions against the Japanese home islands. It was also an early-warning radar station that could alert the Japanese military to American bomber missions.

The U.S.A.A.F., for its part, saw this island as an ideal base for the planned fighter escort that was badly needed for the B-29s raiding Japan. Plus, bombers could also use the airstrips for emergency landings and refueling. The same applied to Okinawa, which could serve as an important base, supporting any future invasion of Japanese home islands.

The task of defending Iwo Jima was given to Lt-General Tadamichi Kuribayashi and his 22,000 men, who immediately set about building and digging a vast array of underground tunnels and fortifications. The volcanic rock of the island was ideal for such constructions, being soft enough to dig easily but sturdy enough to withstand heavy shelling. Kuribayashi also took a different approach to the defense of Iwo Jima compared to other islands assaulted by the Americans. Instead of attacking the first wave of soldiers as they waded ashore,

Kuribayashi would allow the first wave to reach at least 875 yards inland before hidden machine-gun emplacements would put them under fire from the rear and flanks. This would be costly to the Marines who, after seeing the massive preattack bombardment, were likely to assume that this invasion would be easy.

Attacking the island would be the 5th Amphibious Corps made up of 5th Marine Division, which would land on the left of the invasion beach; 4th Marine Division, on the right; and 3rd Marine Division as a floating reserve. These units were to be under the overall command of Major-General Harry Schmidt. The divisions were to land on the south-east beaches then strike inland to take the airfields and cut off the dominating Mount Suribachi from the rest of the island, before moving north-east to capture the rest of the island.

Following days of aerial strikes and naval bombardment, the first elements of the Marine divisions landed on the beaches on the morning of 19 February, 1945. They took heavy casualties as the defenders put their plan into action, and the Marines struggled to dig foxholes on the volcanic ash beaches to escape the withering crossfire. But by the evening of the first day, the Marines had reached the first airstrip and had succeeded in cutting off Mount Suribachi. Three more days of heavy fighting would follow, with the Marines using flamethrowers and explosives to clear the Japanese defenders from their deep bunkers, before Suribachi was taken, and the Stars and Stripes raised. The fighting continued as the Marines moved north, the Japanese always refusing to give up

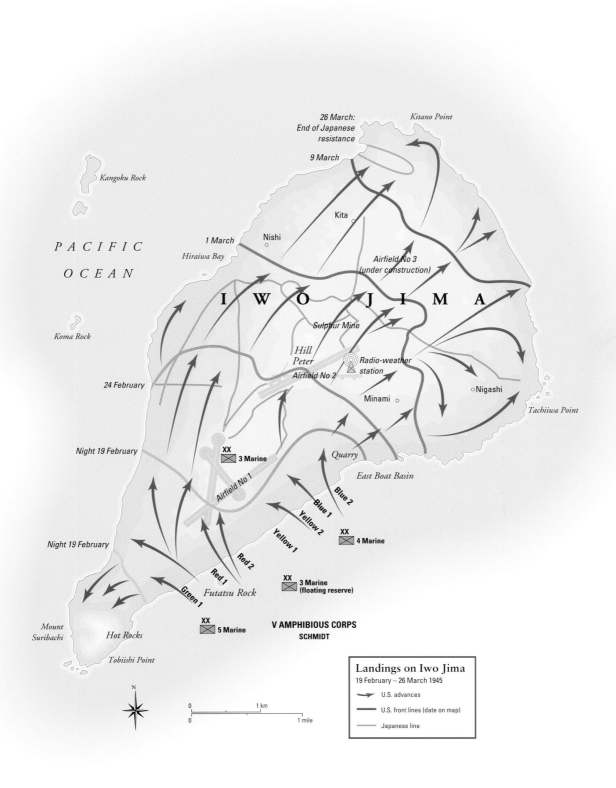

26 March:
End of Japanese
resistance

Kitano Point

9 March

Kangoku Rock

Kita

P A C I F I C

Nishi

1 March

O C E A N

Hiraiwa Bay

Airfield No 3
(under construction)

I W O   J I M A

Koma Rock

Sulphur Mine

*Hill
Peter*

Radio-weather
station

24 February

Airfield No 2

Minami

Nigashi

Tachiiwa Point

Night 19 February

XX
3 Marine

Quarry

East Boat Basin

Airfield No 1

Blue 2

Blue 1

Yellow 2

XX
4 Marine

Night 19 February

Yellow 1

Red 2

XX
3 Marine
(floating reserve)

Red 1

Futatsu Rock

Green 1

*Mount
Suribachi*

Hot Rocks

XX
5 Marine

V AMPHIBIOUS CORPS
SCHMIDT

Tobiishi Point

N

0   1 km

0   1 mile

Landings on Iwo Jima
19 February – 26 March 1945

U.S. advances

U.S. front lines (date on map)

Japanese line

their defenses. On the evening of 25 March, the Japanese launched one last attack against the second airfield. By the morning there were few Japanese survivors and the island was finally in American hands. Of the 22,000 Japanese defenders on Iwo Jima before the battle fewer than 200 remained alive, and many of these were badly wounded. The U.S. forces incurred nearly 6,000 killed and over 17,000 wounded.

The invasion of Okinawa would be the largest amphibious assault in the Pacific theater and also the last battle fought in World War II. Okinawa, unlike Iwo Jima, had a large Japanese population and the civilian casualties in the campaign were extremely high. A third were killed, or chose to commit suicide, convinced by Japanese propaganda that the U.S. troops were savage killers.

The invading U.S. forces totaled 170,000 men, made up from 24th Corps commanded by Major-General Hodges, and the 3rd Marine Amphibious Corps commanded by Major-General Geiger. These units would make up the U.S. 10th Army under the overall command of Lt-General Simon Buckner. The Japanese were 100,000-strong, and commanded by General Mitsuru Ushijima in the south, and General Takehido Udo in the north. Ushijima took on the most important area of defense around the area of Shuri Castle toward the south of the island and the Motobu Peninsula in the north, ordering his men to hold until the last man and last round. This battle was a battle he knew he could not win, but he wanted to hold the Americans for as long as possible in order to slow the impending invasion of his homeland.

The landings occurred on the thin neck of the island toward the center on 1 April. The Marines swept through the north with relative ease and captured the Motobu Peninsula by 20 April. Fighting in the southern part of the island was much more difficult. The islands were honeycombed with caves that served as natural bunkers. The defenders refused to give up, often leaving the Marines and infantry no choice but to use flamethrowers or simply blow the cave entrances with explosives, burying the defenders alive.

Shuri Castle was eventually taken on 29 May, with Ushijima leading his men to the Oroku Peninsula as a final defensive position. Ushijima committed suicide on 22 June—the same day the island was deemed secure by U.S. forces. The U.S. forces suffered badly from combat fatigue in this bitter, no-quarter struggle. Disease, as well as casualties inflicted by the enemy, numbered 72,000, of which 12,500 were killed in action. A few Japanese were now prepared to surrender, seeing the hopelessness of their situation. Of the Japanese garrison about 7,000 survived to become prisoners of war.

AVENGER OVER OKINAWA
An American TBM Avenger banks over Okinawa, above the ships offshore. This aircraft is on photographic reconnaissance, but Avengers were also frequently deployed as bombers.

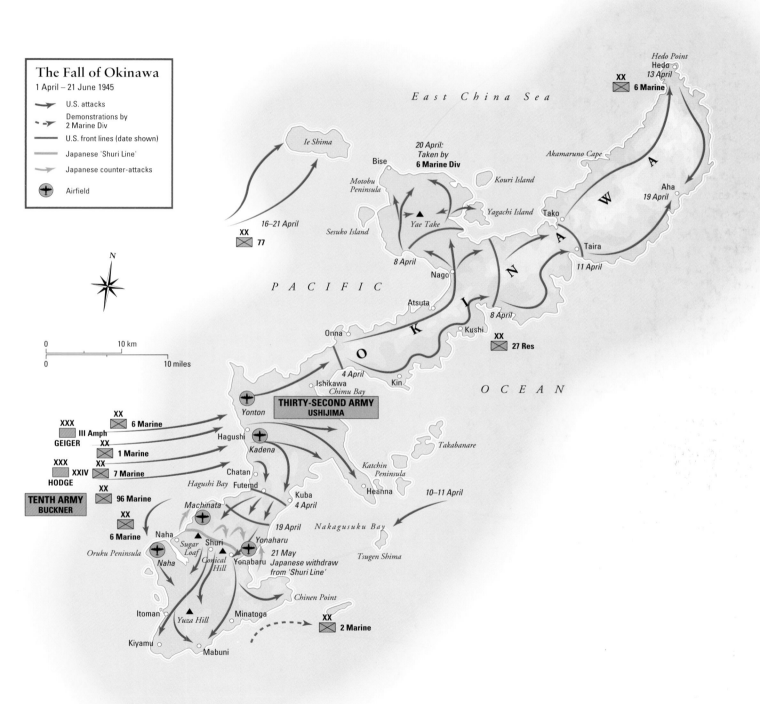

The Fall of Okinawa
1 April – 21 June 1945

→ U.S. attacks

-→ Demonstrations by
2 Marine Div

— U.S. front lines (date shown)

— Japanese 'Shuri Line'

⇢ Japanese counter-attacks

⊕ Airfield

East China Sea

Hedo Point
Hedo
13 April

XX
6 Marine

Akamaruno Cape

O K I N A W A

Ie Shima

20 April:
Taken by
6 Marine Div

Kouri Island

Motobu
Peninsula

Yagachi Island

Tako

Aha
19 April

XX
77

Sesuko Island

Yae Take

8 April

Taira

11 April

16–21 April

PACIFIC

Nago

Atsuta

8 April

Onna

Kushi

XX
27 Res

Ishikawa
Chimu Bay

4 April

Kin

OCEAN

⊕
Yonton

THIRTY-SECOND ARMY
USHIJIMA

Takabanare

XXX
III Amph
GEIGER

XX
6 Marine

⊕
Hagushi

⊕
Kadena

Katchin
Peninsula

XX
1 Marine

Chatan

XXX
XXIV
HODGE

XX
7 Marine

Futema

Heanna

Hagushi Bay

Kuba
4 April

10–11 April

XX
96 Marine

Machinata

19 April

Nakagusuku Bay

Tsugen Shima

TENTH ARMY
BUCKNER

XX
6 Marine

Naha

Sugar
Loaf

Shuri

Yonaharu

⊕
Yonabaru

Oruku Peninsula

⊕
Naha

Conical
Hill

21 May
Japanese withdraw
from 'Shuri Line'

Chinen Point

Itoman

Yuza Hill

Minatoga

XX
2 Marine

Kiyamu

Mabuni

N

0   10 km
0   10 miles

THE ATOMIC BOMB

"Now, I am become death, the destroyer of worlds."

J. ROBERT OPPENHEIMER, PHYSICIST

On 6 August 1945 "Little Boy"—the first atomic weapon to be used in war—was dropped on the Japanese city of Hiroshima, instantly killing an estimated 80,000 people. Three days later another bomb, "Fat Man," was dropped on Nagasaki, creating a similar death toll. Much debate has gone into the question: did the Allies need to use such destructive weapons? Many felt the Japanese were already beaten, especially with Russia's entry into the conflict, declaring war on Japan and invading Manchuria. The civilian administration of Japan was already pursuing a peace policy and it was only the military that wanted to continue the fight to the bitter end.

With scientific assistance from Great Britain and Canada, the U.S. government had set up the "Manhattan Project" in the race to build the first atomic weapon, a device so destructive that whoever held it in their possession had the strategic initiative. The Allies had chosen a policy of strategic bombing, and this involved the bombing of civilian targets to break the enemy's industrial infrastructure, as well as lowering morale. This bomb would take destruction to a new level.

Many of Japan's major cities had been hit in the raids carried out by the new B-29 bomber, using firebombs that decimated the cities. Most of the houses in the cities were wooden constructions and this, combined with the narrow streets, meant the bombing caused huge civilian casualties, claiming 100,000 lives in Tokyo. In the invasion of Okinawa and Iwo Jima, the American forces had suffered terrible losses, leading to the speculation of even greater losses of U.S. servicemen in the planned invasion of Japan itself, which the American public would find hard to live with. Casualties were estimated to be in the hundreds of thousands. The atomic bomb offered great force and the lowest amount of U.S. casualties. This is the official reason the High Command and government went ahead with its deployment.

At Potsdam, President Truman gave an ultimatum to Japan: to surrender or "the alternative for Japan is prompt and utter destruction." The Japanese declined and Truman gave the order for the bomb to be dropped. The target of Hiroshima was chosen, not just for military reasons, or for its factories and installations, but also for its high

LITTLE BOY
The name of the Hiroshima bomb was borrowed from a character in The Maltese Falcon. *But Little Boy was not so small. The device was 10 feet long, and weighed 9,700 pounds.*

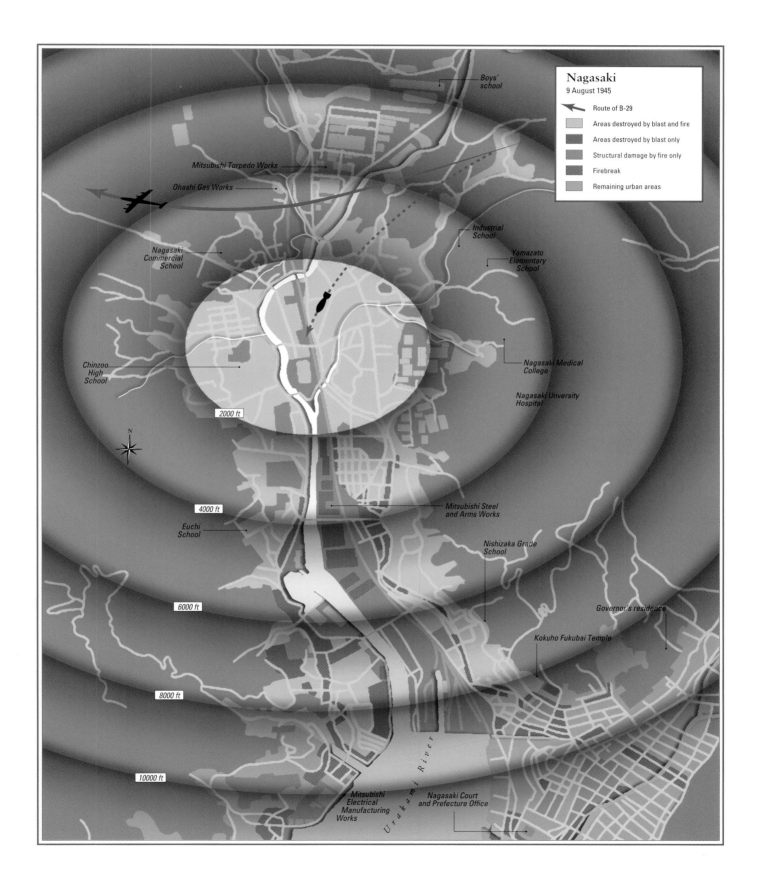

Nagasaki
9 August 1945

Route of B-29
Areas destroyed by blast and fire
Areas destroyed by blast only
Structural damage by fire only
Firebreak
Remaining urban areas

Boys' school
Mitsubishi Torpedo Works
Ohashi Gas Works
Nagasaki Commercial School
Industrial School
Yamazato Elementary School
Chinzoo High School
Nagasaki Medical College
Nagasaki University Hospital
2000 ft
4000 ft
Euchi School
Mitsubishi Steel and Arms Works
Nishizaka Grade School
6000 ft
Governor's residence
Kokuho Fukubai Temple
8000 ft
10000 ft
Urakami River
Mitsubishi Electrical Manufacturing Works
Nagasaki Court and Prefecture Office

population, which would create as large a psychological impact as possible. Until now the city had remained more or less untouched by the bombing campaign and had a minor logistics base for the military. However, other than the central district, which had several concrete constructions, the main part of the city was of wooden buildings, thus lending itself to utter destruction.

Enola Gay, a B-29 bomber piloted by the commander of the 509th Composite Bomb Group, Colonel Paul Tibbets, took off from Tinian on the morning of 6 August, accompanied by two other B-29s whose role was to record the event. At 08:15 am the bomb was released over Hiroshima. It detonated 2,000 feet above the city. Almost all the city was destroyed and 80,000 people vaporized. Many more would die over the coming months and years as a result of the exposure to radiation. The blast radius was one mile with the resultant fires destroying a further four miles.

Three days later Bockscar, flown by Major Charles W. Sweeney, dropped "Fat Man" on the city of Nagasaki, a large port on the south of Japan that was home to several large factories, again largely constructed of wood. The original target was to be Kokura but cloud cover meant that Bockscar had to be diverted to Nagasaki. The bomb was released at 11:01 am and killed 70,000 people. This second bomb led the Japanese government as a whole to accept that there was no alternative but unconditional surrender of their country to the Allies.

The use of these weapons and their destructive power was a source of much controversy at the time, with many of the U.S. commanders, including MacArthur and Nimitz, believing that the bomb should not have been used at all, and that invasion was the better option. Others argue that the dropping of the bomb was a show of strength to the Russians who were, at the time, invading Manchuria and already in possession of large parts of eastern and central Europe. The main official reason for the use of the atom bombs was that—its terrible effects notwithstanding—more lives would have been lost, American certainly but Japanese too, in a conventional invasion of the home islands.

Decades after the event, that debate remains unresolved. But those who live in the shadow of Hiroshima and Nagasaki, which is to say all of us, can at least be glad that atomic weapons, and their even more devastating offspring, have never been used in anger since.

THE MUSHROOM CLOUD AND AFTER

Left, a huge plume rises from the ashes of Nagasaki and into the clouds. Below, the remains of a temple in the vanished city. "I realize the tragic significance of the atomic bomb," said President Truman after Nagasaki. "We thank God that it has come to us, instead of to our enemies."

SOVIET INVASION OF MANCHURIA 1945

"We call upon the government of Japan to proclaim now the unconditional surrender of all the Japanese armed forces."

ALLIED ULTIMATUM TO JAPAN, AUGUST 1945

The Soviet Union had agreed at the Yalta Conference between the three major powers, in February 1945, that it would attack Japanese forces within three months of the capitulation of Germany in the European campaign. Three months to the day after the fall of Germany, they carried out their undertaking by attacking the Japanese in Manchuria. It was to be a one-sided battle that would not last long but which was instrumental in bringing Japan to its knees.

The Soviets were to attack in four places, the main attack in Manchuria, with amphibious attacks on northern Korea, the island of Sakhalin, and the Kurile Islands. Far East Command, under the control of Marshal Alexander Vasilevsky, was enormous, being made up of three "Fronts," the Transbaikal and the 1st Far East, and 2nd Far East. These units totaled 1.5 million men with 5,000 tanks and tens of thousands of artillery pieces.

Opposing these forces was the Japanese Kwantung Army, which was severely depleted of heavy weapons and men, many of whom had been transferred to the fighting in the Pacific campaign. This army was basically an occupying force made up of light infantry numbering some 600,000 men, which had the capability of fighting small insurgency battles. It was nothing compared to the might of the Red Army that had already gained so much experience fighting the Germans.

The Russian attack went ahead on 8 August 1945, between the two atomic bomb drops, deploying a pincer movement. One side of the pincer came from the west through Mongolia, which was too inhospitable to build the required supply lines required for the Soviet advance. However, the Japanese commanders, believing this would be the case, had left the area poorly fortified and the Soviet advance, therefore, was rapid. During this time airborne troops were also dropped behind the lines to seize vital towns and airstrips in order to fly in further men and supplies if required.

With Soviet forces now penetrating deep into Manchuria (Manchukuo), Emperor Hirohito of Japan declared a ceasefire on 15 August, barely a week after the assault had gone in. With this ceasefire the Russians continued their advance and had reached Mukden and Changchun by 20 August, with Mengjiang also being invaded at the same time.

The Russian amphibious landings to the east went according to plan as well, with the island of Sakhalin and the Kurile Islands in their hands quickly, which established Soviet sovereignty in accordance with the Yalta agreements. The landings in north Korea also went well, but a lack of supplies meant that the Soviet advance only went up to the Yalu River, and with the Americans landing in the south at Incheon after the Japanese surrender. As a

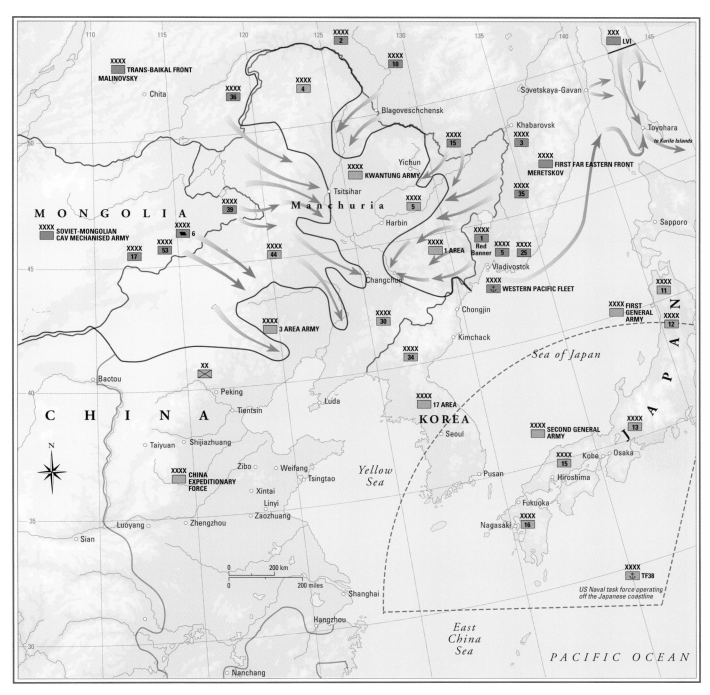

Soviet Invasion of Manchuria
September 1945

—— Soviet front line on 1 September

—— Japanese front line 1 September

↞ Soviet advances

result of the bipartate invasion, Korea was subsequently split into two separate nations.

There is no doubt that the Soviet invasion of Manchuria contributed massively to the surrender of the Japanese, with the rapid and powerful advance showing clearly to the Japanese that they could never hold out against the combined might of the Allies. The anticlimactic conclusion to the fighting in the East was also the last chapter of the conflict as a whole. This war had raged across the globe for six years, like some fiery, nightmarish hurricane. Now, at long last, a kind of calm descended.

INDEX

ACKNOWLEDGMENTS

Maps: Jeanne Radford, P.A.B. Smith, Alexander Swanston, Malcolm Swanston, and Jonathan Young

The publishers would like to thank the following for their kind permission to use their images:

6 National Archives and Records Administration, USA 14 US Signal Corps 16 Private Collection 18 Private Collection 23(t) Popperfoto/Getty Images 23(b) National Archives and Records Administration, USA 27(t) Wikipedia 27(b) The LIFE Picture Collection/Getty Images 30 Sekundenschlaf 34 Wikipedia 39 German Federal Archive 41 German Federal Archive 42 National Archives and Records Administration, USA 45 National Archives and Records Administration, USA 48 German Federal Archive 52 Print Collector/Getty Images 54 National Archives and Records Administration, USA 56 Private Collection 57 National Archives and Records Administration, USA 60(t) Private Collection 60(bl) Topical Press Agency Hulton Archive/Getty Images 60(br) Davis/Hulton Archive/Getty Images 62 Private Collection 75 National Archives and Records Administration, USA 80 German Federal Archive 81 Andgasow 82 Private Collection 92 National Archives and Records Administration, USA 94(l) National Archives and Records Administration, USA 94(r) Polish Archive Marek Tuszynski 95 Polish Archive/Marek Tuszynski 101 Russian International News Agency (RIA Novosti) 105 National Archives and Records Administration, USA 106(t and b) US Navy 115 Private Collection 116 Private Collection 118 US Army 121 US Navy 127 US Naval Archive 128 Imperial War Museum/Getty Images 134 US Air Force 143 State Memorial Museum of Defence and Siege of Leningrad, Saint Petersburg 147 RIA Novosti 153(t) US Navy 153(b) Private Collection 155 US Navy/US Navy National Museum of Naval Aviation 161 National Archives and Records Administration, USA 162 US Army 164 National Archives and Records Administration, USA 168 Bagratan 176 US Air Force 178(t) Leonard McCrombe/Picture Post/Getty Images 178(b) US Air Force 191 Private Collection 192 Private Collection 193 Private Collection 194 US Army 197 Library of Congress 203 US Navy 214(t,b) US Army 216 US Air Force 229(l,r) National Archives and Records Administration, USA 236(l) US Navy 236(r) US Army 242 National Archives and Records Administration, USA 244 National Archives and Records Administration, USA 246 National Archives and Records Administration, USA 247 National Archives and Records Administration, USA

Key: (t) top (b) bottom (l) left (r) right

Every effort has been made to contact the copyright holders for images reproduced in this book. The publishers would welcome any errors or omissions being brought to their attention.